The Taste of Wine

The Taste of Wine

PAMELA VANDYKE PRICE

Random House   New York

For
my dear friends
Edith and Herbert Moore
in whose house I have shared so many good things
and
the wine trade and wine growers of the world,
past and present,
whose happy pupil I have been
with my love

Edited and designed by
Dorling Kindersley Limited
29 King Street
London WC2E 8JD

Published in the United States by
Random House, Inc.
New York

Originally published in the United Kingdom by
Macdonald and Jane's
(Macdonald and Company [Publishers] Limited)
London

Library of Congress Cataloging in Publication Data

Vandyke Price, Pamela Joan, 1923–
  The taste of wine.

  Includes index.
    1. Wine and wine making. 2. Wine tasting.
I. Title.
TP548.V338 1975   641.2'2   75–10309
ISBN 0-394-49819-4

Manufactured in the United States of America

2 4 6 8 9 7 5 3

First American Edition

Contents

CHATEAU LAFITE ROTHSCHILD

When Pamela Vandyke Price suggested I write a foreword to this book, I was at first very reluctant to do so. Especially so at this moment when so many articles and so many criticisms centre on French wines, not always sympathetically or based on any real knowledge. And another book on wine . . .

But yes—a really good one! *The Taste of Wine* is most unusual. Here is someone who did not grow up knowing about or even drinking wine regularly, but who has studied it and now shares the pleasure it has given her in a way that can be understood by the absolute beginner. It may inspire even experienced drinkers to want to know and taste more. The story of her achievement is of great importance.

I met the author when the Fête de la Fleur was held at Château Lafite-Rothschild in 1962. There she was admitted as a Gourmette to the Commanderie du Bontemps du Médoc et des Graves, and I saw her taste our 1961 vintage. To enjoy wine is not uncommon, but to combine this with understanding and the ability to communicate both is unusual. To taste, as it were, sometimes with one's tongue in one's cheek, is an Anglo-Saxon gift, the art of understatement. All of us who know fine wine will be glad of the appearance of this handsome book.

I am particularly glad that such a key to drinking should appear now. In recent years wines have been considered too much as a financial commodity, as if they were stock exchange high-flyers, or objects to be put away in a strong room for speculative capital gain. Fortunately economic trends have brought people back to reality—God created wine to be drunk.

It is important to form your own opinions, with every wine, every vintage; start from scratch whenever you taste and never lower your standards.

So—get reading, get learning—and, for the rest of your lives, good drinking!

ELIE DE ROTHSCHILD

The History of Wine

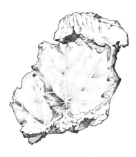

Fossilized vine leaf, above The earliest known variety of vine is *vitis sezannensis*, which was probably growing at least 60 million years ago. Some fossils have been found in the region of Sézanne, in Champagne.

Evolution of the wine press. In the top two illustrations, Egyptians are pressing grapes in a bag and "wringing out the cloth" for the final pressing. Below are a beam press from ancient Greece and a wooden press typical of those used from the Middle Ages to the 19th century.

The vine is an extraordinary plant. It is one of the most useful to man and one of the most beautiful. It is also the parent of perhaps the most fascinating liquid in the world—wine.

There were vines long before there were men. Fossils have been discovered showing that a type of vine flourished in what were then the sub-tropical forests of eastern France before man had emerged. But the first grapes that were cultivated for man's use were probably grown in Asia Minor, south of the Black and Caspian Seas, between 6000 and 4000 BC. How the first wine was made we shall never know, but it must have been the result of some grapes being left, perhaps forgotten, in a crock or pot, where, in the heat, they would ferment within a short time.

The Bible credits Noah with planting a vineyard and there are many ways in which grapes would have been valuable to primitive people: they are high in natural sugar, and therefore would have been a prized food; they can be dried and stored, in raisin form, which would have made them practical "iron rations" for a nomadic people, and also a source of nutrition in the winter or in times of crop failure. Vines can be trained as protection against the sun, and they will grow (like the olive) in regions that are virtually useless for the cultivation of any other crops. So a vineyard, as many passages in the Old Testament indicate, would have been a valuable possession.

The cultivation of vines spread all around the Mediterranean, the Phoenicians probably being responsible for bringing grapes and vinestocks to Greece, Rome, and eventually to France. This was certainly before 600 BC. The vine was also cultivated by the peoples of Mesopotamia, the Ancient Egyptians, the Babylonians and Sumerians, and as soon as men began to depict themselves and their occupations and to write, the vine and wine were constantly shown and mentioned. As well as being an enjoyable drink, wine possesses natural medicinal and disinfectant properties, and it was used as a restorative and sedative and as a precaution against infection in regions where the water supply might be suspect. Foodstuffs could be washed with wine or vinegar, kept edible in a marinade of wine, oil and herbs, and wounds were cleansed with wine before being dressed with oil. The numerous and often mysterious properties of wine made it inevitable that it would also play an important part in many religious rituals. The cult of Dionysus, the wine god, was an important element in the life of Ancient Greece, and sometimes a terrifying one, as witness the appalling Bacchic orgy described by Euripides in the Bacchae.

The Etruscans, Carthaginians and later the Romans, established vineyards and made wine throughout Italy. The vine was always respected; Pliny relates that a vinestock was not merely carried by centurions as a sign of rank and authority, but that Roman soldiers were flogged only with vinestocks, whereas other troops were beaten with any stave to hand. The founder of Christianity referred to Himself as "the true vine", from which time wine and clusters of grapes have regularly featured in all forms of Christian art.

As well as the private vineyards on the estates of the wealthy Romans, large-scale plantations of vines supplied the growing demand for wine. Various forms of presses were used, and the wine was transported in wineskins, the skins of animals, very much as it used to be in Madeira until quite recent times. It might be stored in bulk in a huge jar, rather like a primitive vat, or, if especially good, be put aside in the elongated vessels with pointed bases known as amphorae, which could be partially buried in the earth, thereby keeping the contents cool. The wine was served from small amphorae, fitted into metal stands in private dwellings, and a picture of an individual wine store of classical times shows a row of vessels like squat flasks, dated with what must have been special vintages. The wine shop at Pompeii shows the way the amphorae were held upright in hollows in the counter, ready to be poured for customers. Some of the grapes the Romans grew have even been identified by present-day authorities as the direct ancestors of certain of the classic grapes used for the finest wines: the Argitis of Pliny was probably the Riesling, the Biturica Minor possibly the Gamay, the Helvenacia Minor was the Pinot Noir. Rules for pruning and protecting the vines from pests, as well as maintaining the quality of wine, were highly evolved. As the Romans extended their empire, vineyards were established to supply the army in Germany, the Iberian Peninsula, the Balkan countries and Britain.

Local vineyards, however, were insufficient to satisfy the demand of the far-flung Roman Empire. The navigable rivers, such as the Garonne and parts of the Rhône valley, were used to transport the Mediterranean wines to northern garrisons, and remains of amphorae found in excavations along Roman roads indicate where certain Roman colonies bought their wine and the routes by which it reached them. By then large vineyards were established in what was to become the Bordeaux region, along the Rhône and in the Mosel valleys, and so much wine was made that in the second half of the first century AD prices began to drop. As a result the Emperor Domitian, fearing that vineyards were

Vintage scenes from Ancient Egypt, top and above. They come from the Tomb of Nakht (1372–1350 BC) in Thebes. The vines were trellised as they are in the Minho today. Gardens of vines were status symbols, grapes being grown for the table as well as for wine. After the grapes had been trodden, the wine was stored in jars with stoppers.

The 13th-century stained glass from Canterbury Cathedral, above, shows the two spies returning from Canaan with a bunch of giant grapes. "We came into the land whither thou sentest us, and surely it floweth with milk and honey; and this is the fruit of it."

being cultivated at the expense of the wheat needed to make bread, issued a decree in AD 92 that no new vineyards were to be planted in Italy itself and half those throughout the Empire were to be destroyed. However, although a great deal of fuss was made about this, it seems highly probable that the peasants on the spot managed at least partially to evade compliance with this decree, and in fact by the time Probus repealed Domitian's decree in his short reign (276–282) the vineyards of Burgundy and the Rhône were certainly well established. Casks were coming into use; eight centuries later the Bayeux Tapestry shows William the Conqueror's wine supplies being brought to England in casks that were probably very similar to the casks of Roman times.

The wine containers of the Romans were originally sealed with wax, and they, and perhaps the Greeks as well, would pour a small quantity of oil on top of the open wine, to protect it from deterioration through contact with the air. This practice continued until recent times with many Italian wines in bottle or flask, and those opening them would automatically give the bottle a flick to throw the oil off the surface of the wine before pouring it. In late Roman times cork was used as a closure or bung for wine containers, doubtless as a result of the development of the Roman Empire in the Iberian Peninsula and the western regions of North Africa. Pliny refers to it as a stopper for wine.

With the spread of Christianity, religious establishments cultivated vineyards, supplying

Above, the great mosaic in the House of Dionysus, Paphos, shows Dionysus handing some fermented grape juice to a nymph, who develops the first hangover. In the centre of the mosaic, Icarius, to whom the god taught wine making, is observing the effects of his wares on two shepherds. The mosaic dates from the 3rd century AD.

Right, a harvest scene from a vault mosaic in Santa Constanza, Rome, 4th century AD.

wine both for religious and medical use. Such great estates as existed also possessed vineyards. But with the decline of the Roman Empire and the advent of the Dark Ages they became increasingly isolated and subject to the hazards of war. Many declined—it is known that wolves came into the vineyards of Bordeaux—and the use of corks was forgotten, except perhaps by those actually living near one of the cork forests in Spain or Portugal.

Wine, however, continued to be made. Alcuin (735–804), the Yorkshireman who was called by Charlemagne to become tutor to the Imperial

Court (and certainly the first English wine writer), often acknowledges presents of wine in his letters to various colleagues and gives explicit directions as to how the wine should be cared for while on its way to him. Alcuin ended his life at the Abbey of St Martin of Tours. This was already a well-known wine centre, for St Martin (315–397), the soldier-saint who divided his cloak with a beggar, is credited with rediscovering how to prune vines: when inspecting his Abbey's vineyard, he and his companions found to their horror that their asses had got loose and chewed the vine shoots, but at the following vintage it was these vines that bore most abundantly. Charlemagne was certainly interested in Burgundian wine growing and it was he who ordered that the great slope of Johannisberg on the Rhine be planted with vines, having noted one winter that this particular site was free of snow before all others.

During the period of nearly three centuries when the whole of south-west France belonged to the English crown, the wine fleet would sail from Bordeaux, racing to reach the English and North European ports with the new vintage. Because of the pirates lurking along the French coasts, the English formed a special protective flotilla—this was the beginning of the Royal Navy. The gigantic casks, or *tonnes*, which were loaded in the vessels' holds are no longer in use, but their capacity has given the calculation of size—tonnage—to the ships of the world. Bottles were again in use from about this time, but they served more as carafes, to receive the wine as it was drawn from the wood; if they were not emptied, they would be roughly stoppered with a piece of cloth or wood. New wine was always better than old, because exposure to the air while it remained in the cask caused it to deteriorate and, eventually, turn to vinegar. In some parts of the world snow or ice was kept to preserve and cool wine, but much of the haphazardly made stuff had to be "improved" by the addition of honey to make it vaguely drinkable towards the end of its life. It could also be helped by mixing in mead or hydromel, the resulting blend often being referred to as "bastard". Chaucer makes many references to the different wines available in London; he was the son of a vintner and certainly familiar with Spanish and Bordeaux wines.

Bordeaux was also on one of the greatest pilgrim routes of all time, the road to St James of Compostella. From the pilgrims who passed through Bordeaux, augmented by refugees from the Moors in Spain, and people seeking asylum from religious as well as political persecution in many countries, a polyglot community grew up there. The Bordeaux wine trade tried to protect

The huge Kurfürsten Hoff wine keg, Heidelberg, from the late 16th century. It was one of the three giant tuns from the cellars of the Castle of the Elector Palatine. Its capacity was several hundred hogsheads. Giant casks are traditional in Germany; often the carvings record important events.

"The Shame of Noah", left, depicted in 15th century stained glass in Great Malvern Priory. Noah, first tiller of the soil, planted a vineyard after he had come out of the ark, and his wine made him drunk. Ham reported his naked sleep but Shem and Japheth brought a covering for their father.

St Martin of Tours (315–397), above. As Bishop of Tours, he was the father of French monasticism, but in wine history he is celebrated for rediscovering the benefits of pruning—after the improved yield from the vines which the monastery asses had nibbled.

Blind Dom Pérignon, left. As cellarmaster of Hautvillers in the late 17th century, he evolved the making of the *cuvée* and revived the use of cork to harness the sparkle in Champagne.

itself by insisting that these foreigners live outside the walls of the old city, and that their wine could not be shipped to export markets until the original Bordeaux had left. The term *clairet* was used to differentiate genuine Bordeaux from wine blended with the darker, fuller "high country" wines from the interior and south of France. This piece of medieval legislation gave the word "claret" to the English language and today the quaysides where the "outsiders" had to remain are the centre of the *noblesse du bouchon* of Bordeaux.

When man reached out to discover other countries, wine was an essential part of the ship's stores, even if only to eke out the precious water rations (Rioja wine went with Columbus to America). It also features in the accounts of those early expeditions. When Leif Ericsson travelled to what is now New England in about AD 1000 he described his adventures in the *Saga of Wineland the Good*, being impressed by the enormous quantities of vines he found. But these were not the classic wine vine, *vitis vinifera*, but *vitis labrusca*, a type of wild vine that gives to wine made from it a curious flavour usually described as "foxy". Sir Walter Raleigh's expedition to set up a settlement on Roanoke Island in 1558 mentions the Scuppernong grape, which is particularly large.

In 1522 Cortez sent back to Spain for vine cuttings, and, most interestingly, the Spaniards in Mexico actually grafted European vines on to native vine stocks, as a protection against phylloxera. This is remarkable, but it is described in an account of the settlement of Mexico written in 1536.

The early missionaries followed, planting vines so as to have wine for Mass. In lower California, the Jesuit Father Ugarte planted vines in the late 1690s and many wineries were subsequently established there, including the famous one at the San Diego Mission planted in 1769 by the Franciscan, Father Junipero Serra, and the San Gabriel Mission, in 1771, the oldest Californian winery still in existence. About 1843 the Concord grape, one of the most popular varieties, was evolved in North America and experiments were advancing with both native and imported vine stocks, although European vines did not thrive in the east.

The first settlers in Australia planted vines there in 1788, but vines had been planted at the Cape, in South Africa, with cuttings from Holland as early as 1654. In South America, Argentina, which is the fourth largest wine-producing country in the world, and Chile were competing at international wine exhibitions by the 1870s.

But perhaps the most significant developments

in the history of wine had occurred in France in the late 17th century. In 1658, a young man became a Benedictine monk in France. About ten years later he was appointed cellarer at the Abbey of Hautvillers, in Champagne. From this time, until his death in 1715, Dom Pérignon created a growing fame for the Hautvillers wines, which indeed were often referred to as "Vins de Pérignon". Unfortunately the Abbey records vanished when the monks had to flee in 1790, but it does not seem an exaggeration to claim that this Benedictine monk was responsible, not only for making the blend and harnessing the sparkle in Champagne, but for reviving the use of the cork so that wines could henceforth be bottled and sealed, laid down and developed to maturity and magnificence. One version of the story relates how two Spanish Benedictines, en route for Sweden, spent a night at Hautvillers where the French monks asked them what the curious thing was they had used to stopper their water gourds. The Spaniards explained that this was the bark of the cork oak. Dom Pérignon was by this time completely blind, but still alert to the possibilities of this method of sealing and from that time cork has been the means of keeping fine wine in bottle. Another version of the story says that Dom Pérignon in fact visited the Benedictine Monastery of Alcántara, on the Spanish–Portuguese border, and worked in the cork forests.

Some time in the last quarter of the 17th century a new type of bottle had also been evolved as the result of progress in glass blowing; this bottle was both thicker and more resistant to stress from within than those previously used. The method was evolved in England, and bottles made of *verre anglais* began to be exported, so some came to Champagne.

Early bottle stoppers and even corks tended to fit loosely and projected above the bottle. They were often pulled out by the drinker taking them between his teeth. But about 1750 a corkscrew, then called a bottlescrew, was evolved, so corks could be fitted tightly and bear wax "capsules" for additional sealing. The earliest wine label— for port—probably dates from 1756, but generally labels were rare before the 20th century except for the finest wines. People simply ordered the type of wine from their merchant.

The improvement in wine when kept for a period in bottle was so marked that within a very short period the era of the great bottled wines began. Bottles were not yet standardized, but when they could be laid on their sides (the cork being kept wet by the wine so that it remained swollen, sealing the bottle neck), huge stocks of bottles could be accumulated. Fine

Amphorae in the Punic port of Carthage, probably about 3rd century BC. Used for olives and oil as well as wine, these jars were made to wedge between the ridges of the timbers in the bottom of a boat. They were also for storage and service ashore.

The wine shop at Pompeii, showing the holes in the counter in which the amphorae were held upright. It is possible that the wine was kept cool by water, or wet sand, beneath the counter.

food and appropriate wines became part of civilized living in the capitals of the world during the 18th century, and wines were made so that they should have long lives. For example, the "hat" of skins, pips and stalks that floats on the top of a fermentation vat would, in a region such as the Gironde, be left on the wine for several weeks, so that, when young, wines made in this way would be very hard, extremely dark in colour and require many years maturation when they were bottled—which might itself not be until after several years in wood.

Then, in the middle of the 19th century, two successive plagues struck vines throughout the world and changed both methods of cultivation and the style of wines as they are made today. In 1845 a gardener at Margate sent some diseased vine leaves to be identified and investigated. They were found to be suffering from powdery or downy mildew (oidium Tuckerii—named after the discoverer) and the disease was thought to have been brought to Britain by some plants, either vines or creepers, possibly from North America. By 1852 all the European and North African vineyards had been seriously attacked, but a M. Grison, head of the forcing houses at the Palace of Versailles, who had discovered the oidium on the royal grapes in 1846, managed to keep those grapes healthy by treating them with a spray of lime-sulphur. The mildew did not actually kill the vines, but the grapes that were affected cracked and remained small and acid. Eventually, dusting the vines with sulphur powder was widely adopted and thousands of tons are used as a protective today. The mildew was controlled, but, as George Ordish, a world authority on pest control and a specialist in wine diseases, points out, it was the mildew that, neglected, caused the decline of wine growing in Britain and the remains of mildewed vines that are still found on old walls might have been restored to health by applying sulphur in some form.

Something much more serious began to be noticed in the late 1860s. In 1863 a new vine pest was recorded and investigated at Hammersmith, and shortly afterwards reports came in of a mysterious disease affecting many French vineyards. The ironic thing is that the aphis, *phylloxera vastatrix*, which was destroying the vine roots, certainly came from America, probably brought in on vines imported for research while scientists were trying to combat the mildew. The phylloxera aphis has a complex life cycle, but in general terms it reproduces itself in wingless female creatures that live on the vine roots and kill the roots of European vines or vines of European stock in about three years. It will be remembered that grafting had been used by the

The 15th-century French engraving, above, shows vineyard and wine making activities. The wooden, or wicker, carrier is called a "hotte" and is in use today. Indoors, someone is "spiling" the head of a cask to tap the wine in wood.

A monster sherry cask, above, imported into Britain from Spain where it had been specially made for display at the Great Exhibition of 1851. Giant casks have often been featured at such exhibitions, but they have seldom been used for the long-term storage of wine.

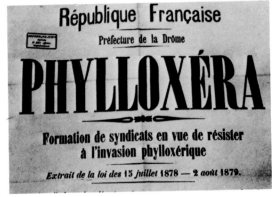

République Française

Préfecture de la Drôme

PHYLLOXÉRA

Formation de syndicats en vue de résister à l'invasion phylloxérique

Extrait de la loi des 15 juillet 1878 — 2 août 1879.

The campaign to organize preventive measures against phylloxera was often violently resisted by growers, who naturally opposed the destruction of their vineyards by officials and were suspicious of treatments. One treatment involved the use of a Vermorel Injector, or "Pal", left. It injected carbon disulphide into the vineyard in the hope that it would destroy the aphis, but there was no guarantee that the vines would not be attacked again. Eventually, free courses in grafting enabled everyone to master the pest.

Spaniards in Mexico in the mid-16th century, but, although a Frenchman, Bazille, suggested that this might be done as early as 1869, the Europeans did not understand the action of the aphis sufficiently to appreciate the difference that grafting might make. Appalling damage was done to the vineyards. In ten years in France alone the area under vines was nearly halved. Once in the soil, the aphis cannot be eradicated, so that very soon almost all the European vineyards were affected. All kinds of remedies, some of them crazy, were tried, and vineyards were flooded or compulsorily uprooted. Chemicals that killed the phylloxera were efficacious, but the vines might then be attacked all over again. Wine as we know it would have become a legend within two generations, had not the resistance of the American *vitis labrusca* to phylloxera been finally recognized. So today the majority of all European wines are made from classic *vitis vinifera* varieties grafted on to American phylloxera-resistant roots.

There are some vineyards still producing that have never had the phylloxera, including most of those in Chile and on the Hunter River in Australia and those on particularly sandy soil, such as Colares in Portugal. The creature has not yet affected English vineyards and Cyprus has also been fortunate in this respect. But increased facilities of transportation continually increase the risk of it being brought in to healthy vineyards already at risk from migrating birds and the chance contact of the boots of someone who has just come from an infected vineyard.

The vines were saved, but was the wine the same? Grafted vines tend to have a shorter life, and at first pessimists considered that wine made from grafted stocks would be thinner and inferior. But there were some superb vintages at the turn of the century in many classic vineyards, and most people today would probably agree that it is not so much the grafting that has changed the styles of wines as the incorporation of progressive techniques of wine making and vine cultivation. The European vineyards where "national" (i.e. ungrafted) vines are still grown do not, as yet, produce and have never produced the very finest wines, so that direct comparisons between grafted and ungrafted stock products are difficult. Even if one is fortunate enough to be able to taste a pre-phylloxera Bordeaux, its very age makes it difficult to know what it might have been like as a younger wine, so this is not fair. But there is one comparison that is possible—in port. Quinta do Noval, in the Douro Valley, is a single estate that has always made fine wines and the late owner, Luiz Porto, contributed much to viticulture. At Noval, by permission, a small

quantity of *nacional* vines, ungrafted, still make a very small amount of wine, which can be directly compared with the estate's wine produced from grafted vines. The comparison does, I think, indicate that wine made from ungrafted stock may have a profounder, at once gentler yet more lengthy, and ultimately more impressive, smell and flavour. It will be interesting to see if experiments with classic vines in Cyprus will enable the same type of comparison to be made with table wines.

Yet there are many other factors to consider here: wine is big business today, the demand for fine wines always exceeds supply, and it is very seldom possible for the owner of even a great estate to tie up capital while a wine matures in the lengthy, traditional way. (Even Château Lafite made no profit until 1948—nearly a century after the Rothschilds bought it!). Wines are therefore made so that they will be agreeable and drinkable at an earlier stage in their lives; science enables them to achieve the quality of good wines in conditions where previously they might have been bad or undrinkable; the skill of the blender will adjust the proportions of non-vintage wines so that they appeal to a huge public instead of only to a local demand; branded wines make consistency of quality possible, whether you order your bottle on a train or an aeroplane or drink it in the Sahara or the Arctic.

People are often disappointed when they visit a modern winery or tasting room and feel that some of the glamour has gone out of wine because science has come in, but, providing the scientist neither distorts the essential character of the wine nor is made to yield so much to commercial pressures as to debase a great name into a bottle of "vaguely alcoholized water with a pretty label", I cannot see that any of the modern developments are bad in themselves. Wine makers are the midwives of wine, not plastic surgeons altering a wine's style, nor dictators crushing a wine's individuality. The fact that such a wide range of wines is available in many cities throughout the world, both in wine-making and non-wine-making countries, is an enriching and civilizing development. There are some things that the scientists still cannot do—they cannot make a great wine in a test tube, nor produce an outstanding vintage from an indifferent site in poor climatic conditions—but they are as important to wine as medical science is to human beings.

Whether it is a pleasant beverage, made within months, or a priceless bottle that has matured for a lifespan equal to that of a human being, wine is, as it has always been and as I think it will always be, a wonderful thing.

A Dutch decorative still life, dated 1627. The pleasure taken in grapes, wine, glasses, jugs and carafes as subjects for the painter's skill is obvious in the masterpieces of the period.

The Grape

Grapes are often difficult to identify, because local names may have been bestowed on them and because they may, early in their development, have evolved several strains. Yet there are grapes made by the *vinifera* vine which influence all the wines of the world, and some of them are listed here, under the names by which they are generally known.

There is an erroneous belief that wines made from single grape varieties are somehow "better" than those to which many grapes have contributed. In modern wineries, the skill of the technician and his laboratory as well as mechanical methods of cultivation, can make quite different styles of wine from the same grape, even on the same type of soil—for example, the Chenin Blanc from different wineries in California—but before the scientists were able to control wine making in such detail, the different grapes could, in certain vineyards, make the resulting wine finer. For example, the finest Mosel and Rhine wines are certainly 100 per cent Riesling and the great red Burgundies are all Pinot Noir; but in Bordeaux, the Cabernet Sauvignon contributes nobility, the Cabernet Franc fruit and vivacity, the Petit Verdot a certain type of acidity, the Merlot charm and bouquet, and so on, to the reds.

When tasting, try to see if there is any evocation of something you already know in a wine. Sometimes, even as little as ten per cent of a classic grape, such as the Sauvignon, can speak through a mixture of other grapes unknown to the taster. At others, the smell of something associated with one grape—such as the Pinot Noir—can immediately make contact with the taster, even if the wine is unfamiliar on the palate. Californian Gamays, South African Steens and some Australian Sémillons, on the other hand, to me usually only relate in the after-taste to their origins. If a great wine grape is included in a wine, it makes its presence felt—somehow.

Anatomy of the Grape

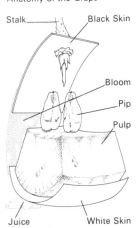

Stalk — Black Skin
Bloom
Pip
Pulp
Juice — White Skin

The grape is chiefly made up of water: 78–80 per cent in the stalk, skin and pulp, 36–40 per cent in the pips. But each part of the grape can contribute to the wine. The stalk and skin contribute tannin, and so do the pips if they are crushed. The skin can provide colour, and occasionally bouquet. The bloom catches and holds the wine yeasts. The pulp contains sugar, necessary for fermentation; tartaric, malic and citric acid, necessary for freshness, and preservation; nitrogenous matters, certain minerals, pectins and pectoses, giving the beautiful roundness to wines made when the juice is reduced.

Aligoté
A white grape used mainly in Burgundy for inexpensive wines, and grown widely elsewhere including California.

Cabernet Franc
One of the great Bordeaux black grapes and the one that makes the finer red Loires, the pink wines labelled "Rosé du Cabernet", and many other wines throughout the world that are just labelled "Cabernet".

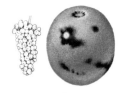

Cabernet Sauvignon
The supreme black grape of the Médoc and Graves, and the one that gives the nobility to most red Bordeaux in general. It can be rather assertive and tends to make wines that are somewhat forceful until they get plenty of bottle age—such as the great vintages of Mouton-Rothschild. In other vineyards, it can have a hardness, even sometimes astringency, that needs time to assuage, but its character always stands out.

Canaiolo
Italian black grape, giving its name to a sweetish wine from Lake Bolsena, and important in Chiantis made to be drunk young—to which it gives softness and fragrance.

Carignan
Black grape with a particularly intense type of smell, much used in the southern vineyards of France. It is also grown in other hot climates, e.g. Algeria, and in California where it is spelt Carignane.

Chardonnay
Sometimes called Pinot Chardonnay, because in the past it was thought to be a white variant of the Pinot Noir. It is not however directly related to the Pinot. The Chardonnay is the great grape of the white Burgundies, one of those involved in Champagne, and is used throughout the world to make fine, often full-bodied very dry and medium dry white wines. It is very successful in California.

Chasselas
White grape, used in Switzerland and to make the more ordinary Alsatian wines, and cultivated in other vineyards throughout the world.

Chenin Blanc
The white grape that makes the fine white wines of the middle region of the Loire, where it can be used for bone dry to very sweet wines, such as those of Vouvray, and to which it

always seems to me to give a slightly honeyed, flowery back and after-taste. Cultivated throughout the world, it makes good, light, fruity wines in California, and has now been identified as the Steen of South Africa, where it can make interesting late vintaged wines. There is always something extra, subtle and slightly intense about the wines made from this white grape.

Cinsaut
Black grape, widely used in many southern French vineyards; also in South Africa, where it is called Hermitage, making robust, full red wines.

Furmint
Extensively cultivated in south eastern Europe, this is the grape that makes both the dry and great sweet wines of Hungarian Tokay. It gets its name because its yellowish colour recalls "froment"—ripening wheat. It is also cultivated in Germany and Italy, the wines it makes usually being both fragrant and with a certain nervous intensity that makes them distinctive. It is supposed to have been introduced to Hungary by Walloon wine growers in the 15th century.

Gamay
The black grape of the Beaujolais, cultivated in many world vineyards, and generally producing wines of marked fruitiness with a light, enticing fragrance, and brilliant light red colour.

Gewürztraminer
The "spicy" Traminer, now called Gewürztraminer in Alsace, and cultivated in many eastern European countries for white wines. It is sometimes used in conjunction with other grapes, but it possesses a particular full fragrance, reminiscent to some of straw or hay, that usually comes through. It can be a good choice of wine when something dry but fullish, is required.

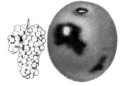

Grenache
Black grape, one of those widely used in the Rhône, where its fairly assertive, occasionally hard character comes through the wines. Elsewhere it can make full, slightly deep wines of obvious appeal.

Malmsey
One of the grapes of antiquity, now associated with the most opulent style of Madeira, but used as Malvasia and Malvoisie in many hot countries and in many blends.

Mascalese
The Mascalese is one of the most important black grapes used for Sicilian wines; also grown in other hot vineyards.

Maurisco
One of the port grapes, particularly suited to very hot vineyards.

Mauzac
White grape chiefly famous for making the sparkling Blanquette de Limoux in the south-east of France.

Mavron
The name means "black" and this is one of the native Cyprus grapes, also, in forms such as Mavrud or Mavroud, making red wines in south-eastern Europe.

Merlot
Black grape, one of those used in the Gironde, which, especially, gives the close-textured subtle fragrance to Lafite, and can be a great attraction in St-Emilion. Cultivated widely, it usually makes a slightly soft, full-bodied wine. It is the grape the Bordeaux vintagers eat, because it is one of the few wine grapes that are pleasant to quench thirst.

Müller-Thurgau
Grape evolved from a Riesling-Sylvaner cross at the end of the 19th century, early ripening and useful in many German vineyards—but never achieving the finesse of the Riesling wines.

Muscadet
White grape, originally the Melon de Bourgogne, grown in the Muscadet area. The locals will say it is the only French wine named for its grape and being reminded of Alsace, will say ''L'Alsace, ce n'est pas la France!''

Muscat
Muscat can be black or white, but is more usually white. There are numerous types of Muscat, the Muscat d'Alexandrie being famous, and the Muskat Ottonel extensively used in eastern Europe, and Muscats, Moscatos and Muscatels are found all over the world. The grape tends to make wines that possess marked fragrance and aroma, actually ''grapey'', not necessarily sweet.

Nebbiolo
Black grape grown extensively throughout Italy, where in Piedmont it makes some of the best reds, including Barolo and Gattinara. The wines of Grumello, Inferno, Sassella and Velgella in Lombardy must be made with 95 per cent of the Nebbiolo grape.

Nerello
Sicilian black grape extensively used for red wines of the island.

Palomino
The great white grape of sherry, making the finest finos, but cultivated elsewhere in the world and known by various names, including Listan or, in some parts of California, Chasselas Doré.

Pedro Ximénez
Often abbreviated to PX, this is one of the grapes used for sherry. It is also the main grape for the wines of Montilla-Moriles, and is used in many Spanish wines, to which it gives depth and style, not simply the sweetening with which it is associated in the Jerez region.

Petite-Sirah
Believed by some to be descended from the Syrah widely grown in the Rhône, it is a black grape planted in California and producing medium quality red wines.

Petit Verdot
One of the black grapes of Bordeaux, used in small quantities to give the red wines a certain acidity and assertiveness.

Pinot
One of the great grape families. Many different varieties of Pinot are grown throughout the world and some are called by national or local names.

Pinot Blanc
The great white grape that is used in Champagne and, with the Chardonnay, makes the finest white Burgundies.

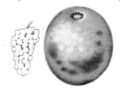

Pinot Noir
One of the world's great black grapes, used solely for all the great red Burgundies, in Champagne blends and for some of the still Champagnes. It is also found in many European countries, in particular Austria, where it is known as the Blauburgunder, and Hungary where it is called Nagyburgundi. It can make a red wine with wonderful bouquet and profundity, able to age excellently, and in smaller-scale versions, wines that give great pleasure for their distinctive fruit, velvety style and a smell that one would like to say was unmistakeable—but it can be deceptively elusive. Used in many New World vineyards, including California and the Cape.

Poulsard
Referred to in the Jura locally as the Plant d'Arbois, this grape makes the best red wines, light in colour, in that region.

Rabigato
Rabigato is one of the grapes used to make white port.

Roussanne
White grape used extensively throughout the Rhône and among the grapes of Châteauneuf-du-Pape.

Rheinriesling
See Riesling.

Riesling
One of the greatest—some might even say the greatest —white wine grapes of the world, and cultivated world-wide. There are several

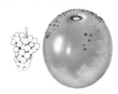

members of the Riesling family, the noblest being the Rheinriesling, which makes the finest Rhine and Mosel wines and is sometimes called the White Riesling or Johannisberger in the United States. The Wälschriesling makes many of the wines labelled simply ''Riesling'' in the Balkans. The great characteristic of the Riesling is its superb delicate fruity smell and capacity to make noble wines, including very sweet ones.

Ruländer
A type of Pinot, sometimes referred to as Pinot Gris, cultivated in Germany, Austria and Hungary, where it is known as ''Grey Friar'', and elsewhere.

St-Emilion
See Trebbiano.

Sangiovese
Black grape extensively cultivated throughout Italy, where it is the foundation of Chianti, and elsewhere.

Savagnin
Grape used for the *vins jaunes* of the Jura, notably those from Château Chalon.

Sauvignon Blanc
One of the great white wine grapes of the world, used in the great white Bordeaux, dry

and sweet, and in many parts of the world. It is the ''Blanc Fumé'' of the upper Loire, and, used alone, makes distinctively fruity but fine, firm wines, that always remind me of cold steel.

Scheurebe
A recently evolved grape which makes fragrant wines of quality, particularly in the Palatinate.

Sémillon
One of the grapes used for

the white Bordeaux, dry and sweet, and cultivated throughout the world. It usually makes wines that are rather rounded and notably fragrant, but can be dry.

Sercial
The driest of the four main grape varieties grown on the island of Madeira and producing the lightest in colour of the Madeira wines.

Steen
See Chenin Blanc.

Sylvaner (Silvaner)
This is another great white wine grape, making fine wines in Franconia and often in the Palatinate, light, crisp wines in Alsace, and fresh, sometimes fruity wines elsewhere.

Syrah
One of the black grapes used widely in the Rhône, where it supplies finesse to many wines. It is also cultivated successfully for robust red wines throughout the world.

Trebbiano
Italian white wine grape, especially successful in Latium, giving dry, very definitely scented wines, usually straw-coloured. It is cultivated in south-eastern Europe and in other countries. It is in fact the same as the St-Emilion grape grown in Cognac, and the Ugni Blanc of southern France.

Ugni Blanc
See Trebbiano.

Viognier
White grapes used in some of the Côte Rôtie Rhône wines and exclusively for Château Grillet and Viognier white wines made there.

Wälschriesling
See Riesling.

Xynisteri
Native to Cyprus, a white wine grape making crisp, dry wines.

Zinfandel
Possibly the leading Californian red wine grape, the Zinfandel is also probably a native grape, although some theories have been advanced that it was originally the Zierfandel of Hungary. It produces a rather open-textured agreeable red wine.

15

Soil and Climate

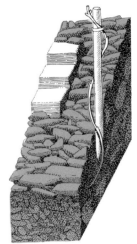

Chalk
Chalky soil, light for the vine to penetrate, reflecting the sun, as in Champagne. This kind of vineyard is good for elegant white wines with some vivacity and crispness. Chalk also drains well, another factor which can affect the taste. When tasting always try to recall something that may be conveyed by the composition of the vineyard.

Clay
Clay soil, which can be used for vines making everyday full-bodied reds. In certain circumstances it produces assertive wines, such as some St-Emilions, or richness in expansive white wines in areas where the sweeter wines are made. But, because it drains badly, and the vine does not like being waterlogged, too much clay or heavy soil is rarely ideal for producing the finest wines. This can apply to the subsoil as well as the topsoil.

Volcanic
The fine, darkish soil of a volcanic vineyard, such as can be seen in Sicily and around Naples, where the wines, red and white, demonstrate a certain odd flavour and evocative after-taste. As with all soils, the water source that feeds the roots is influential; the mineral content will affect the constitution of the grape.

Slate
The slaty topsoil of a steeply terraced Saar vineyard—with steps to facilitate working. The slate holds the heat and gives the wines great finesse and steely authority.

Chalk
Vines in chalk soil in the undulating "Champaigne"— open country of Champagne —gracious countryside though in a northern region, often vintaging in late autumn.

Clay
Planting vines in the heavy clay soil of the Coteaux du Layon region of the Loire, where they will produce fine, sweet to very sweet white wines.

Volcanic
Open landscape on volcanic soil in the Etna vineyards, east Sicily, where modern terracing and cultivation have greatly improved the quality of production.

Slate
The precipitous slopes and slaty topsoil of a vineyard on the Mosel. Here the vines are grown in vertical rows for maximum exposure to the sun.

The vine in profile
The various ground level and subterranean sources from which the vine draws its nourishment: pruned low— in a fairly hot vineyard—its roots first penetrate a thick layer of stones, then pebbles and gravel on limestone, a line of compacted gravel and then a mixture of sand and clay. The roots reach out into the different sorts of soil, but the tap or main root goes down almost to a layer of clay. Each layer into which the roots extend will contribute something to the ultimate wine—sometimes a wine off an apparently heavy soil owes its elegance to a gravel subsoil, as with certain Médocs. Do not simply think of the topsoil when you are tasting—try to imagine what may be underneath.

Soil can affect wine in many ways: the light, almost white albariza soil of Jerez, the pale vineyards of Champagne and similar fine white wine regions reflect the light upwards onto the grapes, resulting in elegant wines. Stones hold the heat— as at Châteauneuf-du-Pape—acting like night storage heaters on the grapes, and giving the baked, almost roasted flavour to many of the wines. Rocks, such as those seen at Solutré in southern Burgundy, can give an almost stony flavour to some of the wines, as they affect the roots. The granite of the Douro Valley, where growers have to blast to get the vines in, holds them firm and makes them seek deep for nourishment. Ironstone, such as comes through to the surface in the Rheinhessen, gives a firm quality. The powdery surface of some Saar and Mosel vineyards gives the finesse to the Riesling, and the Côte Brune and Côte Blonde of the upper Rhône Valley not only look blonde and brunette, but

Drainage in a vineyard
The effect of different soils. Left, water drains straight down, as in a fairly flat vineyard with plenty of gravel in its composition. Centre, the water encounters a layer of clay and its course is diverted. Right, water draining downwards to a river or nearby water table, or, in light soil, being re-absorbed upwards by heat into the atmosphere.

taste accordingly—the darker slope gives a slightly heavier wine, the lighter one a wine that is more gracious and sunny. Volcanic soils can produce wines with a curious minerally after-taste, and usually wines from vineyards where the soil is friable, crumbly and with some pebbles can make very fine wines—as in the Médoc.

The subsoil can be of equal importance, for this is where the vine draws its nourishment; it does not like wet feet, so too much clay or heavy soil seldom produces fine wines. The drainage of the vineyard is a critical factor; vineyards on a slope, however slight, are generally superior to those on a plain, and the sites half or two-thirds up the slope are most advantageously situated: at the top, they are too exposed and the water drains away too fast, at the bottom they may get waterlogged.

The climate naturally affects vines in general and, when it varies very much, vintages. Sunshine alone does not make a fine wine: the aspect

of a vineyard and the type of sun it receives is important. Generally, where there are distinct slopes, a vineyard that looks south (in the northern hemisphere) and gets some of the afternoon sun will give wines that smile more than those that look north and east. Compare even the best Montlouis with a Vouvray. But valleys can provide shelter, and the variation of climate—such as in California—the windings of rivers such as the tortuous Mosel, and the mountainous ridges of, say, the Alsatian vineyard areas, can make vineyards even a hundred yards apart produce totally different wines.

Climate
Two contrasting climates and terrains. Above, the regulated expanse of a Champagne vineyard; left, typical peasant cultivation in the Troödos Mountains in Cyprus, with isolated stony plots. In a chilly vineyard, the vines have to get maximum exposure to the sun, in a very hot vineyard they may need the shelter—albeit slight—of slopes and trees.

Terracing
Terracing in two completely different vineyards. Left, Quinta do Noval, Portugal, perhaps the most famous single Douro estate, and, above, the slopes of the great Doktor vineyard above Bernkastel on the Mosel. Terracing serves to keep the topsoil in place as well as assisting drainage. But the steep slopes can make life hard for the worker.

The Vine through the Year

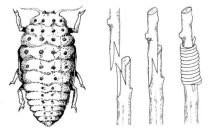

The history of a bunch of grapes—the first shoot, followed by the flowering of the vine, then the formation of the grapes and eventually the fruit, as shown at St-Emilion. Classic wine grapes mostly have perfect flowers—male and female organs in the same flower—making self-pollination the rule, although cross-pollination is also possible.

Above left, the aphis *phylloxera vastatrix*. Almost impossible to eradicate from the soil once it has arrived, it would have destroyed all the vines in the latter part of the 19th century had it not been discovered how, by grafting (as shown above right and below), the vines could be grown on phylloxera-resistant American stock.

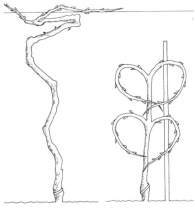

The vine is trained and pruned according to its needs, and according to local regulations. In different vineyards the different climate and type of landscape may require a trellis (above left), or bush, or the single stem, to give the yield of grapes according to the quality desired.

It it rightly said that it takes two years to make a vintage—in other words, the quality and character of the yield in one year is at least partly established in the previous year. For example, the vine roots accumulate starch in their tissues in late summer and autumn, to use as food in the next year and even the year after that.

Young vines do not yield grapes of sufficient quantity or quality for wine making and, in very general terms, they are usually only able to make grapes for good to fine wines when thoroughly mature; the age may vary, but for most fine wines the vines will be at least 5–7 years old. They usually bear for both quantity and quality for up to 20–25 years; after that quantity declines, but quality can remain good for much longer—a lifetime. But then the yield is uneconomic.

The vine buds and then flowers, the base of each cluster blooming first; the fragrance of a vineyard is strange—elusive but slightly pungent. Ideally, the flowering should be over quickly, uninterrupted during 8–10 days. During the flowering and afterwards the weather should be dry and fairly sunny, although a very high temperature can retard the opening of the flowers.

The fruit set then takes place and the berries develop quite rapidly, passing from green to ripe. Sugar content increases with maturity, acidity decreases; in great heat, the grapes ripen very fast, with more gradual heat, slowly; flowering should ideally be fast, ripening fairly slow—but the vintage almost always occurs 100 days after the flowering.

Throughout the year, some moisture is required for the vines, and as the food supply in the leaves virtually ceases in August, a little gentle rain is then needed to augment the supply from the roots and, just before the vintage, to plump out the grapes. All the while the vineyards must be tended, usually tilled at least four times a year, to remove weeds, aerate the soil, facilitate drainage; fertilizers must feed the soil so that it can nourish the vine roots, pruning will control quality and check for any disease on the vines which can be dealt with by spraying. Just before the vintage, dead leaves are removed so as to allow the grapes to get adequate exposure to the sun. In the winter, the vines and vineyards are again tidied and put in order after the vintage.

Frost, which can kill the embryo grapes, is why the mid-May period of the "Ice Saints" (Pancratius, Servatius, Boniface and Sophid) is a critical time; it can also destroy the vines, as happened in many vineyards in 1956. The other enemy is hail, which can batter the vines, maiming them for that year, or shatter the formed grapes. Hail and heavy rain are often localized, sometimes affecting one vineyard while leaving its neighbour wholly unscathed. Excessive rain and heat are also hazards, but excessive humidity, producing fog and possible rot (not the "noble" type) is perhaps worse. The commercially-producing English vineyards have suffered a great deal from this, like those of the US eastern seaboard; obviously even excessive rain can soon be absorbed in a dry climate, but it will make soil heavy and prevent ripening in a damp one.

The Vintage

It is true that there are often picturesque ceremonies associated with the inauguration of a vintage, such as the release of thousands of doves when the first pressing of the grapes is made in front of the Cathedral at Jerez, and the proclamation of the Ban des Vendanges in various regions of the Gironde, a reminder of the time when it was an offence to start vintaging before the time considered best for making quality wine. There are also usually parties for the workers, proprietors and all their colleagues when the vintage is finished.

But the process of gathering the grapes is essentially a hard agricultural task. Although mechanical harvesting machines are in use in some vineyards, in general wine is made by grapes picked by hand, often and ideally under a hot sun. With vines trained low, the task is back-breaking; when they are trained high, equally so. On very steep slopes it may be impossible to stand on a level surface at all, on flatter vineyards the workers may be stumbling over stones or ankle-deep in moist earth. Different types of grapes have to be picked at different times as they ripen, and with the sweet wines workers may have to pass through a vineyard many times, gathering the grapes in small bunches, or, literally, grape by grape. Although a grower will wait until his grapes are ripe, by waiting for an extra day or more he may risk the beginning of autumn rains, or, in northern vineyards, an early frost—yet a slight additional wait may mean vastly superior quality in some fine wine vineyards.

After the vintage, the vines change colour spectacularly, those planted with single grape varieties being most dramatic, brilliant red and gold, until the leaves fall. In the winter the vines have a dark, twisted, bleak appearance—many people looking at a vineyard at this stage suppose the vines to be dead. But even when a vine does die, its roots and stem provide the finest fuel over which to grill meat—often traditional fare at vintage parties—to which a unique flavour is imparted.

Above, at Château d'Yquem the grapes are being inspected for the progress of ripening and action of the *botrytis cinerea* or noble rot.

Right, a traditional vintage scene in a vineyard in Greece.

Below, the workers who pick grapes affected by noble rot must know the exact stage when the fungus has made them suitable for harvesting, and special scissors are necessary to pick grape by grape or small bunch by small bunch. It requires skill and experience.

Table Wines I

The grapes are gathered when ripe and crushed or pressed to release their juice. This pressing is nowadays seldom done by workers treading the grapes, although the action of the human foot is effective because it is important that the pips and stalks of the grapes should not be split and incorporated haphazardly in the must or unfermented grape juice, as this can make it too high in elements that can make the wine hard, astringent and generally unpalatable. Modern presses can be finely adjusted to the grapes they handle and the sort of wine required.

The wine yeasts act upon the sugar in the grape juice and convert it into alcohol. Most freshly pressed grape juice, whether from black or white grapes, is lemonish-yellow and the period during which it becomes wine is a critical one: if the temperature rises too high or drops too low, the yeasts will cease to work. This is why in modern wine making many vats have their temperature controlled automatically; in former times, it was only possible to light fires in the vat or press house to warm things up, or shovel blocks of ice into the must to cool it down. Heavy rain at vintage time also makes it difficult for the yeasts to work satisfactorily, and rain and cold may make it necessary to help the fermentation by the addition of sugar—such as is permitted (though strictly controlled) in many vineyards situated in northern regions or in regions vulnerable to abrupt vicissitudes of the weather. This process, known generally as chaptalization, is not the same as sweetening finished wine to please commercial demands; done skilfully, it should not be in any way obtrusive.

There are a few grapes that yield a pinkish juice, but in general white wine is made from white grapes, red wine from black grapes, although in some regions—notably Champagne and the Rhône Valley—both white and red wines are made from a mixture of black and white grapes. The colour of red wines derives from the pigments in the skins of the black grapes, which, at the time of fermentation, are allowed to remain in contact with the must for a period and impart their colour. For pink wines, the skins of black grapes are left in contact with the must for just long enough for it to acquire a pink tinge. Usually this is about 24 hours; the practice of letting the colour take overnight is the explanation of the expression *vin d'une nuit* sometimes seen on the labels of wines made in southern France. Another method of making pink wine is simply to blend in some red wine with the white—a perfectly pleasant drink if the components are good and harmoniously combined. With white wines, the skins of the grapes are not left in the must during fermentation; with red wines, they

Egrappage à main—rubbing the grapes through a wooden grid, avoiding all contact with metal. Used still in certain Bordeaux estates.

are left, sometimes together with the stems (usually whipped off the grapes in the de-stalking process preliminary to the pressing), so that the colour and the additional tannin—the element that enables certain wines to live as long as a man—may be incorporated in the wine. In former times, this "hat" of grapeskins and débris would be left on certain wines for several weeks; nowadays, when wines are required for earlier consumption, it may only remain a few days or hours. From the vat into which the pressed grapejuice is directed, the finished wine may then be directed into other vats to mature, or into wooden vats or casks—although this is something that is now reserved only for the finer wines. The wine must be run off the lees—the débris and general deposit—and, before it is ready for bottling, it will usually have been subjected to several rackings—the process of running it off its lees in cask—plus fining, when a substance is added to fall through the wine, to clarify it by attracting any particles in suspension. Eggwhite is perhaps the most famous fining element, but fish finings, blood, water and various chemicals may also be used.

Most fine wines undergo three stages of fermentation: the first fermentation, which may with ordinary wines be the only one, is usually rather vigorous, and dies down with the advent of the cooler weather after the vintage. There is also a process known as malolactic fermentation, whereby the malic acid in the wine is converted into lactic acid: this usually only lasts a short time and may with some wines coincide with the first fermentation. With the majority of the finer European classic wines, there is another, secondary, fermentation in the spring after the vintage, during which time the yeasts revive and work again. Unless special precautions are taken, or unless the carbon dioxide given off during fermentation is to be retained in the wine (as with Champagne), it is unlikely that wines will be bottled until they have stopped "working" or fermenting. But how long they remain in the vat, in the cask, or in any blending vat depends on the individual wine and requirements of the wine maker to accommodate his markets. In some areas, such as in very hot vineyards, the malic acid should, ideally, be retained in the wine to make it fresh and crisp; with other wines, the fermentation is over quickly, in a single stage, and the wines can be bottled soon after they are made. Some wines remain in casks for years, some never go into casks at all, others, such as the fine German wines, are made literally cask by individual cask. There is no one single way to make all wines, for what suits one would be inappropriate for another.

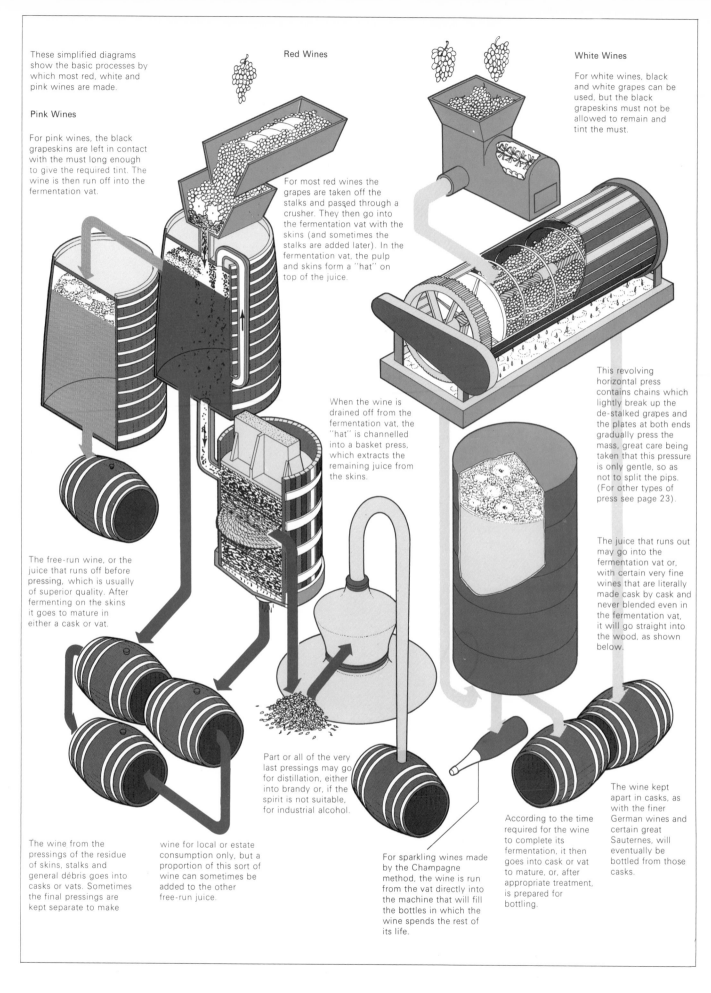

These simplified diagrams show the basic processes by which most red, white and pink wines are made.

Red Wines

White Wines

Pink Wines

For pink wines, the black grapeskins are left in contact with the must long enough to give the required tint. The wine is then run off into the fermentation vat.

For white wines, black and white grapes can be used, but the black grapeskins must not be allowed to remain and tint the must.

For most red wines the grapes are taken off the stalks and passed through a crusher. They then go into the fermentation vat with the skins (and sometimes the stalks are added later). In the fermentation vat, the pulp and skins form a "hat" on top of the juice.

When the wine is drained off from the fermentation vat, the "hat" is channelled into a basket press, which extracts the remaining juice from the skins.

This revolving horizontal press contains chains which lightly break up the de-stalked grapes and the plates at both ends gradually press the mass, great care being taken that this pressure is only gentle, so as not to split the pips. (For other types of press see page 23).

The free-run wine, or the juice that runs off before pressing, which is usually of superior quality. After fermenting on the skins it goes to mature in either a cask or vat.

The juice that runs out may go into the fermentation vat or, with certain very fine wines that are literally made cask by cask and never blended even in the fermentation vat, it will go straight into the wood, as shown below.

The wine from the pressings of the residue of skins, stalks and general débris goes into casks or vats. Sometimes the final pressings are kept separate to make wine for local or estate consumption only, but a proportion of this sort of wine can sometimes be added to the other free-run juice.

Part or all of the very last pressings may go for distillation, either into brandy or, if the spirit is not suitable, for industrial alcohol.

For sparkling wines made by the Champagne method, the wine is run from the vat directly into the machine that will fill the bottles in which the wine spends the rest of its life.

According to the time required for the wine to complete its fermentation, it then goes into cask or vat to mature, or, after appropriate treatment, is prepared for bottling.

The wine kept apart in casks, as with the finer German wines and certain great Sauternes, will eventually be bottled from those casks.

Table Wines 2

Above, a typical old-style wine press and, right, a basket press being loaded with grapes. The disadvantage of these basket presses is that they take time to load and empty.

Right, a series of horizontal presses such as may be seen in many wineries. These presses can operate in different ways to crush the grapes, depending on the type involved and the sort of wine ultimately required—too severe a pressing splits the pips, too light a pressing is obviously wasteful.

Above, a typical wooden fermentation vat, such as is still used for many fine wines, requiring skill to maintain but considered by many to endow the wine with special quality because of the wood.

Right, a series of modern vats in a winery, which may be lined with glass, enamel or, as here, consist entirely of stainless steel, easy to clean and with the temperature thermostatically controlled for the ideal evolution of the wine.

Grape juice becomes wine by the action of the yeasts, which are yellowish substances produced by the propagation of a fungus, *saccharomyces cerevisiae*, found floating in the air in many regions. In areas where new vineyards are being created, however, yeasts may have to be brought in, such as wine yeasts of a special type. Wild yeasts, of which *saccharomyces apiculatus* is the most common, can start off the process of fermentation, but they are not strong enough to make satisfactory wine; the wine yeasts, *saccharomyces ellipsoideus*, can do this, working on the natural sugar in the grape to convert it into alcohol, and fermenting up to about 12–14°C, sometimes a little higher, but ceasing to work at 16°C, whereas the wild yeasts usually die at 4°C.

The yeasts are caught and retained by the bloom on the skin of the grapes, where they excrete enzymes which act as catalysts. This is why rain during the vintage can be a disaster, washing off the bloom and possibly halting the action of the wine yeasts, so that the wine may even have to be started off on its process of fermentation again with outside assistance. The fact that the yeasts need sugar on which to feed is the reason for the chaptalization or sugaring of the must in many northern vineyards, so that the wine can be properly made. But this should be skilfully done, so that the taster does not become aware of the smell of beet sugar.

Above, a Muscat grape, abundant in bloom on its skin. Below, wine yeasts (*saccharomyces cerevisiae*) which will attach themselves to the bloom and excrete enzymes, causing fermentation to take place.

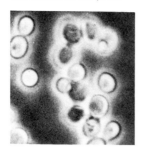

Below, a glass of red wine must, being examined while the wine is being made. The condition of the must has to be carefully supervised, its sugar content having to be satisfactory else the yeasts will not work well. A wine that is too low in alcohol

may lack a strong enough constitution to resist infection —but a wine that is too high may stop the action of the yeasts, so that fermentation halts. Some residual sugar can ultimately remain in the finished wine without it necessarily being obviously sweet, but throughout the entire process of fermentation the wine must be watched for anything untoward occurring.

Wine yeasts vary considerably, those that make sherry being particularly vigorous and inducing a tumultuous fermentation. But the enzymes of the yeasts cannot work if the temperature rises or falls suddenly (think of the use of yeast in baking), and their action will also be arrested by the rise of the alcohol in the wine above a certain point. Yeasts native to certain regions will, as might be expected, work best on the wines of those regions, but very often yeast strains that have proved particularly successful in making certain wines will be sent to other wine regions or wineries where they can be used to improve the wines there, or to enable different styles of wines to be made. For example, in Cyprus, one first-rate Cyprus dry sherry subject to the action of *flor* is made from a native Cyprus wine yeast; but another very good Cyprus dry sherry is made using an Australian yeast strain, and certain fine South African sherries are made with Jerez yeasts. The whole subject is quite complex and chemical, but it is the yeast that brings wine into being.

The taster may sometimes be aware of a smell of yeast in a wine: this can be a stage in the evolution of a young wine and will pass, but a dull, flat yeasty smell can mean the presence of dead yeasts, which should not have remained in a properly made and correctly treated wine. In wine making, dead yeasts can attract the action of the vinegar bacteria and therefore, when fine wines are first made, they are run off from the débris of pips and skins and general mass of solids in which the dead yeasts may remain.

Above, red wine in a vat, during its first fermentation. The surface is moving and giving off carbon dioxide; if you lean over a vat in full fermentation, you should not breathe in and risk a stomach upset. Workers who go into empty vats to clean them can be overcome by fumes.

Louis Pasteur (1822–1895) at work in his laboratory. Pasteur contributed as much to modern wine making as to modern medicine by his work on bacteria. He was asked by Napoleon III to discover why so much wine deteriorated before it reached the customer. It was because Pasteur was born in the Jura region of France, the only one where certain table wines grow le voile, or veil, of fungus on their surfaces, similar to sherry flor, that he was able to relate this process to certain traditional methods whereby wine had been made—and to know why they had certain results. Among other things, he succeeded in identifying the micro-organisms which make grape juice ferment, and he established the role of oxygen in the maturing of wine and the way in which it affects colour. In 1874 Pasteur bought a small property outside Arbois and here he wrote his great Etude Sur Le Vin *in 1878.*

Table Wines 3

The containers in which wine matures and in which it may eventually be shipped vary greatly and, which may surprise drinkers, can contribute enormously to the ultimate quality of the wine. While the enzymes in the wine live, they respond to atmospheric conditions. The porous nature of wood enables air to act on wine.

With still table wines, the container cannot be sealed until the fermentation is complete—the wine must have the space to work and give off any gas (sometimes the violence of a fermentation expels wine down the sides of casks). Therefore fine wines put into casks just after they are made, before the whole fermentation process is finished, must be able to expand; the bungholes are uppermost and bungs put in very loosely. As the fermentation finishes, the casks are topped up (the wine having been racked off any lees), then the bungs are driven home and the casks moved so that the bungholes are at the sides. For wine to be drawn off, either a special cask is kept bung up for the purpose, or else a tap has to be inserted in the head of the cask, prior to bottling. With fortified wines, their strength provides some protection against infections from the atmosphere.

With all wines the condition of the casks is of great importance, a faulty stave, dirty cask or unclean vat can all affect wine seriously; the taste can come through and never be overcome. Some wines are put into new wood, others into wood previously used, for maturation in cask, but the wood of the casks will always have been seasoned before it is used and ideally any cask is made of close-grained hard wood, preferably oak; the finest cask staves are cut with the grain of the wood. It does not matter so much if a cask used for transporting or short-term maturation of the wine imparts some of its natural character—chestnut can do this markedly—as, with a little time and correct handling, this will disappear; but for long-term maturation and for casks to be used for the most sensitive wines no alien flavour should be risked, although it is quite normal for wines to assume a slight flavour of the new casks while they are young and only recently in wood. With wine kept in steel or glass-lined vats, of course, the problem does not arise, and this is perfectly satisfactory for many delicate wines and most wines of everyday character easily affected by contact with the outside atmosphere. Vats, of course, also have to be kept scrupulously clean, but old wooden vats, like casks for certain wines, can add to the quality of the wine in a curious and definite way. (Old wine casks are much sought after by the makers of Scotch and Irish whiskey, who can detect, when making up their blends, the type of cask in which the spirit was matured.) In different wine regions, different casks are used, most, nowadays, being of moderate size, as few huge ones are practical for long-term maturation.

Bottles
Bottling must be done so that the wine runs no risk of being affected by dirt in the bottle; some of the finest German wines are bottled under sterile conditions, the bottling line looking rather like a mechanised operating theatre. Most bottles arrive for use having been sterilized. They should be filled up to the level at which the cork meets the wine, but obviously it is not possible to do this without any air at all being in the bottle; with time, and if a cork is very old, the level of the wine may go down slightly—this space between cork and wine is called ullage, and although a fairly ullaged bottle may contain perfectly drinkable wine, the presence of more than a small amount of air in the bottle can eventually make a wine oxidize.

There is no reason why inexpensive wines should not be put up in metal or plastic containers, providing these do not impart any flavour to the wine. Plastic stoppers of various kinds are perfectly satisfactory for many wines, including such sparkling and fortified wines that are going to be drunk soon after they have been offered for sale. Cork becomes increasingly expensive and crown corks (metal caps with a thin inner lining of cork) are also quite acceptable for cheap wines. The only reason to object to an innovation of this kind is if you think it affects the wine's taste. Many sparkling wines, including some Champagnes, have a crown cork instead of an agrafe and first cork nowadays; you can tell whether this is so by the neck of the bottle, which will have a smooth bulge just below it, like a tonic bottle, whereas a neck that has had to hold an agrafe will have a much more definite ridge.

Wine matures faster in a small bottle than in a large one, but although large sizes—up to 2 litres—are becoming very popular for cheap wines, the good to fine wines are obviously at risk in a large bottle, in case this should break. The magnum size is generally considered ideal for the finest wines, but this requires a number of drinkers, and the standard wine bottle, generally assumed to be the 75 cl size, is therefore the most usual today.

The capsule on the bottle is to protect the cork, but, as it is important for the wine to be able to "breathe" through this, capsules are often pierced for ventilation. In the past, wax was often used to seal bottles, but even wax seems somehow to be more porous than plastic, which is often used today—and which often presents problems about getting it off the bottle.

Stripping and Sterilizing Cork
Top, stripping the bark from the cork oak—at its best in the Iberian Peninsula.

Above, the stripped cork has to be matured outdoors and then sterilized before being graded and cut for whatever type and size is required.

Firing a Barrel

In the cooperage, a cask with its staves held together by metal hoops is "fired". The heat of the fire makes the staves contract and join tightly together.

Cork Weevil
Above, the cork weevil's action. A capsule affords some protection against it, but its tunnelling can allow air to reach the wine.

Champagne Corks
Sparkling wine corks, below. The *agrafe* or metal clip; the cork from a 1964 Roederer Cristal, with a new cork showing the layers and bonded top; a Krug cork, with an unused one hand-made in layers without bonding; the metal muzzle and the long metal capsule, pierced to allow the cork to breathe.

Standard Cork Sizes
Above, basic wine corks. Left to right, "full long", 2", for vintage port and the very finest reds; $1\frac{7}{8}$", for Bordeaux and Burgundies; "short long", $1\frac{3}{4}$", for wines for early drinking; shorter cork for inexpensive wines. Crown corks and plastic stoppers are now also much used.

Old Corking Machine
Above, a machine with a needle at the side of the section that inserts the corks; to allow expansion when the cork is in the bottle neck. In very old machines, the capsule is smoothed and secured round the neck by a string, looped, pulled, and then released.

Old Bottling Machine
Right, an old type of bottling machine still often used. The bottles are held in rows and then filled, after which they can pass through machines that attach the various labels.

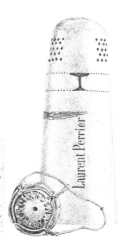

Bottling
Right, a simplified diagram of a bottling line, which usually takes up considerable space. Left to right, the huge vats release their contents into a filter—its plates hold asbestos filter sheets. The wine then goes into the automatic bottling machine, filling the bottles evenly. They arrive sterilized, then pass on to be corked and labelled, the machine attaching label, capsule and further labels (on the back or neck). Finally the bottles are packed in cartons.

At each stage in the process, inspectors examine them for clarity, quantity of wine per bottle, and proper labelling.

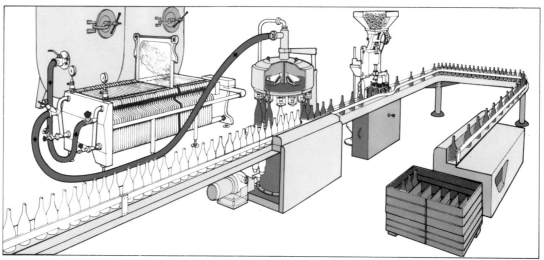

The Champagne Method

Grape picking in Champagne requires special skill, because a severely bruised grape will immediately start to ferment, and Chardonnay grapes in particular have fragile skins. Each vintager is armed with an *épinette*, a type of scissors and they work in teams, one on each side of a row of vines, each with an attendant who carries off the filled baskets to the bigger ones for despatch to the presshouse. In case of any imperfect grapes being included, a preliminary sorting is often done in the vineyard—this careful selection ensures the quality but inevitably puts up the price of the wine. The women are wearing *bagnolets*, the traditional Champagne sunbonnets.

Pressing must be rapid and the press is a special one, called a *maie*, made of oak. The Chardonnay yields slightly more juice than the Pinot, but the juice of the different pressings is kept separate, the juice of the first pressing making the finest wine. The loading, pressing, breaking up of the mass of squashed grapes in the press and final unloading of the press will take six hours or more and the work is extremely hard.

Champagne bottle sizes
From left to right a quarter-bottle, half-bottle, bottle, magnum, jeroboam, rehoboam, methuselah.

¼   ½   1   2   4   6   8

Although the regulations governing the use of the term "Champagne" and "Champagne method" only prevail in the European Community, it is probably most convenient to assume that, for the purposes of this book, they apply throughout the world; the differences in wines that are quite legally termed "Champagne" in certain countries but which do not come into the definition as understood in the EEC, will be easily appreciated, and it is no reflection on the quality of the numerous wines which may be offered as "Champagne" to know why they are different.

Champagne is made from the grapes grown within the various vineyards of the Champagne region, either the Pinot Noir or the white Chardonnay being used, and, for the majority of Champagnes, a combination of the two. The first fermentation dies down at the beginning of the cold weather after the vintage and in the spring, before the wine starts to ferment again, the different vattings or *cuvées* are blended according to the type of Champagne that each individual house wishes to make. (It should be remembered that each establishment will have its own style and its own variations on the basic method). The wine then goes into bottle, the first cork is inserted and attached to the neck of the bottle by a clip going over the flange at the top, this being known as an *agrafe*. The Champagne will spend all the rest of its life in this bottle. The secondary fermentation therefore takes place after this, having been given a little incentive by the addition of what is known as *liqueur de tirage*—a little still Champagne in which a small quantity of sugar has been dissolved. The carbon dioxide subsequently produced cannot come out of the bottle, which is now sealed, and therefore it remains in the wine—which incorporates its sparkle.

The wine must now mature, for at least two to three years for non-vintage Champagne, three to five for a vintage. During this time it is subjected to a process known as *remuage*, whereby the bottles, placed with their necks pointed down in racks called *pupîtres*, are rotated and shaken by hand, both to shake up and blend the wine thoroughly and also to release any deposit clinging to the side of the bottle. Each day the shakers of the bottles given them an additional turn and a slight additional inclination downwards, so that, after about three months or more, they are standing upside down in their racks, and any deposit in the wine will have slipped down the bottle and be resting on the cork. After this, they can be binned away, still upside down, the cork of one bottle resting in the punt or hollowed base of the one below it—very curious they look. How long they remain like this depends on the type of

In the spring, before the fermentation can start again, the different vattings or *cuvées* are blended according to the style of Champagne the establishment wishes to make. Each house has its own style and variations on the basic method. The wine then goes into bottle, the first cork is inserted and held down by a metal clip, called an *agrafe*. It will spend the rest of its life in this bottle.

The sort of sediment, composed of both light and heavy substances, that has to be shaken down on to the first cork by rotating and oscillating the bottles. A professional can rotate 100,000 bottles a day and oscillate 40,000.

The process of rotating and oscillating the bottles is known as *remuage*. It takes years to learn this skill. The *remueurs* work in miles of underground galleries—where car rallies are sometimes held. There are over 26 kilometres under one Champagne house, 20 under another. The bottles are in frames, in which they are both turned and inclined at an increasing angle. The original frame or *pupitre* was possibly cut from Madame Clicquot's kitchen table.

wine and the quality of the house. When the wine is required for sale, the bottle will be subjected to the "disgorging" process. The *agrafe* is removed and the first cork taken out; a little lump of ice comes with it and this contains the sludge and deposit. The second cork is then inserted, and also any "dosage" required: this is sweetening dissolved in wine, according to whether a wholly dry or slightly sweet wine is required. Once the second cork is in, the wire muzzle goes over the top of it, being prevented from biting into the cork (the *agrafe* bites deep) by a small metal disc; the cork is further protected by a capsule, which has its origin in times when the rats in the cellars would bite through the wine-soaked cord used for tying down the corks before wire came into common use. The bottle is then "dressed", receiving its label or labels, wrapped in tissue and put ready for despatch; ideally the wine should have a further short period to settle down after disgorging.

The important thing to remember is that the age of Champagne depends on the date when the second cork went in: a wine that is on its first cork and in the cellars where it has been made can have its life very much prolonged, but once the second cork goes in the wine will begin to age markedly and eventually decline. Old Champagne, which tends to go slightly flat and become darker in colour, can, if originally a fine wine, be delicious, but people who want something light, young and very fizzy may consider it past its best.

The process whereby Champagne is made is lengthy, requiring much skill, and therefore the wine can never be cheap. The cost of the special corks, of the bottles (to resist the pressure inside) and of everything to do with a sparkling wine made by the process is unavoidably high. In addition, the base wine has to be of high quality. It is never worthwhile subjecting any inferior wine to the process whereby it is made sparkling —sparkling wines of inferior quality are even worse than they would be in still form.

After the process of *remuage* (see above), the wine, resting on its first cork, is stored for maturation with the bottles upside down. In the cellars cut out of the chalk, it can remain like this for many years—depending on the type of wine to be made and the quality of the house making it.

When the wine is matured and ready to be offered for sale, it is subject to a process known as disgorging. This used to be done entirely by hand, the *agrafe* being removed with pliers, the deposit clinging to the cork coming with it; the bottle is topped up with any wine lost and the dosage—the amount of sweetening required according to the type of wine made—is added. The second cork goes in, topped with a metal cap to resist the pressure of the wire muzzle, the bottle is then "dressed" with capsule and labels and, after further maturation, is ready for sale. Nowadays most houses pass the necks of the bottles through a freezing solution so that, when the cork comes out, a pellet of ice including the deposit comes too and the topping up can be mechanically achieved.

Fortified Wines I

As their name implies, fortified wines are those that are "stronger"—made so by the addition of spirit. The most important ones are sherry, port, Madeira and Marsala. They are essentially different from table wines because of the way they are made, but all start as wine.

Sherry

For the making of sherry, the grapes are sometimes dried in the open, on esparto grass mats; after pressing, the grape juice is put into new casks and moved to the bodegas.

Sherry yeasts are strong, and the fermentation begins almost immediately, making a noise in the casks like a crowd of giants chuckling. When the sherry has been fully fermented, all the natural grape sugar will have been converted into alcohol. Essentially, all sherry is a bone dry wine; any sweetness in it to satisfy the demands of the market will be added later. Indeed, the sweet sherries so popular on export markets are virtually unknown in Spain itself. The solera system, which is used for sherry making, is the means whereby different wines are matured and blended so that a consistent and individual type of sherry will result. The term solera also describes the place or store where the actual solera system is in use. A particular solera will produce a particular wine, and the sherries which make up that particular solera will never have passed any period of their life in another solera.

The young sherry, when fermentation is completed, receives a first slight fortification with alcohol. It is then classified. There are only two main sherry types, fino and oloroso, and no one can decide in advance what a cask of wine will become. In the process of classification, the potential finos are marked with a chalk sign known as a "palm" because of its shape; wines that show signs of the oloroso style are known as *rayas*; they receive a stroke cut across with one or more other strokes according to strength and delicacy.

After classification the wine goes into the solera system and progresses through casks stacked in tiers, also known as scales. It is not moved simply from cask to cask, upwards or downwards, but is used to replenish each of the casks in proportion when older wine is drawn off; these in turn replenish the casks from which wines have been drawn, up to the final selection, which will be the consignment selected by the shipper. If wine were a constant commodity it would be possible to move it through the solera in identical progressive patterns, but one of the mysteries of sherry is that it does not remain the same, and the refreshment of the casks must consequently also vary.

The solera system could be likened to a large school with the wines representing the pupils: some of them at the outset go into different forms, or different divisions of the same form, others start at the bottom; as they mature, some progress straight up the school, others vary in their progress, sometimes skipping a stage, or being put into some specialized division.

Port

A large number of different grapes, both white and red, are used to make port which is always a blend of various musts. The grape juice is pressed *in situ*, in the Douro, where it also goes through the fermentation process. Not all the natural sugar is converted into alcohol, for fermentation is arrested at a certain point by the addition of grape brandy, supplied by the Portuguese authorities. With this fortification, fermentation stops, and the port wine remains sweet, to a greater or lesser extent.

In the spring of the year following the vintage, the young port wine comes down to Vila Nova de Gaia, opposite Oporto. Here it goes into the shippers' lodges where it is sorted into different "lots" according to style. The wines are tasted, blended and matured in these lodges, and with the exception of vintage port, which spends most of its life in bottle, port, like sherry, spends its life mostly in wood.

Madeira and Marsala

For Madeira, when fermentation has taken place, some fortification with spirit is given to the wines, according to type; Madeira then goes into a heating chamber known as an *estufa*, where it is gradually heated up and then gradually cooled, over a period of about three months. Madeira is matured in cask before being bottled, but it first goes through a stage similar to the solera system.

For Marsala, after the wine has been made and blended a concentrate of great sweetness is added as well as a heated concentrate known as *sifone* or cooked wine. The Marsala blends are then made up, and the wine is matured in wood in a solera system.

Development of the Port Bottle
The earliest port bottle (left) is squat and bulbous. Over the years (left to right) the bottle develops into a shape more suitable for binning on its side in the cellar. The neck is also slightly bulbous, to permit expansion of the "full long" port cork (essential if the wine is to be kept for many years). Individual houses and even private customers often had their own medallions on the side of the bottle. Today there is a trend to return to the 19th century shape, both to distinguish port from other fortified wines, and, with more being bottled in Portugal these days, from a natural sense of national pride in the use of the traditional bottle shape.

1708   1739   1753   1780   1807   1812

Sherry

A simplified diagram of the making of sherry. The grapes are previously dried on mats; in the old days they were trodden in wooden *lagares* and then pressed again in a sandwich device. The men wore boots with nails angled in the soles, designed to avoid crushing the grape pips into the mixture and affecting its taste. The diagram also shows a modern balloon press, in which pressure is applied by compressed air, while the drum rotates to loosen the "cake" of solid matter. The aim is still to extract the maximum juice without splitting the pips. The juice then runs into the fermentation vats below.

Port

A simplified diagram of how port is made. The grapes used to be trodden in the *lagar* by barefoot workmen. This practice is dying out, in spite of the feelings of traditionalists that modern methods are no improvement on the naked foot. The must starts fermenting at once in the *lagar*. Again, the more modern method, the autovinificator (see below), aims at the same effect, with the must running off into the *tonels*, or vats, for the fermentation to be stopped by the addition of grape spirit.

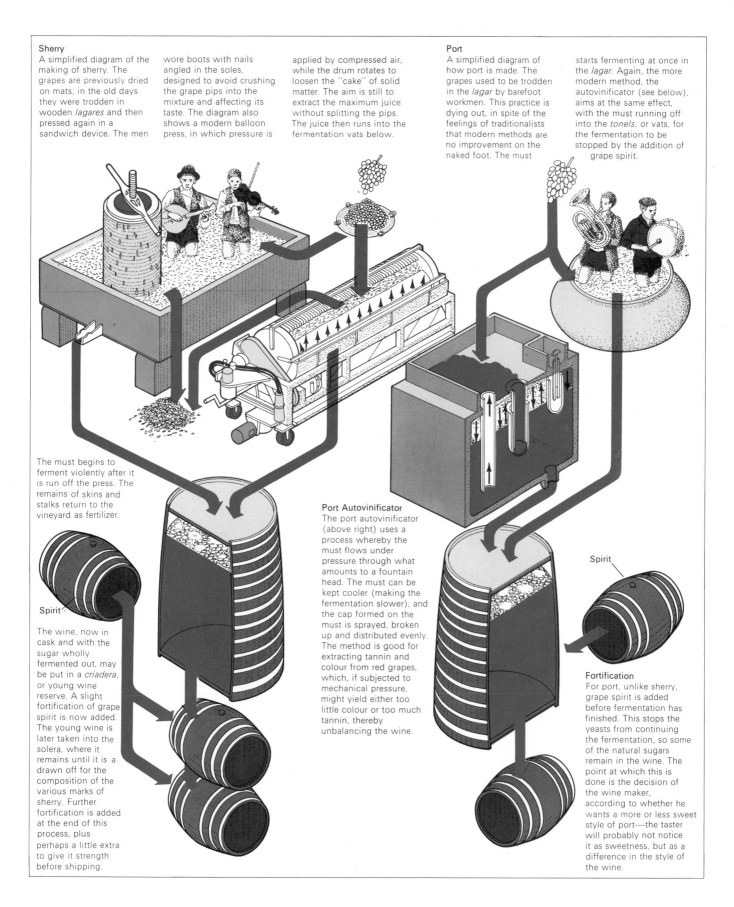

The must begins to ferment violently after it is run off the press. The remains of skins and stalks return to the vineyard as fertilizer.

Spirit

The wine, now in cask and with the sugar wholly fermented out, may be put in a *criadera*, or young wine reserve. A slight fortification of grape spirit is now added. The young wine is later taken into the solera, where it remains until it is drawn off for the composition of the various marks of sherry. Further fortification is added at the end of this process, plus perhaps a little extra to give it strength before shipping.

Port Autovinificator

The port autovinificator (above right) uses a process whereby the must flows under pressure through what amounts to a fountain head. The must can be kept cooler (making the fermentation slower), and the cap formed on the must is sprayed, broken up and distributed evenly. The method is good for extracting tannin and colour from red grapes, which, if subjected to mechanical pressure, might yield either too little colour or too much tannin, thereby unbalancing the wine.

Spirit

Fortification

For port, unlike sherry, grape spirit is added before fermentation has finished. This stops the yeasts from continuing the fermentation, so some of the natural sugars remain in the wine. The point at which this is done is the decision of the wine maker, according to whether he wants a more or less sweet style of port—the taster will probably not notice it as sweetness, but as a difference in the style of the wine.

Fortified Wines 2

Right, grapes drying in the open on esparto grass mats before being pressed for sherry. The same preliminary drying is used for various other wines, as the reduction in the water content has the effect of concentrating the juice. The hot dry atmosphere of the south of Spain enables this to be done without adversely affecting the grapes.

Left, one of the bodegas of Zoilo Ruis Mateos, at Jerez de la Frontera, showing why such bodegas are likened to cathedrals. The air must circulate freely, and in the summer heat the bodegas are closed in the afternoon and the windows shielded by blinds. The range of casks form the solera, from which the great blends of wines are composed according to the style of the establishments.

Above, *flor* on the surface of a fino. It will thicken or almost vanish according to the time of year, but the constantly stirring bacteria is one of the most awe-inspiring sights—here the life of the wine is seen, protected by the curious, woolly-looking covering.

Above, topping up a sherry butt in a bodega belonging to Sandeman in Jerez. The dry heat of the region causes vast quantities of wine to evaporate annually, so the butts of older wine are continually being topped up with wine that is younger but of the same style.

Above, picking the port grapes on the terraced slopes of the Douro. Left, the first stage in the making of port. With few exceptions, the traditional method of men treading the grapes up the Douro has been superseded by the autovinificator, which enables the grapes to be crushed and the juice released without splitting the pips.

Madeira

Before roads facilitated the transport of the newly made wine from the vineyards in the mountains of Madeira to the shippers' lodges in Funchal, it was human labour which brought the wine down the steep pathways, carrying the wine in whole goatskins. This was done until comparatively recent times, but now most vineyards are accessible by modern transport. The goatskin is one of the earliest means of carrying wine. The Spanish porrón, the glass vessel with a handle and spout, evokes the time when wine was carried in a skin, easily attached to a saddlebow, and the wine could be squirted into the mouth of the drinker without his lips having to touch the aperture.

Above, up in the Douro Valley, these baskets of grapes are to be ferried across the river between Pinhão and Regua. The Douro, a "sly river", runs deceptively fast between many rocks and gorges. Left, a port lodge in Vila Nova de Gaia, across the Douro from Oporto, centre of the wine trade. These lodges are often remarkably beautiful, as the Portuguese coopers are skilled in making even the most utilitarian woodwork handsome. The wine stays here until it is ready to go into bottle or to be shipped in bulk to markets abroad. The pipes of port are kept topped up with fat-bellied copper jugs, of different sizes.

31

Selling and Shipping Wine

When the wine has been made, it must be sold. People are often romantically-inclined about wine, but in fact it is a business commodity and must have a purpose—to please the customer and profit the maker. It is no use for the owner of a great estate to have vast stocks of past vintages on hand—after the wine has gone into bottle, it ought to leave the property, either to mature further in the cellars of a shipper or merchant; if it is not bottled at the estate, it must then be bottled by the shipper or merchant.

It is sometimes difficult to understand that grower, shipper and merchant may be all the same person or firm; but a merchant usually ships some wine himself, and a shipper may also either make it in his own vineyards or buy it direct from peasant growers, to handle it in his own establishment. A shipper or merchant may have an exclusivity as regards certain wines, or have particular lines made specially for them.

In countries where there is a state monopoly, such as Canada and some of the Scandinavian countries, wines are selected from ranges submitted; elsewhere individual firms buy from the producers, often visiting the regions to do so, or having samples submitted to them in their own establishments. Much depends on the kind of sales they wish to make: a big retail chain, for example, may require quite different wines—and far greater quantities—from the needs of the independent and more specialist merchant. Many harsh things have been said about big firms, but in fact they have often made it possible for the public to enjoy a wide range of good cheap wines, simply because the quantities they can order enables a lower price to be passed on to the consumer. They can keep up quality: the Italian wine bargains which will provide equal value vineyards, and Nicolas, the biggest merchants in the world, have enormous influence on many classic areas, notably Chablis. At the same time, an independent smaller firm may find individual wine bargains which will provide equal value and interest to its customers, and estate wines in inevitably limited supply. Both have parts to play.

Where the wine is bottled is naturally of interest, and there is an increasing tendency to bottle in the country where the wine was made, if not actually at the estate. With wines in the medium and low price ranges, it is not of great importance where the bottling is done and, obviously, the shipper who has vast technical resources at his disposal may be able to handle a wine to its advantage better than a small concern or grower unfamiliar with the most modern techniques. The great wines are certainly all bottled at the estates where they are made, but bulk wines may advantageously be shipped in bulk, and bottled where they are to be drunk: unkind remarks are made about tankers, but in fact a wine is likely to resist the hazards of a journey far better if it travels in bulk, even the specially constructed hold of a ship, rather than in a small container. The delicate wines, naturally, are not subjected to this sort of treatment, but everyday wines need take no harm from it. Indeed, if there are delays or strikes or sudden changes in the weather, these hazards to the good condition of wine are better resisted by it when it is in a large container.

Wines bottled where they are made and those bottled in the country of their origin are not to be judged in the same way: estate wines are handled close to their own vineyards, but a wine can be moved several hundred miles and still be bottled in the country of its origin.

If you do get the chance to compare an estate bottled wine with the same wine bottled elsewhere, remember that the estate bottling need not always be superior; it should, ideally, be a more distinctive version of the wine. It probably will be evident that the wine bottled after making a longish journey will be slightly in advance of the estate-bottling.

As far as the finest wines are concerned, buyers usually start by looking at them where they are made, although they generally want to examine their potential purchases again in the austerity of their own tasting-rooms where they do their work. Samples of wines still in cask or vat are obviously in a state of transition and much skill and experience is necessary to be able to divine the potential progress and capabilities of young wines that may need long maturation after bottling. The ability to taste wines at this stage is very much the rôle of the shipper; some of even the best merchants find it difficult, though they may be able to pick out wines that are nearing their point of sale with great accuracy in relation to the needs of their markets.

The relationship of drinker to source of supply is delicate but important: if you live where there are several retail outlets for wine, it is a pity not to take advantage of all—no single merchant, however good, can list every fine or good wine in the world, or have every sort of bargain. The supermarket, retail chain, big firm, small concern, mail order house—all can give the individual drinker value and enhance his experience of wines. The lines of the independent concern can provide great value, the finer wines of the big firm can be advantageous in price—and vice versa. Buying in bulk, even if by the single case lot or dozen, can save money; buying the odd bottle that is part of a special offer can do likewise.

Tasting Wine

Tasting Wine

There is nothing mysterious about tasting. It is a method of approaching wine that can be learned, although only experience and intelligent practice can give authority.

The prime aim of tasting is to find a wine that is enjoyable, whether you are tasting with a view to buying wine for domestic use, to gain enough knowledge to order wine with confidence when dining out, or to try new wines so that they will please rather than disappoint. Eventually you should hope to be able to buy young wines for long-term maturation and improvement, and to form intelligent ideas about suitable wines for long-term laying down.

Tasting is a refinement of the process of drinking. Once the basic ways of approaching a wine have been learnt, few people find it difficult to register at least a few of the sensations they experience. The significance of these experiences and what they mean needs interpreting and relating to known factors about the wine under consideration. The language that describes tasting experiences is both learned by and personally created by the taster, for the language of wine, like the language of the creative arts, is specialized. It should never degenerate into jargon or meaningless technicalities, and the beginner should not pretend to understand incomprehensible terms, A new, simple vocabulary of wine has been created for the readers of this book (see page 180) to help them understand both technical and personal tasting terms.

A good sense of smell is an asset, nearly as useful as a good memory and the ability to make notes. Taste is at least 75 per cent smell and it would obviously be very difficult for anyone with no sense of smell to taste wines properly. But it is possible to cultivate what sense of smell you have, and even if this has deteriorated, it will often be found that other senses, such as sight and the feel of the wine in the mouth, will be developed in a compensatory way.

A good memory is as important as a good sense of smell. It is a great help if you can relate what tasting experiences you already have to those you are in the process of acquiring. Several outstanding tasters have told me that as they got older their memory let them down, and while they could relate wines they were tasting to those they had tasted ten or twenty years ago, they could

Above, using a *copita* to check a cask sample of sherry in a *bodega* in Jerez.

Below, a 1539 tasting scene in Germany. The types of taster are the same today: salesman, producer, self-styled expert, bored man looking for a drink—and the one who really knows wine.

Bottom, serious work in Taylor's Lodge in Vila Nova de Gaia, appraising samples of port.

less easily remember those they had been looking at the previous month. In the language of wine tasting, one "sees" or "looks at" a wine.

The memory can be cultivated by notes, which should be made at the time of tasting—they are never as useful made even an hour or so later. When reading about wine, pause to relate your personal experiences to the views of the writer. Any tag or direct association is of the greatest help in aiding taste memory: some legend or historical fact will give personality to what may previously have been only a wine name. For example, the tradition, created by Colonel Bisson in the late 18th century, that army regiments should salute and present arms when passing the Clos Vougeot vineyard is memorably linked with this famous Burgundy.

Memory can also be aided by evoking the place where the wine is made. "The climate, the feet, the ferments", the late Allan Sichel would say, recommending his students to extend their sensory antennae in order to "listen to what the wine has to say". Anyone who has felt the soil of a great vineyard in his hands, known the heat that strikes down and is reflected from the earth, stood in a presshouse hazy with the living dust of grape bloom and yeasts, or sniffed the atmosphere in a cellar where fine wines are growing up, will never again feel that wine is just an ordinary drink.

Sometimes the taster, without being aware of a series of thoughts, will hear a wine speak directly to him and identify it, just as one human being will in a second identify a single face, already known and loved, in a crowd.

The right attitude of mind is perhaps the most important asset. Honesty is essential, for the insincere taster can be tricked by a fancy label, a great reputation, a high price, or by the assumption that a good or great wine is being presented. He may also remain uncertain about quality if he never differentiates between what he likes and what he thinks is good. True humility is also essential; the serious taster must be prepared to learn by his mistakes. Many people will assert that they can always tell red Bordeaux from red Burgundy. I once asked two of the most admired tasters of their day how many times they had mistaken a claret (red Bordeaux) for a Burgundy, and the reply was "Dozens of times". The subtleties of Bordeaux can deceive many into

thinking that certain wines, such as some of the greater estate St-Emilions, are Burgundies.

There is no serious taster who has not often been deceived by being led to expect that he is tasting one type of wine when another is in the glass, by being given an uncharacteristic vintage or an untypical estate wine or a wine made by some specialized individual process. But I have also seen people identify a long line of wines with absolute authority, and all the wines accompanying a dinner without hesitation. This is a game that wine lovers play; not in itself a gauge of knowledge, but an indication of sensitivity, experience and memory when one is on form.

Above, the use of the *tastevin* in Burgundy.

Left, the *velenche* or pipette used to draw a sample through the bunghole, demonstrated in the Hunter River Valley in New South Wales.

Wine Tastings

There are two kinds of serious wine tastings: those given by wine merchants showing a range of wines that are ready or nearly ready to drink, and those given by shippers of young wines, many of which may be far too immature to drink. Some wine lovers find it difficult to taste fine wines while they are young, and if you, after a little experience, share this view, keep to the other type of tasting. If this too interferes in any way with your actually enjoying wine, then simply taste wines as you drink them with food, even if they can never be as severely judged as at a professional tasting.

Tastings to which the public are invited may be picturesque, taking place in a cellar, by candlelight, with bits of cheese to nibble, sometimes with a commentary on each wine by someone of authority. At this type of tasting, the tasters may even sit down. This can be a valuable way of learning, if after a little while you can form and maintain an opinion about a subject and not merely accept the opinions of someone else, no matter how respected. Always avoid the risk of becoming the dupe of someone who may inform you that something is good when your instincts and judgment tell you that it is bad. To hear someone talk about wine *after* one has tasted or to take part in a discussion during a tasting can be illuminating, and professional tasters are always interested in the questions and differences of opinions of beginners.

The more serious and professional type of tasting is less atmospheric simply because tasting is demanding both to the senses and intelligence, and noise, distracting smells of flowers and food, social chat, dim or coloured lights can seriously interfere with the contact of the taster with the wine. For various reasons buyers sometimes have to taste in a grower's cellar, but usually they appraise wines in what looks like a cross between an operating theatre and a chemistry laboratory. There will be plenty of white light, daylight or artificial, white surfaces against which colours can be sharply determined, space for bottles and glasses to be arranged so that tasters do not jostle each other. There will be a sink or spittoon easy of access, possibly a few pieces of bread or dry biscuits to refresh palates; no one will talk much and then only in moderated tones. Serious wine tasting must be done like this; the annual turnover of a huge business may depend on the decision of one or two people.

Finally, there is the tasting party, an agreeable new style of entertaining. This may begin with a fairly serious study session and then turn into a buffet party, the wines continuing to be drunk. Alternatively, it may feature a range of wines with a theme: a holiday country or a region, a selection from one winery, a series of different

Tasting vessels. Top, the Burgundy *tastevin*, still in use. In dimly-lit cellars it shows the colour of wine as it glints over the indentations. The wine hits the mouth in a different way, too, and for some this sharpens the taste impressions. Next, the Bordeaux *tasse de vin*, no longer used; shaped like a saucer, it has an interior bulge for colour comparison. Bottom, two views of the newly evolved Chianti tasting cup, in the shape of the cockerel that is the Chianti emblem.

vintages or makers of wines all bearing the same names. People may select wines for buying from such tastings, or they may use them as the basis for a party, or fund-raising activity. An evening of music by Schubert was once arranged with an interval tasting of Herr von Schubert's superb Ruwer wines, the only connection being the coincidence of the name. Such tastings are enhancements of civilized life and may well introduce wines to people who form a life-long love for them.

At a professional tasting the wines will usually be restricted to those from a few regions and frequently from one only, such as a range of hocks and Mosels from a single vintage or at most a pair of vintages. Occasionally, a greater progression of vintages is shown; even if the oldest wines are not offered for sale it is possible for the tasters to observe the type of progress the wines make as they age. Non-vintage and young table wines are tasted before older and finer wines; if the wines are the same age the cheaper ones are tasted first.

At tastings of both white and red table wines, it is a matter of personal taste as to which are approached first. If the white wine tasting line ends with a wine that is in any way sweet, such as a great sweet German wine, a Sauternes or a very spicy or luscious Alsatian, ideally the red wines are tasted first. It is difficult to go on to dry red wines after sweet white ones. If no sweet wines are included among the whites, most people will take the white wines first. Personally, I find certain wines more difficult and tiring to taste than others, and I tend to take the difficult ones first, for example white Burgundy before Rhône, red Loire or Bordeaux.

Tasting in Vineyard Regions

Many famous properties have special reception-cum-tasting rooms for the benefit of visitors where samples of wine may be stored and either drunk, or tasted and spat out. At a tasting in a cellar or specific wine store, such as the above-ground *chais* (wine stores) of Bordeaux or the bodegas of Jerez, tasting samples will usually be drawn directly from the cask. People who visit cellars are often surprised that old bottles are not broached for tasting, but by the time the wine is in bottle it is usually already sold and has been sent away; any remaining bottles will be either the owner's personal reserve or such recent bottlings as are still on sale. For a cask sample, the wine may be drawn from the cask with an instrument resembling a large-scale pipette and known in France as the *velenche*. The wine is drawn into it by plunging the *velenche* in the bung-hole: the liquid flows into the vessel and is retained in it

Tasting rooms, old and new. Left, the arcaded cellars of Hatch, Mansfield, under London's Pall Mall; in use for wine at least since 1802, and possibly long before that. Above, the London tasting room of Sichel, an independent family firm famous for their French and German classic wines. In the austerity of such surroundings details of colour, bouquet and flavour can be rigorously examined, and wines selected for world markets.

while the end is stopped with the thumb; gradual release of the thumb will also release the wine from the end of the pipette and direct it into the tasting glass. In Jerez, a different instrument for drawing up sherry from the cask is used. This is the *venencia* and consists of an elongated metal cup on the end of a long, whalebone handle, which is plunged through the surface coating of *flor*. At Sanlúcar de Barrameda, where manzanillas are made, the *venencia* handle is made of bamboo. Sometimes a sample may be drawn from a spigot in the head of the cask, one of the staves being levered inwards so as to increase the pressure behind the tap and force the wine through.

When you are tasting in vineyard regions, remember that the wine will not yet have passed through the various processes that make it star bright and as it will later appear in the bottle. It may have been racked off the lees (pumped from cask to cask, so that each cask is kept filled to the bung), or fined (the process whereby any loose particles in suspension in the wine are collected to be removed). Wines undergoing this kind of treatment will not be at their best and any wine that is still going through a stage of fermentation is impossible to taste.

Impediments to Tasting
It is useless, whatever the type of tasting session, to try and gain anything from the wines if you are in a distracted frame of mind. Any malaise,

irritation or preoccupying emotion will interfere. Noise, bad light, social interruptions all make tasting difficult, even impossible. The most obvious distraction, however, is smell. Everything and everyone has its own particular smell; as you become more experienced in tasting, you will discover that your sense of smell becomes more alert. Everyone tastes against their own smell: the smell of the body itself and anything associated with it. It is other people's smells that may cause the distraction.

On one occasion, a layman commented that, with my entrance into the tasting room, he would be unable to smell the wines. I was able to reply truthfully that I could smell his hair and after-shave lotion, shoe polish, the cleaning fluid used on his suit and the pipe and tobacco in his pocket. No one can help having their own smells but when they intrude on the tastings of others it is considerate to try to minimize them. Women invited to a serious tasting will not use any form of scent, and they will beware of scented soaps, hair lacquer, talcum powder and lipstick.

No serious taster would smoke at a tasting, or smoke heavily before a tasting, any more than they would eat curry or drink fruit juice before-hand, the acidity of which will make wines taste too bland. Anything very sweet will make wines taste bitter, and a chocolate before tasting makes it virtually impossible to taste anything for several hours afterwards.

Tasting Techniques

No art should be taught by dictating absolute procedures and there is no one way that is best in learning to taste. Several methods are adopted by those reputed for their teaching ability, but these are not always easily followed by wine lovers outside the trade.

Some instructors find it helpful to be scientific, commenting on each aspect of the wine in technical terms, assessing its chemical composition. As the purpose of wine drinking is enjoyment, this scientific approach can be less than useful and often leads to a clinical method of analysis, fault-finding and drawing on technical skills.

Other teachers insist on pupils keeping rigidly to a set routine: no tasting before the wine's bouquet has been dealt with, no smelling before the colour has been fully discussed. Some even allocate a definite time for each stage! This, like a commentary on a wine before you taste it, can be irritating, and pupils may be unable to work in such a rigid way. Also, if you are made to draw definite conclusions, in a set order, from colour, smell and flavour, you may find all your justified theories upset — because wines are individuals. It can often happen that, whereas a colour and/or smell might lead you to expect a certain sort of wine, the flavour or even just the after-taste will be wholly at variance with your previously formed convictions; as it is always unwise to work over a taste to excess—you will end by knowing little or nothing about the wine—a too suddenly formed and frequently changed opinion can mislead you utterly.

Many academically inclined tasters will take a fair time appraising colour, smell and taste before coming to a general conclusion about a wine. Others, including myself, work from the general to the particular, and you may eventually find that you adopt one method for certain wines and change it when tackling others.

When I began to learn to taste, I was simply told "Let the wine talk to you". Whether you are tasting with a view to buying or recommending wine to others, begin by asking yourself the question, "Is this wine good or bad?" and then ask yourself "Do I like this wine?". In both instances, you should try to answer the further question "If so, why? If not, why not?". Never pretend to find something in a wine that you do not really see.

When tasting young wines, it is necessary to try and see what they may become, which is why it is helpful if you can also study the mature versions for certain traits indicate certain possibilities. A wine that ought to improve with age can often be a disappointment if it begins by being delicious. A wine cannot be reasonably appraised when it is

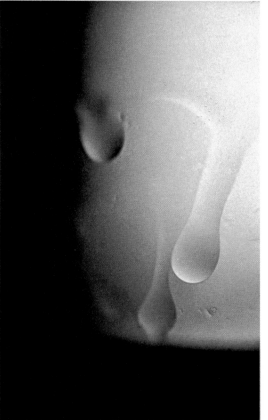

Above, the colour of a wine —Château Gazin 1960— looking straight down into the glass. The curious blue outer ring is the outside of the tasting glass at its widest, the apparent blue mark in the wine is the rim of the glass superimposed on the colour. Note how the wine shades from its edge down to the "eye" in the heart. With this fine Pomerol, of a lightish year, the aureole at the outside is beginning to turn tawny, though there is plenty of assertive red in the middle, and, at the centre, the heart of the colour is beginning to lighten. If the glass were tilted sideways, the tawny edge would be more apparent, but this view indicates the infinity of tones of a fine wine—the more different shades that can be noted, the finer the wine.

Left, the "legs" or traces of glycerine as they slip down the sides of the glass in a sample of 1967 Taylor vintage port. The presence of signs like these on the glass indicates a quality wine, red or white.

Above, busy bubbles indicating the wine is still "working" or fermenting in the bottle.

Right, a star bright Sauternes, Château Rieussec 1966, alongside a maderized and cloudy sample of white wine —note the more orange tinge typical of this condition.

Above, crystals of potassium bitartrate in a fine Mosel. These, which need not affect taste in any way, can also glitter on a freshly-drawn cork, and indicate a quality wine that has been subjected to certain conditions. No cheap ordinary white will contain them.

Below, the effect of age on the colour of white and red wines, as they are examined at an angle. The 1973 Alsatian Gewürztraminer (left) is very pale, almost colourless at the edge. The 1961 sample of the same wine is deeper in colour, with an almost butter-yellow tone at the centre. As such wines age beyond their peak, they can maderize and acquire an orange tinge, though this need not make them undrinkable. With the two red wines, the Château Yon Figeac 1970, St-Emilion (right) is still assertively red, with a purple tone in the centre of the wine. The edge is just beginning to lighten. The vintage was a fine one. The Château Grand La Lagune 1940, on the left, is the great growth of Ludon in the Médoc, but this vintage was a light though often charming one. Note the deep aureole of light orange darkening to tawny, and the several shades of light red down to the still fairly deep heart.

Age and Colour

still in cask and has just been racked or fined, nor if it has only just gone into bottle or if the bottle has been violently agitated or subjected to recent sudden changes of temperature.

When tasting mature wines, you must consider whether not merely you, but also the people with whom you will share them are likely to enjoy them — "commercial" wines are sometimes sneered at, but many people have found that widely advertised brands and wines made to cater for certain markets are exactly what those markets want.

The taste of wines may be considerably affected by the atmosphere (I find it hard to taste on a heavy, cold, wet or humid grey day), and if you are disappointed by a wine being less good than expected, check the time of year. At the flowering of the vine in spring and at vintage time, wines tend to be less than at their best even after many years in bottle: they are preoccupied with the two most important events in the vine's cycle of life.

Samples for Tasting

Several types of glass are used for serious tastings: the Paris goblet, the tulip-shaped glass and the dock glass, which is like a larger version of the sherry copita. Glasses should never be stored upside down as they will tend to smell of the stale air shut up inside them, and they will possibly also pick up the smell of anything on which they are standing, such as plastic, paper or wood. In many tasting rooms, glasses are hung up by the feet so that dust cannot get in but so that the air can circulate. If an empty glass smells musty and it is impossible to wash it on the spot, swing it about in the air to freshen it.

Only a little wine is poured into the glass for serious appraisal, about the equivalent of two small mouthfuls. With young wines, it is necessary to aerate them by swinging them vigorously around the glass and even a third of a glass would be too large a measure; with older wines, it is economical not to pour too much. Should it be necessary to warm a wine up in any way, the person conducting the tasting will either have arranged this or set an example by cupping his hands round the bowl of the glass. However, the temperature at which most wines are examined in a professional tasting room is that at which they might have been brought from a cool cellar. Red wines are never heated, and white wines are seldom markedly chilled, although some salesmen may hope to impress laymen with white wines that have been chilled in advance. If the tasting is taking place on a very hot day or in a centrally heated room, some chilling is probably advisable for white wines, especially the sweet ones.

The Smell of Wine

There are four main stages in tasting which can be taken in any order, and at any rate. There is the appearance and colour of the wine (page 42), there is the smell, the feel and flavour in the mouth, and finally, there is the finish and after-taste. Not all stages will have the same amount of things to say, for some wines go through periods when they are virtually dumb and seem to have very little to reveal.

Smell

Twirl the wine round in the glass so that the smell is released and comes up to your nose as you sniff over the rim. This is easiest done by holding the glass by the stem or the foot; the latter looks difficult, but is in fact the most comfortable way of handling a glass once you are used to it. Put the thumb on the top of the foot of the glass and place the first two or three fingers underneath, so that you can exactly control the amount of agitation you want to give the wine. Do not attempt to have the nose over the glass while you are moving the wine about, but as soon as you stop twirling, take a few short sniffs at the wine and try to ascertain what the smell is like.

The analysis and interpretation of smells is exacting and often exasperating. The wine should smell pleasant; it may smell strange, but it should have nothing disagreeable about it. Surprisingly, few wines smell "grapey", although those made from any variety of the Muscat are generally easily identifiable by their grapiness. When you have begun to register the smells of different wines, try to gain the experience of smelling one or two outstanding examples that may be taken as typical: a great Riesling, red Bordeaux, red Burgundy, whether young or mature, so that the backbone smell of the grapes that make the classic wines will be recognizable again.

Does the wine remind you by its smell of any other wine to which you can relate it? Do you get the impression that the wine is the product of a vineyard that is either very hot or very cold? The finest wines come from regions where the vine has to struggle for existence, and whether a wine is dry or verging towards sweetness, the smell tends to have an atmosphere which can often indicate the climate. Sometimes you may feel that the wine must definitely come from a cold vineyard; at other times, there is an impression of coolness overlying heat, and this may well indicate that the vineyard is generally cool, but that the particular vintage was a hot one. Again the impression may be of coldness and even damp when the vintage has been poor, or an atmosphere of sun and baked earth will immediately come to mind as you stick your nose in the glass. This is why sensitivity and alertness are important aspects in tasting. There is no need to be exaggeratedly imaginative, but if your only reaction to the smell of a wine is that "it smells like all red wine", there is little point in attempting to taste.

There may be a pronounced smell or the wine may have to be vigorously shaken to get even a whiff of smell. The latter can indicate that the wine is still very young and is, as it were, "making itself". Does the smell lead you to think that the wine will be dry or sweet? Does it convey an impression of lightness of style or weight and profundity? Does the smell develop gradually but magnificently, and does it come to a climax in the glass, like a flower opening, or is it merely evident, agreeable, but with nothing more to tell the nose? The more important the wine, the more complicated the smell, and sometimes there will be a number of different smells which do not yet appear to have joined together in harmony; this can occur with certain great wines tasted while they are still very young.

If the wine is very difficult to smell, swirl it round as quickly as possible and sniff again. This additional aeration should bring out whatever smells are there. You will want to go back and smell the wine again after putting it in your mouth, but do not necessarily make up your mind at once; a vivid first impression in tasting can usually be relied on, but if in doubt bring the other tasting senses into play.

The notes people make about the smells of wine can be highly individual, and if it is helpful for you to associate a certain smell with a certain wine or type of wine, there is no need to work out some polite phrase if your meaning is adequately expressed even by something crude. If the Traminer grape smell reminds a taster of newly-ironed laundry this is a perfectly delightful and vivid description. The Traminer, to me, smells like a haystack but I have known it remind people, pleasantly and satisfactorily, of a midden. Do not try to find a number of smells in a wine, but let the ones that are there reach your nose and discover what tags you can put on them.

Extremely old wines, especially the red wines of Bordeaux, sometimes have what is known as "a mushroom nose". This is evident as a slightly dampish smell, such as you might notice in a cellar; some people find this particularly charming when it is combined with the delicacy and complexity of the aristocratic qualities of a noble wine, but others may consider that it is almost a smell of decay and would prefer the wine to be younger. There is also a close-textured smell which I describe as "heavy velvet curtains" and which usually means a great red wine, generally Bordeaux, that has not yet reached its peak. Burgundies, too, can smell, and taste, velvety, but

I often find a greater sweetness and opened-out smell about them than in Bordeaux, possibly because of the way they are made. Sometimes red wines can smell a little "green" when some of the vines are still very young, and occasionally wines that have been sugared (chaptalized) badly will smell of the beet sugar that has been injudiciously added to them. A chemical smell that indicates some rather drastic treatment may also be apparent, and some cheap white wines can smell slightly of sulphur. This chemical is used throughout the wine trade as a disinfectant and as a means of keeping wines in condition, but its presence should never be obvious; if you find your nose begins to wrinkle and if you want to cough when you are smelling a wine, this may well be the effect of sulphur.

A smell of rotten apples can be indicative of a wine undergoing fermentation, and it cannot be smelt or tasted properly at this stage. The soggy smell that reminds some people of wet cloth and takes me back to childhood when I would suck my woollen mittens, can be a sign that the bottle was dirty; if the soggy smell evokes wood there may have been some imperfection in the cask. A wine that smells violently of vinegar is probably half way to turning into this liquid, having been infected by the vinegar bacteria. A wine that smells strongly yeasty like yeast tablets or the smell of a brewery may have dead yeasts in it, but a vague smell of yeast can be present when a wine is completing but has not quite finished its fermentation.

The smell of a corked wine has been described in various ways, and for some people the smell of cork is actually present. I must admit that no corked wine I have ever smelt or tasted reminds me in the slightest of cork; if a wine completely lacks the smell I expect and if I at the same time detect a vague, flat, chemical smell reminiscent of swimming baths or chlorine, then the wine is definitely corked to me.

No wine should be finally judged when it has just been poured from a bottle from which the cork has only that moment been drawn. The small quantity of air between the cork and the wine may markedly alter the smell of the first glass poured; the curious smell that results is known as "bottle stink", and if the wine is shaken about for a few seconds, the stale smell will vanish.

Appearance

A wine should be bright although it is not essential that it should be star bright. Every time a wine is passed through a filter, in order to satisfy the public demand for absolute brightness, something of the wine's character is taken out together with bits of deposit. With many great wines, white as well as red, the presence of certain particles in the wine can be a sign of great quality; these particles may also be in tasting samples because the bottle, in which there is a certain amount of deposit, has been shaken.

Has the wine a lively, living appearance or does it seem flat, like a liquid that has been long standing? The difference between the appearance of these two types of wine can be appreciated by comparing, in reality or in the mind's eye, a glass of spring water with a glass of tap water that has been standing in a carafe for several days.

As you move the wine about in the glass, it should show a certain amount of density. A fortified wine will be thicker in substance than a table wine, and a sweet wine will display a certain viscosity, clinging more to the side of the glass than a bone dry wine. Some wines leave trails of transparent liquid on the glass, which fall straight down again to the wine; these trails are known as "legs" and relate to the glycerine content, usually signifying a wine of quality.

Small bubbles evident in the wine and clinging to the glass at the edge of the wine and also seen inside the bottle, may indicate either that the wine is still undergoing a slight fermentation or that it possesses a natural liveliness. This may happen at tastings of young wines and can be distinguished from bubbles formed by wine being splashed into a glass by the fact that fermentation bubbles will remain and not burst. Fermentation can be detected by other means, but it is sometimes possible to confirm what the nose and palate suspect by looking at what is happening in the glass and the bottle.

Colour

The easiest way of examining the colour of a wine is to tilt the glass so that the bowl is at an angle of about 45° away from the body, the wine in it forming an oval pool. Hold the glass over something white such as white paper, a napkin or any dead-white surface, preferably under an ordinary white light or in good daylight, and look down on the wine rather than up at it. At a cellar tasting it may be necessary to hold the glass up against the flame of a candle, but to eyes accustomed to daylight and artificial light, candlelight can be as deceiving and flattering to wines as it is to women. (I have seen a good amateur taster kneel down in front of a tasting sample so that he could get an impression of the wine across the level in the glass, but this is rather affected.)

Looking down at the wine, note the tones of colour in it, from the point at which it makes contact with the glass down to the centre, or "eye" of the wine—which is like the shading on the eyes of a peacock's tail. In a cheap wine, probably only three or four distinct colour tones will be noticeable, but with a wine of high quality there will be many more, whether the wine is old or young. This is useful to bear in mind if you are "tasting blind" and may be asked which of two wines is the more expensive.

In general, red wines lighten in colour with age and white wines darken, but all show the shading of the tones from the rim of the wine down to the eye, which is always the darkest point. Sometimes the rim of the wine, whether red or white, is almost transparent.

White wines

Young white wines can be very pale in colour, and they generally tend to be paler when they come from northern vineyards; the drier they are the paler they will be. Awareness of colour is as personal a matter as taste, but I find that young dry wines from cold vineyards, such as those of the Mosel, often have the pale, shimmering colour of a segment of lemon; a slight golden tinge comes into the dry wines of the Loire, and the white Burgundies are very pale gold. The one exception to the latter example is Chablis which has an odd greenish gleam to it, almost as if there were two colours, the green shining through the pale yellow. White wines from southern vineyards may be distinctly gold and some, such as certain of the white Rhônes, have a pale straw-coloured tinge to them. It is, however, unwise to be too definite about colours as they can be considerably affected by the grapes that make the wine, the juice of some white grapes being different in hue from others. When wines are made from blends of black and white grapes, as with certain Spanish and Rhône wines, the resulting white wine will be different from one made with white grapes only. It should also be remembered that wine laboratory technicians can work wonders, and as there are often fashions for very pale or rather dark wines in certain markets, the tone of a wine can be modified to suit their requirements.

Most of the sweet wines begin by being pale to light yellow-gold. The term "buttercup" appears in some of my tasting notes for these wines because their hue reminds me of the childhood "Do you like butter?" practice of holding an open buttercup under the chin; the reflected yellow on the skin is immediately evocative of the soft gold of many sweet wines.

The difference between a fully sparkling and a *pétillant* wine. Top, a Champagne, St Marceaux Brut, taken just as the *mousse* or foam on the surface is subsiding, but showing how the tiny bubbles rise in profusion, fast and for some time. The only things that will prevent this beautiful sight in a sparkling wine are a greasy glass, or one that has not been rinsed free of detergent. Below it, the 1964 Vouvray Clos Naudin, *demi-sec, pétillant*, of A. Foreau. The bubbles are miniscule and rise fast, but there are not as many of them.

The variety of "white" in white wines. Left, the 1973 Chablis of Louis Michel—there is a slight tinge of green, but only just as yet. Then the 1973 Crozes-Hermitage, Mule Blanche of Paul Jaboulet, shows a slightly warmer though still very pale yellow colour. The 1969 Wachenheimer Schlossberg Riesling of Dr Bürklin-Wolf, a Palatinate of supreme quality, is beginning to turn silvery-gold with some age. Finally, the 1966 Château Rieussec, Fargues, exemplifies the near marigold colour of a Sauternes beginning to be at its best. The two 1973s have a long way to go and will deepen slightly in colour, the Rhône turning the colour of light straw, the Chablis a more definite but always delicate lime yellow.

Two pink or rosé wines showing a typical difference between such wines from cool and sun-baked vineyards. The Anjou Rosé du Cabernet (left) has a more pronounced colour than an ordinary Anjou Rosé, but there is a shade of blue in the light pink—to me this indicates cold. The 1969 Château de Fonsalette Rosé, 1er Grand Cru Côtes du Rhône, (right) is darker in general, with more flame in its pinkish-red, and, as shown here, more shades of colour which indicate the greater quality of the wine.

Typical colours of three classic reds. Left, the 1973 Beaujolais Villages of Jacques Dépagneux is brilliant pink-red, and vibrant with appeal, but there is not much more than one tone here. Centre, a Burgundy, the 1970 Corton-Bressandes of Tollot-Beaut, and right, a Bordeaux, the 1970 Château Palmer. The Burgundy is already beginning to lighten somewhat; the Bordeaux is still completely dark. The Corton wines tend to be lightish in colour, and Burgundies usually do look more red than purple when side by side with Bordeaux. The Burgundy is beginning to drink well; the Bordeaux is hardly ready to taste.

Maderization

As white wines age, they darken in colour, and they may acquire a distinct brownish tinge if they are affected by air, even the small amount in the bottle under the cork, or any air that may have penetrated the cork through the protective capsule. A wine with this characteristic is known as being "maderized", and implies that it resembles Madeira though in fact the resemblance is slight. Even if a wine is maderized, however, it may still be perfectly drinkable and will have lost little in the process of ageing except the beautiful colour which it developed with maturity. Great Sauternes, for example, may look almost like an amontillado sherry, but taste none the worse. Some medium dry to sweet and even some dry white wines can also acquire an odd and not unpleasant orange tinge with age, and the wines of Tokay are possibly the supreme examples of this characteristic.

Red Wines

Unless you are acutely sensitive to the finer shades of colours, you will probably find it easier to appraise red wines than white. The range of red hues is very wide, the pigments in different grape varieties giving different tones, from the vigorous, assertive bright red of Beaujolais to the profounder red of Burgundy and the subtler shading of red Bordeaux. In general, wines from northern vineyards tend to be lighter red than those from the south, but this generalization should be cautiously applied. Some red wines, for example certain 1967 and 1970 Côte d'Or Burgundies, began by being so light in colour when they were first bottled and shown at tastings that comments were made about them being pink rather than red. Not until they were some time in bottle did they gain colour. Many red Bordeaux, too, deepen and intensify in colour as they develop in bottle. When they reach their prime, the edge of the wine may begin to assume a beautiful tawny colour, which gradually spreads throughout the rest of the wine; a very old Bordeaux can be most delicately shaded like the tinges of colour on fine velvet that deepen towards a shadow on the cloth. Red Burgundy, which usually ages faster than red Bordeaux, will also lighten with age although matured old red Burgundies tend to be slightly redder than the same kind of wine from Bordeaux; very old wines from both regions can pale down to what is almost an apricot colour. With wines that show this extreme age, it is difficult to be more precise than to say that they are very old.

Many red wines when young have a distinct purplish tinge to them and the mouth of the taster will be temporarily stained by the wines.

Taste and After-taste

The process of actually tasting a wine is accomplished by taking a small quantity of wine rather slowly into the mouth, feeling it as it runs over the top and the sides of the tongue, squeezing it between the tongue and top palate, under the tongue, around the gums and inside the cheeks of the bottom jaw. In this context, the term "palate" does not relate specifically to one region of the mouth, but rather to the whole physical tasting apparatus of the mouth; it would, though, be hard to draw a line between tasting and smelling. The feel of the wine on the lips and teeth is also important, as is the angle at which it actually reaches the mouth; for this reason some tasters find glasses of a particular shape more useful than others, and some prefer to use the Burgundian *tastevin* even when tasting other types of wine because the wine hits the mouth in a different way. Most tasters find that the sensations made by the wine in the mouth are sharpened if a little air is drawn in at the same time as admitting the wine. It is not necessary to make a loud, sucking noise while doing this, and, as with spitting, nobody takes the slightest notice at a serious tasting.

Let the wine flow about in the mouth, try to register its general shape and constitution, its texture and anything that seems outstanding about the flavour. Then spit it out and immediately you have done so breathe down your nose and note the echo, as it were, of the smell and the taste of the wine in your nose and mouth. This is known as the after-taste. Thereafter it is permissible immediately to put a little more wine into the mouth and repeat the process, if necessary taking a little longer over the second taste.

With a complex and fine wine, even when it is still young, the taste will have a beginning, a middle and an end, like the shadow of the flavour, and the after-taste may be similarly divided. From these points it is possible to draw the shape of a wine like a graph. Sometimes there is a large peak at the beginning, a straight flat section or even a hollow in the middle, and then the end may droop down or rise to a magnificent climax. Sometimes the first taste of a wine makes a tremendous impression, while other wines have to work up to their climax. The final taste and the after-taste can be the most fascinating although the most delicate of all, or a wine can finish abruptly and fall away.

After spitting out the tasting sample, numerous questions present themselves to the honest and serious taster. Does the wine feel clean and agreeable in the mouth? Does it feel unevenly put together or sticky? Does it seem thick, almost chewy? Or is it too thin and slight, lean and angular when you might have expected it to be

The Shape of Wines

Great wine at its peak

Pleasant and pretty

Dull

Promise not performance

The sort of "profiles" I sometimes find it helpful to draw of different wines when a large number of the same type and vintage are being tasted at once—such as a showing of 30 to 60 Bordeaux or German wines of the same year. At the top, there is a great wine at its peak; with a beginning, middle and end. Then a wine that is small-scale and pretty, making a pleasant, perhaps flippant impression. The third is a dull wine—there is little to say. Finally, a wine that demonstrates a lot of promise, and then disappoints with a mean performance. The shape of wines can help the taste memory, especially if you find it hard to make detailed notes when tasting.

rounded and forthcoming? If it is a mature wine, do you want to drink it and drink more of it? If it is a young wine, do you foresee it becoming attractive and has it something in reserve which you want to discover, or does it immediately reveal itself?

Acidity

There are two elements in wine that sometimes put off the taster who is faced for the first time with immature wines: acidity and tannin. A young wine that is going to be a pleasant drink should not taste "acid", but in order to be a refreshing wine it must have the right kind of acidity. The acidity which is very obvious in, for example, young dry white wines is one of the things that makes them so tiring to taste; if you have to taste several hundred they can upset the stomach for inevitably some drops go down the throat. Acidity, however, must be present for it is part of the wine's constitution. I personally never find it helpful to concentrate on acidity, but for the taster who is just beginning it is useful to recognize that there is good as well as bad acidity; a little experience will enable him to appreciate the proportion in which it should be present. Generally, you notice acidity as a slightly sharp effect on the parts of the mouth with which the wine first makes contact: the tip of the tongue and the inside of the lips.

Tannin

Tannin, on the other hand, is chiefly experienced on the sides of the tongue and the cheeks; it pulls the mouth rather like when you are eating rhubarb. Great red wines, in particular, need tannin to give them long life; unfortunately popular demand for some famous named wines to be made drinkable while they are still young has resulted in wines that are initially softer than wine lovers would wish to see them. Tannin is far more likely to be noticeable in young red Bordeaux than red Burgundies, because Burgundy, to which sugar is added as a matter of course, will be a little softer, even when young.

There are certain subtleties of taste that, once you have registered them, require a little more explanation: for example, when tasting a particular wine you may find that it reminds you of pebbles; try to discover if the vineyard from which it comes has a gravelly soil. If you get an impression of a baked, almost roasted quality in a wine, does this mean a hot vintage or a hot vineyard that produces similar wines in most years?

The wines from great estates generally have outstanding individuality, but there can always be the odd year when they are not typical. If you intend to follow the progress of the wines from a

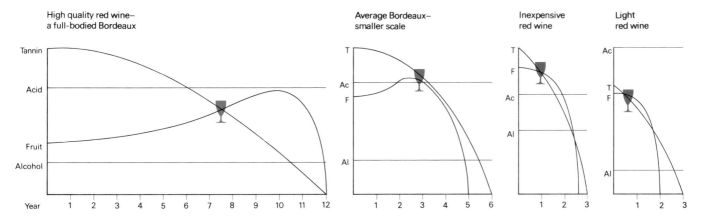

High quality red wine— a full-bodied Bordeaux

Average Bordeaux— smaller scale

Inexpensive red wine

Light red wine

certain estate seriously, you should try to inform yourself of any changes of ownership, replantings of vines, installations of new machinery or general modifications of wine methods. When you are tasting the finest German wines, remember that the cask number, which will also be shown on the label, indicates even more individuality because the style of one cask may differ radically from that of another. Similarly, from certain other estates that number their bottles, such as Mouton-Rothschild, a bottle bearing a very high number may well have been bottled weeks, or months, later than one bearing a low number. All these additional details are of interest to the experienced taster; for the beginner it is sufficient to learn to answer the simple questions before tackling the more difficult ones.

After-Taste

If you breathe out through your nose immediately after spitting out the wine that you are tasting you will get an impression like an echo of the taste of the wine. This after-taste can also be experienced in a different way by breathing out through the mouth. Personally I think that breathing down the nose gives a sharper impression of the after-taste, but blowing air through the mouth can sometimes be helpful in giving a final impression of a fairly viscous or high-strength wine. Some people like to swallow a very little of the wine before they breathe, but after too many swallows the palate may become blunted and the senses confused. I find some aspects of mature wine are only revealed as it goes down the throat, but I usually have a fair idea of what they are going to be before I do swallow. The value of swallowing, for anyone advising on buying wine, is that you can more easily put yourself in the place of the customer. Remember, though, that many wines are hard to appreciate when drunk on a completely empty stomach; it is therefore advisable to eat a morsel of something neutral, such as a biscuit or a piece of plain bread.

Diagrams evolved by Clive Williams, MW, for use by the students of a wine school. They show the action and evolution of a wine's natural preservatives: tannin, acid, fruit (sugar) and alcohol. Left, a fine full-bodied Bordeaux is shown, at its peak when the loss of tannin reveals the fruit. Thereafter the fruit increases and suddenly declines, leaving a wine which, without the support of the tannin, merely maintains its high acidity and little else. Next, a smaller-scale Bordeaux shows only a slight increase in the fruit as the tannin begins to drop, and then both decline fairly abruptly together. Third, a cheap red wine shows how the fruit is really the only positive asset of the wine— when this drops, everything declines, the fruit fading before the tannin. Right, a lightish red wine has comparatively high acidity, but the initial assertion of fruit still drops, more rapidly than the tannin. Such a wine might seem harsh and shrill as it aged.

Tasting Language

It is always better to use your own terms in making notes about wines. If you associate certain wines with, say, flowers or fruit, or if they remind you of a particular smell or flavour, these associations will tag the wine forever in your mind. In conversation or in writing about a tasting, you will make yourself better understood if you use terms in common use in the world of wine. (As an amateur you are not often likely to be tasting so as to note market potential, appraise length of life or go into technicalities.)

Many people mark wines for excellence on their tasting sheet, giving them a certain number of marks, usually 12 or 20. If there is nothing to say about a wine except "horrible" or "seems perfect" there is no need to invent more descriptive phrases. A personal "wine language" may be both vivid and evocative, but for the beginner some trade terms and the definitions I have formulated (see page 180) provide a useful guide. Some people use the language of the country when tasting its wines, others note wines in terms of people, and men frequently describe wines as having feminine characteristics (all fine wines have personalities).

I sometimes draw the shape of a wine in a miniature graph, indicating any jagged traits, roundness, whether it finishes short, trails away or flicks up at the end. Not all wines need lengthy descriptions; great wines may have many attributes, but for little wines a few words may suffice.

Sparkling Wines

These should be tasted exactly as still table wines. For serious appraisal, taste them once while they are fully sparkling or *pétillant*, and then leave some wine in the glass, cover it with a piece of paper and taste it the following day. You will then have an exact idea of the quality of the base wine when the wine has gone flat. Apart from that, judge the wines for their cleanliness, pleasant smell, balance and an agreeable taste and after-taste.

Fortified Wines

Tasting fortified wines is essentially the same as tasting still table wines—you look at the wines to discern their basic quality and appraise them personally in relation to your own likes and dislikes, and the purpose they should fulfil in your drinking pattern. Each of the establishments making them will have an individual style, conforming with the wine makers' ideas as to what is good, and each establishment will also probably have a range of lines differentiated according to price. When you are making up your mind as to which sherry or port you prefer, you should compare like with like—for example, a fine old amontillado or tawny from several houses, not a cheap blended amontillado with one that has acquired its style by maturation.

Sherry

Sherries are judged very much on the way they smell: the manzanillas, finos and amontillados should have a marked freshness. Sherry that smells flat or of hardly anything may be coarse and inferior, or it may have been left open in a bottle or decanter for weeks. Some people notice a saltiness about manzanillas; I sometimes detect an iodine or ozone tang. A good fino to me has a cool, slightly soapy smell, which tends to be flattened if the wine is much sweetened, but this spreading out of the style is not necessarily unpleasant. Amontillados are traditionally associated with hazelnuts; they, and fine dry olorosos, have for me an assertive but subtly substantial inner smell and taste. All these wines should come off the palate cleanly, leaving it refreshed. The sweeter sherries should gain in depth and profundity, not simply get sweeter; age adds complexity and there can be a wonderful dying away of something that is the essence of sherry, something that can cling to an empty glass for up to an hour.

Port

Because of the natural sugar left in the wine, port is not hard to taste, but, with the great wines, their subtleties and shades of smell and flavour make them taxing. The finer they are, the more they have to give—to those who can appreciate them. White port should primarily be refreshing; ruby port smooth, comforting and reviving; fine old tawny is a port to discuss, from colour to after-taste; vintage port combines the quality of the house style with the individuality of its year. Old tawnies and vintages are definitely special occasion ports, for leisured enjoyment after a meal. No port should be sweet and sticky: you should perceive the inner structure of the wine, firm and flexible, note the distinction of the colour, detect the separate components of the

| Manzanilla | Fino | Amontillado |

Sherry
The sherry "scale" ranging from light lemon-yellow to deep brown. The colours, varying for each sherry establishment, indicate the different wines. Reading from left to right is a very pale manzanilla followed by a fino with a slightly sunnier tinge. With maturing the fino can become the amontillado, with its beautiful coppery hue. Colour does not necessarily indicate sweetness: the oloroso.

Port
The colour of port is of great importance. In the shippers' tasting rooms, white enamel sample saucers are used for meticulously matching the ports of various houses.

A white port, lightly golden in tone and more of a buttercup yellow than a sherry. It may be lighter or darker according to the house from which it comes.

Tawny

Fine old tawny, developed by long maturing, the ultimate achievement of fine ruby port (see below). The younger wine's tones have faded gradually into the exquisite shading of the tawny, from the aureole of gold down to the red-brown diamond of the wine's heart.

Ruby

The younger, ruby port has vigorous, assertive and defined tones that, with long maturing, will fade gradually, like silk velvet, into the tones of tawny (see above).

Vintage

A Cockburn 1963. In 1975 it is beginning to be charming and drinkable, but still with a fine future. The tones are more intense than in fine old tawny, the aureole is narrower and as yet the wine is dark red.

Oloroso   Fine rare oloroso   Cream Sherry

shown next, could be bone
dry in Spain, but is usually
sweetened for export
markets. The one illustrated
here displays the colour of

a sweet chestnut. It is
followed by a wine that is
brown rather than golden
and that could indicate a
brown sherry or a fine rare

oloroso aged for years in
bottle. Last comes the dark
brown milk or cream sherry
with an intensely dark gold
rim around the wine.

Sercial   Verdelho   Bual   Malmsey

Madeira
The tones of Madeira are
marked although each
establishment will have its
own style. From left to right
are Sercial, the driest and

lightest, next to Verdelho,
sometimes associated with
the colour as well as the
flavour of hazelnuts. Third is
Bual, luscious and velvety,

and last is the dark rich
Malmsey. This can look
almost black; in the finer
samples there is a hint of
dark gold at the rim.

Marsala
The dry Marsalas as shown
here are usually lighter in
colour than the sweet
Marsalas. The latter have a
more substantial, brown or
reddish-brown hue and are
the more popular wines.

Vermouth
Chambéry, on the left, is the palest of all vermouths;
although some biancos can have the same, near lime
tinge, most are essentially pale yellow. The dry vermouth
in the centre could come from France or Italy or from
anywhere that wine and hence vermouth can be made.
The reddish tone of the sweet wine on the right is typical
of Italian vermouths. Each house has its own range and
traditions as to colours, some being light and others
darker, implying sweetness or body.

bouquet which, to me, relate directly to the taste
and after-taste more than with any other wine.

If you are comparing several vintage ports,
remember that the assertive nature of younger
wines can overwhelm the more sensitive older
ones, so taste old before young. With tawnies
remember to appraise equal qualities; the long
matured fine tawnies will make even the best
blends of less expensive tawnies seem inadequate,
though the wines may actually be sound and
good value.

Madeira and Marsala
Madeiras made from single grape varieties can
be appraised like other fortified wines as regards
colour, nose, flavour and after-taste. With the
blends, the proportions of the different wines
involved and their age can, with a little practice,
be detected. Madeira usually has a fairly obvious
burnt or heated back-taste. Again, even the most
luscious wines should have a cleanliness about
them, and their profundity should never cloy.

Marsala, as far as the dry and medium dry
versions are concerned, also tends to have a
burnt or scorched back-taste. It can be a fairly
intense wine, with moderate viscosity, but
although the styles of the different establishments
vary, it never seems to me to have the complexity
of port, but to have a more straightforward
appeal.

Vermouth
When appraising vermouths that are to be drunk
as apéritifs, the fresh palate-stimulating and
digestive qualities should be evident. The lightly
herby style of Chambéry is distinctive, even in the
version made with Alpine strawberries, but
other vermouths vary considerably, those of
Marseilles being particularly aromatic, the biancos rather spiced. Vermouths from wine regions
naturally vary according to the wine on which
they are based and the other ingredients included;
in some, the herbs, spices and aromatics are
pronounced, in others the flavour is straightforward. Consider how you are going to use the
vermouth, whether straight or in mixtures (and
which ones), as a long drink base or mainly as
an apéritif. For serious comparisons, chill the
bottle of vermouth, rather than trying to taste it
with ice in it.

Other fortified wines
Apply the standards by which you taste all wine
and, with wines made like the fortified classics, do
not compare one directly with the other. Is the
Cyprus sherry, South African port type or the
vermouth from anywhere in the world good in
its own right? That is all tasting should tell you.

Studying Wines

Any enthusiastic wine lover, and the shrewd buyer too, will want to gain as wide an experience as possible of all wines. But it is generally best to take one particular wine for serious study from the beginning of one's concentrated tasting. In the struggle to develop and interpret all that is involved with tasting, there are so many aspects to concentrate on that it is a help and simplification if one studies just one aspect of the subject at a time. It is thus possible to learn about the particular region, something of its history, come to know a range of its wines and, by beginning the acquisition of experience with the enjoyment of wine, be encouraged to learn more. Confusion at the outset can result in people deciding that they can never learn much about wine and wondering if there really *is* much to enjoy. A thorough knowledge of one wine can also be used in the appraisal of others, but a superficial experience of many is hard to deepen.

My own recommendation would always be to begin learning about a particular table wine. The fortified wines are fascinating, but, apart from their characteristics being very much the style of the house that makes them, side by side with their regional traits, it is not as easy, physically, to taste large numbers of them. They are also sometimes appraised in a different way from table wines (see page 46), while the person who can taste table wines can taste anything else. Sparkling wines are also specialized according to the establishments that make them, and their sparkling quality can also complicate the impression they make on the novice taster.

If you live in a particular wine region, detailed study of the wines is easy; for the majority who do not, study of rare or special wines can be expensive and difficult to pursue. For that reason the table wine chosen for study should be fairly widely available, in different qualities and from different sources. Even if your wine merchant has vast stocks of the finest wines, you should try as wide a selection as possible, though you may return eventually to your original preference. The complacent "I only ever drink So-and-so's wines" is both chauvinistic and unrealistic for you do not know how good a particular commodity is until you have compared it with others.

While it is not necessary to taste only the most expensive and top quality wines, it is certainly wise to "drink a little more expensively than you can afford"; by basing your ideas of what is good on what others have considered first-rate, you will have a good standard against which to compare other wines. But there are several reasons why the finest and rarest should not be the only wines you taste in whichever classic region you have decided to specialize. First, such wines have definite personalities about which it is impossible to be indifferent, and second, you must also be able to taste small-scale wines if you are to be a good taster; they are harder to select but often more exciting to make as discoveries. Third, you should not limit yourself too much if you wish to differentiate not only between the wines that you like and those that you think are good, but between the wines that are true to themselves, typical of the grapes and the region that make them, and the versions that are commercially produced for public demand.

White or Red Wines
Whether you select a classic white or red wine is a personal matter. Bear in mind that it is more difficult for the beginner to analyse differences of vintage, site and grape variety in wines from a region where the influence of the shipper—and the grower—can make a vast difference to the wines of a parish or vineyard that bears the same name. Narrow down your wines for study; in white wines, make the Mosel or Rhine wines, the Côte de Beaune white Burgundies, or the white wines of the middle and upper Loire your speciality. In reds, choose between red Burgundies in general, Beaujolais, possibly the red wines of the Loire, Chianti, different Barolos or red Rioja, but from at least seven or eight shippers.

I must, however, declare my own conviction that red Bordeaux is both the easiest and most practical of the classic wines on which to cut one's tasting buds. There are thousands of wines, available world-wide, the majority of them wines of quality, yet the different regions can demonstrate the individuality of the wines, and the different single estates within the regions can be even more individual. Each vintage is different, and although the wines of each shipper and each proprietor have their own character, these characteristics are still contained within the definition of what is typical of the area.

I was taught by an authority who, in saying that Bordeaux still remained the most natural wine in the world, further asserted that "If you can taste claret, you can taste anything". I have seen him identify soils of vineyards making wines with which he was previously unfamiliar, and describe the traits of vintages of wines he had never regularly drunk; I have watched him identify growers' and shippers' styles in wines, detect a single row of one vine variety in a vineyard otherwise dominated by another grape, and heard him observe, when tasting from a vat, that a vineyard had suffered hail, which even the grower himself did not know. As the late Allan Sichel could and did do this, I think that he may have had good reason for speaking as he did about Bordeaux.

Classification of Wines by Taste

In the following pages, the wines have first been classified according to the basic categories of still table wines, white, red and pink; sparkling and semi-sparkling; fortified and other wines, particularly vermouth and those that do not fit naturally into any of the categories. Within each of these categories the wines have been subdivided according to their general style—the factor that first influences your choice. The subdivisions of white wines, for example, will inevitably be different from those of red wines; the factors that determine your choice of a still table wine that is white will not be the same factors that determine your choice of a still table wine that is red. The next sub-division concerns the range of types of taste, and these may be numerous or few; in many instances the dividing line between them tends to be shadowy, so that the terms sometimes overlap. Beside each of these final sub-divisions are lists of examples which should guide anyone with access to a wine list or a retail outlet. My choice of examples has been dictated by a number of factors: many wines bearing brand names may be on sale under different names in different countries, and they have therefore been omitted, as have most names of wineries, many of which make a complete range of many styles of wines. Also omitted are most specific estate wines and vintages; these are not usually available in vast quantities, and, as they are generally at the top of the price ranges, anyone wishing to become acquainted with them will usually do so by means of an informed source of supply and personal advice

The majority of examples are provided by wines made from one particular grape (varietals or cultivars), a particular wine making method, or coming from one defined region, large or small. It would be possible to place some wines in several different divisions; Vouvray, for example, can range from very dry to very sweet, from fully sparkling and semi-sparkling to still. Similarly it would be possible to go on subdividing the parish or commune wines of great classic vineyards, such as those of Burgundy and Bordeaux. In these classifications, I have been guided by what seemed most helpful, and if a certain style seemed best exemplified by citing a particular vineyard sub-division, it has been included. The well-known wines of Europe predominate, partly because they are world-famous and available in many parts of the world, and partly because, once having gained experience of them, few difficulties will be encountered in tasting other less well-known wines.

Descriptive terms
A full glossary of the descriptive terms used here, both technical and personal, will be found on pages 180–184. It will be noted that two types of terminology are involved: terms that describe the wines in relation to smell and taste, with my personal tags as possible help to people struggling to translate their experiences into language; and terms, such as weight, distinction and firmness, that in general classify a certain type of wine. In using terms that relate to taste whereby the drinker can classify wines, I am aware of running a considerable risk, for one man's "dry" may be another man's "medium dry", not only according to the measurable degree of sweetness in a wine—or its absence—but also due to the preferences and the metabolism of the individual. These may be conditioned by experience, state of mind and health, place, climate, what has recently passed over the palate—and what the drinker thinks he is drinking.

It is also essential that anyone outside the wine trade should appreciate that someone buying or selling wine will also be affected by considerations relating to the economics of his business. It would be foolish for a wine buyer to select wines that only he likes; his customers must also like them, and the wines must be in the ranges in which customers are interested and at prices that enable them to keep buying wine. People do not continue to buy wines they do not really like, but a large proportion of the public will buy wines that they think they *ought* to like; many wines may be made with this safe, anxious-to-please policy in mind, with the result that they will be so vaguely amiable and undistinguished that definite classification can sometimes be misleading.

It does, for example, require a certain amount of experience in sincere drinking to like a *truly* dry wine which has qualities that may elude the beginner. There is nothing discreditable about admitting this, and it is usually easier to begin by appreciating even slight sweetness. The sweetness may be wholly natural, or the wine may have been adjusted to be sweeter than it might originally have been so as to appeal to a wider public. One example of this is Anjou Rosé, which when it is made from the Cabernet Franc grape, should be a truly dry pink wine; today Anjou Rosé du Cabernet is popular on a large scale, with the result that most examples are only medium dry and not wholly dry. Muscadet, which like real Chablis should be very dry indeed, is unlikely to be the type of wine most people could honestly say they enjoyed at the outset of their drinking experience. But the vogue for Muscadet has encouraged descriptions such as a "nice round wine" and "full-bodied and mellow", none of them applicable to Muscadet in its basic form. The consequence of its popularity has been that, as with Anjou Rosé and many other wines, the basic style and character have sometimes been adapted to the requirements of the mass market; a great deal of cheap Muscadet today is far from resembling the crisp, almost bitterly dry white wine of old style Muscadet.

No one is to blame for these distortions, but because of them it is all the more important for the wine lover to cultivate an approach to wine unaffected by any opinions as to what "ought" to be drunk, and to establish a set of personal standards of quality based on enjoyment. In this way, the potential wine lover will be able to sort out the types of wine he wishes to drink and appraise them accordingly. The provisional acceptance of someone else's terms of wine classification will, I hope, enable the drinker to communicate his wishes to those who deal in wine until he has gained some experience.

In order to register in the mind a particular wine or type of wine, it will be necessary to utilise all three sets of wine terms: those that tell you what the wine is, those that detail its attributes, and those that tell you in general what the wine is like. Serious wine lovers can make general use of the classifications of wines even if they happen to be in a place where the so-called classic wines are not available, for these classics have established the style and standards of various types of many wines and are, in a sense, the progenitors of all the wines of the world.

Using the classifications
Decide what you want to drink or think you may enjoy by way of a still, sparkling or fortified wine, either to accompany food or fit into some social occasion, or to verify the type of taste sensations you may expect from certain wines. Be honest about the style, linking dry, slightly sweet, moderate personality, straightforwardness, to what you can enjoy or begin to understand.

There are so many wines and so many variations within each main category that it would be possible to find exceptions to every general statement. This does not mean that a statement is in any way untrue; it will serve as a guide when you are considering unfamiliar wines. Use the generalizations first, then incorporate within them any exceptions or modifications you have personally learnt. Bear in mind that wines are as individual as human beings. They are affected by where they are made, how they are made, by whom they are made, from what they are made, and when. A different grape variety, different method of vine cultivation or wine making, different proprietor of an estate, and unexpected weather conditions can cause infinite variations in the personality of a wine.

Accept that some large wineries will make an entire range of wines, red, white and pink, of several degrees of sweetness and dryness, as well as sparkling and semi-sparkling wines, and fortified wines of various types. This should particularly be borne in mind when appraising wines of the New World as compared with the classic areas in Europe; in many countries where good medium personality wines are made (eastern Europe for example), a wide range of different types will also be produced in the same region and by the same winery. Such wineries are catering for a demand for wines in the medium-priced to inexpensive ranges, and, even when it is possible for them in theory to produce wines of quality as fine as any of the established classics, it may not be economically possible for them to do so. Even the greatest wine estates may have to put any profit back into the cost of running the estate. No profit was made by Château Lafite, one of the greatest Bordeaux estates, until more than a hundred years after the Rothschilds bought it in 1859. Wines in the medium ranges, however good, should not form the sole standards of quality for the drinker. Not only have they potentially less lasting enjoyment and interest, but they are usually less clearly defined and less impressive. It is always important to drink the best, especially when beginning to learn about wine; great wines will make an impression against which others can be appraised in due course, while second-rate wines can only form second-rate standards.

For this reason, most of the examples in the classifications have been drawn from established classics, coming from vineyards that may make a variety of wines, but which have won their reputation for only one or two. They may have their imitations, and many wines may claim kinship with them, but there can be only *one* red Bordeaux or Burgundy, only *one* Champagne, only *one* port or sherry. In future centuries there may be other classics from newer vineyards.

White Wines

Main Taste Categories

Bone dry

All the wines in the bone dry category are without any trace of sweetness, and all, from the most modest to the greatest, possess a certain direct character, uncompromising and quite distinct. You may not like them when you first begin to drink wine, and you may find them taxing even when you are experienced in wine-drinking. They are clear-cut in style but you do not *have* to like them. Even if you do not care for them, try to understand why some people admire them so much and why they have gained their reputation. Is it the cleansing effect they have on the palate? Is it the strung-out range of subtle flavours some possess? Or is it the refreshing smell and taste, which may prepare you for eating or for drinking other gentler wines?

A bone dry wine can give several kinds of pleasure: it can freshen and tone up the palate before eating and drinking, stimulate the digestion, prepare the way, gastronomically, for wines that may be gentler in appeal and perhaps more lingering. Taken with food, bone dry wines may balance the heaviness of some foods, such as roast goose, or they may complement the fresh sharpness of others, such as chicken or fish cooked with tarragon. They can bring out fine, often hidden flavours in delicate or subtle dishes, rather as a squeeze of lemon does, and they can, because of their dryness, effect an ultimate harmony with some dishes that might, on their own, be bland, such as baked fish and boiled chicken.

Because of their uncompromising dryness, these wines are usually better with some kind of food—as apéritifs they should be served with a few biscuits or olives, as some may be considered too hard and assertive to drink on an empty stomach. Those with a little fruitiness to them can be enjoyed on their own. Usually, however, the lighter and crisper wines are perhaps better before luncheon rather than dinner.

When you taste a bone dry wine, try to apprehend its coolness; even if the wine comes from a vineyard that you associated with a sun-baked region at holiday time, the cold will be there, at its back, imparting the acidity that freshens and balances even the most fruity, weighty wine in this category.

Dry and Medium Dry

This division includes all the wines that are generally thought of as "dry" because they are made without special vinification stressing the sweetness and without the conspicuous addition of sugar to the must or to the finished wine.

Many dry and medium dry wines possess charm—even to the inexperienced they are pleasant—and in the finer ranges they can have an enormous number of subtle attributes, in addition to being refreshing drinks and agreeable accompaniments to food. This can make them confusing to choose—a certain white Burgundy, for example, can be five times the price of another bearing a similar name from a neighbouring vineyard.

Often people simply smell a wine and make up their minds what it is going to taste like before they even put it in their mouths; then, of course, it *will* tend to taste as they have predetermined it should. This can result in the condemnation of a fine dry wine with a big flowery bouquet as "sweet" or "heady". On the other hand, it can also lead to the praise of something that should rightly possess a certain fragrance and full-bodied style, but which has been badly made or is the product of a poor vintage. The shrill, unripe, almost bitter style may lead some people to thinking the wine is praiseworthily dry. They may not be able to like it at first, but if they force themselves, they will eventually come to accept this type of indifferent or bad wine as the standard.

It is usually wiser for the beginner to sample wines that are mostly medium dry and easy to like at once, and carry out occasional experiments with dry wines, always drinking something of admitted and reputed quality.

Many people indignantly reject the idea that they do not like truly dry wines. But there is no reason why they should like them. Far more regular wine drinkers, whether they drink for casual enjoyment or for what they think is wine appreciation, are in truth drinking medium dry wines rather than those that are really dry or bone dry. Sales figures, laboratory statistics and commercial advice contradict the supposition that to love wine you must first love only *dry* wine.

Medium dry or even sweet wines are becoming more popular. They were always a favourite in the cold damp of Scotland, and Scandinavia, where a glucose-rich diet is essential for energy. The North American public, perhaps influenced by the popularity of the dry martini, has been slower to accept that medium dry wines can be good. For one reason, it is difficult to appreciate a delicate dry wine after several rounds of a spirit-based drink. Appreciation is also made more difficult by the centrally-heated atmosphere of many homes, with the result that something truly cold to drink is called for. A medium dry wine, served chilled or even iced, is, however, better able to withstand such treatment and still have something to give than a wine that is truly dry. Excessive chilling of a dry wine will not only

Planting the vine.

Vintaging in Switzerland.

remove most of the bouquet but, if the drinker imbibes too much, the acidity in the wine may react unpleasantly afterwards. Over-chilling can mask faults in a wine, but may also destroy anything very delicate and fine; thus the more robust dry and medium dry whites have often more to contribute by way of enjoyment when chilled.

Dry and medium dry wines can be drunk at any time, before meals and with a huge variety of food, for casual and formal occasions; they are available throughout the world and in all price ranges. As apéritifs, they can discreetly perk up the palate or revive the appetite; they may complement rich food or enhance a modest dish. Many are assertive and grand, but, especially in the middle and lower price ranges, they are frequently pleasant, sometimes pretty wines.

If you are hesitating before a list of unfamiliar wines that may bear descriptions, either on the wine list or on the labels, remember that one firm's "dry" may well be the same as someone else's "medium dry", which again may really be "slightly sweet". However, the majority of world-famous, classic, dry wines in the upper price ranges *are* truly dry, even when they are also quite fruity and full-bodied. A cheap wine, aimed at appealing to a wide market, will probably be slightly sweet even if described as "medium dry" because the merchant is trying to attract a public that prefers a touch of sweetness, but may be hesitant about ordering a wine labelled as such because of the snobbery of "dry being better".

Implicitly Sweet

There are many wines that are sweet either because of the grapes that make them or the time when these grapes are gathered, or a combination of both reasons. These are the types of sweet wines defined as implicitly sweet, and they may often have a fresh flowery smell and crisp finish, verging on the dry.

Many of these sweet wines earned their reputations in the past when sugar was rare and expensive and when people who led more active lives valued the natural sweetness and encouraged wine makers to accentuate it. The attraction of such wines for people living in cold damp areas is obvious. Today, too, they can make a valuable contribution to the general enjoyment of wine for they can be drunk at almost any hour. Before the day of the apéritif, implicitly sweet or even definitely sweet wines were frequently served with the first course of meals. The cocktail only came into social drinking comparatively recently; certainly before 1920 a drink was not automatically served before dinner in any traditional English-speaking household. There was a much shorter interval between diners assembling and the meal beginning. Even today and even in many wine-producing regions in Europe, it is by no means invariably routine to serve a drink before a meal.

The fashion for dry wines, or at any rate for wines that seem to be so, has in some instances resulted in wines produced in areas formerly renowned for their sweet or very sweet wines, now being made drier or even very dry. There are dry versions of many of the great sweet classics; in the implicitly sweet category are included the wines that producers aim to market as sweet wines and in which crispness and acidity are apparent, rather than sweetness. The latter will, of course, be there behind the primary impressions on nose and palate. This does not mean a distortion of the character of the wine, and in many instances a more commercially accepted version of a wine can be enjoyed and appreciated as an advance in wine making, and may even revive a classic tradition.

Visitors to regions famous for their slightly sweet or sweet wines should remember that, side by side with updated modern wines, there may also exist examples of wines made in an older way. The palate of today, conditioned to clean-cut, star-bright, light-coloured, crisp wines may not find such wines more than merely interesting as antique survivals. But there may be other wines, utterly uncommercial and sometimes expensive because they are only made in small quantities, that are rarities worth seeking. They may demonstrate why certain sweet wines deserved their fame: not likely to be everyday drinks, these, but such as to make a lasting impression on the interested drinker.

There should always be an essential unity within an implicitly sweet wine, and the sweetness should never fall heavily on the palate or leave the drinker with the feeling of a sticky mouth and generally cloyed senses. Compare the sweetness of a wine to that of many fruits: there is a toned-up sensation in the mouth after you eat them and this is the kind of pleasure a slightly sweet wine should give. Unless people know that a wine is supposed to be slightly sweet, they may often assume that it is dry, but more delicious than expected.

Sweet and Very Sweet

The wines in this section are, as far as commercial availability is concerned, restricted to the classics of Europe—classics because the history and traditions associated with them go back a long way in time. When sugar was rare and costly even for the wealthy, the great sweet wines were prized as much for their tonic and revitalizing properties as for their flavour. The Muscat wines of Samos were praised by the poets in classical times—Homer in the Odyssey and Mago of Carthage refer to sweet wines from grapes slightly dried after picking; Cyprus Commandaria was the tipple of the Crusaders. The great Sauternes and Barsacs, Hungarian Tokay and the superb German sweet wines were drunk with gusto and discrimination in the 19th century. To those who may say that such wines have no place in the contemporary drinking scene, I would refer them

Transporting wine in Yugoslavia.

to the menus of dinners given in the White House in Washington as recently as the late 1950s, when great Barsacs accompanied the first courses, including hot lobster, just as they might have done half a century or more ago. Luckily, within the last few years wise drinkers of all ages have dropped the snobbish "wine must be dry to be good" attitude and enjoy the great sweet wines on many occasions.

Try to distinguish wines that are just sweet from those that are sweet with the addition of noble rot. The primarily sweet wines may have some grapes affected by noble rot, but there is a profundity and a distinctive after-taste to those that are chiefly made with nobly rotten grapes. The latter have always seemed to me to be longer, subtler, with a complex smell and a more delicate intensity about the flavour than those that are simply sweet.

A sweet wine should satisfy, not sate, and should be able to be appraised slowly by all the senses of taste. As certain of the great sweet wines are fairly high in alcohol, they are not for indiscriminate drinking. The alcoholic content varies a great deal, and most people are unlikely to suspect its exact degree by tasting until it is too late. The Tokay Essence and the finest German Trockenbeerenauslesen do not generally exceed 8° Guy Lussac (percentage of alcohol by volume), and the German wines are often assisted to reach this strength necessary for their survival. The great Sauternes, however, will quite naturally go up to 14–15° or even 17°, which makes for trouble with the Customs and Excise from time to time. If you finish off the contents of a bottle of Sauternes after a dinner, you will be likely to feel the effects the next morning!

Intensely Sweet
The demarcation line between very sweet and intensely sweet is, I think, one of intensification. There is something more to intensely sweet wines. This is evident in complexity, profundity, and grandeur, not in greater sweetness, with the exception of the great Sauternes. In fact, some of these wines may not give the impression of being as sweet as some of the very sweet ones. It is almost as if they had reached such a point of sweetness that they have gone over their peak and are beginning to be dry again. I think that the analogy with certain types of honey helps here: honey is sweet, even very sweet, but some fine honeys have an inner assertive flavour that seems to intensify itself in the mouth and leave the palate tingling with a stimulating freshness.

I often experience this with the great wines made from slightly dried grapes left late on the vine and acted on by the noble rot. Great care is needed to make such wines, and some may achieve no more than rich sweetness. If they lack balance and proportion, the imperfection will be marked to the taster who knows what they can be like. This is the reason why some people do not

like the greatest sweet wines, for if the integral intensity is lacking, there may be little except sweetness to enjoy. A great wine of any kind that is less than good will, because of its distinct character and importance, suffer far more by faults in its making than a wine that is quite good but slightly unsuccessful. Some very poor wines have been made at certain times, in particular circumstances and by those who have been responsible for making some of the very greatest. The honest taster, undeterred by a great name, a world reputation and a high price, may still find a particular wine less admirable than it should rightly be—and he may well be right, whether he actually likes or dislikes it.

It is also worth bearing in mind that it can be difficult if not impossible to enjoy and appraise intensely sweet wines in certain situations. As these wines are often served at the end of a meal, it is important to avoid stunning or markedly altering the palate and impairing the general ability to taste them with moderate discrimination. After spirits or quantities of wine apéritifs before a meal, followed perhaps by curry-flavoured food and a pudding containing a great deal of chocolate, eggs and especially egg yolks, and liqueurs, no fine wine will taste of anything much, and the great sweet wines may seem positively unpleasant. This applies even more if an intensely sweet wine follows salads dressed with malt vinegar or with much wine vinegar in proportion to the oil. Intensely sweet wines can be the climax of a fine meal, but they should be progressively introduced by the food and wines before them, and when they are drunk they should be sipped in a leisurely way, in small or moderate quantities.

All sweet wines must be served cold. The sweeter they are the colder they should be; this does not mean that they should be virtually frappé or part-frozen. Chilling freshens them and brings out their lusciousness while minimizing the obvious sweetness; no wine should be chilled so much that it loses its smell.

A wine that is sweet can be a pleasant drink, a wine that is nobly sweet can be a great one. To my mind, all are wasted on elaborate sweet food, and most are excellent on their own, with a plain biscuit or piece of sponge cake. Great sweet wines may also be served with fine dessert fruit, except for oranges or pineapple which are too acid.

Small-scale sweet wines do not demand so much attention and can be served with some of the simpler sweet dishes. In the Sauternais district, however, certain of the more aromatic sweet wines may be served with slightly gamey food, such as Poulet Béarnais, a strongly garlic-flavoured chicken dish. Following the precept that wine should either complement or contrast with food, the locals sometimes serve a single glass of a Sauternes with foie gras. The first time I met this I was apprehensive, but it is a possible combination although you must be careful in the

Groot Constantia winery at the Cape of Good Hope, established in 1679 and still in production.

choice of food and drink that follows; one very rich course in a meal is usually enough. A well-known English wine merchant was firm about the happy partnership of sharp British matured cheeses, such as farmhouse Cheddar, Lancashire and Double Gloucester, with the great Sauternes, and I admit this is also possible. But I prefer them on their own.

The Principal Wine-Producing Regions

The vineyards of the Rhine and the Mosel, the north of Italy, north Portugal, the northern half of Hungary, Switzerland, the Champagne area, certain slopes in the Loire and Rhône, the Rioja vineyards of north Spain, and much of the Napa Valley in California are some of the many vineyards of the world where **bone dry** wines are made. All these areas, including those with warm summers and even extreme heat, experience periods of cold weather and some have heavy falls of snow. Frost is the enemy of the vine as of most other plants, but snow and a certain amount of cold can be healthy for a vineyard.

Coolness of climate can be echoed in the crispness of the wine, provided the grapes get enough sun to ripen them in due course. The establishment of vineyards in Canada and the revival of them in England shows what the vine can do at these northern limits. Certain vineyards in Australia, South Africa and Argentina, from where bone dry wines also come, demonstrate the vine's versatility in the southern hermisphere.

Many of the finest bone dry white wines are produced along river valleys; these are the corridors of the winds that freshen and cool the vines, either in shallow valleys, as in the Loire or the Marne, or on the gradual slopes above the lakes of Switzerland and north Italy, as well as in the deeper cut windings of the Mosel, the Douro and the Rhône. The water of rivers and lakes is not only important as regards the atmosphere of the vineyards, but, by reflecting light, can have a distinct effect on the ripening of the grapes. The alteration of the level of the Mosel, when the Rhine-Mosel canal was constructed, caused serious concern among vineyard owners of river-bank sites as the water rose slightly. However, it does not appear that the change in the angle at which light is reflected off the river has adversely affected or coarsened the quality of wines from such renowned vineyards as that of Wehlener Sonnenuhr.

The vineyards that produce bone dry wines may also produce many more that are **dry** or **medium dry**. The assertive dryness of the bone dry wines is softened, the wine is slightly more easy-going, sometimes because a different grape or combination of grapes is used, sometimes because the wine comes from a special estate or from a site of particular character and quality. There are, however, some absolutes: you will not, for example, find a dry or medium dry wine in the middle of a Chablis vineyard where only bone dry wines are produced, nor can a dry or medium dry wine be made from grapes that possess quite a high proportion of natural sugar. In general, vineyards that make good and fine, dry and medium dry white wines will be in cool regions, or regions where the atmosphere for at least part of the year is fresh, and a certain amount of chill pervades the vineyards.

There are also regions, slightly south of those making bone dry wines or in particularly sheltered areas, that produce dry and medium dry wines, such as the Côte d'Or and southern Burgundy, certain sites in the middle and upper Loire, the Gironde and the regions of the Lot and Dordogne, parts of central Italy, southern Spain and Portugal, southern Yugoslavia, Romania and parts of Greece and the Greek islands. Most English vineyards also produce dry to medium dry wines and there are vast quantities of wines of this type made throughout vineyards outside Europe because they appeal to a wide public and because they can be well made from vineyards that are not at the extreme limits of cultivation for the particular vine.

Sweet and **very sweet** wines come from vineyards that concentrate on growing grapes of a high sugar content, such as the Riesling, Sémillon, Muscat and Furmint. The vineyards are situated in warm, sunny regions, such as southern France, Italy, Spain, central and south-eastern Europe, California, and South Africa.

Some of the vineyards that produce bone dry and dry wines may also make **implicitly sweet** wines from grapes left on the vines until they are over-ripe. There are a number of vineyards, especially in Germany, where late-vintaged, implicitly sweet wines are now made. The revived popularity of this type of wine has caused some individual producers and firms to increase the production of sweet wines, although as yet not on a large commercial scale.

Lastly, **intensely sweet** wines are made in certain vineyards, north and south of the bone dry and dry regions, which have been exposed to the action of noble rot. The Sauternes and Barsac districts, the Rhine and Mosel valleys, and the Tokay region of Hungary exemplify this.

Vineyard Characteristics

Bone dry wines come from vineyards about which it might be said that there is a bone in the landscape: friable (crumbling) or sharply stony surface soil, sand, gravel of granite or slate, chalk or limestone. The soil will often be light in colour, indicating that wines of crispness, even vivacity will be made—the texture and colour often relate to what the wine is like. The precipitous slopes of the Mosel, the outcrops of rock at Saumur in the Loire, the pale undulations of the Champagne vineyards are examples of this type of landscape. The light soil bestows delicacy and grace on the wine, the pale colour reflects such sun as the vineyards may receive, encouraging the wines to develop charm.

The vineyards will be situated on slopes. Some of these may be as steep as railway cuttings, on which it is difficult to keep a footing, such as those of the Saar and above some of the north Italian lakes; others may slope more gradually, such as those of the Palatinate, the Muscadet region at the western end of the River Loire, and the Chablis vineyards above the little River Serein in Burgundy.

The cultivation of the vines will depend on the locality of the vineyards. Generally, the nearer to the cold, the higher the vines will be trained if they are to produce bone dry, crisp white wines. They need to be in the air away from the chill remaining in the ground, and exposed to any warmth and freshness in the atmosphere. If they must endure the heat of a southern vineyard as well as any seasonal chilliness, they may be trained and pruned like sun-shielding bushes or grown along low trellises instead of high ones, but they will usually be clear of the ground. If the vines are to make good bone dry white wines, they must avoid contact with lasting cold and wet and the air must circulate freely among them in the heat.

Most of the vineyards making **dry** and **medium dry** wines resemble those making bone dry wines, but they tend to have more of a smile to them; the countryside is usually gracious rather than impressive, undulating rather than precipitous. Other forms of agriculture and vegetation may be more evident than vineyards. Sometimes the soil may be darker in colour than in the bone dry regions but it will, in good white wine regions, never be very dark, and it will almost invariably be friable and light-textured, often stony or sandy or a mixture of the two, and sometimes pale and chalky as well. Unless there are steep slopes, or unless the region is still dominated by antique methods of vine cultivation, the vines are usually trained quite low. Even where the use of mechanical cultivators is possible, the vines are grown along low trellises or wires, trained either sideways in the Bordeaux style, or as bushes, varying in height, but seldom taller than the average person.

Wherever medium dry wines are made, **sweet** white wines can be produced. Good white wine country is good country for all types of white wines, depending, of course, on the variety of grapes and the way in which the wine is made.

Sweet Wines

Great sweet and very sweet wines are all white, and for the most part they are made from white grapes only. The tannin that gives long life and profundity to fine red wines is not as significant a constituent in white wines; although some is present, it is seldom noticed in white wines, whether dry or sweet.

Grapes vary according to sugar content. Some, such as the Muscat, are high in natural sugar, while others are capable, in certain conditions, of developing a pronounced additional but natural sweetness. In some grapes the natural sugar may actually arrest the action of the yeasts so that this innate sweetness remains in the wine.

The Chenin Blanc along the Loire in France and in many modern vineyards throughout the world, can make wines that are delicately sweet. Its local Loire name, Pineau de la Loire, is sometimes used elsewhere as Pineau, but it should not be confused with the Pinot Chardonnay, which is more correctly known as Chardonnay.

The Sémillon, one of the grapes used to make Sauternes, is also found throughout the world making slightly sweet and sweet wines. In the classic vineyards it is not often used on its own, but many modern wineries use it to make balanced and agreeable wines bearing its name. Wines made with it or principally from it are sometimes described on American labels as "Sauterne". The final "s" of the French name of that wine region and its wines is excluded, a fair method of differentiating the styles of wine, for I have never tasted a wine labelled "Sauterne" that really had anything more in common with "Sauternes" than its sweetness.

In Californian vineyards, the Sauvignon Blanc grape is used to make slightly soft, even sweet wines. In most European wine regions, however, the definitely dry, albeit full, noble style of that particular grape comes through in blends of

Right, pruning and tying the vines in a California vineyard. Far right, typical terraced vineyards on the steep hillsides of the Middle Rhine.

grapes in wines made as far south as Sicily and Cyprus. I have known it used for some sweet, late-vintaged Austrian wines, however.

The Furmint, the great grape of Hungarian Tokay, makes a wine that can be slightly sweet. It is thought to have been introduced into Hungary in the 13th century from France or Italy. In parts of Italy the Trebbiano grape makes slightly sweet wines. Here it is used in many of the wines labelled *abboccato* or *amabile*, although other grapes may also be used with it. There is also the Malvasia (Malvoisie or Monemvasia), a grape known centuries ago in Greece, which is more associated today with dessert wines, such as Madeira and Marsala, but which is often used with other grapes in many Mediterranean sweet wines.

Perhaps the most universal of all grapes that make slightly sweet or even very sweet wines is the Muscat (Muscatel, Moscato, Muskat). This, together with its different varieties, is used throughout the world, and although it can make a truly dry wine with carefully controlled fermentation, it is mainly associated with wines that are markedly scented and slightly sweet. The Muscat is one of the very few grape varieties that makes a wine that distinctly smells of the grape.

Other grapes can, in certain regions and certain circumstances, such as late vintaging, make wines that are implicitly sweet. These include Riesling, Gewürztraminer and Traminer, and some of the newer grape varieties becoming popular in Germany, including the Müller-Thurgau and Scheurebe. The Morio Muskat is also among these and its almost piercing, scented bouquet is usually easily noted. Remember, however, that one person's slightly sweet wine may be someone else's dry or medium dry. Extreme fruitiness can be confused with definite sweetness, especially when this is also associated with a wine with a pronounced flowery smell. All grapes contain sugar, some more than others, but this sugar need not inevitably make a wine that is sweet.

Sweet Wine Production

A wine may be made sweet by blending it with a very sweet, concentrated wine, and this can produce a good if not a great wine. The sweet wine that is added, even in small proportion, will usually have been made sweet in one of the following ways:

The grapes may have been dried outdoors, usually on straw mats, shortly after they have been picked and before they are pressed. This will make them wrinkled and the juice will be verging on syrupy.

Alternatively, the must or unfermented grape juice may be slightly concentrated by heating, before adding it to other must or finished wine. If the grape juice is from sweetish grapes, heating will intensify the sweetness and this will spread throughout the wine to which it is added. Very sweet grape juice may also be added or even *mistelle*, which is must plus the alcohol that would have resulted if the must had been allowed to ferment normally.

In the past it seems probable that many of the very sweet wines were made by one or a combination of the first two methods—drying and heating—especially if the vineyards were situated in a region that enjoyed fine, dry weather after the vintage so that the grapes could dry outside. If a concentrated must or wine was added, it had to be done at an early stage in the wine's life, to ensure eventual harmony. When the science of wine was in its infancy and the different stages of fermentation were recognized, but the problems they presented had not been solved, the concentrate would have had to be made at the same time as the wine and added immediately.

The sweet wines of the Mediterranean countries, and those from the southern parts of France and Spain, could formerly have been made in one or both of these ways. Every means available was used to make wines of the desired or accentuated sweetness and to preserve them as such.

In regions where cold and sudden variations in climate are to be expected, these methods of sweetening or intensifying wine are not reliable, although laboratory technicians can correct almost all the deficiencies of nature, without always making a wholly satisfying wine. For the normal vintage, the wine grower may, in certain conditions, postpone picking some of the grapes and leave them for late vintaging. Grapes left on the vine will, unless destroyed by frost or rain or hailstorms, contract, even shrivel, but there will still be juice within them. This juice,

Right, vineyards in the Rhône valley at Aigle, Switzerland. Far right, the regimented precision of part of the Château d'Yquem vineyard, as seen from the Château itself.

held within the grape by the contraction of the grapeskin, will have a more intense flavour than that of an ordinary ripe grape. The atmosphere around the vine and the autumn sun will dry the grapes slightly, reducing the content, just as drying the gathered grapes on straw mats might do.

Late Vintaging

Grapes for making wine are usually picked when they are fully ripe. If bad weather threatens the harvest, they may be picked earlier and this unripe quality may later be detected in the wine unless this has been skilfully made. Advancing picking by one or two days will not usually affect the wine adversely, although it may make it different, and sometimes a slightly unripe crop may be picked because a wine high in acidity is required. Otherwise, picking will begin according to the judgment of the producer, depending on the grape varieties and the location of the vineyard. If grapes are left on the vine after the time for the normal vintage they may rot and in time drop off. If they are over-ripe, they may actually burst their skins. There is usually no point in leaving grapes on the vines after they are fully ripe, although wine makers prefer to leave them ungathered up to this point because grapes that are fully ripe make not only a better wine but also a greater quantity.

Certain grapes, such as the Riesling, can, in vineyards with a long, fine and dry autumn, be left on the vines after the main vintage, to be gathered later. Such late-picked grapes are known in German as *Spätlese*, in French as *vendange tardive*. A chance of losing them through heavy rain or frost is taken, but the resulting wine, made either with a proportion of late-vintaged grapes in a blend with others or by itself is a chance worth taking.

In Germany in particular, selected bunches of grapes are chosen for late vintaging (this special selection is termed *Auslese*). First, single grapes are selected (*Beeren* (berry) *auslese*); last of all to be selected and picked are overripe grapes (*Trockenbeerenauslese*).

The wine has what I think of as a distinct smile, the characteristics of the grapes and the vineyards being slightly intensified and resulting in something that is truly different from wines that are just sweet. The natural sweetness that would anyway be there gains a profundity, the smell possesses subtle undertones that might not be noticeable at all in a dry wine, and the after-taste often lingers in flowery freshness that may surprise those who associate sweetness in wines with a syrupy or cloying effect.

Wines from late-vintaged grapes differ from those made from grapes subjected to the action of noble rot. A late-vintaged wine from grapes with noble rot has an additional smell and flavour, certainly a back taste and after-taste, that can usually be detected. Some growers do not separate grapes on which the rot is present from those grown for late picking. It costs a great deal in labour and time to separate the grapes with noble rot on them, in small clusters or even grape by grape, and the producer may put all the grapes of a late vintage together so that the odd additional smell and taste of the "noble rot" may be present in an *Auslese* or even *Spätlese*.

Noble Rot

In many wine regions, the climate can change abruptly. First there is the heat of summer lasting to the vintage, then may come cold, rain and possibly snow or frost. This means that at least in fairly exposed vineyards, the grapes can only be left after the usual vintage date (usually 100 days after the flowering of the vine in the spring) at great risk and they will seldom yield more in juice of quality. However, at the extremes of where the finest dry and sweet white wines can be made, to the north and south of the vineyard regions, certain areas enjoy a curious semi-sheltered climate, often connected with their proximity to a river. The formation of the countryside protects them from severe and immediate changes after the harvest; the water not only reflects the sunlight, but, when the warmth of an autumn day changes to the cold of an autumn or winter night, it gives off mist or even fog.

This is when the action of a fungus called *botrytis cinerea* (noble rot in English, *pourriture noble* in French, *Edelfäule* in German, *muffa nobile* in Italian) can work wonders in vineyards where the grapes are still on the vines. Rot in the ordinary way is rot, and the grapes fall off the vines. They cannot make good, much less fine wines. But noble rot settles on the grapes like fur or fluff, and the surface of the grapeskins resembles rather coarse suede leather. By the action of this rot, the grapeskins wither and shrink, the juice within concentrating and taking on something extra, a flavour that in the wine lingers and tantalizes and is distinctly additional to sweetness as such. There is a profundity about the smell of such wines, and their after-taste has, for me, a barleysugar flavour; glucose more than fructose (both of which are components of the natural sugar in a grape) comes out strongly in wines on which the noble rot fungus has acted.

It does not automatically follow that a year in which fine sweet wines have been made in a region will invariably set the scene for the development of *botrytis cinerea*. Rather it is as if nature has a consolation prize for certain vineyards in regions at the mercy of climate and weather and develops noble rot in an ordinary or even poor year. The result, however, is so fine as to make a lasting reputation for wines that can receive the noble rot. They are never cheap, even when whole small bunches of grapes can be gathered together, instead of being picked one by one, because it is necessary for the pickers to pass up and down a vineyard many times. They also need to know the exact degree of over-ripeness so as to pick only these grapes. In the Sauternais region, special long-bladed scissors are used to snip the grapes off the bunches, and usually only trained and skilled workers are employed on this specialized type of vintage. In many instances, too, these wines remain longer in cask than the ordinary sweet wines from the same vineyards, so that capital is tied up for a long time.

Experiments in several vineyards outside Europe have not really been able to establish the action of *botrytis cinerea* by contrived means, such as by blowing the fungus on to grapes left late on the vine. According to the authoritative Leon D. Adams in *The Wines of America* (Houghton Mifflin, 1973), this was done at Cresta Blanca in California in 1956 and made a much-praised wine from Sémillon and Sauvignon grapes, called Premier Sémillon; however, this was not made after 1966. Some California vineyards have been subjected to artificial fog, but so far the wines made have not been successful enough to warrant making them commercially even on a small scale.

The fungus was reported in the Arroya Seco vineyard in the Salinas Valley in 1969, on white Riesling grapes. Leon D. Adams tasted this wine, marketed as a Spätlese Riesling (the grapes had been left on the vines for an extra three weeks) and reported that he could not detect the botrytis flavour. The California climate is too dry for the damp, foggy conditions that are welcomed in European vineyards where the noble rot can take hold. In the Finger Lakes region of New York State, however, the fungus has occasionally been found at Hammondsport. The Gold Seal winery used late-vintaged Riesling grapes to make a Spätlese Riesling; and in 1961 a Trockenbeeren-auslese was made. In Australia and South Africa, the dryness of the atmosphere does not permit the fungus on any large scale.

The Effects of Noble Rot

Grapes on which the noble rot acts tend to have rather thin skins; this is necessary so that the rot can penetrate them easily, although the skins must be tough enough not to split when completely ripe. The grapes must be fully ripe, otherwise the rot could not act beneficially; by the time it settles on the grapes they must not only be ripe, but the various acids within them must be diminishing. The acids, which must be present in the first place if a flabby wine is not to result, are, as it were, breathed out of the grapes, and the sugar content will rise at the same time; the grapes begin to have a pinkish-brown tint.

The noble rot, once settled on the skins, draws off even more acid, and the water content of the grapes is reduced. The grapes will shrink progressively until they virtually dry up on the vine (in Germany these are the grapes that make the Trockenbeerenauslese as compared with the Beerenauslese wines). In appearance, the grapes look as if they have a plague, the bunches are patchy with a fuzzy fungus, and some grapes are still green and normal in size, while others are wrinkled like raisins. These latter look as if all moisture has been sucked from them, and many, with the botrytis heavily on them, give the impression that they are being eaten up alive. If you taste such a grape, however, the fungus merely melts in the mouth, by no means unpleasantly, and the single drop of almost syrupy pulp is everything that is implied in the word nectar.

The History of Noble Rot

Obviously *botrytis cinerea* existed before its nature and actions were known, but it would not have been practical to have made wines with noble rot on them until comparatively recently. Before bottles and corks were invented, it was new wine that was most sought after, because as wine aged it became sour. It might even turn to vinegar if it had remained in a dirty or unsound cask, exposed to the air. This was why new wine was prized and why the harvest date was officially proclaimed in the wine regions so that no one could steal a march on his neighbours by picking early and making wine that could be offered for sale days before anyone else. The wine ships from Bordeaux would race each other to the British ports, where in London no one could buy until the royal butler (*bouteiller*) had made his choice. As wine got old in cask and perhaps almost undrinkable, it would be doctored or "cut" with honey, mead, hydromel or fruit juices that might make it palatable. This cutting enabled everyone to keep on drinking and the product was known as "bastard" because it was a cross of several things.

Not only would wine makers in those days have been unable, economically, to wait and lose the chance of selling their new vintage if they delayed picking, but they would certainly have despaired of trying to make wine from grapes apparently rotten with mould.

However, it is possible that grapes bearing the noble rot *were* used for wine making in ancient times, just as the use of cork and the use of *flor* to make certain wines were known and then forgotten. My deductions from certain references in more learned works must be considered as a personal view and not, as yet, a theory of substance. In various works about wine in the ancient world there are quotations from the *Deipnosophists* by Athenaeus, dating from about 200 AD. H. Warner Allen, himself a fine classical scholar, quotes copiously from this in *A History of Wine* (Faber, 1961) and notes the high reputation of sweet Chian wines, with one called ὁαπρός or "Saprias". This, he thinks, was the finest of the Chian growths. He cites a much older writer, Philyllius (c. 400 BC) mentioning, among other wines, "mellow Chian . . . so that there may be no danger of a headache next morning". Warner Allen uses the word "mellow" to translate the Greek word ὁαπρός which means "rotten", and he

Vineyards at Würzburg on the river Main, Franconia.

deduces by stages that this is associated with food that is high; he quotes Horace as describing wild boar that was gamey using the Latin word *rancidus*. This, Warner Allen rightly notes, could relate to the word *rancio*, which is Spanish but which is also used in the Catalan area of both France and Spain.

Allan Sichel, however, in *The Penguin Book of Wines* (1965), refers to this word as used in connection with the Grand Roussillon wines. Here it means roughly the same as tawny when applied to sweet Grands Roussillons which have matured for longer than usual in wood; in all other southern wines in this region, *rancio* "takes on only its basic meaning of 'old developed'". I was present when Allan Sichel was tasting these wines and when, with the local authorities, he worked out the definition of *rancio* for his book. But as my own notes indicate, there was nothing whatever rotten about the wines in the sense that Warner Allen assumes that this is "the razor edge of perfection between going up and going down", or anything to do with noble rot either.

But the Greek word anglicized as "Saprias" does mean "rotten". This was the word used by a writer who seems to have been more than a casual lover of wine. What he meant seems perfectly clear from a passage Warner Allen goes on to quote, but which he, the gentle exploratory scholar, finds obscure, while I, the novice trying to study Greek, can only take one way. The quotation, by a character in Athenaeus, says of Saprias, "From the mouth of its jar, when the stopper has been levered up, there rises the scent of violets, the scent of roses, the scent of hyacinths. A divine fragrance fills the whole house to its lofty roof, ambrosia and nectar in one". If that account of a smell that combines freshness, opulent lusciousness and lingering fascination is not of a wine made with noble rot on the grapes, then I do not recognize the voice of another wine writer, translating the sensations of this remarkable smell and flavour into words. Hugh Johnson says about a tasting of great Mosels in the 1970s, "I felt like a queen bee; glutted with honey . . . the rose and carnation scent of the wines became intolerable". Draw the cork on a great German or French wine or a fine Tokay and let the fragrance waft from the bottle like the genie in the fairytale. Given a certain climate and grape, there would seem no reason why the Greeks could not have made nobly rotten wines, and perhaps a scholar will one day trace more of their history.

There are several versions of how the great sweet wines were made later. One is that the monks of Johannisberg in the Rheingau, despairing because they had no authorization from the Prince-Bishop of Fulda to begin the vintage, produced a wine from grapes that were apparently rotten—the resulting wine was superb. This is recorded for 1716. But in the Tokay region of Hungary it seems that the noble rot was recog-

nized for the magician it is as early as 1650. The first *aszu* or wine made from nobly rotten grapes came from the vineyards of Mount Oremus, which at that time belonged to the widow of György Rákóczi I, Prince of Transylvania. Hungary at that time was threatened with war, the vintage was delayed, and thus the first great sweet wines were made. Tokay is admirably situated to make them for its vineyards are on a hill, at the foot of which flow two confluent rivers, the Bodrog and the Ronyva.

In the Sauternes district, nobly rotten, sweet wines were first made comparatively recently. There the story of their origin relates to a messenger of the then owner of Yquem, who issued strict orders that the vintage should not start until his personal instructions were received. The messenger fell ill *en route* and, when he did arrive at the vineyards, the workers made the vintage, despairing of any wine resulting. Edmund Penning-Rowsell, in his great work, *The Wines of Bordeaux* (Wine & Food Society, 1969) comments that the late Marquis de Lur-Saluces, owner of Yquem, believed that the use of grapes bearing the noble rot started about 1860 and that the work of a German wine specialist in the Sauternes vineyards at that time helped to establish what is now a tradition. The late *maître de chai* or cellarmaster at Yquem, however, reported that the earliest Yquem he had ever drunk (and he would certainly have been in a position to try many) was that of 1845, which, he thought, was made in about the same way it is now, with the noble rot. Certainly the wines of Sauternes, inclined to be luscious anyway, were already popular; when studying old menus, it should be remembered that the lusciously sweet wines would not have been in existence or at least not widely exported until about the last quarter of the 19th century.

In Germany, even late vintaged wines were singled out comparatively recently, as Dr O. W. Loeb points out in his book *Moselle* (Faber, 1972). The term Spätlese was not known until 1910 and not in general use before the 1920s. He thinks that the term Beerenauslese was first used in 1783, after a particularly fine vintage, but he wisely points out that it is entirely the responsibility of the grower as to whether he "declares" a Beeren or a Trockenbeerenauslese. After the great vintage year of 1921 not one of the Mosel growers made a Beerenauslese again until 1934; since 1959 the only suitable year was 1971.

It is pertinent to state here that, at this level of quality, there can be a great and noticeable difference between wines that are technically very sweet but which have been made to satisfy certain commercial requirements, and between those which are made because a dedicated and conscientious wine maker chooses to produce a great wine. However high its price, its cost can never be recouped, and it will remain a superb curiosity and an unforgettable experience for the privileged drinker.

Christian Brothers' seminary at Mont La Salle, California.

CLASSIFICATION OF TASTE/WHITE WINES

Bone Dry

France	Germany, Austria	Italy	Spain, Portugal	Rest of Europe	Americas, Australia South Africa
Light and Crisp					
SYLVANER, medium quality, from Alsace	SYLVANER, medium quality, from Franconia; some from Palatinate SYLVANER, medium quality, from Austria RIESLING, inexpensive, from Austria GRÜNER VELTLINER wines, from Austria FURMINT, ordinary quality, from Germany	SYLVANER, medium quality, from north Italy RIESLING, inexpensive, from north Italy GRÜNER VELTLINER wines, from north Italy		JOHANNISBERGER, from Switzerland RIESLING, inexpensive, from Yugoslavia, Hungary, Bulgaria FURMINT, ordinary quality, from Hungary	RIESLING, some inexpensive examples SYLVANER, inexpensive
Crisp					
CHABLIS PETIT CHABLIS MUSCADET ANJOU SAUMUR, most examples TOURAINE AZAY-LE-RIDEAU, sec CHINON QUINCY REUILLY JASNIÈRES SAVOIE, still wines RIESLING, ordinary quality, from Alsace	RIESLING, ordinary quality, from Mosel, Saar, Ruwer, Franconia, Palatinate	VERDICCHIO DEI CASTELLI DI JESI VILLAGRANDE estate wines, from Sicily REGALEALI estate wines, from Sicily Inexpensive wines, from Sicily, notably from Etna	MINHO still wines, notably VILA REAL, from Portugal	RIESLING, from central and south-east Europe FENDANT, from Switzerland Most white wines from Luxembourg ARSINOË and other dry whites, from Cyprus TRAKYA and other dry whites, from Turkey	RIESLING, from Australia, South Africa SAUVIGNON, from California STEEN, ordinary quality, from South Africa CHENIN BLANC
Crisp and Fruity					
VOUVRAY, dry MONTLOUIS SAUMUR, specific vintages ANJOU, some estate SANCERRE, ordinary quality POUILLY BLANC FUMÉ GAILLAC, dry Dry white wines from the Dordogne RIESLING, good quality, from Alsace EDELZWICKER, from Alsace	RIESLING, good quality, from Rhine, Mosel, Franconia RIESLING, estate, from Palatinate SYLVANER, estate, from Palatinate SYLVANER, superior quality, from Franconia Some white wines from Nahe	TREBBIANO, and some other white wines, from north Italy VERMENTINO, from Sardinia	VALDEPEÑAS, young, from Spain AZEITÃO, some examples, from Portugal		RIESLING, estate SAUVIGNON, superior quality CHENIN BLANC, superior quality
Medium to Full-Bodied and Robust					
GROS PLANT BOURGOGNE ALIGOTÉ MUSCADET, some estate CÔTES DU RHÔNE—VILLAGES CHÂTEAU GRILLET CONDRIEU VIOGNIER, all wines from this grape ST-JOSEPH ST PÉRAY HERMITAGE CROZES-HERMITAGE TOKAY D'ALSACE PINOT D'ALSACE	RULÄNDER and other regional wines, from Baden-Württemberg	Inexpensive, branded white wines, from Sicily	RIOJA, inexpensive, from Spain DOURO, from Portugal DÃO, from Portugal	TOKAY, dry, from Hungary Some white wines from Cyprus	CHENIN BLANC, special quality
Weighty					
CHABLIS, first and great growths, in outstanding years Still CHAMPAGNE CHÂTEAUNEUF-DU-PAPE, estate			RIOJA, estate, from Spain BUSSACO, from Portugal		CHARDONNAY, estate

Bone Dry

Light and Crisp

These wines are light in terms of body character, with a crispness indicating the acidity of the vineyards from where they come. They include many Sylvaner and Riesling wines, the best being from central and south-eastern Europe, and also wines made from the Grüner Veltliner grape in Austria and northern Italy and from the Furmint grape, notably in Hungary and Germany.

Sylvaner Palatinate Some of the lightest bone dry wines are made from the Sylvaner (Silvaner) grape. In Germany, it produces a great deal of wine in the Palatinate region, sometimes in conjunction with other grapes. It is also much grown in *Franconia* Franconia where it makes some of the *Alsace* finer whites and in Alsace, the French vineyard region that is, in wine terms, a continuation of the Deutsche Weinstrasse of the Palatinate. Although occasionally some late gathered Sylvaners in Germany and Austria are used to make fullish, sweetish wines, the Sylvaner essentially produces a light, fresh wine, at its most enjoyable while quite young. It has a very light colour, crispness and "cool" character being its main charms.

The Sylvaner makes pleasant light, crisp wines throughout many other countries of central and south-eastern Europe, and its name appears on their *Switzerland* labels. In Switzerland, the well-known, *Johannisberger* light white wine Johannisberger (which perhaps gained early fame from having Schloss Johannisberg on the Rhine as a namesake) is made from a type of *California* Sylvaner. In vineyards outside Europe, *Australia* the Sylvaner is also used considerably, but as it is a grape not much liking fierce heat, some wines made from it under those conditions tend to lack character.

Riesling The Riesling, one of the greatest wine grapes of the world, also makes light, crisp wines; it is widely grown in many middle and south-eastern European countries, including Yugoslavia, Hungary, Austria and Bulgaria. It is also extensively cultivated in many New World vineyards.

Rheinriesling There are two main types of Riesling *Wälschriesling* strain: the Rheinriesling which makes the Alsace and German Rieslings, and the Wälschriesling, which is much grown in eastern Europe but tends to make a lighter, slightly coarser type of wine. The great German and Alsatian wines are seldom light and cannot, therefore, be used as a comparison to appraise *Balkan countries* Balkan or other Rieslings, which are characterized by lightness and crispness, with a distinctive bouquet. Riesling wines of special quality can possess a most elegant fruitiness, and this makes them particularly easy to enjoy at any time of day.

Austria Delicate, sometimes slightly fruity, *Grüner Veltliner* bone dry white wines are made in Austria from the Grüner Veltliner grape, which often possesses a touch of liveliness verging on the sparkle. This grape, as well as the Sylvaner and *North Italy* Riesling, is also widely grown in northern Italy, notably in the vineyards of the Alto Adige, Friuli-Venezia Guilia, Valtellina and Valle d'Aosta. Here these grapes produce pleasant, light wines, many of them endowed with a delicate flowery bouquet. This characteristic is associated with vineyards close to high mountains which impart freshness and crispness to the wine.

Furmint In Hungary the Furmint grape *Hungary* produces light, crisp wines, with a particular, almost herby aroma. This grape is also cultivated in other parts of *Germany* central Europe, notably Germany, and its rather assertive bouquet makes some people think it makes a sweet wine. Although it is often possible to get an idea of how sweet a wine is by just smelling it, a very flowery smell does not necessarily denote a sweet wine. Ordinary Furmint wines are bone dry, light and crisp.

Crisp

The bone dry taste of these wines is characterized by freshness and acidity. Some of the best known classic wines are included here, notably Chablis and the Muscadets of France, certain other Loire wines, Mosel and Saar wines from Germany, Alsatian Rieslings and Californian wines made from the Sauvignon grape.

Chablis Possibly the most famous bone dry wine in the world comes from the area round Chablis in central France. Unfortunately its renown has resulted in many wines being called "Chablis type".

Although one can sometimes detect a family resemblance between certain wines and those that wine makers and salesmen think they resemble, it is doubtful that anyone who has ever tasted true Chablis would find that it bears the slightest similarity to any other wine, apart from being white and dry. The type of wine frequently offered as "Chablis" may be either a blend of Chablis and another white wine, or an otherwise perfectly good, cheap, white Burgundy. Chablis proper is a white Burgundy, made from the Chardonnay grape, in comparatively small vineyards, north-west of the Burgundy vineyards in the Côte d'Or. The fact that the vineyards are slightly further north is usually noticeable when you taste a true Chablis against other white Burgundies. It is very pale in colour and, unlike any other white Burgundy, has a greenish glint at the edge of the wine; even as it ages, Chablis never really becomes golden in colour. It can have great nobility, but is generally an austere wine, so minerally dry that few wine drinkers like it at first and most appreciate it only after some experience.

Grands crus

The Institut National des Appellations d'Origins (INAO) has classified the Chablis region into great and first growths. There are seven great growths *(grands crus)* or vineyards: Blanchots, Bougros, Les Clos, Grenouilles, Valmur, Les Preuses and Vaudésir; La Moutonne is considered by many to come into this category though officially it does not belong there. There are 23 further vineyards classified as first growths

Premiers crus

(premiers crus). Both great and first growths of Chablis come into the Weighty sub-division.

Petit Chablis

Petit Chablis, bone dry and crisp, denotes a wine from vineyards behind the main Chablis area and should in no way be thought of as inferior; it will simply be on a smaller scale than a great or first growth. Chablis, which I do classify as a crisp wine, is a label name indicating that the wine will come from one of the vineyards of the Chablis region. The label, however, will only bear a specific name if it comes from an authorized vineyard.

Muscadet

Muscadet is the other outstanding crisp French wine that is bone dry. It is made from the Muscadet grape (originally known as the Melon or Muscadet de Bourgogne, planted after a devastating frost in the 18th century, thus belying the saying that Muscadet was "the wine of Abelard the Breton").

Muscadet des Coteaux de la Loire
Muscadet de Sèvre-et-Maine

The vineyards are at the mouth of the River Loire, south of Nantes in Brittany, and there are three main regions: Muscadet, Muscadet des Coteaux de la Loire and, reputed as the best, Muscadet de Sèvre-et-Maine. Muscadet is usually at its best when quite young although there are a few exceptions; these, however, are the wines of specific estates, whose owners know exactly how to handle the wine so as to display its quality. When tasting Muscadet, think of the nearness of the sea to the vineyards, the west winds coming in from the Atlantic, and the variable,

Muscadet sur lie

often wet, cold climate. There is a current vogue for Muscadet bottled *sur lie*, meaning straight off the lees in the cask, without the wine being racked off, so that there may be a slight "prickle" of sparkle apparent in it. This kind of wine can decline markedly in crispness if it is allowed to get old; the vintage on a Muscadet label indicates how soon you should drink it, usually within two or three years.

Loire
Chenin Blanc

Along the River Loire, the Chenin Blanc grape known locally as the Pineau de la Loire, makes bone dry, crisp

Anjou, Saumur, Touraine, Azay-le-Rideau Chinon, Quincy, Reuilly, Jasnières

wines in many vineyards: Anjou, Saumur, Touraine, Azay-le-Rideau. There is also a white Chinon; this, with the wines of Quincy, Reuilly and Jasnières, all crisp, bone dry wines, is becoming known outside the regions. The vineyards are further from the sea and the wines tend to become slightly fruity, an indication that the vineyards are more sheltered. The Chenin Blanc makes agreeable crisp wines in many other vineyards, too, but exposed to a lot of sun, it seems to broaden its style

California

and, as in some California wineries, can produce a fairly sweet wine.

South Africa

The Chenin Blanc is the grape known as Steen in South Africa and once considered indigenous to that country. The Cape vineyards label wines as both Steen and Chenin Blanc, the latter tending to imply wines of a slightly full style.

Riesling
Mosel
Saar

The medium-priced and cheaper Rieslings from the Mosel and, especially, its tributary the Saar, are deliciously crisp and this attribute is also found in many of the Swiss wines, including those

Swiss Fendant

made from the Fendant grape, a type of white Chasselas.

Alsace

In Alsace, the more ordinary Rieslings are good examples of crisp, bone dry wines and, even in the lower price ranges, it is possible to note the difference between these Rieslings and

Luxembourg those of the Mosel—a slightly more southerly vineyard can be detected in the Alsatian Rieslings. The Luxembourg wines, further north than Alsace, are also crisp, though tending to lightness; they generally possess a freshness that makes them best enjoyed while very young, up to three years old.

Throughout the central and south-eastern vineyards of Europe, the Riesling makes crisp wines, but, at their best, those of Hungary are possibly *Hungary* endowed with the most delicacy and finesse, and those of Yugoslavia with the *Yugoslavia* most amiability.

Italy In Italy, the pale straw-coloured wine *Verdicchio dei* of Verdicchio dei Castelli di Jesi (a *Castelli di Jesi* region in the Marche, near Ancona) is possibly the best known crisp white wine. In its amphora-shaped bottle this wine, made from the Verdicchio grape, was known by Pliny the Younger and *Sicily* Juvenal. In Sicily, there are a number of crisp white wines, notably those from the Etna region made on the Villagrande estate's volcanic soil, and those from the west of the island, particularly the Regaleali estate. The poor soil of Sicily tends to make very good crisp wines, as do certain areas of *Portugal* the Minho region of north Portugal, around Vila Real, where the height and western outlook can give the same kind of freshness that the Sicilian wines gain from the Mediterranean. Even in *Cyprus* Cyprus, the skill of the wineries enables fairly crisp wines to be made from the vineyards on the southern slopes of the Troodos Mountains, and I have sampled *Middle East* crisp wines from Turkey, the Lebanon, and Israel. However, in these Middle-eastern countries, much depends on the skill of the winery and the wine maker to counteract the possible lack of acidity in the wines, even when the vineyards are on mountain slopes; the crispness tends to be short-lived, even when the wines are well kept.

Outside Europe, altitude enables many crisp wines to be made, although certain classic wine grapes may change their original characteristics: the Sauvignon, for example, makes good *California* crisp wines in California, although in Europe a wine from this grape would belong in the dry rather than the bone dry category. In Australia, *Australia* certain wineries achieve wines of marked crispness, particularly with the Riesling grape, and eventually the New Zealand vineyards may make similar quality *South Africa* wines. South African wine makers have produced excellent crisp Rieslings.

Crisp and Fruity

In these wines the freshness of style is balanced with a smell and taste of fruit. Good German wines, the finer Alsatian wines and many from the Loire are included together with some South African and Australian wines.

Riesling The German examples include wines of more than ordinary quality, made from the Riesling grape in the Mosel and *Sylvaner* Rhine vineyards, and from the Sylvaner, Riesling and other grapes in the *Palatinate* Palatinate and in Franconia in the top *Franconia* quality ranges, such as those from the Juliusspital and Jesuitengarten vineyards. The fruitiness is apparent, although there is no trace of fullness or even implied sweetness. All these wines show the traits of crispness and fruitiness while they are young, those of the Rhine being more easily associated with the lusciousness of stone fruits, those of the Mosel with berry fruits. Some of the Franconian wines, made from combinations of grapes, will, in the superior qualities, display more crispness than fruit; those of the Palatinate, especially in fine vintages, will exemplify a fruity rather than a crisp style.

Rheingau The vineyards of the Rheingau on the north bank of the Rhine produce wines that are slightly crisper and more *Rheinhessen* delicate than those of the Rheinhessen, on the west bank of the Rhine, after the river turns sharply towards the south. For crisp, fruity examples of German wines, look for those from specifically defined vineyard regions. In great years widely-praised vintages will make fine sweet wines while the more ordinary vintages can result in excellent crisp, fruity wines from the general vineyards and from certain of the big estates.

Alsace In Alsace, the finer Rieslings admirably exemplify crispness and fruitiness and so do those blends of grapes that produce wine labelled as *Edelzwicker* Edelzwicker. Along the Loire, there are certain estate wines or wines of *Saumur,* outstanding vintages from Saumur, *Montlouis,* Montlouis and even Vouvray that make *Vouvray* crisp, fruity wines, although much here depends on the producer determining the style. The ordinary wines of *Sancerre* Sancerre, made from the Sauvignon *Pouilly-sur-Loire* grape, and those of Pouilly-sur-Loire *Blanc Fumé* (sometimes labelled Blanc Fumé, the local name for Sauvignon) should show the type of crisp and fruity wine this grape makes in a cool vineyard in most

Gaillac years. Some of the wines, however, sold under single estate names, may be rather larger in scale and, in certain years, will come into the dry rather than the bone dry division. Along the Dordogne, and notably in Gaillac, the softer, sunny climate often results in wines with marked fruit which, in the finer qualities, possess true elegance.

From the vineyards outside Europe, there are as yet few truly crisp and fruity, bone dry wines for sale on export markets. The appeal of such wines tends to be to those who already have a discerning wine palate; for the mass market, wines that are dry or medium dry can be made from the same grapes that make the bone dry European wines. *Australia* Recently, however, I tasted an Australian wine, McWilliams' Lexia, made indisputably from the Muscat grape with a full, scented bouquet; it was bone dry on the palate, the fruit never overwhelming the crispness. In *South Africa* South Africa, the cultivated liveliness of certain of the KWV (Ko-operatieve Wijnbouwers Vereniging) Rieslings and the Chenin Blanc wines also come into this category. *Italy* In Italy, certain of the white wines from northern vineyards, made from the Trebbiano grape or with this grape predominating in a blend, can achieve crisp fruitiness. The white wines of *Spain* Valdepeñas in Spain can also come into this division, particularly while they are young, up to two years old.

Medium to Full-Bodied and Robust

These wines are generally straightforward, with perhaps moderate personality and they make a direct appeal to the drinker. Many wines are included, the best known being the dry Tokay from Hungary, Douro and Dão of Portugal, and certain of the white Côte du Rhônes.

Gros Plant There is an enormous quantity and variety of wines in this division, although some, like the Gros Plant from the *Bourgogne* mouth of the Loire, and Bourgogne *Aligoté* Aligoté (both named from the grape that makes them), can be rather coarse in style. Often, in the cheaper ranges, these are the wines that are sold by large retail stores as "Chablis type", or under the Pinot Chardonnay label in the United States. Such wines can be harsh rather than truly dry, although some drinkers like their aggressive style. Many *Sicily* Sicilian wines produced for mass markets

exemplify this robust, full-bodied character, with a bone dry finish.

Finer wines, which will make a clear impression on the drinker, are the dry *Tokay* Tokay from Hungary, and certain of the *Baden,* Baden and Württemberg wines, notably *Württemberg* those from individual estates, and for which the Ruländer grape is used, either by itself or with other varieties. In *Douro* northern Portugal, the white Douro wines, which verge on definite toughness, *Dão* and white Dão come into this category, both being what might be termed yeoman wines. The more ordinary white *Rioja* Riojas could be included here too, although many of these are now softened, if not actually sweetened, to overcome their bone dry nature.

Rhône The white Rhône wines from the north of the region are perhaps the most notable examples of medium or full-bodied, bone dry wines. Château *Château Grillet* Grillet, the only estate in France to have an individual AOC, is world-famous. Today, the uncompromising dryness of its wines, which used to be a faintly pinkish straw colour and are now pale light gold, seems to have been modified. *Condrieu* The white wine of Condrieu, however, made from the Viognier grape is an assertive, full-bodied, bone dry wine, with a profound character; it can also improve with age in bottle, not always an advantage for bone dry wine. There is a similar wine simply bearing the *Viognier* name of the grape.

Côtes du Rhône The straightforward white Côtes du Rhône wines, those of Hermitage and Crozes-Hermitage, which are subtler and slightly bigger, the whites of St-Joseph and the still whites of St-Péray are all in this division, with the possible exception of the Hermitage and Crozes-Hermitage whites in some outstanding years. Many people who like a white wine with a slightly "pushing" style for drinking with heavy food may well find white Rhônes more immediately enjoyable. A mixture of grapes is used, including some black grapes, but the most important grapes here are the white Marsanne and Roussane. The steeply-terraced vineyards alongside the swiftly-flowing Rhône could not make wines other than robust and moderately full-bodied in style: think of the snow on the mountains above the vineyards in winter, the hot sun of summer and the fierce, drying wind, the Mistral, in the rocky landscape and you will appreciate that these wines are the true children of the grapes of this region.

Weighty

These wines are big, uncompromisingly dry and profound, and they need care in choosing and serving. Many do not immediately appeal to the beginner in wine drinking, but it is worth returning to them to discover what has made them renowned. Some of the great wines of the world come into this division—still Champagne, first and great growths of Chablis, the finest estate Riojas, Châteauneuf-du-Pape.

Still Champagne Still or "nature" Champagne, now officially termed wine of the Coteaux Champenois, is usually but not invariably made only from the Chardonnay grape. It is a distant relation of white Burgundy, but the cooler region and the open, chalky slopes of the vineyards are emphasized in this still wine. It is in the luxury price range because comparatively little is made and export controls are strict (at the time of writing, it cannot be imported into the United States). The style varies according to the Champagne establishment making it, and wines that include some Pinot Noir black grapes are usually fuller than those made from white grapes only.

Grands crus, premiers crus, Chablis First and great growths of Chablis are austerely magnificent bone dry wines, often needing a fair amount of bottle age to overcome their initial reserve and predominantly green character. They possess great profundity and, even in otherwise unripe vintages, are never superficial, always, to me, retaining a certain mystery. Whereas the still white wine of Champagne is a good accompaniment to foie gras truffée or salmon in a wine sauce, the finer Chablis wines seem to be best with simpler dishes, such as oysters and lobster, sole, turbot and halibut. Chablis is rather aloof, reserved and always with a tantalizing finish and after-taste that endows this otherwise huge wine with finesse.

Rioja The estate wines of the Rioja region, in the valley of the River Ebro, can also attain weight, although they may maderise early if carelessly made. The stern character of this region makes these wines big, filling and gripping the mouth, lingering on the palate, even if sometimes they have a rasping finish. The very finest white Riojas are unlikely to appeal widely to Anglo-Saxon palates at first, for it is noticeable that the "bone" in the landscape is almost like this in the mouth as well. They are wines for a dry atmosphere; in a damp climate they can seem angular.

Rhône The white Rhônes, from the bottom of the valley, are also weighty wines, but with inner subtlety; some of the estate *Châteauneuf-du-Pape* wines from Châteauneuf-du-Pape possess great delicacy, albeit on a large scale. These white wines from the Rhône evoke sunbaked, wind-dried stones and sand; they have evolved over a very long time from vineyards that have been making wines of reputation for at least a thousand years. They demonstrate a close-to-the-earth, peasant tradition in wine-making which has remained virtually unbroken through the centuries and which is unlikely to be found elsewhere.

Italy It is occasionally possible to find a wine vaguely akin to the Rhônes and the Riojas in Italy, but, if you do, it will certainly be the product of an individually owned property, where someone still makes wines as his ancestors did. These odd exceptions to the rule can be interesting, and I have also had such weighty wines at Bussaco, in the centre of Portugal, and in Sicily; they were wholly individual and uncommercial.

Dry to Medium Dry

Light and Crisp

A vast range of dry white wines is made throughout the world from the Sauvignon grape. The lightest and crispest in terms of acidity usually come from northern vineyards, and are represented in Germany by the Palatinate, Rheinhessen and Mosel wines, and in France by some Loire wines. The Italian Terlano wines and the Californian Chenin Blancs are also dry and medium dry wines.

Palatinate Many Palatinate wines of a fullish style come into this category, notably those from the lower, more sheltered vineyards. Rhine wines of less quality

Rheinhessen

than Spätlese can vary in lightness especially when made from a mixture of grapes instead of Riesling only. The wines of the Rheinhessen, even when light and crisp as in certain years, show a tendency to be less bone dry than those of the Rheingau because of the heavier soil. The wines of Piesport on the Mosel, including the famous Goldtröpfchen, can usually be distinguished by their open-textured, more amiable style.

Piesporter Goldtröpfchen

Loire
Montlouis

Along the Loire, the regional wines of Montlouis and the finer wines of the

Pouilly-sur-Loire

Pouilly-sur-Loire vineyards come into this division. Ordinary Pouillys are made from the white Chasselas grape which generally makes a slightly weightier and coarser wine.

Italy

A vast quantity of Italian wines are light and crisp, including some of the Sicilian whites and many from the south Tyrol. Of these latter, Terlano is the best known and is made up of a mixture of grapes, 50 per cent having to be white Pinot, the remainder Riesling, Sauvignon and Sylvaner.

Terlano

═Dry to Medium Dry═

France	Germany, Austria	Italy	Rest of Europe	Americas, Australia South Africa
Light and Crisp				
MONTLOUIS regional wines POUILLY-SUR-LOIRE of superior quality POUILLY BLANC FUMÉ of ordinary quality GAILLAC, some examples TARN, some examples	SYLVANER, notably some examples from the Palatinate RIESLING in light years from the Rheinhessen MOSEL of ordinary quality from the middle Mosel	TERLANO wines from the Alto Adige CORVO BIANCO from Sicily		CHENIN BLANC, some examples RIESLING, some examples from South Africa "HOCK", some Australian examples RIESLING from Chile SAUVIGNONS of ordinary quality
Fruity and Delicate				
MERCUREY RULLY SANTENAY	Wines of named site or estate, and quality below Spätlese, from Germany	TRAMINER from north Italy SOAVE, some examples	TRAMINER from Yugoslavia FURMINT from Yugoslavia and Bulgaria SYLVANER from Bulgaria CHARDONNAY from Bulgaria MUSCAT, some examples, from south-east Europe	CHARDONNAY, some examples, especially from northern sites
Fruity, usually Robust				
GRAVES GRAVES DE VAYRES RHÔNE wines of ordinary quality BOURGOGNE ALIGOTÉ ST-VÉRAN MÂCON BLANC POUILLY-FUISSÉ POUILLY-SUR-LOIRE, estate wines SANCERRE estates PREMIÈRES CÔTES DE BORDEAUX of special quality	ENTRE-DEUX-MERS of special quality VOUVRAY, dry, of special quality JURANÇON BLANC, dry ROUSSILLON, some examples LANGUEDOC, some examples JURA, ordinary quality from Etoile, Arbois, Poligny VIN JAUNE from Jura CHÂTEAU-CHALON GEWÜRZTRAMINER from Alsace	MÜLLER-THURGAU single-vine wines SCHEUREBE single-vine wines	FRASCATI of ordinary quality CASTELLI ROMANI of ordinary quality SOAVE, superior quality VALPOLICELLA, superior quality TREBBIANO, superior quality ORVIETO, dry TORGIANO, dry ALBANO, dry White wines from Tuscany LACRIMA CHRISTI, superior quality TORBATO SECCO	TOKAY, dry MUSCAT OTTONEL, from Balkans White wines, ordinary quality, from Greece CAP BON, from Tunisia COLARES from Portugal VALDEPENAS, some examples, from Spain	CHARDONNAY, some of superior quality, from United States CHENIN BLANC, some of superior quality, from United States STEEN, some examples, from South Africa
Medium to Full-bodied, often with Distinctive Elegance				
BURGUNDY from Côte d'Or in general VOUVRAY, some estate or site examples SANCERRE, some estates in outstanding years	SAVENNIÈRES estates GRAVES from specific estates RHÔNE wines from specific sites			CHARDONNAY, some estate wines CHENIN BLANC, some estate wines

United States

The use of a blend of grapes demonstrates how difficult it is to generalize about wines, American wines in particular. In the United States, wines from "Varietals" or single grape types are labelled as such and might be categorized according to the characteristics of the grapes. However, according to Federal regulations, a varietal wine need only contain 51% of the grape type. The variations of taste can therefore be enormous, irrespective of what one might expect from the location of the vineyards. I have had a Chenin Blanc from one California winery that was indeed dry, light and crisp, while another from a nearby winery was definitely sweet.

Australia, Chile, South Africa

Many South African and Australian wines come into the crisp, light division, including many from reputable wineries sometimes labelled as "hock". The Chilean Riesling wines, too, are light and crisp.

Fruity and Delicate

In these wines, acidity and fruit are balanced for maximum enjoyment, and there are extra shades of smell and flavour that are never obvious or overpowering. Some of the finer Mosel, Rhine and Palatinate wines come into this division.

Germany

The estates in fine vintages and the most respected growers produce wines that are immediately attractive as regards bouquet and general "grapiness", plus a refinement and complexity that delight the experienced as well as the beginner in wine. The natural ripeness of the grapes make them wonderful wines, best enjoyed on their own, without any food.

Traminer

In northern Italy, the Traminer grape makes fruity, delicate wines, and this is also true for a number of the central and south-eastern European Traminers, notably those from Yugoslavia.

Pinot Chardonnay

Throughout the world, wines sold simply under the grape name of Chardonnay will be wines possessing fruit and delicacy; these vary according to where they are grown, but those from the more northern sites of the northern hemisphere tend to be the more delicate.

Fruity, usually Robust

These are popular, straightforward wines in which the fruit is fairly assertive, giving a roundness and weightiness to the wines. Many Rhine wines, Alsatian Gewürztraminer, white Beaujolais, southern Burgundies, some Loire and Bordeaux wines come into this category. So do the Jurançon and Jura wines, the Italian Castelli Romani, Orvieto, Torgiano and Tuscan wines, as well as the Lacrima Christi and Spanish Valdepeñas. Many American dry Pinot Chardonnays and Chenin Blanc wines can also be classified as fruity.

Müller-Thurgau

The Müller-Thurgau grape, now planted in fair quantity in the Rhine vineyards, makes a fruity and fairly assertive wine. Traditionalists often lament its presence in classic vineyards—where the Müller-Thurgau can actually be distinguished from the trim, regulated Riesling vine as being much tuftier and more exuberant. However, although the appeal of the high yielding Müller-Thurgau may be primarily sensuous, its use facilitates the production of vast quantities of wines in the middle ranges.

Scheurebe

The Scheurebe, another new grape, is very fruity indeed; when successful, its scented, lush style can be very enjoyable, but it cannot be directly compared with any of the finer Rieslings.

Gewürztraminer

In Alsace, the Gewürztraminer makes a spicy, fullish style of wine in the ordinary ranges; it is a sound choice if you are in doubt about the wine list or the taste of guests.

Beaujolais

Wines of a definitely robust style, with moderate fruit which increases in very ripe vintages include the fairly new white Beaujolais, made from the Aligoté grape, and St Véran wines from the same region which are made from the Chardonnay. Many southern white Burgundies come into this category, including Pouilly Fuissé and white Mâcon, although some of the less successful examples may lack fruit.

St Véran

Burgundy Pouilly Fuissé, Mâcon

Loire

In the Loire, the wines from the centre of the region can display great fruit, notably those from individual estates. Fruity styles of Vouvray, which can be made in all the styles in which a white wine is made, are widely available, with a smell of honey and flowers and a slightly full character. The estate wines of Pouilly-sur-Loire, and even more so those of Sancerre in ordinary years, are elegant examples of a robust wine.

Vouvray

Pouilly-sur-Loire, Sancerre

Bordeaux Graves de Vayres, Premières Côtes, Entre-Deux-Mers

The small-scale white wines from the Bordeaux region, such as those of Graves de Vayres, the Premières Côtes and Entre-Deux-Mers can, when well made, be fruity although indifferent examples tend to lack character.

Jurançon

Languedoc, Roussillon, Hérault

Greece

Jurançon wines from the Pyrenees can be fruity and robust, and so can many of those from the vastly improved vineyards of Languedoc, Roussillon and Hérault. Most of these wines should be drunk while young as any crispness they possess tends to fade. They come from hot vineyards, as do the Greek white wines which are robust although sometimes the fruit seems to have been almost baked out of them.

Bulgaria

Yugoslavia

North Africa

Cap Bon

In the south-east of Europe, the Bulgarian whites usually possess a modicum of both fruit and sturdiness, and so do those of the Serbian region of Yugoslavia down to Macedonia and the Greek frontier. The fruit tends to be reduced in wines from the really hot vineyards of North Africa, and the whites there are perhaps best regarded as holiday drinks, with the exception of a few Tunisian wines. The wines from the Cap Bon peninsula are particularly well made and the vineyards there enjoy the fresher atmosphere of the coast.

Jura

A group of wines that generally come into the fruity and robust category are those of the Jura in France although they bear only the slightest resemblance to wines of other regions. They come from a thickly forested, mountainous region, and a coniferous, slightly aromatic element can be detected in the after-taste of many.

Etoile

Arbois
Poligny

The limestone of the Jura soil is favourable to the production of subtle white wines; probably the best come from the Etoile region. This area is only eighty miles from Burgundy proper and approximately at the same latitude, and therefore the wines all possess an assertive style as well as true delicacy in the finer qualities. Arbois, famous for the work of Pasteur, and Poligny, are other wine towns, and their products are beginning to feature on export markets. The grapes used are the Savagnin, the white Pinot and the Chardonnay.

Vin jaune

Château-Chalon

A curious wine made in the Jura is *vin jaune* (yellow wine), made entirely from the Savagnin grape. It is made by letting the wine rest in casks and allowing it to ferment very slowly. A type of fungus known as *le voile* forms on the surface of the casks. This is similar to the development of *flor* on the surface of fino sherries, and the film remains on the wine for up to six years. The wine is then bottled, and the result is unusual, not unlike an unfortified sherry. *Vin jaune* is pungent, dry, yellow and quite forceful. The finest come from the region of Château-Chalon.

Italy

Castelli Romani
Frascati
Orvieto, Torgiano

Tuscan, Albana, Soave, Valpolicella

Wines made from the Trebbiano grape in central and northern Italy usually combine fruit and a fairly assertive style. The dry Castelli Romani wines from south of Rome, notably Frascati, are good examples. So are the dry Orvieto and Torgiano wines from Umbria. Others in this category include the better white Tuscans, Albana from Emilia-Romagna, and Soave and Valpolicella from Veneto. The last two can be lighter in style than the others, but the better wines fit more appropriately into this section. For all these wines, the Trebbiano grape is much used and, in some instances, the Malvasia, which gives aroma and a slightly broad style. Sardinia's most famed white, Torbato Secco, would also fit in here, although it also possesses a slightly delicate style. The Trebbiano is a grape that can be reminiscent of toffee, and it can give an enticing full, flowery bouquet to the wine.

Torbato Secco

Lacrima Christi

Lacrima Christi is a wine of superior quality from the Bay of Naples in the Campania. Deep straw or even golden in colour, it displays the full-bodied, assertive style of a southern wine as well as a more subtle quality that can give it a dry taste and a lingering, almost profound after-taste. It is clearly a wine from a hot vineyard, but the soil from the slopes of Vesuvius is volcanic and this modifies the full style that might otherwise have verged on the flabby. The Greco grape that makes white Lacrima Christi is capable of producing wines of good acidity and more bouquet than might be expected so far south.

Sicily

In Sicily, the Grecanico vine produces wines surprising for their bouquet and elegant, dry style at the same time as being full-bodied and assertive. Sometimes the new wineries hesitate to produce wines for the vital export trade that are too assertively Sicilian, and may modify them to accord with the market preferences for light dry wines.

Portugal

Valdepeñas

Iberian Peninsula wines now appearing in export markets may include a few from the centre of Portugal, although white Colares is seldom found outside this region near Lisbon. The finer qualities of Spanish white Valdepeñas wines display that slightly buttery flavour that to me typifies many wines in this category.

United States

The wineries of the United States that produce fine, dry and medium dry white wines tend to concentrate on those made from the Chardonnay and Chenin Blanc grapes for the weightier wines.

However, because such a wide selection of all types of wines is available from many wineries, the very fine shades of difference are not always easily distinguished. The potentially good and great full-bodied, dry white wines may be made in small quantities only because the demand for them is economically inadequate.

Medium to Full-Bodied, often with Distinctive Elegance

The wines in this category, which include white Burgundy, Loire and Graves wines, have an aristocratic bouquet, delicious fruit, and a pervasively mouth-filling style and lingering flavour.

Côte de Beaune
Côte de Nuits

The finest white Burgundies are made in the Côte de Beaune, many very good ones in southern Burgundy and a very few in the Côte de Nuits. All are made from the Chardonnay grape and possess profound and subtle characters. They can last a surprising time for white wines, up to 20 years although few wines are made to last so long. Interestingly, many of the vintages in which they are outstanding do not invariably coincide with the finer vintage years for the red wines of the region. There are many complexities about getting to know Burgundy wines. The differences between the main vineyard regions in Burgundy break down first into the differences between the communes or parishes (such as Meursault, Savigny, Chassagne-Montrachet), and secondly into differences between any named vineyard or *climat* within these (such as Meursault Charmes, Savigny les Marconnets).

The plots within the vineyards are usually divided between numerous proprietors, each of whom will cultivate his vines and make his own, slightly individual wine. Variations again occur when the wines are bought and handled differently by the merchant or shipper. Only the finest individual wines are estate bottled by the proprietor. All these implications make generalizations about white Burgundy difficult and sometimes misleading. Some people will find a special lightness in the wines of Pernand Vergelesses, others detect a particular delicacy in those of Puligny-Montrachet and a sunny charm in those of Meursault. But only considerable experience with wines in the top grades will enable you to pronounce on the various regions.

Pernand Vergelesses, Puligny-Montrachet, Meursault

Côte d'Or

Chardonnay

Meanwhile, the prime thing to note about white Burgundy from the Côte d'Or is the way in which the climate (neither too chilly nor too sunny), the location (curvy sloping vineyards), and the Chardonnay grape combine to make remarkable white wines. The bouquet and aroma harmonize with the flavour and after-taste; like many wines made in cooler regions, the Chardonnay can have more smell than taste. Further south it can lose much of its smell and have almost too much flavour and no elegance as regards after-taste. A fine white Burgundy from the Côte d'Or may be on a larger scale than the fine wines from slightly further south, in the Mâconnais and Côte Chalonnaise, but all these wines possess a gracious freshness and balance of fruit and acidity. As they age, these wines darken from their original pale or light gold to medium gold, but even when they become slightly maderized, they can still be wines to admire.

Mâconnais
Côte Chalonnaise

Vouvray

Certain great Vouvrays can possess a full-bodied, but still dry or medium dry character and can also last for a surprising time. The Clos Naudin of A. Foreau, for example, will, as far as the dry wines are concerned, last for up to 30 years. Such wines, however, are seldom widely available; they come from small growers or estates and are in the higher price ranges. The wines of Savennières, too, from nearer the sea end of the Loire, can be delectably dry but full-bodied, and so can the greater estate Sancerres.

Savennières

Sancerre
Graves

The fine estate white wines of the Graves region, just south of Bordeaux are wines of great distinction, which possess a delicacy and finesse to delight the wine lover. The grapes are chiefly Sauvignon and Sémillon, and sometimes Muscadelle. Many of the great estates here make red as well as white wines, but the whites, lighter and gentler in appeal than any northern white wines, are quite different from the reds. They all come from vineyards of a light, pale soil, often gravelly, as the name Graves implies. Near the River Garonne where the pleasant, small-scale Premières Côtes from specific estates are made there are chalky banks and cliffs of limestone. The greater white Graves, some of them from estates which also make fine red wines, darken while still fairly young, but age gracefully. They can possess great profundity, and their "smiling" character should not make the drinker overlook this additional attribute.

Premières Côtes

69

Implicitly Sweet

Light

This section lists those table wines that have an underlying sweetness; they are never assertive, often having considerable freshness. They include the Sémillon, Malvasia, Muscat and South African Steen wines, and can be drunk on many occasions, even as apéritifs if you do not serve a dry wine immediately afterwards.

Sémillon Straightforward, light and implicitly sweet Sémillon wines are made throughout the world, notably in

Malvasia California. The Malvasia wines of Italy, in the more ordinary quality ranges, can also be light and sweet, but in the finer ranges they tend to be full-bodied.

Extremely scented, light and sweet wines are made in central and south-eastern Europe from the

Muscat-Ottonel Muscat-Ottonel grape, a Muscat variety. The wines make an assertive, initial impression and then, in my experience, tend to give little more.

Misket The Misket, another type of Muscat, is a red grape making a light, slightly

Furmint sweet Bulgarian wine. The Furmint, also extensively cultivated in south-eastern and central Europe, makes light, sweet wines in Italy and in Germany. It can produce scented wines, but to me Furmint wines always have something more important than sweetness lurking behind the first flavour which can be detected.

From Austria several implicitly sweet wines are now becoming known outside their regions of production, notably

Gumpoldskirchen those from the Gumpoldskirchen area. They are made from the local grapes Spätrot and Rotgipfler which make a close-textured wine that most people find easy to like. In Yugoslavia, the sweet Radgonska Ranina, made near

---

Implicitly Sweet

France	Germany Austria	Italy	Rest of Europe	Americas Australia South Africa
Light				
COTEAUX DU LAYON of ordinary quality COTEAUX DE L'AUBANCE of ordinary quality QUART DE CHAUME of ordinary quality GAILLAC LIQUOREUX MONBAZILLAC of ordinary quality CÉRONS Late vintaged wines from Alsace	SPÄTLESE wines from Germany GEWÜRZTRAMINERS of superior quality MÜLLER-THURGAUS of special quality SCHEUREBES, some of special quality GUMPOLDSKIRCHEN from Austria Late vintaged wines from Austria		MORIO MUSKAT from Balkans MISKET from Bulgaria TIGER MILK (RADGONSKA) RANINA)	"SAUTERNE" SÉMILLON STEEN, late vintage, from South Africa
Medium-Bodied				
Superior late vintaged wines from Alsace	AUSLESE, from Germany SPATLESE, superior quality estate wines from Germany AUSLESE from Austria AUSLESE from Baden-Württemberg			
Full-Bodied				
COTEAUX DU LAYON, estate wines COTEAUX DE L'AUBANCE, estates QUART DE CHAUME, estate wines MONBAZILLAC estates VOUVRAY, certain fine "sweet" examples		AMABILE wines ABBOCCATO wines VIN SANTO CANNELLINO FRASCATI TREBBIANO, some examples MALVASIA, some examples	MUSCAT, some examples from east Europe	MUSCAT, some examples

Tiger Milk Kapela in Slovenia, is certainly the best-known white wine, under its name of Tiger Milk.

Muscat In many vineyards outside Europe, some of the Muscats, as well as those made from the Sémillon and the Chenin Blanc grapes, possess the implicit sweetness that can make for most agreeable occasional drinking. One of the significant things about nomenclature, especially in relation to wines possessing slight sweetness, is the story of the Christian Brothers' Californian wine which, while it was called "light sweet Muscat" did not sell. *Château la Salle* The firm changed the wine's name to Château la Salle—without changing the style of the wine at all and without disguising in their descriptive material that it is made from the Muscat. It became their best-selling single wine!

Steen One wine of increasing importance in export markets is the unusual, late-vintaged Steen, from South Africa. The Steen grape was thought to be native to the Cape, although some theories were advanced that it might have been the result of an early crossing of the Riesling with a wild vine. Steen is recorded as a quality wine and exported as early as the beginning of the 19th century; its roundness and fruitiness make the wines bearing its name popular. It is now established that the Steen grape is a type of Chenin Blanc, and although I have not recognized this grape in the ordinary Steen wines, the "honey and flowers" of that great Loire grape is manifest at the Cape in the late-vintaged Steen of the Ko-operatieve Wijnbouwers Vereniging (KWV), lightly fragrant, pleasing in what might be described as a well-bred way, never obvious.

Medium-Bodied

Sweetness is one thing, the slight intensification resulting from late picking of the grapes another. Together the two can make a wine with shades of fragrance, flavour and after-taste rather than a wholly straightforward wine. But from vineyards in which good and fine wines can be produced, it is also possible to make implicitly sweet wines that are medium-bodied. Austrian and German Auslese wines, late-vintaged Alsatian Rieslings and German Spätlese are examples of these wines.

Auslese Some Austrian wines and some Franconian and Baden-Württemberg wines are now being made in the Auslese category. However, these tend to be

Alsace Riesling late vintage curiosities or specialities to enjoy in these regions. The late-vintaged Rieslings of Alsace, with their lingering fruitiness and concentrated bouquet, clearly exemplify this type of medium-bodied wine. Some of the Alsatian wines from specific vineyard sites where individual vines may be very old, can also display this medium-bodied implied sweetness especially in certain years when the Riesling gives of its best. "A Riesling year" say the producers when the elegant fruitiness of the noble grape develops to the full. In certain vineyards, mixtures of grapes are still grown so that the sunny, smiling character may derive from a combination of grape flavours. In particular vintages, it is not necessary for the grapes to be late picked to achieve the underlying, almost honeyed character.

Spätlese In Germany, the Spätlese (late-gathered) grapes make medium-bodied wines of implicit sweetness. The wines are usually crisper along the Mosel, gentler and sometimes more delicate along the Rhine, rather fuller and softer in the Palatinate and markedly flowery in the Nahe. Elegant, gracious and aristocratic, they are some of the most delicious white wines in the world.

Full-Bodied

The wines in this category, albeit slightly sweet, have a profundity combined with delicacy and finesse that resound in the senses with an appreciative melody. The wines from the Loire and Monbazillac, the Italian Vin Santo and *amabile* wines are the finest examples.

Vouvray In the Loire, Vouvrays can typify the full-bodied, slightly sweet wines. The "honey and flowers" smell and flavour is pronounced in the wines the Chenin Blanc makes in this vineyard. Nearer the *Coteaux du Layon* sea, the Coteaux du Layon wines, from the little slopes of the south bank of the Loire below Angers are, albeit honeyed, slightly crisper—the vineyards are more exposed. Along the banks of the Layon, *Coteaux de l'Aubance* in the Coteaux de l'Aubance around *Bonnezeaux* Bonnezeaux and especially in the Quart *Quart de Chaume* de Chaume region nearer the Loire, the Chenin Blanc makes wines that, in the past, were prized for their sweetness. In certain great vintages for white wines, they will come into the category of very sweet. Prevailing fashions in wine, however, as well as the cooler situation of the vineyards generally mean that these wines are implicitly sweet, though with delicious fruitiness. If you think of the cool, subtle sweetness of a peach grown outside as compared with the more obvious sweetness of the same fruit grown in a hothouse, you may be able to distinguish these wines from those that are more straightforwardly sweet.

Monbazillac The wines of Monbazillac, just south of the Dordogne River and the Bergerac region, but approximately on the same latitude as Bordeaux, are also capable of great sweetness and elegance. The chalk and limestone of the soil make for good white wines, but with the rising demand for dry wines the finest examples of sweet Monbazillac have become comparative rarities.

Italy In Italy, many of the wines labelled *amabile* or *abboccato* will be sweet without necessarily being luscious, and in many of the white wine areas a sweetish as well as a dry wine will be made. In the *Frascati* Frascati region there is in addition a *cannellino* (definitely sweet) among the

Malvasia several sweet wines, and in some areas the use of the Malvasia grape gives wines that are verging on the very sweet. As the sweetness depends greatly on the individual producer and the type of market being catered for, it is difficult to generalize about these wines. Vin Santo, *Vin Santo* made in different parts of Italy with the most reputed coming from Tuscany, is usually made from Trebbiano and Malvasia grapes. It is left in wood for up to five years, achieving an eventual alcoholic strength of about 15°, just above that of ordinary table wines. Vin Santo is a long drawn-out, smooth, sweet wine which, in the better examples, often has a distinctly dry after-taste, almost a minerally flavour. It is seldom seen on export markets but, for the traveller in Italy, it is worth noting that it can sometimes be a bone dry wine as well. As a sweet wine it is usually more suitable for drinking at the end of a meal.

Sweet and Very Sweet

France	Germany Austria	Italy	Spain Portugal	Rest of Europe
Light to Medium-Bodied				

VIN DE PAILLE from
  Jura
VOUVRAY, superior
  "sweet" examples
CERONS, special
  quality
LOUPIAC
STE-CROIX-DU-MONT
COTEAUX DU LAYON,
  finest quality
BONNEZEAUX, finest
  quality
QUART DE CHAUME,
  finest quality
Outstanding late
  vintaged wines from
  Alsace
	AUSLESE, some
	  examples from
	  Germany
	BEERENAUSLESE,
	  some examples from
	  Germany
	RUSTER AUSBRUCH,
	  from Austria
	EISWEIN, some
	  examples
	Outstanding late
	  vintaged wines from
	  Austria
		PASSITO wines,
		especially MOSCATO
				MUSCAT, most
				  examples from
				  northern Europe

Medium to Full-Bodied				

JURANÇON *doux*
SAUTERNES, regional
BARSAC, regional
			GRANDJO, from
			Portugal
				COMMANDARIA from
				  Cyprus
				MAVRODAPHNE from
				  Greece
				SAMOS
				MUSCATS from the
				  Mediterranean

Sweet and Very Sweet

Light to Medium-Bodied

These wines often have a complex bouquet, with a superb after-taste that combines the sunshine of the vintage with the effect of noble rot. The German Auslese and Beerenauslese wines, the Austrian Ruster Ausbruch, some wines from Bordeaux and Monbazillac, the Italian *passito* and Mediterranean Muscat wines all come into this category.

Auslese, Beerenauslese The Auslese and Beerenauslese sweet German wines can vary enormously in style and quality, not merely because of the different regions from which they come, but because of the style of wine produced by the individual grower or firm. It may be said that one man's Auslese can be a greater as well as a sweeter wine than someone else's Beerenauslese. There are also some admirable growers who do not find it economically possible to make the exalted sweet wines and who therefore simply put any over-ripe grapes or those attacked by the *Edelfäule* (noble rot) into their Spätlese wines. On the Rhine and Mosel, however, the principal grape permitted for use in Spätlese wines is the Riesling. It makes wines of complex bouquet and aroma, with great length and after-taste.

Austria In Austria, the Bouviertraube, a new grape, makes light-bodied sweet wines. Experiments have also been made with the Sauvignon grape although such wines seldom reach export markets. The town of Rust, in Burgenland, is the centre for the production of a more famous sweet wine, Ruster Ausbruch. *Ruster Ausbruch* This almost syrupy wine is made from Furmint and Muscat Ottonel grapes which have been allowed to shrivel and partly dry. Some visitors have thought they detected the presence of noble rot in these wines, but I have not found this in such wines as I have tasted elsewhere. However, the dry atmosphere in this region and the limestone soil indicate that fine white wines may be made, and there are sheltered areas near water that make it possible for *botrytis cinerea* to *Rust, Apetlon* develop. Rust and Apetlon, where pleasant, straightforwardly honeyed wines are made, are not far from the Tokay region of Hungary, where noble rot certainly works on the vines.

Bordeaux The small-scale sweet Bordeaux come into the light to medium-bodied category. They are produced in vineyards along the Garonne, the *Cérons* Cérons region being on the west bank, north of Barsac. Cérons wines, some of them made with noble rot, come from a gravelly, flinty soil and possess a freshness and a smell that to me suggests citrus fruits. Like most of the wines in this category, they are pleasant drinks for any time of day and can be enjoyed as apéritifs. On the east bank of the river *Loupiac* are the regions of Loupiac and Sainte Croix du Mont, on soil that is a mixture of stones, clay and chalk, with some gravel. The Loupiac wines are often lightly spicy, like the greater ones of Barsac, the region that faces them on the opposite side of the river. The wines *Sainte-Croix-du-Mont* from Sainte-Croix-du-Mont are more assertively sweet, like Sauternes. Noble rot does not seem much in evidence as far as most wines for export are concerned, and the more open, higher vineyards do not seem as favourable for noble rot as the sheltered, often stuffy vineyards of the west bank where the greatest sweet white wines, the Sauternes and Barsacs, are made.

Other sweet wines of quality from France include Monbazillac from the Bergerac region and the Coteaux du Layon wines and Vouvray from the *Monbazillac* Loire. The great Monbazillacs are to me slightly honeyed, with a softer intensity than the Loire wines; at the same time they have a less opulent lusciousness than the sweet Bordeaux wines. They come from inland vineyards where fine white wines can be made, and they might be described as agreeable rather than enticing.

Coteaux du Layon The fine Coteaux du Layons can be remarkable, with fascinating smells and flavours that are reminiscent of fruits, such as quinces, nectarines, certain types of pear and even figs. They can age remarkably too, but these fine qualities relate only to the type of expensive wine that will bear the name of an individual estate, not to the pleasant, more ordinary wines.

Vouvray Great sweet Vouvray is also rare but, in my experience, slightly nobler, a wine with reserved charm; unfortunately few growers now make it with the noble rot.

The sheltered, small vineyards lie on the north bank of the Loire, on light soil, and the wines are usually matured in cellars dug out of the local rocky outcrops. The resulting wines are as profound and complex as any of the great sweet wines I know. Again, the grower and the particular site are all-important.

Italy   In Italy the very sweet wines are highly complex and grapes affected by noble rot are often considered a nuisance and harvested as soon as possible. However, the *muffa nobile* (noble rot) has been noted in Tuscany and Piedmont, although the grapes used there may not be ideal for supporting its action. In Austria, the word Riesling used on its
Riesling   own on labels is synonymous with Walschriesling or White Riesling, and this is often the type of Riesling found in north Italy.

Passito   The passito wines are the best known fine sweet Italian wines and may be produced in various regions. Different grape varieties are used including the fruity Moscato, which itself makes a straightforward, sometimes very sweet dessert wine. Passito wines are made from the grapes that have been slightly dried in the sun after they have been vintaged. They vary in flavour and style according to the region from which they come.

Around the Mediterranean coast of France many fruity, sweet wines are made, a great deal of them from the
Muscat   Muscat grape which ripens here to yield luscious, uncomplicated wines. Our ancestors enjoyed the Muscats of Banyuls, Frontignan and Lunel, but these, together with the better-known Muscat de Beaumes de Venise, are not included in table wines as the majority receive some form of fortification or strengthening.

Medium to Full-Bodied

Most of these sweet wines come from southern hot vineyards and often have a sun-baked after-taste. They include the Jurançon and Grandjo wines, the Greek Samos and Mavrodaphne, and the famous Commandaria from Cyprus.
Jurançon   The sweet Jurançon wines from near Pau, in the French Pyrenees, were once highly sought after but today it is the dry Jurançon that visitors are likely to meet. Made from the curious local grapes Manseng and Courbu, which account for 85 per cent of the blend, Jurançon is highly fragrant, with a

smell that has been likened to quinces, nectarines or plums. This slightly sheltered region, where fogs can form from the Atlantic, can be affected by noble rot. Some authorities have maintained that they detected noble rot in the flavour of fine Jurançon, one eminent wine merchant even noting a resemblance to Tokay, and Warner Allen associated it with the Coteaux du Layon wines. I have never found this in the agreeably sweet, but fresh Jurançons I have tried; it is however, a rare wine, and it may now be wholly uneconomic to make with noble rot.

Grandjo   Sweet Grandjo wines come from Granda d'Alijo, high up the River Douro Valley in north Portugal. Several Portuguese wines, including some reds from the northern part of the country can be sweet. The damp, often very cold climate of this country, with its Atlantic coast and granite soils, make it reasonable that sweet wines should be made to satisfy national demand. However, I have never heard of any Portuguese or Spanish sweet wines made with noble rot. Grandjo was popular at the court of Edward VII, possibly on account of the King's friendship with the Marquis de Soveral, the then Portuguese ambassador, and possibly because it was cheaper than Sauternes. To me it is a sweet wine from a southern country, agreeable but uncomplicated.

White wines tend to darken as they age and sweet white wines usually start by being darker than dry ones. With age, the finer examples can become a beautiful brilliant gold, like brass with the patina of years of cleaning. Generally, the farther south sweet wines are made, the deeper they will be in colour, even at the beginning of their lives. The sweet wines from the Greek
Samos   island of Samos are medium to deep gold with the sun-baked after-taste that is often perceived in sweet wines from hot vineyards. Samos wines have been known for centuries, even before the Turks conquered the island in 1453; the wines were so luscious that the Turks spared the vineyards. Today a dry Samos is also made; both must by law
Muscat   be 100 per cent Muscat.
Mavrodaphne   Mavrodaphne, which is usually almost brown, is another sweet wine made in Greece and some of the Greek islands from the Monemvasia grape. It produces a distinct, velvety sweet wine with an almost burnt after-taste. The name Mavrodaphne has been evolved from the Greek word for black or dark-haired

Daphne, apparently after an attractive brunette. Old Mavrodaphne can be profound and lengthy, but the peasant version, as compared with anything commercial, is nowadays the only one that will show why this wine won its reputation for greatness. Mavrodaphnes made by the great wineries have never seemed to me more than amiably sweet, uncomplicated drinks.

Commandaria   The same cannot be said about Commandaria, the sweet wine of Cyprus. This has been highly esteemed since classical times and has, on account of its antiquity, been called the apostle of the wines. The name comes from the Grande Commanderie, dating from the 12th century when the Knights of St John of Jerusalem had their headquarters in Limassol, and when some regions of Cyprus were divided into Commanderies or commands. Commandaria is made from black and white grapes in certain villages on the southern slopes of the Troodos

mountains. In the heat the wine ferments naturally to a high alcoholic strength; the wine yeasts of Cyprus are particularly strong, otherwise this rising alcoholic strength would slow down their work or even kill them.

In some village versions, Commandaria is matured in huge jars, thought by some authorities to be the ancestor of the sherry solera system. In the wineries, Commandaria is made more scientifically, but the result is an intensely pungent wine, evocative of heat and grapes of assertive flavour, brown in colour and sometimes as it ages with a golden rim. Although no vintage Commandarias are made, the type of wine an individual farmer may make can remain, topped up, as a fine wine for fifty, even a hundred years. The wineries, too, make special blends in which all the wines will be very old. This wine is perhaps the nearest one can come today to drinking the kind of wine once enjoyed by the Greeks and Romans.

Intensely Sweet

Medium-Bodied

These sweet wines have a pronounced, concentrated type of sweetness which, in fine qualities, is never cloying. They are usually made from late-picked grapes, sometimes with the noble rot on them. Rising labour costs have caused a diminished production of these sweet wines with a subsequent rise in price. The German Trockenbeerenauslese and Eiswein, and the Hungarian Tokays are the finest examples.

Trockenbeeren-   The German wine regions make their
auslese   Trockenbeerenauslese from grapes shrunken on the vine through the evaporation of the water in each grape and through their longer than usual exposure to the atmosphere. The grapes are picked one by one over several weeks, and it has been estimated that it could take 20 experienced vintagers up to two weeks to collect grapes to make 300 litres of must for a Beerenauslese. The grower decides whether he will make a Beerenauslese or a Trocken-beerenauslese—the Beerenauslese of one grower may be a finer wine and a better example of intense sweetness than someone else's Trockenbeerenauslese. It is not essential for the noble rot to act on the grapes, although it usually does. In

the outstanding summer of 1959, the rot did not form on the grapes, but both Beerenauslese and Trockenbeerenauslese were still made. They were rightly named as such on the labels, for they had been gathered grape by grape or else in small bunches and had become shrunken and dry.

Eiswein   Intensely sweet wines also include that curiosity known as Eiswein or ice wine, originally made by chance but now suddenly fashionable. Ice wines are fetching such high prices that many are now made irrespective of whether the proper conditions exist under which they may be produced. Confusion exists about Eiswein, but it is essentially a wine made from fully ripe grapes picked very early in the morning while they are lightly frozen. Harvesting may be as late as November or December, and the grapes are late in ripening; good Eiswein is usually made after a vintage which is not generally satisfactory. The ice forms on the grapes after a sharp night frost because they still have water in them (they must be rushed frozen to the presshouse). The temporary freezing means that the sugar and elements remaining in each grape are concentrated. A vagueness may be noticed about the inner and back-taste of a good Eiswein, like the shadow of a

75

Intensely Sweet

France	Germany Austria	Rest of Europe
Medium-Bodied BARSAC, small-scale estates SAUTERNES, small-scale estates BOMMES, small-scale estates FARGUES, small-scale estates PREIGNAC, small-scale estates	TROCKENBEEREN-AUSLESE EISWEIN, most examples	TOKAY, four to five *puttonyos*
Weighty and Profound BARSAC, great estates SAUTERNES, great estates BOMMES, great estates FARGUES, great estates PREIGNAC, great estates		TOKAY ESSENCE

presence, hard to apprehend, as the wine is delicate in style. After a tasting of eight of them I wrote, "fascinating, but like the ghost of a wine of sunnier years". In certain wines that ordinarily seem noble but uncompromising, I noted that their austerity had been softened.

Tokay   Hungarian Tokay, made since 1650, comes from 28 hill villages on the low-lying slopes of a range of volcanic hills. The climate is dry with warm sunny days in September and October, cool, even cold nights and early morning mist that, rising above the Bodrog River at the foot of the Tokay hills, makes ideal conditions for the satisfactory formation and action of the rot. The grapes are Furmint, with its slightly aromatic style, together with the Hungarian Harslevelü and a type of yellow Muscat. The grapes on which the botrytis works reach the stage where they are called *aszu*, meaning syrupy. The grapes are gathered in wooden vessels called *puttonyos*, and the juice that oozes from these is collected separately and put into casks; this is the juice that makes Tokay Essence or Eszencia (which comes in the Weighty sub-division).

The rotten grapes are trodden by barefoot workers into a paste, while the others are pressed as for ordinary wine. There is a curious and unique element in the making of Tokay in that the grape stalks are put into the must and stirred for six hours; this sappy addition possibly accounts for the inner firmness detectable in Tokay. The sweetness is the result of the varying number of *puttonyos* of *aszu* paste put into each container, known as a *gönc* and containing 120–140 litres of must. The more *puttonyos*, the sweeter the wine. The wine is then fermented, filtered and put into *gönci* for maturation in the local rock cellars, so low that it is rightly said "One must bow before Tokay".

The result is an odd, compounded wine, complex and sometimes giving the impression it is about to turn around and be positively dry. Dry Tokay, *Tokay Szamorodni*   Tokay Szamorodni, can be medium sweet or medium dry to dry. There is something very positive and at the same time delicate about Tokay; almost bronze in colour, its bouquet is freshly sweet, its flavour more so, and the after-taste and finish clean and long-lingering.

Weighty and Profound

These wines, known as *liquoreux* by the French, have an assertive bouquet, sometimes a little spicy, and there is a roundness to the feel of the wines, in their depth and developing sweetness. Noble rot gives the subtle, lingering after-taste. Tokay Essence and the great Sauternes and Barsacs come into this category.

Tokay Essence   Tokay Essence has won a reputation

as an elixir of life, its restorative powers having been called on for people apparently dying. Since the Iron Curtain descended on Hungary, only minute quantities of it have, however, been released to the West. The flavour is quite unique. The drippings of the *aszu* grapes ferment slowly; R.E.H. Gunyon, whose former firm is one of the great shippers of Hungarian wines, thinks it never stops. Although it is comparatively low in alcohol, 5°–8°, it is rich in natural glucose which may account for its reputation as a restorative. The enzymes in *aszu* must probably resist both the yeasts that would turn the sugar in the grape juice into alcohol and the inimical yeasts that would make it into vinegar. In the rock cellars, the wine is never topped up in its casks, and these have loose bungs, admitting the air. The heavy blue-black mould on the cellar walls sprouts on the top of the bottles of wine. Tokay Essence can only be made when the *aszu* grapes are not merely ripe but will "take" the addition of the fermentation of the drippings satisfactorily, and this does not invariably occur.

The taste of Tokay Essence has been described as indescribable, but this is no help to the wine lover who may never get a chance to try it but who would like some indication. Whereas Tokay of five *puttonyos* has a distinct sweetness and one can detect the noble rot, albeit translated into slightly more delicate, or pungently sly terms than in the great German sweet wines, the flavour in the Essence is quite different. A description of brown toast and butter with brown sugar is one that may be understood. The wine is naturally sunny, open in character, but the association with bread seems inevitable because of its wholesome appeal, a minute quantity lingering around the mouth and trailing its flavours away. It is the demands it makes on the drinker to resolve its enigmatic character that makes it great.

Sauternes   The great Sauternes which, within the defined area on the west bank of the Garonne south of Bordeaux, include the Barsac region, are possibly the most weighty of all the great sweet wines.

This is fine white wine country, slightly richer in soil than that of the adjoining Graves region; in this low-lying, stuffy, shut-in countryside the sub-soils are extremely important for drainage and for supplying the vineyards with water. Sauternes and Barsac have sub-soils containing some chalk, but the French adjective *moelleux*, often applied to them, means pithy or from bone marrow.

Barsac   The term mellow is more often used, and while the Barsacs have an odd flick of a dry finish, the Sauternes at their best have an established firm lusciousness all the way from bouquet to after-taste. Neither are merely weightily sweet; if a Sauternes is a peach, a Barsac is a nectarine, both grown outside against a sunny wall and not in a hothouse. Apart from the Sauternais and Barsac areas, the regions

Preignac,   of Preignac, Fargues and Bommes have
Fargues, Bommes   their own individuality.

The grapes used are all predominantly Sémillon, Sauvignon and sometimes a little Muscadelle, the two first giving the wines their honeyed but firm style. At the 1867 Paris Exhibition the judges, composed of both nationalities and adjudicating sweet German and French wines, gave the award to a Sauternes, Rayne-Vigneau. This was interesting because the wine was blended from all the casks in which it had matured, as happens today, while in Germany separately vintaged casks are kept apart and numbered.

In the subtle after-taste, the great Sauternes and Barsacs compare with the fine Beerenauslese and Trockenbeerenauslese of Germany, for there is the same refinement and underlying extra assertiveness of the concentration. They are, however, weightier (note the long streaks of legs or glycerine trailing down the sides of the glass) and more alcoholic. Their enticing charm may not immediately indicate that this is so, but while an average drinker can consume a bottle of a great German wine and usually wake refreshed the next morning, the after-effects of even half-a-bottle of a big Sauternes are likely to be much more devastating.

Red Wines

Main Taste Categories

Whereas all but the finest dry and sweet white wines are mainly to be enjoyed for their freshness and crispness, or their fruit and sweetness, red wines have subtleties of flavour and style in even the more modest ranges. They are also usually considered in relation to food, seldom being drunk on their own. In most countries red wine is usually served with meat of various kinds, although there are occasions when a formal meal, with the stress on fine wines, is planned for a programme of fine white wines. Another reason for a preference for red wines with food in northern countries is that people who endure cold, damp climates find the fruit and cosiness of even modest red wines easy to enjoy; if they suffer from rheumatic conditions the constituents of most red wines are more readily assimilated than the acidity of many whites. Finally, while white wines of the highest quality ranges can be discussed, argued about and appraised *ad infinitum*, this rarely occurs with wines of lesser quality. And to me it seems that it is possible to find more to talk about, study and ponder within a far wider range of reds. I also find them easier to taste in great numbers, and I can drink certain red wines on any occasion and with anything. There is always, for me, something cerebral, something to think about in even the most obviously sensual red wine, just as there is something sensual about even the most intellectual of whites. It is the wine with the appeal to the mind that endures in my memory.

Although there are some sweet or sweetish red wines, the majority may generally be described as dry or medium dry, with more or less fruit. They are here classified as straightforward, of medium personality and weighty, according to their importance.

Straightforward

These include the type of regional wines that formerly would hardly have been palatable even on the spot, as well as the huge quantities of branded wines that now make it possible for millions of people to drink wine with quite ordinary meals. Although branded wines are carefully made up to satisfy majority demand, they inevitably vary according to the availability and quality of supplies, so that the version and components of "Body of Bacchus" 1975 may be different in 1976. As with the greatest wines, no "once and for all" attitude should be adopted for the humblest.

Straightforward red wines should provide pleasant drinks to accompany everyday food or else provide the introduction for a more complex wine if two reds are to be served. They are the types of wine to take on a picnic, serve with bread and cheese, even to drink with a hamburger. If they are correctly aired and decanted they will seem, if not actually taste, better and will enhance any ordinary meal.

They should have smell, taste, a slight follow-up of the flavour, as well as a pleasing, living red colour whatever the tone. Does the wine smell pleasant, possibly a little fruity? Is the flavour agreeable, confirming what has previously been indicated by the smell? Is the wine moderately supple and round or does it seem slightly harsh or thin? As you swallow, does something extra make you want to swallow again? Or does the wine seem dead and flat, without much smell or taste and does one mouthful suffice? Do not make too hasty a judgment; leave the bottle uncorked for an hour or more and then taste the wine again: you may find it both different and much better.

Most straightforward, crisp red wines stay in the modest price ranges, but they are generally more distinctive and give more pleasure than the straightforward light ones. They possess a slight, but distinct inner vitality or lift that distinguishes them from the more ordinary wines. If you particularly note a wine poured from a carafe, this is possibly a crisp, slightly assertive, straightforward red wine. Many 'little regional wines", have this crisp and assertive character and provide pleasures and memories for the traveller in wine regions; however, those of sufficient character to feature on export lists will be rather more assertive.

People who like wines with bite or obvious smoothness will probably not appreciate straightforward, fruity and robust wines. These should all have at least a suggestion of roundness, however robust and pushing they may seem, and they should never make a violent onslaught on the palate and then slide away; if this kind of red wine is "gutsy", it should display this characteristic from the first sniff through the flavour and into the after-taste. If the wine is predominantly fruity, its shape should display this fruitiness by initial freshness of bouquet, the taste itself and the clean finish. If at the back of an otherwise ordinary wine there seems to lurk a suggestion of something more important, this may be because the wine is made from one of the great classic grapes. I have found this in a Yugoslav Pinot Noir, some Italian Merlots, a Hungarian Cabernet Franc and the ordinary little clarets of Bourg and Blaye.

There may also be smells and tastes, sometimes vaguely but occasionally distinctly evocative

Porrón, used in Spain, evolved from the wineskin. The liquid is directed from the spout straight into the mouth, allowing several to share a bottle.

The Chevaliers du Tastevin in Burgundy celebrate the feast of St Vincent, patron of French wine growers, on January 22.

of a vineyard that makes more important wines, such as Côtes du Rhône-Villages, ordinary Riojas, Mâcon Rouge. This sensation is even more curious with wines made from classic grapes and coming from vineyards of which the taster has no experience, such as when I taste ordinary quality Californian Cabernet Sauvignon, or certain Australian reds. Finally, there are wines which, small-scale and possibly only in the ordinary category, nevertheless introduce the taster to completely new taste experiences: the native grapes of certain regions or countries, such as the North American Zinfandel, the South African Pinotage, Hungarian Kadarka, Bulgarian Mavroud, Cyprus Mavron, and the Yugoslav Plavac, Postup and Dingač. Tasting these wines, one must free the mind from associations with other wines and decide whether one likes them or not. Try to determine what makes such a wine individual, its smell, taste or general composition, and if you can link these to any familiar taste experience.

Medium personality

An enormous quantity and variety of wines come into this category. It includes wines that are slightly more important than the straightforward because of the quality of the vineyards; wines from vineyards previously little known but now able to make wines of a style acceptable to export markets; wines from certain grape varieties that can now make wines in many diverse vineyards that are capable of improving with maturation; and wines from "little" estates previously only known locally or used for blending. In addition, some vintage wines that can exemplify an agreeable robust style if matured for a time and those that can develop elegance and charm can also have medium personality.

All wines have something to tell the drinker, even if only whether they are pleasant or not. But wines of medium personality are notable by their smell, taste and after-taste, and they are sufficiently complex for these components to be separate and relate only indirectly to each other. For example, a Pinot Noir from a Californian winery may smell utterly characteristically of the grape, but the taste is unexpected (at least to somebody experienced in tasting red Burgundy), and only the after-taste may link with the smell. Certain wines can turn round sharply from bouquet to taste to after-taste, as when a classic grape, made in a vineyard not always associated with it, can only be detected in the after-taste. I have found this with certain Gamays made in the New World.

Tasting a wine from a classic grape, try to discover how the vineyard and its climate have affected the performance of the grape; you may, of course, be deceived when the wine has been affected solely by the wine-making process, but at least you will register that there are

differences. The Cabernet and Pinot grapes show great diversity when grown in vineyards that are either very hot or fairly chilly. Mixtures of grapes can be varied in proportions so as best to adapt to the vineyard and climate; surprise is sometimes expressed that the wines of Bordeaux should be made from several grapes, but this is precisely why they are so varied and so complex, even with the "little" wines.

Wines of medium personality from specific estates or labelled as the produce of the special reserves of specific wineries can highlight some interesting points: small-scale but individual wines from areas where greater red wines are produced can point to the giants and introduce the drinker to them. This is of enormous use where vintage wines are concerned because the smaller-scale wines will develop faster and can give some indication as to the progress of the bigger ones. Non-vintage wines can give a clear general impression of a region or a specific vineyard: because they are of moderate personality, their impression is likely to be easy to register, and remember that the wine of a great estate, affected by its vintage, may be so complex and so unlike the wine of another estate a few hundred yards away that it is hard to pick out anything that the two may have in common until you have gained some experience.

With wines of moderate personality, it is of great importance to "drink above what you can afford" because these are the wines that make a lasting impression on the mind and the senses. As price generally relates to quality, second or third rate wines will produce second or third rate wine standards. It is always wiser to be honest and admit preference for, say, a Beaujolais at the top of its form rather than a Burgundy that may bear a famous name but which you do not truly appreciate. At the same time it is also important to bear in mind that, although you may not like a particular reputed wine, it has nevertheless won its reputation through the praise of many people. Try to find out why they like it and you do not, and remember that, while you may not like it now, you may come to understand and like it very much as you get more experienced. Never dismiss a "little" wine as "bad" or automatically praise a great wine as "good" until you have begun to distinguish between your personal preferences and accepted and objective standards—insofar as taste can ever be objective.

Weighty

Into this category come the greatest red wines of the world. These are wines to be treated with respect and care, for their qualities can easily be lost if they are served incorrectly, in a hurry, or in the wrong context. Nor should potentially great wines be served casually or substituted for carafe or everyday wine in a misguided attempt to increase the glamour of a special occasion; even the owners of great estates do not do this.

Burgundy grape baskets. These can be suspended from a pole if too heavy when full.

Château Latour, Pauillac.

Among all the wines of the world it is the weighty red wines that have produced the best and worst of wine writing, the affectations of the wine snob and the inspiration of the wine lover. They are not just drinks, just as a Mozart opera or a Beethoven symphony are not just sounds. At their best, they give stimulation and satisfaction to the mind and the senses. Even if they were not as expensive as they are, it would be extravagant to regard them as beverages to serve with food—they merit careful partnering with appropriate dishes to show themselves off to advantage. Although certain of the more robust weighty wines can accompany elaborate food and withstand a complexity of food flavours, the simplest food of finest quality will generally be the most suitable, especially for wines of outstanding delicacy and elegance. It is pertinent to refer here to one of the points in the perpetual argument of red Burgundy versus red Bordeaux: whereas Burgundy at its finest does seem to require serving in combination with fine, even rich food to make a harmonious gastronomic experience, the lover of great claret will drink the very finest with the simplest of dishes, such as lamb cutlets, steak and even roast chicken. I am not the only one who would happily make do with bread and cheese with all but the oldest and most outstanding red Bordeaux. It is rightly said that while, given the means, it is possible to drink a fine claret every month or even every week, you are lucky if you drink a very fine red Burgundy more than once a year; less is made, and very little in the top qualities.

It is essential to listen to what the weighty wines have to say; people who "don't see what all the fuss is about" are invariably those who never listen, only voraciously want the wine to do something for their benefit. Do not look at such wines in a hurry; they need time for you to take detailed note of them, and you should be in a relaxed, receptive and humble frame of mind. Savour each instant of appraisal, for each stage can present a complete pleasure, and together the colour, bouquet, taste and after-taste can stir the senses. (It is true that the ear is not appealed to by wine, and according to legend it complained about this to Dionysus; the God of Wine suggested that, as men drank, they should in thankfulness clink their drinking vessels so that the sound might please the neglected ear.)

With each of the greatest red wines it should be possible to appraise each single aspect of the wine in as much detail as might be devoted overall to an entire wine of lesser importance. For example, there is an opening, middle and after-smell, a beginning, continuing and concluding flavour, and an after-taste that can also be divided into several sections: the opening, sustaining and final impression.

It is usually easy to personalize the wines: one may be fully mature, another an adolescent as yet not fully developed, a third still a baby, while some others may be beautiful old people or persons just passing their prime. Comparisons can make the taste memory vivid by personal notes that liken a particular Pauillac to a guards officer, a St Julien to a diplomat; the mind will remember that the 1967 Bordeaux are friendly but that the 1969 rather lack charm, that the Burgundies of Firm X are slightly tarty and those of Firm Z too shy to possess wide appeal.

Try to relate a great wine to its vineyard in general and to determine if it is true to this. However much appeal it possesses, does it remain well-bred and in harmony with itself? Some Burgundies are made so as to be what I call "woofy" or superficial: they smell fatty and taste flabby, with an anticlimax of an after-taste and a lingering treacly trace on the palate; they may command high prices, but they are not aristocratic Burgundies. Does the wine make you want to discover more about it? This is *the* definition of finesse, but some Bordeaux, especially in certain much publicized years, are sometimes made to feel no more than plummy and stalky in the mouth. Do adjectives like "big", "strapping", even "blackstrap" spring to mind? No fine Rhône, however majestic, should be associated with such coarseness or ponderousness.

Right, Château Lafite-Rothschild, Pauillac.
Far right, Château Mouton-Rothschild, Pauillac.

Above, Château Margaux.
Below right, Château Palmer,
Margaux.

In thinking of the vintage, discover whether you associate it primarily with heat (an over-baked vineyard can give a rather hard wine as the grapes may be too small), or does the ripeness seem to have combated the cold? Does the smell feel full of sun that builds to a ripeness and seems to bloom in the mouth and then trail lengthily away? This can be the impression in great vintages. Is there a touch of wetness, even an unripe smell and taste, or a curious hollowness in the middle of the taste indicating lack of cohesion between smell and the end flavour? These can be signs of wet weather at the wrong time or rain in the middle of the vintage so that picking may have had to stop. This is true of some of the 1964 Médocs. Does the wine seem smaller-scale than it should be, compact but not generous, or is it mouth-filling and a bit too easy-going? The former may indicate a rather chilly summer, the latter generally too much rain.

A strange smell, especially in Burgundies, can be due to bad wine making in a difficult year and this smell, which usually reminds me of stale treacle, can be that of the sugar beet used in the chaptalization of the must. A lack of balance in a Bordeaux and too much hard stalkiness can indicate that for one reason or another the Cabernet Sauvignon is too predominant and that perhaps the Merlot in the vintage has failed or been unsuccessful in bestowing its beautiful smell and charm. This is what gives the unique quality to Lafite, but the Merlot is not always an ideal grape to cultivate elsewhere. Does the natural crispness of a young Bordeaux in a good year seem backed by something too "green"? This can indicate immature or young vines, and the wine may soften and become harmonious with a little age. Great profundity, on the other hand, can indicate very old vines, maybe with a small yield, but with much quality.

Wines that are well-balanced and pleasing, but seem to be on a small scale compared with the great vintages, can be good examples of light years of famous wines. It is important to realize that a light year is not an off year, and even an off year wine from a grower reputed for quality can be a delicious, rewarding wine, on its own or used to introduce a more important wine. The light years, such as 1960, of estates like Latour, can be superb and charming. And the 1962 Palmer was a very great wine in its year.

Principal Vineyard Regions

Vast areas are coming under vines to keep pace with the growing demand for wine, and areas where wine has always been made, though perhaps not exported, are being extended. In the traditional old-established vineyards **straightforward** red wines may simply be the wines of more ordinary quality, from sites that before modern methods of cultivation and wine making could yield only a little poor wine. This is true for many wines of southern France, such as in the Hérault, Languedoc and Provence, where much wine went for vermouth making or distillation until quite recently. There are also many Italian and Spanish vineyard areas, and some Portuguese, where good rather than ordinary wine can now be produced, the lesser wines being straightforward. And there are many straightforward non-vintage wines from vineyards now able to sell their vintage and estate wines.

There are other regions where vineyards carpet what might otherwise have been un-productive soil; North Africa, many North and South American wine regions outside the finer wine areas, and huge expanses of South Africa and Australasia. In many of the south-eastern European countries the State has undertaken the role of wine maker and, by equipping the vine-yards with the most modern installations, has provided work and exportable quantities of wine. Sicily is an interesting example of this, although private estates and vast tracts owned by large concerns also exist.

A number of vineyards making straightforward and especially crisp wines are at fairly high altitudes and some are in cool, even cold regions, such as the Jura, Switzerland, north Portugal and the hills near Rome. Increasing numbers of some of these wines are made partly or wholly by *macération carbonique*, a technique used in the Rhône valley and now adopted with variations in many regions. Essentially, it consists of allowing the fermentation process to begin while the grapes are still whole; after they have been pressed or crushed, the method of wine making is adapted so as to produce wine typical of the region and grapes. This type of wine will be ready to drink almost immediately, instead of having to undergo long-term maturation. Some "little" or peasant-made wines are harsh and not capable of developing to please export markets if produced in the traditional manner, and other wines with a high tannin content, such as certain small-scale Bordeaux and southern French reds, can be off-putting. In these cases the *macération carbonique* method or the use of it for part of the crop vintaged can result in wines that are delicious drinks when still very young; they are attractive because of their fruit and

Château Pichon-Longueville.
Pauillac.

fragrance and are what might be exactly described as "quaffing wines".

Some southern hemisphere wines, in which the malolactic fermentation is not allowed to take place, can also possess a marked freshness and fruitiness.

Hot vineyards make straightforward but firm, fruity and robust wines. Thanks to modern methods of cultivation and controlled vinification the resulting wines need not be astringent or unbalanced. In regions where some of the medium personality or fine weighty wines are made, there can also be areas where the richness or heaviness of the soil will produce wines of less subtlety and finesse which can still be good everyday drinks.

Although the art and craft of the wine maker can make good wine where formerly only bad ones could be produced, there are limits to what the most expert technicians can achieve. Red wines of **medium personality** need certain types of soil and climate, usually a soil that is not good for much else besides wines, a certain amount of warmth and sun, sufficient moisture to feed the vines and swell the grapes, and enough cold to keep the vineyard healthy and produce a moderately high acidity or freshness in the wine. Too heavy a soil may be too rich or it may drain badly; the ideal soil is usually composed of sand, gravel, chalk and silica, as for whites. Stones are never removed by workers but kicked on to the vineyards so that they may hold and reflect the heat, sending it up on to the grapes; they also facilitate drainage.

Violent extremes of heat and cold can be found in these types of vineyards, but usually these climatic extremes are balanced so that a very hot summer is followed by a cold or at least a damp or windy winter. Too much sun can make a red wine on the harsh or astringent side, too little and the grapes' unripeness may betray itself in a sourness or excess acidity. Vineyards making wines of medium personality are most often within a fairly temperate zone, in which

there is a fair amount of sun in the spring and again during the weeks immediately before the vintage.

The climate may be variable in regions where the vintage is of some importance. It would obviously not be sensible to make wines for medium or long-term maturation if the weather were likely to flood or freeze them every other year, but some of the wines of medium personality are smaller classics from regions where the greater reds are made, and the chance is therefore worth taking. Producers are often urged to make wines for "laying down", but even where storage space is inexpensive and easily available, capital is tied up in such reserves, which have to be supervised, insured and eventually marketed so as to show a profit. The profit factor means that it is impracticable to make wines that are never going to be more than odd showpieces, however much the wine lover may long for the contrary to be the case.

The majority of **weighty** red wines come from Burgundy and Bordeaux, although there are small areas in Spain, Italy and elsewhere that also produce them. In general, these are areas where the vine has to fight to live and fight hard to succeed. The climate will mainly be variable and unpredictable, especially as vintages are of great importance; the vineyards are usually small, often being contained within other vineyard regions.

Vineyard Characteristics

The look of vineyards likely to yield **straightforward** mass-production red wines will be slightly undulating or apparently flat to the eye. The soil colour will be medium; if it is dark or very reddish it may be too rich, if light, then finer wines can probably be produced. Because of its economy, mechanical cultivation will be used, and the vines will therefore be planted so that a tractor can move between the rows. In some vineyards outside Europe, mechanical grape pickers resembling high tractors with the kind of inner workings associated with a car wash, are used to flick the grapes off the vines. On steeply sloping vineyards, the tractors and cultivators are attached to overhead cables working up the gradient; only in regions where cheap manual labour is still available are the vineyards terraced.

Grapes that make good, inexpensive, red wines like sun and dryness; they include the Carignan, Grenache, Syrah and Cinsaut grapes and are cultivated in many parts of the world. They are grapes meant to yield quantity rather than outstanding quality. The Italian Grignolino, Nebbiolo and Sangiovese grapes, among others, can also produce pleasant wines of ordinary quality, but the Gamay makes a better wine when subjected to a little cold. The two great red wine grapes, the Pinot Noir and the Cabernet

Château Cheval Blanc,
St-Emilion.

Château Corton André.
Aloxe-Corton.

(both Cabernet Franc and Cabernet Sauvignon) have so influenced the European wine lover that it is difficult to disassociate them from their most famous vineyards, Burgundy and Bordeaux. The Cabernet Franc, which can make vigorous, fresh and fruity wines, is possibly the most widely used in many world vineyards, but the Cabernet Sauvignon is often better reputed. Personally, I think that the latter grape seldom gives of its utmost when used alone, and unless it can also be given a fairly long maturation in wood, the astringency predominates unpleasantly. The Cabernet Franc, however, can make delicious wines by itself in vineyards that are either chilly as on the Loire or hot and dry as in many New World regions.

The Merlot, the grape that gives fragrance and charm to certain Bordeaux, makes appealing wines in Italy and many New World vineyards. The wines I have tasted from the Zinfandel grape certainly have an inner firmness, but so far they have not demonstrated lasting charm, profundity and elegance although they might attain these qualities. There can be no doubt that New World wines could challenge European classics on their own ground if economics permitted but wine makers have to make wines they can sell. Certainly some of the North American red wines already stand up very well in comparison; but they are, naturally, expensive.

The extensive vineyards of the New World mostly produce straightforward, crisp and slightly assertive wines, but lightish and fruity red wines generally come from vineyards that are not too sunbaked, or at least not all year round, and with friable, fairly light soil. A little cold helps to make the wines fresh.

In some vineyards, such as those of the Beaujolais and the Beaujolais Villages regions, or the sub-divided wine districts in parts of Italy and separate regions in the Roussillon and Languedoc areas, detailed care can give sufficient individuality to a wine to attract buyers and eventually command higher prices. With vineyards such as those of many of the Balkan countries or North Africa extremely costly methods would not be worthwhile because of local preference for cheap wines. Soils may be light to reddish in colour and, in the more northern regions, where the finer sites will be those getting the morning sun, vineyards making the more ordinary wines are often those that face west or south-west, and the vineyards may also be on the lower levels of any slopes, or even on the plains below the finer vineyards.

Wines of **medium personality** will usually come from very carefully kept vineyards, perhaps those in classic regions, or from small regions cultivated according to old-fashioned ideas. The vineyards will also usually be sloping; if the area produces very fine weighty classic wines, those of medium personality will be grown towards the top or bottom of the slopes, and in the middle or two-thirds up if the vineyard is a small-scale classic in its own right. The crisper, more delicately fruity wines will generally come from a lightly coloured soil, the more assertively fruity wines from darker soil, and sometimes from vineyards with a sterner type of landscape, such as the terraced vineyards of parts of the Rhône Valley, Italy and some regions of Spain.

It is unlikely that any vineyard making **weighty** red wines will be wholly flat, although the slopes on which red wines are made are not usually as steep as those from which, for example, the great Mosels come. The soil will be poor, the ground will undulate, and there may be a vast difference between the vines of one small plot and another within yards of it because of the difference in subsoil and topsoil, and the particular angle affecting the time of day when the sun will strike it. When such individuality exists, it is obvious that even more differences will occur by the smallest variations in the grape varieties, the way they are cultivated, the proportions that go into the blend and finally the various individual variations in the making and maturing of the wine. Usually, such vineyards are very well tended and, even when much of the cultivation is mechanized, a certain amount of manual labour is inevitably involved; the vines are seldom trained high, generally only up to waist level. The different methods of pruning aim at producing grapes that will make quality wine rather than vast quantities; therefore the bunches must have sufficient space to expand, they must avoid dragging the branches down and must be reasonably protected from the elements. Sometimes the earth is banked up round the vine roots to protect them and facilitate drainage between the rows of vines; weeds and vegetation that might take nourishment away from the vines will be regularly removed. The vines are meticulously sprayed against pests, and sometimes with particular mixtures the leaves may turn blue, without affecting the grapes.

Hospices de Beaune.

Straightforward

Light

This category includes a few German and Alsatian wines, Languedoc, Provence and Cassis wines as well as ordinary quality Bordeaux and Italian reds. Some Californian red wines also belong here. They are all intended for drinking as soon as they are offered for sale. They have moderate freshness and light body with a little fruit.

In general, the very chilly vineyards that make fine white wines, such as in *Germany* Germany, make light reds, if they make red wines at all, and so do a few *Alsace* vineyards in Alsace, particularly those using the Pinot Noir grape. The wines *Corbières,* of more ordinary quality from Corbières, *Minervois,* the Minervois, Languedoc, Cassis

Straightforward

France	Germany Austria	Italy	Spain Portugal	Rest of Europe	Americas Australia South Africa
Light					
LANGUEDOC, some examples PROVENCE, some examples CASSIS, some examples CORBIÈRES, ordinary quality MINERVOIS ENTRE-DEUX-MERS ordinary quality PREMIÈRES CÔTES DE BORDEAUX ordinary quality PINOT NOIR from Alsace	Most red wines from Germany	Red wines of ordinary quality from Italy Mass-market red wines from Sicily			GAMAY NOIR from California GRIGNOLINO from California Branded wines sold as "CLARET" or "CLARET TYPE"
Crisp, Slightly Assertive					
JURA, ordinary quality GAMAY DE TOURAINE FRONSAC GRAVES DE VAYRES, most examples ENTRE-DEUX-MERS PREMIÈRES CÔTES DE BORDEAUX Wines made by *macération carbonique* method from southern France		LATIUM CASTELLI ROMANI VALPOLICELLA, ordinary quality BARDOLINO, ordinary quality NURAGUS from Sardinia	VILA REAL Some red wines from north Portugal	DÔLE, and many other red wines, from Switzerland PROKUPAC from Yugoslavia GAMZA from Bulgaria Some red wines from Romania CABERNET, ordinary quality, from Balkans and northern Europe	PETITE SIRAHS from California CABERNET from Chile
Firm, Fruity, Robust					
CABERNET FRANC, ordinary quality, from Loire BEAUJOLAIS BEAUJOLAIS VILLAGES CÔTES DU RHÔNE VILLAGES BÉARN BANDOL BOURG, ordinary quality BLAYE, ordinary quality CAHORS, ordinary quality MÂCON COSTIÈRES DU GARD Red wines of ordinary quality from Corsica		MERLOT CHIANTI, non-vintage, most examples CANNONAU from Sardinia Most red wines from Sicily	RIOJA, ordinary quality VALDEPEÑAS, ordinary quality DÃO, and most ordinary quality wines from Portugal	DEMESTICA and other quality red wines from Greece OTHELLO, AFAMES, and other ordinary quality red wine from Cyprus MAVROUD from Bulgaria KADARKA from Hungary CABERNET from Hungary PINOT NOIR from Hungary PLAVAC, POSTUP, DINGAC from Yugoslavia	"BURGUNDY" or "BURGUNDY TYPE" ZINFANDEL, ordinary quality CABERNET SAUVIGNON of ordinary quality from California PINOTAGE from South Africa Red wines from Argentina

Languedoc, Cassis, Provence, Hérault
Northern Italy
Premières Côtes de Bordeaux

and Provence, as well as certain regions in the Hérault come into this category, and so do the reds from northern Italy and the ordinary red wines from the Premières Côtes de Bordeaux region. These wines are all "little" reds, but can be pleasant light drinks.

"Claret type"

Many branded wines or wines from various countries sold by retail chains and described vaguely as "claret" tend to be light and straightforward, although none in my experience relates more than very remotely to Bordeaux itself. A number of South African and Australasian wines have in the past been similarly labelled, but even if they are made from the Cabernet, they usually come into the fruity and robust category. Spanish wines labelled as "claret" are usually much more assertive than anything should be from Bordeaux. But many popular blends made for drinking as everyday

Vin rouge

"Vin rouge" are light and straight-forward, as are some Sicilian wines.

Sicily

There are some straightforward

California

Californian wines, (above the jug or carafe quality) made from the Grignolino grape or the Gamay Noir; here these grapes yield a lighter, less obviously fruity wine than in Europe.

Crisp, Slightly Assertive

There are probably hundreds of wines in this category, reds with a certain fresh liveliness that appeal slightly more than those that are merely pleasant and light. I usually find that they possess moderate acidity but not much tannin, making them wines for short-term consumption, but in some instances they benefit from a few months' additional bottle age. Their delicate fruitiness is one of their most attractive traits. All these wines have a mouth-filling flavour, and the category includes many from little known regions whose wines deserve exploration and wider appreciation.

Cabernet

The Cabernet wines, often named as such, from most northern European vineyards possess a distinctive, implicitly "pushing" style. Often, as in many

Balkan countries
Chile
Loire

Balkan vineyards and in Chile, it will be the Cabernet Franc which results in fruit and moderate to definite acidity. In the Loire region, the ordinary regional Cabernet Franc wines and the Gamay de Touraine come into this category, as do the more ordinary

Jura

qualities of Jura reds, the Swiss Dôle

Switzerland

and most Swiss red wines. Southern French wines include those made mainly from the Carignan grape and certainly those made partly or mainly by the *macération carbonique* method.

Vila Real
Prokupac, Gamza

The reds of Vila Real in north Portugal, the Yugoslav Prokupac, Bulgarian Gamza, some red Romanian wines, the markedly fragrant Sardinian

Nuragus
Valpolicella
Bardolino
California

Nuragus and the ordinary qualities of Valpolicella and Bardolino should be included. I would also add the better Californian Gamay Noirs and certain Petite Sirahs.

Latium
Castelli Romani

The Italian Latium wines, notably those of the Castelli Romani, admirably exemplify this category; they have a delightful smell but it leads directly to the taste, with no surprises or develop-ments in store. From France, the unfairly neglected Fronsacs and Graves

Fronsacs, Graves de Vayres

de Vayres should be included, as well as the few red estate wines of the Entre-

Entre-Deux-Mers, Premières Côtes de Bordeaux

Deux-Mers and Premières Côtes de Bordeaux. They have a pleasant, underlying lightness and crispness from the light, sometimes pebbly soil.

Firm, Fruity, Robust

This category probably includes the greatest number of wines bought as everyday drinks with food when something special at low cost is required. Service is of great importance; a cheap wine of this type can taste impressively better if served in the right context. Most benefit by decanting or at least airing, when their smell can make itself evident and any inner hardness or astringency can be softened. They are admirable drinks with simple coarse-flavoured dishes—cold pies with pickles, Scotch eggs and salad, meatballs and ketchup, and virtually any sort of robust snack and stew. The wines to accompany these foods need a fairly obvious smell and taste, with no delicate complications, but enough guts not to be overwhelmed. They can have a perfumed bouquet, but they are acceptable if mouthfilling in style and often have what I think of as the "iron filings" back-taste or a certain amount of tannin. These wines are not only enjoyable to drink, on or off their home ground, but they also provide good exercise for anyone who wishes to practise tasting.

"Ordinary quality"

Many of the wines listed in this category have the prefix "ordinary" because they are the small-scale versions of wines that might be included

in the medium personality or weighty categories. Others are not associated with capabilities of more quality; in many holiday regions, the occasional ordinary wine may stand out but it is usually best enjoyed on the spot. The large wine shippers and merchants are alert to the possibilities of "new" wines for export markets, but if a wine has not been discovered, exploited and exported, this may be for sound commercial reasons. Only a very limited quantity may be made, which the supplier prefers to keep for the home market, or the wine, such as ordinary *Cahors, Béarn,* Cahors, Béarn and much Bandol, may *Bandol* be unlikely to appeal to a sufficiently wide public to warrant large-scale exports.

Red wines of this kind, with a certain freshness and good acidity, may often be traced to vineyards with a cool or cold climate for at least part of the *Mâcon* year; the ordinary red Mâcons, Dão *Dão* and many Portuguese reds made in the mountains, exemplify this, as do the *Hungary,* Hungarian reds, some Corsican and *Corsica,* Sardinian wines and the non-vintage *Sardinia, Cyprus,* Cyprus reds that get freshness from *Loire,* the sea. The ordinary red Loires *Beaujolais,* (Cabernet Franc), ordinary Beaujolais *Côtes du Rhône* and Côtes du Rhône are yet other examples. In certain southern wines, and those made in a hot climate, the aggressive style is modified by modern wine making methods; this is true of *Shiraz,* Corsican wines, the Shiraz and *Grenache* Grenache wines in many New World vineyards and others often described *"Burgundy* or labelled as "Burgundy", possibly *type"* because of their fruitiness and slightly spread flavour. The ability of South African, Australian, and I believe of some north Italian wine makers to

prevent the loss of acidity during the malolactic fermentation that takes place in classic European reds, leads to wines that can keep their style and proportion. Fruity and robust wines made by old-fashioned methods may be heavy, unbalanced and harsh as evidenced in some casually made Greek and certain Spanish red wines.

Argentina, Many Argentine reds, certain *Sicily,* Sicilian wines, those of the Costières du *Costières du* Gard south of Nîmes, and non-vintage *Gard, Chianti* Chianti recall a sunbaked earth just as *Cannonau* the Sardinian Cannonau and the *Patrimonio* Corsican Patrimonio wines are slightly herby, the back-taste indicating the atmosphere of the maquis and the scented plants of the respective islands. Similarly, the mountain table wines *Douro* of the Douro Valley, harder, more austere and recalling the granite of the soil, are recognizable as wines of their landscape, as are the north *Merlot* Italian Merlots with their agreeable smell and slight freshness.

In appraising the ordinary wines of huge areas such as North Africa, South Africa, California and much of Spain and Sicily, the differences bestowed by the wineries should always be borne in mind. Unless these differences distort the character of the wine, they should all enhance the result and contribute something. When, for instance, I taste the non-vintage *Afames,* Afames and Othello of Cyprus, I can *Othello* see the difference made by skilled and conscientious wine makers to wines from vineyards within the same region. I do not know what they do in detail; I can see the details of what they achieve, and I think I can understand *why* they make their wines in their individual ways.

Medium Personality

Fruity, Assertive, Moderately Robust

These are wines where the finest classic grapes really make their presence felt even when made into wines simply bearing their names, often without specific vintages or general vineyard areas. Some come from great wineries, each of which will endow the different wines with their own individuality— in the United States, a wine may bear

a "varietal" or grape name as long as it is made with as little as 51 per cent of that grape. Some Californian wineries also make different qualities of wines bearing the grape names, in the same way that many European wine makers label their wines according to quality. (The term "reserve" is in some places controlled by legislation, in others it may simply imply that the wine is of superior quality.)

Cabernet The Cabernet, both Cabernet Sauvignon and Cabernet Franc, makes

Medium Personality

France		Italy	Spain Portugal	Rest of Europe	Americas Australia South Africa
Fruity, Assertive, Moderately Robust					
BEAUJOLAIS, parish wines of Juliénas, St Amour, Chénas, Chiroubles, Fleurie	MERCUREY, non-vintage	NEBBIOLO	VALDEPEÑAS estates	Hungarian BULL'S BLOOD	CABERNET FRANC, vintage wines from specific regions
CHINON	ST-ÉMILION, non-vintage	SANGIOVESE		Vintage wines from specific regions of Greece and Cyprus	PINOT NOIR, some examples
BOURGUEIL	BEAUNE, non-vintage	BARDOLINO of good quality			CABERNET SAUVIGNON, some examples from specific regions
ST NICOLAS DE BOURGUEIL	CÔTE DE BEAUNE, non-vintage	AMARONE of good quality			SHIRAZ, ordinary quality
SAUMUR-CHAMPIGNY	CÔTE DE BEAUNE VILLAGES, non-vintage	PIEDMONT wines of good quality			GRENACHE, ordinary quality
CAHORS, estate	BOURG, estates	FREISA of good quality			
CÔTE RÔTIE, non-vintage	BLAYE, estates	VALPOLICELLA of good quality			
SANTENAY, non-vintage	BOURGOGNE, BORDEAUX, and BORDEAUX SUPÉRIEUR, non-vintage	BARBERA, most examples			
CORBIÈRES and estate wines from southern France	Corsican estate wines	DOLCETTO, most examples			
		Estate wines from Sicily			
Firm, Fruity, with a Certain Elegance					
MÉDOC non-vintage, or vintage in light years	BORDEAUX bourgeois growths, in light years	CHIANTI of superior quality	RIOJA, vintage, small-scale, in light years		ZINFANDEL, estate
GRAVES non-vintage, or vintage in light years	Southern BURGUNDY vintages, in good and light years	BARBERA, some examples			PINOTAGE, estate
ST JULIEN non-vintage, or vintage in light years	BURGUNDY non-vintage parish wines from Côte d'Or	BARBARESCO			Other estate wines of long maturation
MOULIS non-vintage, or vintage in light years	LOIRE, estates, in good and fine years	GATTINARA			
LISTRAC non-vintage, or vintage in light years	MOULIN-A-VENT, vintage				
MARGAUX non-vintage, or vintage in light years	MORGON, vintage				
	LIRAC				
	CAIRANNE				
	RHÔNE, some regional wines				

medium personality wines throughout the world, though I would think that the Cabernet Franc is generally the more successful. When the Cabernet Sauvignon makes a good wine, it is so good that it verges on great, but sometimes there is a heavy firmness about it so that it may taste harsh, astringent or bitter, especially if the wine is not aired before being drunk. The Cabernet Franc, however, can make delicious wines in very many regions: the fruitiness and the "zing" of the acidity when the grape is grown in the chalky, limestone vineyards of the Loire, make the red Chinon, Bourgueil, St Nicolas de Bourgueil and Saumur-Champigny delicious, crunchy wines in most years. In sunny years when the Cabernet Franc yields particularly well there is an added fascination and finesse. Unfortunately these wines, even in good vintages, are seldom made to last for more than five or six years, but they can, when suitably made, last for ten or twenty, developing subtleties that are perhaps charming rather than beautiful.

Chinon, Bourgueil, St Nicolas de Bourgueil, Saumur-Champigny

Pinot Noir The Pinot Noir grape also makes very good wines of this category, from vineyards throughout the world; in *Yugoslavia* Yugoslavia an excellent one is made. They do, ideally, need at least a little maturation in bottle to show the bloomy appeal associated with the black Pinot. This also applies to the well-known red Hungarian Bull's Blood, *Bull's Blood* which is made chiefly from the Kadarka grape. Significantly, this is grown in the same region of Eger where the Pinot Noir, Merlot (both also used for Bull's Blood) and the Cabernet are very successful in making good Hungarian *Gamay, Shiraz, Grenache* reds. The Gamay, Shiraz and Grenache grapes make wines of medium personality throughout the world; Europeans may associate the Gamay solely with the Beaujolais (although

Bourgogne Supérieur, Bordeaux Supérieur, Beaune, Côte de Beaune, Côte de Beaune Villages, Côte Rôtie Santenay, Mercurey

Corbières, Roussillon

Bandol

Corsica

Bourg, Blaye

Robert, Guionne

St-Emilion

Beaujolais

Chiroubles

Chénas, St Amour

Fleurie

Gamay de Touraine is successful in the Loire) and Shiraz and Grenache with the Rhône and the Garnacha of Rioja. However, these grapes make robust, fruity, usually assertive wines in many warm to hot vineyards and are extensively used in the New World vineyards; indeed, here the Shiraz and Grenache can make wines of greater finesse than their usual European counterparts.

Into this category also come non-vintage wines, made from these classic grapes and in classic regions, such as Burgundy in general, Bordeaux (the "Supérieur" categories of both), non-vintage Beaune, Côte de Beaune and Côte de Beaune Villages, the non-vintage Côte Rôtie reds, and the non-vintage southern Burgundies, such as those of Santenay and Mercurey. Personally I used to find many non-vintage wines from large vineyard areas rather dull, as they seemed to imitate the finer wines without having even a limited contribution to make of their own. But good shippers of non-vintage wines can now establish the character of a region very satisfactorily, and it is possible to find some that might be mistaken for more expensive wines.

The estate wines from Corbières and the Roussillon and southern France in general, including the outstanding vintage wines of Bandol, such as those of Dr Dray, and the Domaine des Tempiers, are fine examples of good wines within their own quality ranges. Some of the estate wines of Corsica can come into this category as well if they have been carefully made so as to avoid a violently assertive and clumsy style. I would also include the estate wines of Bourg and Blaye in the Gironde; virtually unknown until the last ten years, they are sturdy little ponies of wines that can give much pleasure, and estates such as Robert and Guionne often make wines of great interest, with much to say. The non-vintage St-Emilions are easy to enjoy with a fullish style and slightly earthy background.

Certain of the commune or parish Beaujolais, made from the Gamay, are typical of fruity, assertive and moderately robust red wines. Chiroubles is to me invariably associated with fruit, Chénas is similar but with an extra firmness, St Amour has a particular amiability and slight fat, Fleurie the obvious floweriness

Juliénas

Cahors

Spain

Italy

Freisa, Bardolino, Amarone, Valpolicella, Dolcetto, Barbera

*Greece
Castel Danielis*

Othello, Afames

Domaine d'Aherà

associated with its name, and Juliénas has a moderate to full-bodied, fleshy character.

Finally, from the French wines I would select the estate Cahors when these are made according to the old traditions of *vins noirs* or "black wines". Today, and especially since they were promoted from the VDQS to the AC category, Cahors usually means an agreeable, rather full, not particularly fine, slightly southern-style red. But I have sampled the traditional black wines, some of them able to remain for up to 50 years in wood and still retain their profundity and long-lasting vitality. Popularity and the interest of a French President has made the greatest Cahors a commercial wine today, but some of the true black wine is still made from hundred-year-old, ungrafted Malbec vines. An admirable and sustaining drink, it is known locally as "old men's milk" and is supposed to possess recuperative properties.

Spanish wines in this category include Cariñena and Galician reds with a pleasant freshness, and the better wines from Priorato, Torres and Alella. These have too often in the past been sold as Spanish "Burgundy" and "claret", but it is to be hoped that they will make individual names for themselves on export markets.

Numerous Italian wines belong in this category, especially those made wholly or with a high proportion of the Nebbiolo and Sangiovese grapes. They include many of the medium to fine wines of Piedmont and Tuscany. Quality Freisa, Bardolino, Amarone, Valpolicella, Dolcetto and most Barbera also come into this category, and so do the finer Sicilian estate wines and certain Sardinian reds, though these are not often found on export lists.

Certain Greek red wines could be included here although only one, Castel Danielis, is found on UK export lists. Some Cyprus reds, such as the vintage wines of Othello and Afames and the non-vintage but specific regional mountain wine, Domaine d'Aherà, are also robust and fruity. They are not subtle, but possess depth and finesse.

Firm, Fruity, with a certain Elegance

These wines speak assertively but with subtleties of tones as well. By elegance no softness or prettiness is implied but rather an innate style. In this category there are some non-vintage wines, but a greater number of those that bear a vintage have developed to advantage in both wood and bottle. The wines listed here come from only a few vineyard regions. At this stage of experience, the wine lover inevitably concentrates on the detail of certain areas, as knowledge begins to deepen. It is possible that a specialist in Tuscan or Piedmont wines, the greater estate reds of California, South Africa or Australia could draw all the examples from just one of these regions, where there are shades of differences between the estates, and plots within the estates and vintages. A lover of Burgundy could certainly limit himself to Burgundy wines and I might venture to do so entirely from the Médoc. But this is not helpful to the drinker who cannot easily buy many of the wines of one region, although if you know a region with a certain thoroughness, you can appraise another one with much greater ease. I have attempted to refer to as many of the main regions that merit detailed study as possible.

Médoc, Graves, St Julien, Margaux, Listrac, Moulis   Non-vintage Médocs, red Graves and St Julien, Margaux, Listrac and Moulis wines all come into this category. The parish or commune wines are of more distinct style than those of the general regions; some parishes, such as Ludon and Macau, do not have a separate AOC; their wines, even the greatest, are therefore simply classed as AOC Haut-Médoc.

Côte d'Or   The non-vintage parish wines from the Côte d'Or also come into this category. It is important to handle all these parish wines correctly; they can show to great advantage, especially if they come from a reputable source, but they should not be treated simply as carafe wines, when the beginnings of their more subtle attributes may not make themselves apparent. To find out more details about these wines, ascertain if there is a great name or estate wine of renown in the parish: Haut Brion and La Mission Haut Brion in the Graves, Léoville-Lascases, Léoville-Barton in St Julien, Le Chambertin in Gevrey-Chambertin. If you read what various people have written about such great wines, you may be able to detect something akin to them when you taste the non-vintages of a lower category.

There are also the small-scale vintage wines from certain regions that make the bigger classics; these include the parish wines of the Côte d'Or, which, in the Côte de Nuits, can demonstrate the slight blackcurrant taste with an inner firmness that is typical of these fine wines. In general terms, those from nearer Dijon tend to be slightly more reserved and sensitive, those of the middle of the Côte fuller, and those nearer to Beaune a little more expansive and fruity; the Côte de Beaune reds are straightforwardly fruity and robust wines. In southern Bufgundy, the finer examples of the wines of certain shippers from Santenay and Mercurey and some red Mâcons can in some years speak assertively and elegantly to the drinker. It is possible to note the slight softening in the air in the more southern wines where the vine does not have to struggle so much. The vintages that make delicious wines of this category have enough sun to provide sound ripeness, but not so much that the wines coarsen and broaden; one should feel the skeleton of their construction, not simply appreciate their amiability.

Santenay, Mercurey Mâcon

In the Beaujolais, the wines of Moulin à Vent and Morgon are those that always possess a certain reserve and take longest to mature, the Moulin à Vent wines possessing distinct elegance. those of Morgon being firmer and often beginning hard. They seldom give of their quality while very young, but a truly sunny year can with care make them long, finely proportioned wines with an extra finesse to their bouquet. Seven to ten years can be their life although they seldom last more than five years after their vintage.

Moulin à Vent, Morgon

The wines from the bottom of the Rhône Valley are now becoming known outside their region. Vintages are not greatly variable in this region, but, except for the wines produced in the lower price ranges and intended for drinking soon after bottling, most benefit greatly by a little extra maturation after you have bought them. The wines of Lirac and Cairanne, to the west of the Rhône, are lighter than the Châteauneufs and might be described as pretty peasant girls in the elegantly becoming dress of the region. Those of Vacqueyras, east of the Rhône, seem to display a slight additional freshness from their proximity to the slopes of the mountains that form part of the Alpes Maritimes. Thanks to modern wine making methods, the Grenache grape can here give of its fruit without too much of its assertiveness, and the Syrah can show its slightly

Rhône

Lirac, Cairanne

Vacqueyras

Gironde

seductive bouquet without too much fat and coarseness.

In the Gironde, I would cite the bourgeois growths from most regions in vintages that might be categorized as light to good. Many bourgeois growths make wines that are perfect miniature Bordeaux, giving an impression of their regions and their vintages, interesting in regard to bouquet, flavour and after-taste; their appeal may be limited, but it combines sensuous and cerebral assets. Some of them, such as the recently rehabilitated and scrupulously made *d'Angludet, Chasse-Spleen, Gressier-Grand-Poujeaux, Brillette, Fonréaud, Fourcas-Hosten, La Tour de Mons, Loudenne* d'Angludet in Margaux, Chasse-Spleen in Moulis together with Gressier-Grand-Poujeaux, all rated as *crus exceptionnels*, Brillette in Moulis and Fonréaud and Fourcas-Hosten in Listrac, La Tour de Mons at Soussans, and Loudenne at St Yzans in the Bas-Médoc, are much more than "little wines". They can be beaten on the heights of Bordeaux only by the classed growths in fine years, and they can show ranges of wines that last as long as the *crus classés*, and may sometimes give more easily appreciated pleasure if not quite as profound a fascination.

St-Emilion

Across the Garonne, the St-Emilion classed growths in average to good years come into this category, and I would personally rate the finer *Pomerol* Pomerols as wines with even more to say; they have a trace of elegance because of the sand and gravel that sometimes, in blind tastings, can confuse them with Pauillacs. In the *Graves* Graves, the lighter years of the classed growths may be included, but the spicy complexity of these wines in good years takes them into the Weighty category. By their delicacy, they tend not to be wines for beginners, because they have under-currents that need a little experience to appreciate.

Many estate wines from the New World can be included here, especially those that have been given longer than usual maturation in wood and/or bottle. Wines made from the classic *Cabernet Sauvignon, Pinot Noir* grapes, such as the Cabernet Sauvignon and Pinot Noir are the most impressive, but the style followed by the estate or winery must be taken into account as well as the grape. The vintages do not usually display marked individuality, only indicating the length of time since the wine was made. This can be of interest, but an old wine is not necessarily a good wine,

and while certain red Bordeaux and Burgundies can go leisurely and gracefully downhill in their old age, many New World wines tend to decline suddenly and sharply. The fact that they may be kept in ideal conditions in the wineries until they are sold, and then be stored in a dry, heated atmosphere will naturally hasten this sudden decline. It has also been my experience that, whereas these New World wines can possess great vigour in their youth and prime, they somewhat lack the subtleties of bouquet and after-taste that attract and charm. These characteristics can of course develop and then pass in a dry, clean atmosphere, whereas in a dampish, cool climate, like that of the British Isles, they remain and linger, sometimes when the wine is virtually a ghost.

Australia, South Africa Pinotage, Zinfandel

The special red wines of certain Australian estates, some South African Pinotages, and the Zinfandel wines must be classified here. The wines made from the Zinfandel grape have given me the impression of a grape that makes firm, fruity wines, with a certain robustness and an angular harshness at the back of the main taste that might evolve into something interesting or fascinating.

Rioja

The Rioja region in the north east of Spain makes the finest reds of this country, but many of the best should be classified as Weighty. In this category of firm, fruity and elegant wines come the medium ranges that are sold under a vintage which sometimes means that a wine is topped up while in cask, and not necessarily with the same wine. The different establishments have their style of wine making but the sunbaked smell, "red earth and slightly iron back-taste" is always noticeable. Most of these wines benefit enormously by decanting before drinking. It is sometimes unfairly said about Rioja wines—and about other red wines from regions with long-established and proud traditions—that they are reminiscent of wines of better-known classics. Riojas are fine wines in their own right and should not be compared with wines from other countries. Rioja wines probably cheered Columbus and his crew, and as early as 1635 the Logroño authorities prohibited wheeled traffic in the town so that the wine, lying below ground, might not be disturbed by any vibration. Elderly people still recall the days when vast quantities of Rioja wines were sold to famous French wine regions to "improve" the robustness of the French wines.

Chianti   Many Italian wines must be listed here, such as Chiantis entitled to be called *vecchio*, which means they will have had two years in wood, and from producers or estates making moderate to forceful red wines, usually 70 per cent from the Sangiovese grape; also wines of similar superior quality from certain regions. In the Valtelline region of *Valtelline* Lombardy, the wines of Grumello, *Grumello,* Inferno, Sassella and Velgella must be *Inferno,* made with 95 per cent of the Nebbiolo *Sassella,* grape; the Castel Chiuro red of Nino *Velgella* Negri is said to be outstanding. *Castel Chiuro* Piedmont, good and fine wine country *Piedmont* in general, makes good Barbaresco and *Barbaresco,* Barbera wines, and Barbera d'Asti, *Barbera,* which must be made solely from the *Barbera d'Asti* Barbera grape, is considered the most interesting. The Grignolino d'Asti is *Grignolino* also much praised. My personal *d'Asti* impression of these wines is that they can age attractively up to a certain

stage, retaining their fruit as well as increasing their various qualities, but that they tend to decline rather suddenly. It should be remembered that they can be slightly higher in alcoholic content than some French wines that may, superficially, seem similar in style; a $12.5°-13°$ wine will seem more assertive to the taster than one of below $12°$.

Gattinara   Gattinara, made from the Nebbiolo grape is another Piedmont wine, from the Novara hills; it usually possesses a fairly dominant bouquet and a nervous, variable character, sometimes straightforward, sometimes flirtatiously charming. The occasional Latium *Latium* wines might be listed here, but the area is generally too far south, the wines respond to the heat and sun so as to expand and smile abundantly, whereas in a cooler vineyard they possess the withdrawn quality when young that can mean there is a reserve of fascination and interest to be developed if they are properly made and cared for.

Weighty

Moderately Fruity and Robust

These great wines are characterized by their direct appeal to the senses, coupled with a fruity smell and flavour. They are wines to study for although they are usually immediately likeable there is much to discover in them.

Pauillac   The wines of Pauillac possess what I think of as a steel framework; famous for their nobility, they can be both graceful and gracious. The bourgeois growths, such as Fonbadet, Haut-*Fonbadet,* Bages-Monpelou and Pibran, *Haut-Bages-* demonstrate this nobility in good and *Monpelou,* even great years. The St Estèphes are *Pibran,* harder and slower to show any charm, *St Estèphe,* and Pomeys, Tronquoy-Lalande, *Pomeys,* Haut Marbuzet, Les Ormes de Pez, *Tronquoy-* Houissant, Andron-Blanquet and *Lalande, Haut* Château de Pez itself have a more *Marbuzet, Les* robust style than the Pauillacs. *Ormes de Pez,* Virtually all the classed growths except *Houissant,* the very greatest of St-Emilion should *Andron-* be listed here; the wines demonstrating *Blanquet,* a robustness and open-textured style *Château de Pez* that most northern people find very acceptable, even if they may sometimes lack finesse. The small-scale Pomerols *Pomerol* could also come into this category,

though in great years they can merit inclusion in the Assertive Fruit and *Moulis, Listrac* Character category. The Moulis wines in good years and those of Listrac in good to fine years are also wines of moderate fruit.

Classed growths   Among the classed growths of the Médoc, certain wines in light years, *St Julien,* especially of St Julien and Margaux, *Margaux* possess everything that this category implies: fruity charm that makes them very easy to like and understand. With the St Juliens, there is also a delicious close-textured smell, and with the Margaux wines an inner sunniness. It is impossible to mention all the wines, but one should generally look for the lightest vintages of well known estates, such *Léoville,* as the three Léoville estates in *Palmer,* St Julien, and the estates of Palmer, *Rausan-Ségla,* Rausan-Ségla and Lascombes in the *Lascombes* Margaux; the lesser known classed growths of these parishes should also be tried, together with the light years *La Lagune,* of La Lagune from Ludon and *Cantemerle* Cantemerle in Macau. In the Graves, *Graves* the lesser-known growths in light to good years can show a sunny charm, with a back-taste of spice typical of the region.

Côte d'Or   In Burgundy, the Côte d'Or wines may generally be divided into those of

Weighty

France				Italy, Spain	Americas Australia South Africa
Moderately Fruity and Robust					
CHÂTEAUNEUF-DU-PAPE, estate vintage CÔTE RÔTIE, vintage CROZES-HERMITAGE, vintage PAUILLAC, bourgeois, in good years	ST ESTEPHE, bourgeois, in good years POMEROL classed growths in light to good years ST-ÉMILION classed growths in light to good years	ST JULIEN classed growths in light years MARGAUX classed growths in light years BURGUNDY parish wines from Côte d'Or in light to good years	Southern BURGUNDY, some of special quality, in outstanding years CÔTE DE BEAUNE, some special sites in good to fine years	BAROLO estate wines CHIANTI special vintage RIOJA, certain estates	
Assertive Fruit and Character					
CHÂTEAUNEUF-DU-PAPE of outstanding quality HERMITAGE in most years GIGONDAS of special quality BURGUNDY single sites from Côte d'Or, in good to fine years	CÔTE DE NUITS single sites in light to good years CÔTE DE BEAUNE single sites, in good to great years GRAVES classed growths in light to good years PAUILLAC classed growths in light to good years	ST-ÉMILION classed growths in good to great years POMEROL classed growths in good years MARGAUX classed growths in light to good years ST JULIEN classed growths in light to good years	ST ESTÈPHE classed growths in good years MOULIS estate wines in good years LISTRAC estate wines in good years LUDON estate wines in good years BORDEAUX first growths in light years	CHIANTI of outstanding quality BAROLO of outstanding quality	CABERNET SAUVIGNONS of outstanding quality PINOT NOIRS of outstanding quality
Elegant, Profound, usually with Charm					
BORDEAUX, great classed growths in good to great years, including the finest ST-ÉMILION, POMEROL and GRAVES	CÔTE DE NUITS, the finest individual vineyard wines in great years				

Côte de Beaune

Côte de Nuits

Gevrey-Chambertin, Chambolle-Musigny, Morey-St Denis, Nuits-St Georges

Aloxe-Corton, Savigny-lès-Beaune, Volnay, Monthélie

Montagny, Mercurey, Givry

the Côte de Beaune and the Côte de Nuits. The Côte de Beaunes in good to fine years are assertive but the name of the grower and shipper is all important. In the Côte de Nuits wines there is greater subtlety and, to my mind, finesse, even in light to good years, and some of the parish wines can also attain this level. The wines of Gevrey-Chambertin (except for the greater sites), Chambolle-Musigny, Morey-St Denis and the site wines of Nuits-St Georges should also be included here.

Wines such as those of Aloxe-Corton, Savigny-lès-Beaune, the site wines of Volnay and Monthélie come into this section, and I have had wines from the southern part of Burgundy, such as those of Montagny, Mercurey and Givry from shippers of repute such as Louis Latour and Marcel Amance that challenge the Côte de Beaunes for quality in good to fine years. The only

exceptions have been when the Côte de Beaunes came from shippers of equal distinction.

Rhône

Crozes-Hermitage

Châteauneuf-du-Pape

Château Rayas

In the Rhône, there are some outstanding vintages, such as 1961 in Crozes-Hermitage, though the different style of the shippers has to be taken into consideration. Those of Paul Jaboulet are usually outstanding, those of Jaboulet-Vercherre very good. Various estates in Châteauneuf-du-Pape make the top category of classic reds. The association known as *Les Reflets de Châteauneuf-du-Pape*, a union of estate owners, produces wines of outstanding qualities. In most years the wines of Château Rayas, where extraordinary white wines are also made, display the same traits. The astonishing characteristics bestowed by the vineyards are at once noticeable; although parts are sand and gravel, they are famous for the enormous orange-brown stones, like baked potatoes, on which it is difficult to walk without turning the ankles; they retain and reflect the heat on to the grapes which have been shielded from direct sun by the method of training. Our ancestors loved these wines which, although they may never attain great finesse, can achieve true nobility and superb stylishness, especially with age. If the Bordeaux are the thoroughbred racehorses, and the Burgundies the glorious hunters, these Rhônes are the magnificent shire horses in all their pride and engaging qualities.

Red Champagne

Bouzy Rouge

One other French red wine must be mentioned here, although it is perhaps more important than fascinating or profound: the red wine of Champagne. The light soil of the region and the Chardonnay and Pinot Noir make wines of fine bouquet, delicacy and mouth-filling quality. Bouzy Rouge is often cited as the outstanding red Champagne, but there are red wines of great quality made at Ambonnay, Ay, Cumières (very elegantly scented), Dizy, Rilly, Verzenay and Villedommange. For economic reasons red still Champagnes are not easy to find, but the passionate lover of wine will certainly find them well worth trying when visiting the region, especially those of Ay.

Ambonnay, Ay, Cumières, Dizy, Rilly, Verzenay, Villedommange

Rioja

Vega Sicilia

Some well-matured estate Riojas, with their back-taste of roasted vineyards, come into this category. I would also include that curious wine, Vega Sicilia from Old Castile, for which the Garnacha grape is also used. It is a remarkable wine with subtleties of smell and flavour to provoke and astonish the lover of great classic wines. It possesses attributes that make the drinker want to plunge more deeply into it to understand it. Some authorities would also list the Valbuena wines in this category. The vintages of both are said to be as individual as a Bordeaux lover could desire, and, unlike the slightly defiant style of most fine Riojas, these wines have a smiling charm.

Valbuena

Chianti

Among the great Italian wines certain estate Chiantis will come into this category, certainly the *riservas*, which have been three years in wood. From Barone Ricasoli's Brolio estate, Brolio Chiantis marked as *riservas* will have been five years in wood. The countryside is portrayed in the wine: small hills, markedly undulating, light soil, a great deal of sun in summer and fresh cold in winter with a moderate amount of rain.

Brolio Chianti

Montepulciano,

Other reputed wines include Vino Nobile de Montepulciano and Brunello

Brunello

di Montalcino, both also from Tuscany; they have long matured in wood, the best Brunello for at least four years and Montepulciano for three years, two of them in wood. These are wines to be tried if possible in their regions, for such very unusual wines can be difficult to appraise away from their home ground. Once their acquaintance has been made, it is possible to put them in perspective as great wines.

Assertive Fruit and Character

These wines are now predominantly French, but others certainly exist that give the same detailed and subtle pleasure. Wine lovers all over the world should seek them out on their travels.

Rhône Hermitage

The outstanding Rhône wine, especially in good years, is Hermitage, provided the assertiveness is never allowed to overwhelm the wine's balance. It is a great pity that now, for economic reasons, such wines cannot be allowed time to develop over many years, and that long-term maturation in bottle is seldom possible. They have an underlying severity, and the firm, enduring qualities that make for very long wines, with bouquets that waft from the glass and lead naturally to a taste that is but a prelude to the after-taste. Certain outstanding vintages of Crozes-Hermitage and, occasionally, Châteauneuf-du-Pape estates can also attain these qualities, but usually only the privileged visitor to the region may be able to try these aged wines. It is occasionally possible to buy and lay down wines of outstanding years when they are first offered for sale.

Crozes-Hermitage, Châteauneuf-du-Pape

Côte de Beaune

In Burgundy, the greater Côte de Beaune wines from specific sites in fine to great years come into this category and a few from certain growers may even come into the Elegant and Profound category. The Pommard sites, those of Volnay and the 29 first growths of Beaune itself—and those of the Hospices—as well as the charming wines of Pernand-Vergelesses and Aloxe-Corton can possess all the qualities of assertive fruit and character, together with a certain elegance. The lightness of the soil around Pernand-Vergelesses as reflected in wines such as the few reds from Chassagne-Montrachet (the Clos St Jean is not the only site) and Santenay les Gravières, to me attain a finesse in fine to great years that is far more

Pommard Volnay, Beaune, Hospices de Beaune, Pernand-Vergelesses, Aloxe-Corton

Chassagne-Montrachet, Santenay les Gravières

interesting than the obvious style of other better known red Burgundies. Some of the more famous sites have pandered to the public demand for what they consider is fine Burgundy: soupy, heavy, obvious, "woofy" and sticky-ended wines, with a headache in every bottle, in short a travesty of the wines that made the names for these sites in the past. Just as a fine unpretentious Rhône is better than an over-priced Burgundy, so also is a Burgundy with a modicum of publicized praise but a straightforward style on the palate. True great Burgundy should have silk at its heart, and the delicacy and sensitivity of a finely-bred and well-educated individual. The "big" wines are big because of the lasting impression they make, not because they hit you over the head when you drink them.

Côte de Nuits

In the Côte de Nuits, the different regions feature with certain basic traits in my mind: Chenove and Marsannay-la-Côte with a certain lightness and sprightliness; Fixin has distinct elegance; Gevrey-Chambertin shows a type of depth and profundity which is most marked in the great sites in good years, though perhaps they have a type of austerity that needs a little experience of Burgundy to understand. At Morey-St Denis the wines open out, beginning to charm—the Clos de Tart and Bonnes Mares in good years have great depth and a roundness that is easy to like even for the beginner. The shipper's name is of great importance for the natural traits of such wines can be hideously exaggerated. Chambolle-Musigny makes wines that are attractive for their fruit and what I note as an apricot smell: a little acidity at the back but a beautiful roundness.

Chenove, Marsannay-la-Côte, Fixin, Gevrey-Chambertin

Morey-St Denis Clos de Tart, Bonnes Mares

Chambolle-Musigny

Clos Vougeot

The Clos Vougeot vineyard is, to me, a little rigid; it needs a very good year and a shipper who will leave the wine alone, otherwise it can lack charm while displaying breed. At Vosne-Romanée, the wines risk distortion of their character like all great wines for which the demand is greater than the supply; this also applies to some of the wines of Flagey-Echézeaux. In many recent vintages they have shown a hot, concentrated style, with the wine rushing at the drinker, aggressive to please, as if maturation has been hastened. Great care has to be taken to avoid this lack of proportion, yet the profound, infinitely flowery, fruity delicacy of great Burgundies from this

Vosne-Romanée

Flagey-Echézeaux

region can make any trouble and any search to discover the quality wines worthwhile.

Beaune

Near to Beaune, the lightness in the soil is obvious to the eye and in the nervous finesse of many of the wines; this quality makes the reds of Aloxe as *fin* as some of the Côte de Nuits; the Pernand wines come into this category as well. Those of Savigny tend to have a slight but elegantly sinewy style, and those of Volnay are to my mind more gracious than the Pommards, which are nevertheless excellent, straightforward, fine Burgundies for the beginner. The red Chassagnes can also demonstrate great elegance in ripe years; they have the lightness that might be expected from wines made in a vineyard chiefly renowned for its great whites, but also a generally more straightforward style than the great wines from the sites of the Côte de Nuits.

Aloxe

Pernand Savigny

Volnay, Pommard

Chassagne

Bordeaux St-Emilion, Pomerol, Pétrus

In the Gironde, I would put all the St-Emilion and Pomerol fine wines of good to great years into this category. They include Pétrus, usually very fruity and with a great amount of body, Ausone, more subtle, and Cheval Blanc, which to many Bordeaux lovers can outdo the Médocs in certain vintages, such as the 1947, with its heavy fruit but admirable balance and profundity. I would also include Gazin (Pomerol), which in years such as 1945 and 1953, possessed great charm as well as distinction.

Ausone, Cheval Blanc

Gazin

Graves Haut Brion, La Mission Haut Brion, Pape Clément

The red Graves in good to great years, moderate to good years of Haut Brion, La Mission Haut Brion (a beautifully made, close-knit wine with infinite finesse), and Pape Clément, with its outstanding fragrance of flowers and spice and its gentle aristocracy, are excellent examples of fruit and firmness. Generally they are a little subtle and reserved to be beginners' Bordeaux, although the light to good years of Haut Brion are easier to appreciate; in many vintages, such as 1964, they can make wines quite different from those of the Médoc, because being further south they vintage a little earlier. The gravelly soil from which the area gets its name gives the wines marked delicacy and, outside the Médoc, they are perhaps the favourites of the moderately experienced Bordeaux lover because of their shades of smell and taste. They do need to be ripe, but when they are, their sunniness and breeding pleases the palate like a cat stretching for

Médoc
Moulis, Listrac,
Ludon

pleasure in the sun. The wines of the Médoc that are nearest to Bordeaux, such as those of Moulis, Listrac and Ludon, are not as well-known as they deserve to be, but the good and great vintages with their fine-drawn style are admirable.

Margaux
St Julien

The classed growths of Margaux and St Julien in good to great years generally belong in this category because of their superb fruit and expansive charm; the greatest vintages from a few estates can be so elegant that they can outclass nearly all other Médocs.

Margaux

The Margaux wines in a good year have a wonderful noble amiability; their fragrance is reminiscent of very ripe mulberries in a walled garden, their gracious fruitiness is never too pronounced nor does it conceal the fineness of their construction; Château

Château
Margaux

Margaux itself for some years after the war seemed less gratifying than it should be, but now seems to have evolved the right balance between nobility and friendliness. Lascombes,

Lascombes

especially in recent vintages, makes very fruity wines, with a bouncy appeal, easy to like and understand. Palmer,

Palmer

which perhaps I know best of any Bordeaux, is also easy to like and, for the discriminating it is possible to see how scrupulously it is made (the de-stalking here is still done by hand) and how the bones of the wine are finely proportioned. Two estates whose wines were often shown to me as superb examples of their styles in particular vintages are La Lagune,

La Lagune

at Ludon, with a beautiful fragrance and light but lingering fruity charm;

Cantemerle

and Cantemerle at Macau, another wine so well made that it teaches the drinker a great deal. Cantemerle makes wines that are often slightly withdrawn, but invariably rewarding if correctly handled; they have finesse even in years when the charm is not outstanding, plus great delicacy.

St Julien

The St Juliens are possibly the wines I might suggest after the Margaux for anyone beginning a study of the finer Médocs. The silkiness of Léoville-

Léoville-Barton

Barton, the slight additional firmness

Léoville-Lascases
Beychevelle

of Léoville-Lascases, and the forthcoming character of Beychevelle make them excellent with a variety of foods. Although care should be taken in handling any fine claret, I think that perhaps the St Juliens are less easily prevented from giving of their best than the wines of some other parishes.

Ducru-
Beaucaillou,
St Pierre-
Sevaistre,
Langoa-Barton,
Gruaud-Larose

Other excellent St Juliens are Ducru-Beaucaillou, St Pierre-Sevaistre, Langoa-Barton, and Gruaud-Larose.

Pauillac

The Pauillacs, which can be very big wines, should be included here in the moderate to good vintages—the greater ones make them so important that they must come into the next section. But there are a number of estates that, while they seldom seem to reach the top heights, make uniformly good Bordeaux, of assertive nobility; they can be especially attractive in good to fine

Pontet Canet,
Grand Puy
Lacoste,
Batailley,
Pédesclaux,
Duhart-Milon,
Pichon-
Longueville
Mouton

years. Pontet Canet, Grand Puy Lacoste, Batailley, Pédesclaux, Duhart-Milon (which now belongs to Lafite) and the two Pichon-Longuevilles are good examples.

The lighter years of all the first Bordeaux growths come into this category, and I would also include even the good years of Mouton, which makes a very big wine, with the Cabernet Sauvignon well in evidence. Latour,

Latour

with its slight extra reserve and nobility, is sometimes not immediately forthcoming in the good to great vintages until it has had sufficient maturation, but its light to good vintages come into this

Lafite

section. Lafite, with its superb bouquet and close-textured subtle taste, is almost always too elegant to include here, although there is the occasional great vintage, such as 1961 and perhaps 1970, when it is such a big wine from the outset that, drunk young and before its time, it can be said to possess

St Estèphe

assertiveness. In St Estèphe I would put the good to great years of most of the classed growths in this section, although I have tasted a few vintages of

Montrose, Cos
d'Estournel,
Calon-Ségur

Montrose, a few more of Cos d'Estournel and several Calon-Ségurs that exemplified elegance more. Cos d'Estournel is the Bordeaux that the Lafite staff say they like to drink if they must drink anything except Lafite, and it usually possesses great breeding. Otherwise, the St Estèphes do not, in my experience, achieve the great profundity and supply the intense intellectual pleasure that can be had from many fine Pauillacs and Margaux wines.

Chianti, Barolo

The Chiantis and Barolos of out-standing vintages, capable of developing infinite subtleties of bouquet and flavour with maturation must be included here. It is sometimes said that Chianti is the Bordeaux of Italy, and Barolo the Burgundy, but this is a confusing statement. The notable difference is that, whereas Barolo, from

Piedmont, is made wholly from the Nebbiolo grape, Chianti, from Tuscany, is largely but not wholly made from the Sangiovese, and Tuscany is farther south than Piedmont. In addition, I would say that the greatest Barolos have an assertiveness and the greatest Chiantis a complexity, and that both should be enjoyed as often as possible.

Elegant and Profound, usually with Charm

From personal preferences, this category could be entirely devoted to Bordeaux, which I find interesting, stimulating, fascinating to talk about and delicious to drink. There are more great Bordeaux available to the ordinary drinker than great Burgundies, but to many people the latter speak more eloquently than the Bordeaux; they are indeed very great wines too.

Bordeaux

In this category all the wines available will be mainly estate or domaine bottled. With the clarets it should be appreciated that it is traditional in Bordeaux wine making to blend the different vattings after the wine is made, having first made sure that each vatting is worthy of inclusion with the *grand vin*. Apart from the slight variations that may occur between bottlings done early and later (sometimes over two or three months) the particular wine of a certain vintage will be the same as any other that bears the same label—insofar as any single bottle of a great wine can be like any other single bottle.

Burgundy

In the Burgundy region, however, the different owners of the various sections of different sites make a great deal of difference to wines of the same name, and to create further differences, buyers may specify after detailed study of the wine in different casks, that they will have certain particular casks. This can make an additional difference to Burgundies that are bottled by anyone except their grower.

Although I have had many very great Côte de Beaune wines, I have never had one that could, even in the finest years and from the most impeccable sources, achieve the ultimate in finesse and magnificence of the wines of *Côte de Nuits*. These superlatives must not be restricted to the great Romanée-Contis, for while they possess one type of glory that is Burgundy, there are others. Sadly few of the finest Burgundies are allowed to be made and

mature for the length of time of which they are capable. In the past, I have had old Burgundies, old even by Bordeaux standards of 20 to 30 years old, that show how much delicacy, finesse, polished quality and almost intellectual distinction they can possess. All this in addition to the more apparent qualities of complex floweriness, silky flavour and a crescendo of finely-wrought charm that never deteriorates into mere opulence. To my mind the greatest Burgundies, possibly because of my love for claret, include the following: Fixin La Perrière, Charmes-Chambertin and Latricières Chambertin, Bonnes Mares, Clos de la Roche and Clos de Tart (the last three in Morey-St Denis), Chambertin Clos de Bèze, Le Musigny, Chambolle-Musigny Les Amoureuses, Les Bonnes Mares and Les Charmes, a very few Clos de Vougeot, the Suchots and Malconsorts of Vosne-Romanée and, at Nuits-St-Georges, Les Saint-Georges, Les Vaucrains, Les Cailles, Les Pruliers and La Richemone.

With Le Chambertin and Chambertin Clos de Bèze, as with Clos de Tart, there is perhaps more at the back of the wines, more precise detail and more reserved nobility. Much depends from whom they come, but they can fascinate the mind as well as the senses and, should ideally never be accompanied by foods that can mask their detail; nor should they be served without a wine of nobility though lesser stature, to introduce them.

Le Musigny is called "the wine of silk and lace" and its 25 acres are shared between ten owners. There is an exquisite Musigny Vieilles Vignes from Comte Georges de Voguë, but the Musignys in general combine delicacy and velvety assertiveness. The wines of Bonnes Mares, Charmes and Amoureuses are perhaps a little easier to understand at first taste; the wine on which my experience of the greatest Burgundy was started was a Les Charmes of 1929, drunk in 1957. The slight extra fat of the Chambolle wines gives them a gentleness that insidiously makes itself memorable.

Romanée-Contis

The Romanée-Conti wines are interesting even if you never succeed in drinking them, because this vineyard was one of the last to keep the old, ungrafted vines. Unfortunately they never recovered from the shortage of carbon disulphide during the Second World War and eventually they had to be uprooted in 1946; the wines began to be made again in 1952 from grafted stocks. Their bouquet has been associated with violets and cherries; they are distinctive wines, opening out hugely on the palate like a peacock's tail, with the deep, increasingly profound flavour becoming apparent in the older vintages. The Richebourg is a very finely proportioned wine, though others may prefer the slightly more open-textured style of La Tâche. Grands Echézeaux are rated by some authorities above Echézeaux, and Romanée-St Vivant and La Romanée slightly below Romanée-Conti and La Tâche.

For anyone who can afford to study the great Burgundies, my advice would be to compare wines of the same vintage from several sources, while the wines are a little more mature than just young and vigorous. Then one can begin to see their skeletons, one can note how they have been made.

Bordeaux   One of the fascinations of great claret is the way it affects the other wines with which it is served, sometimes seemingly making them taste better than one would have thought possible, sometimes revealing the shades of charm and interest of what might have been an overlooked wine, or stressing the way in which the wine of a light or not previously considered great year can soar above an expected taste. The great wine will irradiate all the others that are well chosen to accompany it.

It is not only the first growths that give the memorable experiences of Bordeaux, and in particular years there may be more than one other growth that seems to epitomize all the qualities of that vintage. The 1953 *La Mission Haut Brion* La Mission Haut Brion seemed to me to do this more wonderfully than the Haut Brion, and in 1962 *Palmer* Palmer made a wine that was superlative Médoc when I drank it in 1974. I *Lafite* happen to like the 1953 Lafite more *Latour* than the 1953 Latour, but, discounting personal preference, would say that 1953 was a year when certain Médocs could demonstrate an exceptional, aristocratic charm. This, for me, means Lafite, while Latour tends to show itself memorably in years that have a slightly more noble and reserved style. But the 1928 Latour, a vintage that was hard and withdrawn for a long while, was superb throughout the late 1950s and early 1960s.

A vintage in which most of the great Bordeaux do well is curiously not always one in which the finest wines immediately rise above the level of all the others; the Pauillacs, certain St Estèphes, red Graves and the Pomerols may take time to shed their youth and refine to maturity. This can possibly make the lighter years of some estates *Mouton-Rothschild* more memorable; the 1933 Mouton, for example, was a delicious, sunny wine with something wholly noble at the back of bouquet, flavour and after-taste in addition to its obvious quality. It is this extra something that makes the *Pétrus* greatest Bordeaux. The 1949 Pétrus was to me a very fine wine, when tasted from a magnum a few years ago, but it was too much of a good thing, both as a Pétrus and as a 1949, to possess the outstanding quality of superb Bordeaux. On the other hand, the *Cheval Blanc* 1947 Cheval Blanc, esteemed even by some Médoc lovers as the greatest of that vintage, while having the beauty of the vintage and the class of its estate, also had a length, a profundity, a fascination that seemed outstanding.

Sometimes it is in vintages that begin by being fairly hard that the greater wines later emerge. The 1945 *Gazin* Gazin, for example, seems more aristocratic than some Pauillacs of that vintage, and from the 1961 vintage, the wines that have the staying power and marked nobility of the year may eventually outpace those that made the initial impression and were delicious drinks from a comparatively early stage.

What gives *you* particular pleasure in great claret? The roundness and fruity foundation of such St-Emilions as Cheval Blanc and Ausone in their finest years, or the slight additional lightness and nervous sensitivity of the big Pomerols? Do you find infinite satisfaction in the close-textured red Graves, sensitive and summery in Domaine de Chevalier and Pape Clément, or with a bit more stoniness as in La Mission Haut Brion, or with the assertiveness of Haut Brion? Do you like clarets that are "big", such as Mouton, noble like Latour, *fin* like Lafite, or gracious such as Margaux? Can you find an infinity of pleasure in finely made great vintages from estates such as Cantemerle, Palmer, Cos d'Estournel in years when they outstrip their neighbours? No claret can be all things to every drinker, but, as the Bordeaux region is fortunately the largest area producing the very finest red wines, there is plenty of choice.

97

Pink Wines

Pink wines are frequently known as "rosé" referring to the colour, and this can indeed echo the various pinks in different types of the rose. One of the most charming tastings I have attended was of a wide selection of pink wines, with a vase at each tasting station containing the rose that in colour came closest to that of the wine. Pink wines range from dark, vivid pink a bare shade away from red, through orange and tawny-pink to light bright pink, and from a soft, almost lilac-tinged pink to a clear pinkish-pearl and a faint almost bluish-pink.

Pink wines are not necessarily light in alcohol as is sometimes supposed, and the alcoholic strength cannot be determined by tasting—until afterwards. They are wines to respect in their own right, not the all-purpose "when in doubt" wines that they are sometimes assumed to be. They can be made almost anywhere that wine is made and they are usually non-vintage wines, at their best while young and fresh.

Pink wines are not among the great classics, but they are not meant to be, and because they are light in importance they need not necessarily be so in terms of consideration. They may be described as operetta wines, but they are first-rate operettas. Pink wines are made to give pleasure in a lighthearted, undemanding way. Their freshness and their light fruit should be immediately apparent, and their clean finish should either indicate their ability to introduce more serious wines or simply leave the drinker with an impression of a pleasant experience.

Pink wines are always medium dry or at the most slightly sweet, rarely very sweet.

When you are ordering wine for a picnic, a casual meal, to partner lightly-flavoured food, or if you simply wish to drink something that is pretty and lightly refreshing, the pink, usually inexpensive wines are good choices. A well-made pink wine should have a certain balance, and the discriminating drinker will also try to gain something from the smell and the flavour of the wine. No one, I think, has ever sat discussing a pink wine for more than minutes except to establish whether it is pleasant as a wine in its own right or as a shadow of something else that might be white or red. Pink wines can merely be the shadows of the red or white wines into which they could have been made. If you have previously deduced what a particular local wine may be like, you will know what to expect from a pink wine from the same area.

Generally, the colour of pink wines varies according to the amount of colour in the black grape skins, although wines made by blending red and white may have the colour the wine maker thinks will most appeal. Pink wines from southern regions tend to be darker in hue than those from the north, possessing more fruitiness; pink wines from northern vineyards seem to have less flavour though with freshness, crispness and bouquet predominating. Pink wines from large wineries will also demonstrate the style of the establishment as well as that of the region.

Even the best pink wines are unlikely to be

Pink Wines

Good pink wines are light and crisp, with a certain freshness that often verges on a sparkle. They are usually medium dry wines from hot vineyards possessing additional fruitiness and flavour which can impart a slight sweetness.

In many of the regions famous for their red wines, pink wines will be available, from the pleasant Balkan pinks to the rosés of Bordeaux and Burgundy. The Cabernet Franc grape along the Loire makes vast quantities of pink wine; in "Rosé d'Anjou" wines the Gamay or Groslot grape has been used as well as or instead of the Cabernet Franc, while in "Anjou Rosé du Cabernet" pinks only the Cabernet Franc has been used. There are several Bordeaux rosés, including excellent ones

Balkans

Loire
Rosé d'Anjou

Anjou Rosé du Cabernet

Bordeaux

from the Graves region where the fine white wines are made. In Burgundy, the Pinot Noir grape makes the fairly full and fruity rosés of Marsannay-la-Côte among others, and in the Beaujolais some pink wines are now made from the Gamay.

In Portugal, vast quantities of pink wine are made; as good dry whites are made here, freshness is an attribute of the pink ones. In Spain, good pink wines are produced in the various classic areas. In short, throughout the world pink wines are equal to the quality that may be expected from regions where both good red and white wines are made.

In many regions the pink wines can be small-scale versions of the big reds of the area, and are therefore sometimes

Burgundy

Marsannay-la-Côte
Beaujolais

Portugal

Spain

long-lived or to improve in bottle compared with the white or red wines of their regions; they are essentially made to be enjoyed for their youthful attractiveness and easy-going style. As the colour fades or loses its brilliance, the wines may become flat and lack character. Even if they bear a vintage date, they should generally be drunk while fairly young, at most within a decade or so; non-vintage wines should be drunk within two years of bottling. Pink wines are always served chilled so as to bring out the crisp quality they possess and to accentuate the light fruitiness of the grapes.

Principal Wine-Producing Regions

Many of the classic wine regions and many wineries all over the world make pink wines. Originally they were doubtless catering for a demand for a wine that was cheap and could be made from grapes that might not make anything of particular weight and importance, and the specifically pink wines only occur fairly recently in wine lists. In some classic wine regions the word *clairet* is still used, but this does not necessarily imply a "vin rosé"; the term originally meant a light-coloured or *clair* wine, and was used to differentiate the wines made in the Bordeaux region from the "high country" or inland wines which were darker, hence the word "claret", still used in Britain to mean the red wines of Bordeaux. The Clairette grape, in conjunction with the Muscat, makes the Clairette de Die wines in the Drôme region of France, but these are not pink wines.

Good pink wines will be found in regions that make red wines rather than in regions that make only white, for white and pink wines can be made from black grapes whereas red wine cannot be made from white grapes. Only a few pink wines, for example, are made in Germany which is a white wine country as far as the finer wines are concerned. The type of region that makes good to fine red wines and pleasant to good white wines will usually make good pink wines, the Tavels from the Rhône valley being the supreme example.

Parts of Spain, Portugal, Corsica, Sicily, Cyprus and Greece all make good pink wines, the fruitiness of the black grapes in some balancing any lack of acidity and freshness in the white grapes. In regions chiefly known for their white wines, such as Austria, Portugal and parts of the Loire, the assertively green style of the wines from white grapes can combine with the softer, less assertive character of the reds.

Economic factors may also determine whether or not a wine region makes a pink wine for other than local use; it would for instance be uneconomic to attempt to make pink wines in the Mosel region, where the white wines have established a tradition of quality and can easily find a market. It would be equally impractical if, in the Médoc region of Bordeaux, where red wines predominate, a producer attempted to make a pink wine, although in certain bad years wines of impeccable estates are deep pink rather than red; they are, however, *not* sold as "vins rosés".

Pink wines of character will be found in regions where the wine-making process involves leaving the skins of black grapes to tint the must, and in regions where black grapes have sufficient assertiveness to endow the wines with a light fruitiness of flavour, and with a moderate delicacy of bouquet.

---

useful to introduce the more important wines. Pink wines can also act as "mouthwash" in the form of an apéritif or be used to introduce a more important wine at a meal.

Schillerwein Schillerwein, produced in small quantities in Baden-Württemberg, has nothing to do with the poet Schiller, although his statue is conspicuous in the centre of Stuttgart. *Schillern* means "to shimmer" and implies a pinkish wine made from black and white grapes.

Rhône The most important pink wine of all,
Tavel Tavel, comes from the bottom of the Rhône Valley—with its sunbaked vineyards, freshened by the proximity of the Alpes Maritimes, and the bitter drying Mistral wind blowing down the deep river valley. The Rhône wines are often made from a mixture of white and black grapes and that of Tavel can be made from a number of both black and white, although it is the black Grenache that mostly predominates. The vineyard soil is sandy, stony, gravelly, ideal for fresh, light, almost vivacious wines. Most Tavel comes from co-operatives, but some estate wines reach export markets; these are among the few pink wines that can benefit from a little bottle age, with the result that the wines expand, giving of their fruit, the white grapes meanwhile maintaining a sinewy, assertive character. Estate Tavels can

Cairanne, Lirac age very gracefully. The wines of Cairanne and Lirac, west of the Rhône, are now becoming better known, and also make good pinks.

Sparkling Wines

The curious effect of the river at Ay, where the reflection forms the shape of a bottle of Champagne.

There are three main methods whereby wines are made sparkling: the Champagne method, the *cuve close* or Charmat method, and the process whereby carbon dioxide is pumped into still wines. There are, however, some wines such as the *pétillant* and *vinhos verdes* ("green wines"), which have a natural "liveliness" or inclination to sparkle; thanks to scientific methods of wine making, this type of wine can now be deliberately made and kept in condition, rather than occurring by accident.

The sparkle in any wine is caused by carbon dioxide gas; in a perfectly still table wine this is given off into the air when the wine is freshly made and is either in the vat or in the cask. The process of fermentation is usually vigorous in the autumn or immediately after the vintage and then dies down with the colder weather of winter when the wine yeasts do not work, beginning again in spring, when what is often referred to as secondary fermentation takes place. Sometimes wines that have been badly bottled or bottled too soon can, in the spring after their vintage, become a little fizzy. Such wines are described as "working"; this can happen with certain young Beaujolais, some of which is now deliberately made to be drunk very young, and which *should* be drunk very young unless it is going to start fermenting again.

There are other wines in which a light "prickle" of fermentation as it is often termed, recurs, without any adverse effect. This may occur in the wine at different periods of its life or may remain there. The *vinhos verdes* of the Minho region of north Portugal are typical of one type of this. The vines are cultivated up high trellises, and the wine's evolution includes a special form

A selection of old Champagne bottles.

of secondary fermentation called malolactic which is manifest in the wine as a mini-sparkle. It is present in both the white and red "green wines", but although many slightly sparkling pink wines are made in Portugal, no pink wine can, according to legislation, be a "green wine".

Some of the finest white wines of Germany, Alsace and other great white wine regions, including the Loire and the Rhône, may go through phases of demonstrating a delicious slight sparkle while they are very young and some of the greatest retain it into age. This sparkle should not be confused with the first fermentation or with the malolactic; its presence may not even be noticed with the eye, although occasionally you may see a few minute bubbles in the glass or bottle. There is no fermentation smell on the nose, but as you pull the wine over your tongue you may be aware of a touch of gentle liveliness, as if the wine were tickling the palate to indicate its vigour and charm. The French term for this type of wine is *pétillant*, the German *spritzig*; in Italian the word *frizzante* may be used, although this can often imply a wine that is slightly more fizzy than the two other terms signify. This sort of sparkle should not be confused with the malolactic fermentation, which is part of the natural evolution of any wine unless it is prevented from taking place.

Champagne Method

Champagne is only made in the Champagne district of France, from the Pinot Noir, Pinot Meunier and Chardonnay grapes. The sparkle in Champagne is essentially the result of the secondary fermentation taking place in bottle (see pages 26–27). But other sparkling wines, and especially the finer qualities, are made throughout the world by the Champagne method, and this fact is often declared on the bottle labels. It must be declared in France.

Charmat Method

Champagne is a *vin mousseux* or sparkling wine, but not all sparkling wines are Champagne. By far the greater proportion of fully sparkling wines produced throughout the world are made by what is known as the Charmat, *cuve close* or sealed vat method. This was invented in France in the 19th century, but developed and perfected in 1910 by Eugène Charmat at the Oenological Institute of Montpellier. Today his firm makes one of the best-selling sparkling wines, Veuve du Vernay.

Essentially, the sealed vat method consists of allowing the wine to undergo its second fermentation in a sealed vat instead of in bottle. The carbon dioxide is retained in the wine—in the same way that the cork seals the carbon dioxide into the bottle. There are various processes whereby any deposit in the wine is extracted, and the wine is eventually stabilized, clarified at a lowered temperature, filtered, and bottled under counter pressure. The pressure inside the bottles is the same as that in the tank so that the sparkle is retained in the process of bottling.

As with Champagne, the character of the base wine is of supreme importance, for it must have a certain acidity, otherwise it will go flabby when subjected to the sparkling process. Certain particular problems connected with fermentation have had to be overcome, however. The Muscat grape, for example, which makes the fine sparkling wines of Asti in Piedmont, is high in natural sugar, causing a very violent fermentation; when the Champagne process was first tried in Asti, breakages of bottles and loss of wine were considerable.

There is little advantage in long maturation of such wines in bottle, for many of the wines which make the less expensive sparkling wines will not, unlike Champagne, improve with long term maturation.

Gancia Method

The Gancia method, whereby most of the sweet sparkling wines of Asti are now made, was evolved in the second half of the 19th century after Carlo Gancia had visited Rheims to study the Champagne process; it was, however, not perfected until 100 years later. This method, which has made Gancia so successful that it now has to be made from wines coming from outside the Asti region as well and is simply referred to as Gancia, is an adaptation of both the Champagne

Castello Gancia

and Charmat methods. In general terms, the fermentation of the freshly pressed grape juice is arrested at the stage when the amount of alcohol by volume is no more than about $3°$. The must is then refrigerated, and when the wine is required the fermentation is continued; the wine is then bottled and fermentation completed in bottle. The bottles are eventually disgorged so as to remove any sediment, and the wine is rebottled under pressure from the huge vats into which the disgorging has been done.

This method of fermentation in bottle has been adopted in various forms and with many variations throughout the world. American sparkling wine labels may bear the term "fermented in bottle" to imply the process, while "fermented in *this* bottle" implies that a process closely approximating to the Champagne process has been followed.

Carbonated Wines

These are wines into which carbon dioxide gas has been pumped, exactly as if the wine were put through the type of syphon that aerates still water. In the past, the method has been used to make cheap fizzy wines, unattractive in every way, mainly because of the base wine being inferior. Such wines have large bubbles, slowly rising, and flatten soon. Recently, however, some carbonated wines of quality, such as Langguth's Moselperlwein, have been appearing on export markets. Those that I have tried have not been carbonated to anything like the same extent as fully sparkling wines, and the basic wine to which the carbonation has been applied has been of good quality so that the result has been pleasing and has in no way been a distortion of the wine's character.

Atmospheres

The amount of sparkle in a wine is measured according to "atmospheres"—the pressure behind the cork. The pressure behind the cork of a Champagne bottle is about 5.5 atmospheres, or the equivalent of pressure in the tyres of a double-decker bus. Legislation about what constitutes a fully sparkling and semi-sparkling wine is as yet not rigidly defined in Europe, which is why the whole subject is complex and different sets of regulations apply in different countries throughout the world. In general, however, it may be assumed that a fully sparkling wine will have at least 5 atmospheres pressure and perhaps a little more; a wine that is described as *crémant* or a little less sparkling— like certain wines made in Champagne—will have about 4 atmospheres, and one that is *perlant* or slightly fizzy as little as 2.5 or 1.5 atmospheres. The wines may be differently described on their labels according to the regulations in force where they are made.

Sparkling Wines

Champagne

Non-vintage Champagne

Non-vintage Champagne is the bulk of all Champagne produced, the blends being made up from different years, and the qualities of one year being used to augment and enhance the qualities of others. Most non-vintage Champagne is dry or fairly dry, but the terms used to describe the degrees of sweetness in a Champagne are not as yet subject to legislation and they therefore vary considerably. In general, the main terms indicate the following:

Brut, nature, dry	very dry with little or no added dosage of sugar syrup
Extra-sec, dry	dry or dryish
Sec, Goût Américain	slightly sweetish
Demi-sec, Goût Français	definitely sweet
Demi-doux	very sweet
Doux	extremely sweet

Certain Champagnes are sold as "rich". Although they are sweet, fruity and large-scale in character they are much more than just sweet wines and some of them such as Roederer Rich, should be included in the great dessert wines.

B.O.B.

All Champagne is subject to strict control, and although the great houses are well known, the Champagne houses of authority and importance are not the only names on quality Champagne. Frequently a wine merchant or a restaurant group will order a "Buyer's Own Brand" or B.O.B. This will have been selected by the buyer or shipper to supply a particular clientèle, and all labels must bear an identifying number so that the Champagne can be related to the establishment supplying it, which may even be a famous name.

It is not necessary to keep non-vintage Champagne for any length of time, but it will usually improve a little if kept for a few months after being bought.

Vintage Champagne

This is the wine of a single exceptionally good year, but because of the great climatic variations in the northern vineyards of Champagne, up to 20 per cent of the wine of another year may by law be added to the vintage Champagne of one year. In general, Champagne from a particular vintage is considered to be at its peak for enjoyable drinking when it is between seven and twelve years away from its vintage, although this can vary considerably according to the year. A large bottle of wine also matures more slowly than a small one, and the magnum is often considered to be the ideal wine container. Although Champagne is not usually matured in large bottles because of the possible loss from breakages, a few houses do mature in jeroboams (four bottles). Champagnes destined for larger bottles are decanted into these after having been made and the same applies to quarter bottles or splits.

Pink Champagne

This is a type of Champagne made either by allowing the skins of the black grapes to tint the wine at the time of the first fermentation or by blending in a little red wine of the Champagne region. Most pink Champagne is non-vintage, but some of the great houses make a vintage pink which can be pleasantly fruity.

Blanc de blancs

This is a Champagne made entirely from the Chardonnay grape. In blended Champagnes, the white grapes give delicacy and elegance, the black ones fragrance and fruit. The term *blanc de blancs* alone is not confined exclusively to Champagne and it simply means a white wine made from white grapes. Applied to Champagne, it describes a light and delicate wine, by no means the best. There is also a *blanc de noirs* Champagne made entirely from black grapes; it is not always successful, but interesting to try when you are in the Champagne region, and those of Ay are outstanding.

Luxury Champagne

This is a Champagne made from the finest *cuvées* or vattings, generally from the first pressing of the grapes. The wine is made with even more than the usual scrupulous attention and sometimes with additional refinements such as special bottles like Clicquot's "La Grande Dame", or even in a decanter such as Mercier's "Réserve de l'Empéreur".

The concept of luxury Champagne originated in the depression of the 1920s when Moët et Chandon put on the market a small quantity of a vintage Champagne in a dark green bottle of a shape similar to that used at the end of the 17th century. This, made from their finest vattings, was given the name of Dom Pérignon. Since then many other luxury vattings have been introduced. Some luxury Champagnes are vintage wines, others not, some are *blanc de blancs*; they are all outstanding examples of superlative Champagne. They vary enormously in character, and a comparison of two or three such wines is a wonderful experience. Bollinger's R.D. is unique among these: the letters stand for *récemment dégorgé* which means that the wine has received a greater ageing on its first cork, resulting in a Champagne of greater elegance, nobility and fragrance.

Sweet Champagne Prior to 1914 the majority of Champagnes made for consumption in France and many export markets were at least fuller in style and often sweeter than the majority today. One very great Champagne house would not make what they described as *ce poison* even for the important British market which has always liked a fairly dry wine. There is a right time and place for sweet Champagnes: at the end of a meal, or between times, especially on a cold day.

Single vineyard Champagne Grapes vintaged and made from certain individual vineyards in Champagne are now being made into wines sold as such by their owners. Their individuality has been likened to that of single malt whiskies, and they have great, albeit specialized appeal. The wines of Ay, priding themselves on being those originally founding the reputation of Champagne, are interestingly made from the Pinot Noir, but are of great delicacy and finesse; those of Bouzy, also mostly from Pinot Noir, firmer and capable of considerable development in bottle; those of Cramant, made from the Chardonnay, very light and elegant. These regions also make still wines, red and white, now distinguished as Coteaux Champenois.

Other Sparkling Wines

Sekt Increasing quantities of sparkling wine are being made throughout the world. In Germany, sparkling wine is known as *Sekt*, made chiefly by the sealed vat method, although a little is made following the Champagne process. Virtually any vineyard that can make a fairly dry white wine of a certain

quality can also produce a reasonable sparkling wine. In Italy, Martini, who *Asti Spumante* also make a good, slightly sweet Asti, make a Gran Spumante according to the Champagne process as well as the sealed vat method. There are good wines made by both methods coming on to export markets now from Spain (the *espumoso* wines from Catalonia), Portugal and many other countries.

The white sparkling wines of Saumur *Saumur, Vouvray* and Vouvray are famous for their quality, and the wine makers of this region are particularly proud of the fact that, after the phylloxera plague in the late 19th century, it was they who were invited to assist in the rehabilitation of the Champagne vineyards. The chalk and limestone of these Loire vineyards and the cellars hewn out of the rocks alongside the river make them similar in many ways to those of Champagne; all the quality wines are made according to the Champagne process, but they are not directly to be compared with Champagne, as the grape is the Chemin Blanc.

Non-vintage sparkling wines Only very few sparkling wines that are not actually Champagne bear a vintage date, however they are made; there is no reason why they should do so, for they are at their best while quite young. If you are uncertain about a European wine labelled as having been made by the Champagne method, it can be assumed that it will be moderately to fairly dry unless the label specifically states otherwise. The dryness has nothing to do with the method, but is due to the fact that the public who are able to pay the comparatively high price inevitable with such wines generally prefer a dryish wine.

Inexpensive sparkling wines Sparkling wines made by the sealed vat method are less expensive and therefore appeal to a wider public. They tend to be made in two qualities: dry and slightly sweet. If the label gives no indication one may assume that they will be at least fruity, not bone dry. Wines made from grapes high in natural sugar, such as the Moscato used for Asti, will be naturally sweeter anyway than those from a grape making a bone dry wine, such as sparkling white Burgundy which is made from the Chardonnay.

Fortified Wines

Look-out over the Jerez vineyards, to prevent the grapes being stolen.

Tinajes, big earthenware jars used for fermentation in Montilla.

Barco rabelo, Douro boat formerly used for bringing wine down to Gaia.

Fortified wines are wines that have been strengthened by the addition of a spirit, usually brandy, or in some instances by the addition of a wine concentrate that will bring their alcoholic strength up above the level of table wines. Wines marketed in many wine regions throughout the world often bear the names of sherry and port, but the use of these names is legally protected in many respects. Although some of the wines made in the same way as sherry and port can be good, or very good, I have never tasted one that did not display the characteristics of its own vineyard, its own grapes and frequently variations in the method whereby it was made. At a famous wine tasting which is conducted by the South African authorities, South African sherries are tasted in a range which includes sherry from Spain, but although some confusion is easy in the very sweet ranges, because the sugar masks the basic character of the wine, the finer Spanish wines will stand out in the driest samples—it is not the same when an indifferent Spanish sherry is compared with a first-rate South African.

The detailed methods whereby fortified wines are produced are complex (see pages 28–31). Here it is sufficient to state that sherry is the wine coming from a defined district in Andalucia in the south west of Spain, around Jerez de la Frontera, and that port comes only from a defined region in the upper Douro valley in north Portugal.

Sherry

The sherry vineyards are gently undulating; the finest wines come from the silvery white *albariza* soil that positively shimmers in the sunshine and is the type of chalky soil associated with elegant fine white wines in many regions, as is the sandiness of other parts of the sherry district.

Sherry is made predominantly from the Palomino Blanco grape, sometimes also called the Listan; the Pedro Ximénez, sometimes shortened to PX, grape is mainly used in the sweeter sherries as well as in some of the dry wines. A small amount of Muscatel grapes is also used.

Port

The port vineyards are sloping, often steeply so, and usually terraced; the granite and schist soil is embedded with chips of stone so sharp and tough that the vineyard workers have to wear boots instead of ordinary shoes. In order to plant the vines, it is often necessary to blast holes deep enough to take the roots.

Madeira

Madeira is made in an individual way, although certain of the methods which are employed in port and sherry making are involved. The vines are grown on the steep, terraced hillsides of the Portuguese island of Madeira and trained high, with market-garden crops being cultivated beneath them. There is a slightly toasted flavour to Madeira wines, particularly pronounced in the after-taste. When the island was first discovered by the Portuguese in the 15th century, it was densely covered with trees which they proceeded to burn down; the resulting rich soil seems to give a slightly scorched background taste to the wine.

The four main grape varieties give their names to the principal types of these dessert wines: Sercial, which makes the driest; Verdelho, which is slightly rounder and more subtle, with a fragrance and flavour reminiscent of nuts; Bual (Boal in Portuguese) is fuller and more luscious, darker in colour; and Malmsey, from the Malvoisie or Malvasia grape, makes a dark brown velvety wine with an intense, close-textured fragrance. A few blended wines are also made and sold under the brand names of the houses.

Marsala

This sweet dessert wine was developed by John Woodhouse, the son of a Liverpool merchant, who settled in Sicily in the 18th century and began to export wine from the port of Marsala in 1773. John Woodhouse and his brother supplied Nelson's fleet with the wine, and in 1806 Sir Benjamin Ingham of York founded another *cantina* or lodge in Marsala. In 1833 an Italian senator, Florio, founded a third company and today Florio own the Woodhouse, O'Conner, Ingham and Whittaker establishments. There are many other wine installations in Marsala, and an enormous quantity of wine is still made, although it has declined in fashion in Anglo-Saxon markets since 1851, when 6 per cent of all the wine drunk in Britain was Marsala.

A number of grapes are used in making Marsala, and the soil of the vineyards varies between sand and a pale chalky soil slightly reminiscent of the best sherry vineyards.

Although the different firms produce individual wines, a wine must be aged for at least six months to be labelled Marsala Corrente, three years for Marsala Superiore, and a Marsala labelled Virgine will have been matured for at least five years.

Surprisingly, many different types of Marsala

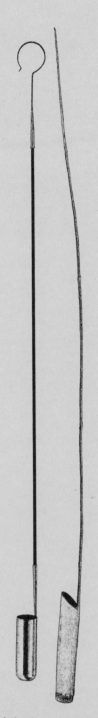

Left, bamboo venencia used at Sanlúcar for manzanilla. Right, whalebone handled venencia for penetrating the *flor* in a fino cask.

are made, from fairly dry and medium dry, to definitely sweet. There is also a flavoured Marsala, known as Marsala all'uovo, blended with egg yolk, and flavours such as almonds, chocolate, coffee, mandarin, strawberry and banana.

It has been my experience that, whereas I have been offered good dry Marsalas with the recommendation that they may remind me of port, I have found them more evocative of an old oloroso sherry with something of the slightly burnt flavour of one of the sweeter Madeiras.

Málaga

The sweet wines of Málaga in Andalucia are out of fashion today, but enormous quantities were drunk before the institution of central heating, when the inhabitants of northern countries needed plenty of full, fruity wines, slightly higher in alcohol than table wines. Bottle labels bearing the name "Mountain" refer to Málaga because the vineyards lie chiefly behind the town of Málaga on the mountain slopes.

The principal Málaga grape is the Pedro Ximénez, with the Lairen, Muscatel and certain others being used in different proportions. Most of the wine is sweet or very sweet, although a little dryish Málaga is also made. At vintage time, some of the Muscatel grapes may be dried on grass mats so as to increase their sweetness by reducing the moisture content. The wine is aged in wood for a year, and during this time it is clarified, graded and then put into smaller casks, from which it may be bottled when it is about ten months old; the finer wines will remain in cask for two or three years. The very best are put through a solera system. Like Montilla, Málaga is not fortified with brandy, because the sweetness of the grapes gives it an alcoholic content varying from 14° to as high as 23°. The labels of Málaga wines may indicate the grapes from which they are made, and also the style, such as seco (dry) and amontillado (medium dry). The most famous wine is Lágrima (meaning a tear), which is a very sweet, dark-coloured wine, intense in flavour.

Tarragona

Up to 1914 vast quantities of the Spanish fortified Tarragona wines were drunk in Britain, where they were often referred to as "poor man's port" or "red Biddy". These were cheap, rather coarse wines, but there are also quality Tarragona wines, notably from one of the most important regions in the area, that of Priorato.

The vines are grown on volcanic soil, from a number of local grapes. Two main types of wine are made, one dry and high in alcohol mainly used for blending, and sweet Prioratos which have their fermentation arrested by the addition of spirit, and therefore come into the category of fortified wines. There are many Tarragona wines that are not fortified, although their strength may well be over that of table wine. They are local curiosities which should be tried by visitors to the region.

Vins Doux Naturels

These sweet wines are hardly ever seen outside the region where they are made: the south and south-east of France, but are well worth trying by visitors to the region. They are above table wine strength and may be made from the Grenache, Muscat, Maccabéo or Malvoisie grapes, fortified by five to ten per cent alcohol, which is added during fermentation. The best known are Muscat de Beaumes de Venise, Muscat de Frontignan, and from the Grand Roussillon region Maury, Côtes d'Agly, Rivesaltes and Banyuls. Some may have their must partly concentrated, and for wines governed by legislation, alcohol, which can be brandy or rum, may be added whenever the natural strength should be increased, though it must not exceed 23°. Vins doux naturels are pleasant drinks, but as they come into the category of fortified wines, heavy customs duty has to be paid on them, and they have never been launched as serious competitors to other fortified wines already established in Anglo-Saxon markets. They are drunk in their own regions as apéritifs, after meals and at any odd time, but they are not easy to fit into the context of contemporary drinking elsewhere. The wines from the Muscat, in particular, are very fragrant, and in the best qualities of the vins doux naturels agreeably honeyed.

Vermouth

Vermouth, which can be and usually is made wherever wine is made, is probably the oldest form of wine in the world and the only one that the ancients would recognize as the type of wine they used to drink. The definition of vermouth is "aromatized wine", and there are references to wine infused with herbs and spices in the records of the ancient Egyptians and on a Sumerian tablet from the end of the third millennium BC. Hippocrates of Cos (460–370 BC), "The Father of Medicine", used wine infused with cinnamon and sweetened with honey for both curative and preventive purposes. Throughout history there are numerous references to vermouth, and as early as 78 AD Diascorides, Nero's Greek surgeon, gives an account of wormwood wine.

It is from the use of wormwood flowers that *Wermut*, the German name for that plant, gave the word vermouth to several languages. For centuries, any wine maker, from peasant proprietors to the owners of great estates, as well as the religious establishments that often acted as hospitals, all made types of compounded wine, using herbs and spices, either for simple, pleasant drinking or for digestive and medicinal purposes.

The best aromatized drinks were made in regions where the ingredients—wine, spices, herbs, berries and certain barks—were easily available and of good quality. In north Italy, Piedmont was not only a wine-growing centre, but the nearby Alps provided a valuable source of supply for the natural ingredients. In 1786 Antonio Benedetto Carpano, who owned a bar in Turin, introduced the first commercially produced, wine-based, aromatized digestive to his customers; it was made up to his own secret recipe which the firm still possesses. At this stage vermouth, as sold in the Carpano wine bar, was individually flavoured according to the orders of the customer: one might prefer a little bitterness, another something sweeter, some preferred certain spices, others perhaps quinine, vanilla or cinnamon. The origin of the famous Carpano drink Punt e Mes dates from a day in 1870 when the bar, opposite the Turin Stock Exchange, was filled with businessmen discussing a drop of one and a half points in certain stocks, and a customer, ordering a particular type of bitter-sweet vermouth, said in the argot of the time "Give me a point and a half" meaning the amount of bitterness he required in his drink.

The Martini and Rossi firm was founded near Turin about 1840, but this establishment replaced a much older concern. The Cinzano family traces its origins back to the 16th century, and a pair of brothers were invested as master distillers in Turin as early as 1757. In France, Louis Noilly was in business near Lyon at the beginning of the 19th century, and, seeing the possibilities of the

Fortified Wines

Sherry

Sherries are classified according to either fino or oloroso style, the finos, which include the manzanillas and amontillados, being drier than the oloroso types. Also included here are the Montilla wines, close relations of sherry.

All sherry is fortified. The degree of fortification, however, can vary the strength of the wine from about 15° to 21°; as the very delicate light wines may become cloudy or even throw a slight deposit when they are subjected to the rigours of travel, a slight additional fortification is often given before shipping sherries for bottling in other countries. The labels of many Spanish-bottled sherries of slightly lower fortification contain a note that, should the wine seem cloudy or have any deposit there is no reason to suspect it is harmful. Of the more delicate sherries, a true sherry lover prefers those that have not been blunted by too much fortification.

Fino Fino is the result of a curious, woolly-looking crust of micro-organisms, known as *flor*, which forms on the surface of the wine in cask. Fino is very pale in colour and so dry that although some of the best selling sherries are also described as dry, most true and wholly unsweetened finos would be far too dry for general taste. Some sweetness is therefore added to the wine, and consequently the term "dry sherry" has virtually no precise meaning, because the permitted limits of sweetness are wide. Very delicate finos can change radically in bottle, and although some people prefer them when they have had a little bottle age, the Spanish taste is for finos with as little bottle age as possible.

Manzanilla Manzanilla is the lightest and driest of all finos and is made and matured at Sanlúcar di Barrameda, on the Atlantic coast. The closeness of the sea imparts what some people find as a saltiness to the bouquet of the wine. It is so delicate that, for export purposes, it may have to be rendered more robust for travel by the addition of fino, or a very slight sweetening. Those who genuinely like a bone dry fino often find manzanilla, away from its home ground, too raspingly dry for their personal taste. It is a curious fact that, if manzanilla is taken to Jerez to mature, it changes its character and becomes an ordinary fino.

Amontillado Amontillado gets its name because it was originally supposed to resemble the wines of Montilla, but essentially it is a matured fino. A true amontillado is a beautiful wine, with a fragrance that is reminiscent of hazelnuts; because of its long maturation it is one of the most expensive sherries. Much of the cheap amontillado sold today is a blend.

Oloroso Oloroso is a full-bodied type of sherry of which there are many styles. It is not sweet, for, as with all sherries, the sugar has been converted into alcohol. A

new Italian drink, set up in business in Marseilles in 1843 with his son-in-law, Claudius Prat. These are only a few of the personalities of the vermouth world.

Vermouth production
There is no detailed procedure or legislation dictating exactly how vermouth should be produced, but the most famous commercial vermouths are undoubtedly those made in and around Turin in Italy, in Marseilles in France and near Chambéry in eastern France. Each vermouth establishment usually makes a specific style of wine, and each may also have a considerable range. Not all Italian vermouth is sweet, nor is all French vermouth dry; indeed, the dry martini, possibly the most famous cocktail in the world, was originally made at Pessione, just outside Turin, where Martini and Rossi have their headquarters.

There are many different methods involved in the making of vermouth, the principal ones being maceration, infusion and distillation, or a combination of two or all of these. Generally, Italian vermouths do not undergo as long a period of maturation as French, but they are made in a different way from the beginning. Such enormous quantities are produced that the local wines of the region do not always suffice to form the base of the vermouth. Some inexpensive vermouths are able to be cheap on export markets by being bottled "high low": imported at two strengths, only a proportion paying the high wine duty. They are then blended and bottled in the country of import.

---

true oloroso is as dry as a true fino or amontillado, but it has more body and a more obvious fragrance and what may be described as a slightly spreading flavour. Oloroso is essentially a matured *raya* which is a type of wine that does not grow *flor*; although some people may think that they detect a slight sweetness in the after-taste, this is caused not by sugar but traces of glycerine produced by the wine. Some olorosos are sweetened for the export markets, but the great—and expensive—olorosos are often drunk in the daytime by many in the sherry trade in preference to the very driest sherries which can be more taxing to the palate.

Palo Cortado
A rarity even in Spain, Palo Cortado is more of an oloroso than a fino, but could perhaps be described as something between the two. It has the beautiful fragrance of an amontillado, with the delicious full flavour of an oloroso.

Dessert Sherries
Brown, milk, and cream sherries were created specifically for the Anglo-Saxon markets, where they are drunk in enormous quantities. The greatest examples of these sweet oloroso wines are magnificent, but they are best drunk with dessert for which they were primarily intended. Cheap sweet sherries which have been created by blending in sweeter wines are not to be despised because they are sweet but the high price of certain world-famous names in the sweet sherry category must be accounted for by their quality. The outstanding example is Harveys Bristol Cream. The port of Bristol has been associated with the wine trade since very early times, and "Bristow milk" is referred to as early as 1634. Bristol Cream, a brand name exclusive to John Harvey, had its origin in 1882, when a lady being shown the firm's Bristol milk was given an even finer oloroso and exclaimed "If that is milk, then this is cream". The then Prince of Wales, later King Edward VII, was offered Bristol milk on one occasion and commented "All I can say is, you've got some damn fine cows".

Old bottled sherry
Earlier generations liked old bottled sherry and laid down enormous quantities of it. For this, a wine of considerable quality that will last well is required; it may well have to be decanted before serving. The sweeter wines are usually the most successful in undergoing long-term maturation in bottle, for anything from 20–90 years.

Sherry-like wines
In many vineyards all over the world there are some very good wines made following the sherry process and the solera system. Sherry producers dislike any of the terms which are used in Spain being applied to these wines, and in all fairness none should be offered as a substitute for sherry. But they can be very good wines, and significantly some of the producers from certain regions are dropping the use of the word "sherry" even with the country of origin on their labels; the wines are simply sold as fortified wines of a particular type.

One misleading circumstance in Britain is that much of the sherry-style wine imported from countries other than Spain may be brought in at two strengths; only a proportion of the imported wine is high strength, and therefore only this proportion pays high strength duty. Fortified wines from what are still generally known as "Commonwealth sources"—South Africa, Australia and Cyprus—enjoy preferential rates of duty. It is therefore not possible to relate quality directly to price as far as this type of fortified wine is concerned, and anyway the finest examples are imported already bottled in the country of origin, ready blended.

Montilla The Province of Cordoba is about 100 miles north-east of the sherry region and the soil is similar. In 1933 when the sherry area was defined, the region of Montilla-Moriles where Montilla, a relation of sherry is made, was independently named. The basic difference between Montilla and sherry results from the colder climate, the higher situation of the vineyards and the variety of grapes, the chief of these being the Pedro Ximénez. Montilla is famous for fermenting its wine in huge earthenware jars, a method used in classical Roman and Greek times. The grapes are not previously dried on mats, but when fermentation finishes the different types of wine are classified as for sherry, and the fino wines grow *flor* like fino sherries. Like the latter, they are pale, delicate and dry apéritif wines. They are matured in wood according to the solera system. The strength of Montilla is sufficiently high naturally to make additional fortification unnecessary except to a very slight extent. The degree of fortification will be according to the style of the house making the Montilla and the export market for which it is destined.

Port

Not very much port is drunk in Portugal, not even the white port which is light enough to serve as an apéritif. It is essentially a wine for colder climates, where the ruby, tawny, crusted, single quinta and vintage ports are among the most popular dessert and after-dinner drinks.

In addition to the English and Scottish names borne by very many world-famous port establishments, there are others wholly Portuguese, making a different but still a quality style of port well worth appraisal.

White port This is made from white grapes only and is therefore not coloured by the pigmentation of the grape skins. It can be dryish or on the sweet side, but should never be pronouncedly sweet, as it is essentially an apéritif wine.

Ruby port This is the young wine, which has probably been in wood for four or five years before going into bottle. It is full-bodied, a bright glowing red and immediately appealing; perhaps it is best enjoyed without much thought, but is at the same time the type of port to order by the glass if you want a warming gentle drink.

Tawny port The finest old tawnies, which are those that port shippers themselves particularly delight in, are specially selected and blended from the very best wines as soon as they reach the lodges. They acquire their beautiful and subtle golden colour by maturation in wood, sometimes for seven years, sometimes for 30 or more. Their smell is as delicious and complex as their colour, the flavour and after-taste fascinating. Fine old tawny can never be cheap, and while other types of tawny port are made by blending red and white ports, the addition on the labels of "fine old" before the word "tawny" signifies the reason for the higher price and the promise of much greater quality. Some tawny ports will also bear the description "twenty years old" or "over forty years old", and this indicates that the youngest wine in the blend must be over the particular age stated on the label.

Vintage-character port Assembled from wines of good years, this type of port has been aged in wood, sometimes for up to four years or until the wines have changed colour. They are ready to drink when bottled, and if you compare them with ruby port, which they may slightly resemble, you will immediately see how much more interesting they are.

Crusted or crusting port This is a full-bodied blend of ports from two or three years, kept in cask for five or six years and then matured in bottle. This type of port forms a heavy sediment known as a crust; it must therefore be decanted before serving. Crusted port can achieve great quality, but should not be confused with vintage port.

Late-bottled vintage This applies to a port of a single year specially selected by the shipper and matured in wood for at least three, but not more than six years. During this time it will have thrown its crust in the cask; it will need no decanting when it is bottled as the crust will have been left in the cask. It is always a very fine wine, a rather lighter version than the vintage port of the same establishment would be and less expensive because of its shorter maturation. It is particularly suitable for contemporary drinking, needing neither decanting nor the extra long-term care of vintage port.

Single quinta port   Quinta is the Portuguese word for a vineyard estate and by extension a Douro estate. Some estates produce port wines of particular individuality which, although rare, are finding their way on to export markets. The most famous estate is indisputably Quinta do Noval, which belongs to the firm of Jose Antonio da Silva, though Quinta da Roeda, "The Diamond of the Douro", is another great name. The late Luiz Porto, who owned Noval, made a number of experiments in wine growing and making and produced the great Noval of 1931 which is regarded by some authorities as the greatest port of the 20th century. The Noval vineyard still contains some of the *nacional* vines of ungrafted vinestocks, even though the phylloxera is still in the soil. A few pipes (one pipe contains 500 litres) are made yearly and privileged visitors are occasionally able to sample this type of old style port.

Vintage port   Each great port house will make its own individual style of wine, and comparisons of these are endlessly fascinating to the taster. But perhaps the most interesting comparisons of all are made with the vintages. Vintage port starts life like other ports, but in the shipper's lodge the head of the firm will decide whether a single wine is of such a quality that he will "declare" it, and set it aside for making into a vintage port. The decision to do this is entirely up to the individual and although in some years many shippers will declare a vintage, only a few will do so in other years. Vintage port is never ready to drink, even in what is described as a light year, for at least eight or ten years, and most shippers are of the opinion that it does not begin to reveal its quality before 12–15 years.

Vintage port remains in wood for only two years before it is bottled—this is the great difference between vintage and other ports. In the past, vintage port was shipped over the bar of the Douro outside Oporto for bottling in the country in which it was to be sold, especially Britain. There a proportion of it would be bottled by the shipper, but wine merchants would also bottle their purchases of vintage port for laying down. Nowadays few merchants have the time, resources and storage space for bottling and storing port, and the shippers handle the wine in increasing quantities. There is, however, a strong tendency for Oporto bottling, unknown before the Second World War but expected to be the rule in the future.

Vermouth

French vermouth from the Marseilles region has a fairly assertive character; it is a robust drink with a pronounced flavouring in which the sun-baked nature of the local vineyards may be detected. Italian vermouths, although well-matured, are not exposed to the atmosphere while they are developing in cask as are many of the French vermouths of Marseilles. They tend always to have a more direct, less subtle style, usually resembling wines from a warm country, immediately appealing and lightly fragrant.

Chambéry   French Chambéry is very light in colour, delicately aromatic and always dry, even in the type that is flavoured with alpine strawberries. This vermouth is sometimes used in mixed drinks, but it should ideally be drunk straight.

Bianco   White vermouth is pale golden in colour and considerably sweetened; people who insist on dry drinks will nevertheless drink quantites of bianco without demur.

Dry Italian   Hardly sweetened at all, dry Italian vermouth nonetheless has a rounder character, quite different from the subtler dryness of a French vermouth.

Sweet Italian   Reddish brown or tawny in colour, sweet Italian vermouth is drunk in enormous quantities in Italy, being the type of restorative to drink after the day's work. In their home regions, vermouths are more often than not drunk straight and not used as an ingredient in a mixture.

Lillet   There are many wine-based drinks such as Lillet, made in Bordeaux; they are really aromatized wines and therefore essentially vermouths although they are categorized as wine-based apéritifs. Vermouths and other wine-based drinks have a place in the world of wine for they fit into the pattern of drinks that has evolved to satisfy social demands, and they also act as palate cleansers, appetizers and digestives. Today, these drinks have lost their medicinal association—except possibly *Bitters* for bitters, which is used in some "pick-me-ups"—and all wine-based drinks can be usefully and agreeably associated with good and fine wines.

Reading a Wine Label

A wine label should give an indication of what the wine is—and preferably more. But regulations governing labelling vary according to countries and even regions, so that there may be more or less information—or information that is of more or less value. (It is also sometimes true that the more elaborate and picturesque the label, the more ordinary the wine. There is an old English proverb which says "Good wine needs no bush", referring to the green branches which used to be hung outside an inn to advertise the new wine.)

Here are some labels that give specific details of wines. Information about how they have been made, the temperature at which they should be served and suggestions as to what they can partner are not necessarily required for the main label, but can be incorporated in tags attached to the necks or back labels. Generally, the basics are: the wine's name, where it was bottled, any vintage or quality or style, and the name of the shipper or importer. Other information is interesting, but only in relation to a particular wine; for example, you may be interested to know the precise alcoholic strength of an ordinary branded wine, but this is hardly relevant to the appraisal of a great wine in the table wine category, unless the importing country requires this. Use labels as guides, not as guarantees or scientific reports—and remember that the marketing man or consultant designer may often, misguidedly, have altered the label of a classic wine in an attempt to give it more "shelf appeal" in a wine shop. But the information the label gives will be subject to detailed control.

Hungary

With this Hungarian wine, the neck label gives the vintage and style, as Szamorodni can be sweet or dry. The label repeats the basic information and gives the wine name—Tokay— plus the makers in Hungary, the exporters, and importers.

Germany

The German labels are possibly the most explicit of all: the three above give contents and alcoholic strength, country of origin and the makers and bottlers. The first label is Tafelwein, simply labelled according to the Bereich (area)— Bernkastel. The second, a Qualitätswein, indicates the general vineyard, Piesport, plus the site—Goldtröpfchen, and the AP number is for ultimate reference. The third, a Qualitätswein mit Prädikat, states the vineyard and site, plus vintage, grape and the way the grapes were gathered—Spätlese—and the fact that it was bottled at the vineyard.

The two German labels above are both estate-bottlings, the first giving all the previous information, plus the fact that the grapes were specially selected—Auslese—and that the wine came from a particular grower. The second actually shows the house, giving the site and particular section of the vineyard— Abtsberg—and the name of the owner—von Schubert— the neck label stating that the grapes were late gathered.

France

The Saint-Véran label—a fairly new AC—indicates the style of wine and from whom it comes, with the address.

The Côte de Brouilly label gives the name and village of the grower, and the name and address of the bottler.

The Loire label specifies the wine and its vintage and states that it was bottled "in the region of production" by the well-known shipper.

The St-Émilion label gives the classification of the wine and its AC in detail, with vintage and the name of the owner, plus the fact that it is a château label. Sometimes estate labels are allowed to be used by firms bottling outside the region of production as a mark of extreme confidence, but then this fact will always be mentioned on the label or overprinted.

The Burgundy labels are both of wines bottled at the estate (mise au domaine), with the name of the particular owner, plus that of the merchant who has selected and shipped the wine. The Corton Charlemagne is that of a specific site, named for the owner, whose address at Pernand-Vergelesses is given.

110

Italy

The Valpolicella label shows the name of the firm making it, states the fact that it is DOC (therefore Italian bottled), indicates the type of wine and where made, gives the address of the firm and the name of the UK agents.

Portugal

The port label gives the shipper, the London and Oporto firms, and indicates the quality—very finest tawny—in addition to the brand name.

South Africa

The South African wine, which in the UK cannot be termed "port", gives the brand name, source of origin and an indication of its style—full ruby—plus the firm handling it in the UK.

Australia

This Australian wine label gives the name and date of the firm's establishment, says where the wine originates and the name of the vineyard, indicates how it should be served, gives the contenance, address of the winery and, at the side, describes the grape variety and gives more details of where it is made.

USA

The two American "Champagnes", which would not be permitted to be so called in Europe, state how the wine has been made and by whom, and give the contents of the bottle plus the alcoholic strength.

The Sauvignon Blanc label also gives the strength, makers and bottlers, and indicates the sort of wine in the bottle and how it should be served.

The labels of the 5 first growths of Bordeaux, that of Lafite being perhaps the smallest label of all for fine claret—and never indicating its position in the classification. The Mouton-Rothschild label, designed each year by well-known artists, gives the number and types of bottles made from the vintage and the specific number of the bottle labelled. Latour gives its position in the classification, so do Haut-Brion and Margaux.

Champagne is the only AC French wine which does not have to bear the words referring to its standing on the label, the term "Vin de Champagne" sufficing. But there is always a reference number, so that the source of any bottle can be traced if required. Here are a non-vintage Bollinger, a vintage Roederer and a bottle of Dom Pérignon, the luxury *cuvée* of Moët et Chandon and pioneer of the use of old-style bottles for such wines.

Spain

The label of this Spanish-bottled sherry gives the name of the establishment, and style of the wine.

The Spanish-bottled Valdepeñas wine gives the vintage, maker (Visan) and their address, plus the type of wine, alcoholic content, bottle content and the name of the importers.

The Shapes of Wine Bottles

Alsace
The flûte d'Alsace, 72 cl capacity and therefore usually slightly taller than German bottles. Green glass. No punt. A similar type of bottle is used for Tavel.

Bordeaux
Classic shouldered bottle for red wines that may have to be laid down. 74/76 cl capacity. Dark to pale green, with punt. Used world wide for red and white wine.

Burgundy
75/78 cl capacity, sloping shouldered bottle, with punt. Medium to dark green for red and white wines. Used for red and white wines throughout the world.

Champagne
Sloping shouldered bottle with punt 80/81 cl capacity and thicker than still wine bottles because it has to resist the pressure inside. Usually dark green. Used also for most types of sparkling wines.

Champagne Magnum
Contains 2 bottles. Magnums of other still table wines exist, but it is worth noting that, although in general they correspond to the Champagne sizes (see page 26), the Bordeaux jeroboam is 5 bottles, and the impériale, also sometimes used for claret, is 8.

Chianti
Flask, holding 1 litre, used for everyday Chiantis, and shouldered bottle for those able to mature for some time when laid down, 75 cl with punt. The Chiantiagianna holds 1.75 litres. The Ruffino bulbous bottle is known as a magnifico. The Orvieto flask holds 75 cl and is called a pulcianello, the 2 litre size is called a toscanello. Usually various tones of green.

Clavelin
Bottle specifically used for the wines of Château Chalon, in the Jura, considered the finest of *vins jaunes*.

Côtes de Provence
Regional bottle for all types of Provence wines.

Franconian Boxbeutel
Used for Franconian white wines and some of the Mauer wines of Baden; evolved from the pilgrim's costrel, or wineskin. Also used for Chilean Rieslings and some other wines throughout the world.

German Wine Bottle
Capacity 70/72 cl. The Mosel bottle is green, the others brown.

Marie-Jeanne
Large bottle used in the Coteaux du Layon, on the Loire, containing 1⅓ litres (1¾ bottles). Dark green.

THE PARTS OF A BOTTLE

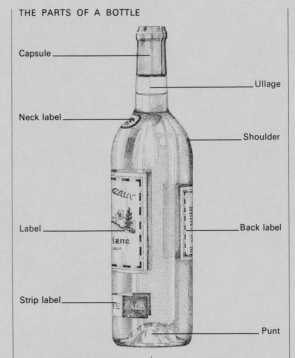

Capsule — Ullage
Neck label — Shoulder
Label — Back label
Strip label — Punt

Port
Left, the sort of bottle associated with port until the present day, but, right, the 19th century type of bottle now being increasingly used in Portugal. The colour is very dark brown, the shoulder definite, the punt deep, and the neck slightly bulbous to take the expansion of a full long cork necessary for a wine likely to be laid down for many years.

Pot
Beaujolais half litre bottle, these days particularly associated with the individual variation used by Charles Piat's establishment, and therefore known as a "Piat".

Tokay
Clear glass half-litre bottle traditional for Tokay, with a very slender neck.

Véronique
Lightly tinted or clear glass, with rings on the neck, used for many different wines, including a number of pinks.

Serving Wine

Serving Wine

Considering that the most modest bottle can be greatly improved by correct service, and that this is in no way difficult, it is extraordinary that even costly wines seldom receive considerate preparation and handling before they are drunk. If the wine is to taste at its best, certain routine procedures are essential. It is true that branded and the most ordinary sort of wines can be bought, brought home and the cork drawn without much impairment of their quality—but they will taste much better if thoughtfully treated.

In order to prepare a bottle for drinking, it should stand up for several hours before required; even if there is no apparent sediment in it, there may be some invisible to the eye which ought to slip down to the base. A fine wine should have at least 24 hours upright, ideally longer, but this depends on the type of wine and the amount of deposit. If for some reason you cannot stand the bottle up, then a red wine should be decanted from its recumbent position.

White, pink and sparkling wines, and all fortified wines intended for drinking before meals, are most enjoyable when cool; some sorts of red wines, such as young Beaujolais and most red Loires are also able to display their fruity charm when cool; other red wines are recommended for serving at "room temperature". But, as has been pertinently remarked, whose room? And what is "cool" as compared with "cold"? These generalizations were first promulgated before the era of central heating, in the days when houses where wine was drunk had real cellars, and when many of the wines that enrich our range of drinks today never travelled beyond their own localities.

The purpose of cooling some wines and bringing others above cellar temperature is so that they shall taste better—some by having their fresh, crisp, fruity delicacy accentuated, others by being allowed to display their wonderful bouquet and lingering flavours as they react to the atmosphere. But a wine that is iced will hardly smell or taste at all, and a red wine that is tepid will not only never recover if it has been hurriedly warmed up, but the drinker will scarcely be able to appreciate its various qualities if it has breathed off most of its bouquet before it reaches the glass and enters the mouth at blood heat. Do everything with wines gently and gradually; they can be cooled or brought to the temperature categorized as "chambré" without any drastic measures.

Wines that are to be cool or chilled may come from a real cellar at almost the ideal temperature for enjoyment. The sweeter they are, the cooler they can be, because obviously they are more assertive and definite, but I think that 7–8°C is

probably the very lowest at which I can enjoy them. Sparkling wines can be 10°–12°C, and most whites and pinks 12°C. Finos and vermouth, and all similar apéritifs come into the same temperature range.

If you draw them from a bin in your home, it is worth knowing that, whereas it will take 2–2½ hours in the middle of most domestic refrigerators to chill them on a warm day, 12–15 minutes in a bucket of ice and water (the mixture is important, ice alone merely chills patches of the bottle), with the level of the water up to the level of the wine, will bring down the temperature perfectly adequately to the same level.

If you are in a hurry to chill a wine, put the glasses into the refrigerator as well—they will be cold when the wine first goes in, and it can be returned for further chilling while you drink the first helping. Don't put ice in wine except for picnics and very informal occasions, but you can use ice cubes to chill glasses beforehand.

Do not keep wines in a refrigerator (the low temperature restaurant dispenser is in a different category) as after some hours they often acquire an odd, flat, unpleasant smell and taste that they never shed.

With apéritifs, such as finos or dry vermouth, the preliminary chilling is really important to polish up the wine; again, the ice bucket is ideal.

Red wines that are young, fruity and crisp, should be lightly chilled—as cool as they might be when brought from a cellar—unless of course you really do prefer them chambré; it is worth experimenting to make up one's own mind, but certainly the wine makers of many hot regions will use the ice bucket for their inexpensive fruity reds on hot days.

In general, red wines of medium and great potentiality show themselves best when at a slightly higher temperature than the lighter reds. If you stand your red wines in your dining room, ideally for 24 hours, they should take on the required "room" temperature. But if you have central heating, or if it is a very hot day, they may become too warm—and can assume an unpleasant, semi-stewed flavour.

But a wine correctly kept, subject to little temperature variation, will retain its prime quality surprisingly: a great Bordeaux shipper kept two exceptional large bottles of very old claret in his office cupboard for 15 years, in the dark but at a temperature of about 18–20°. When opened, they were first decanted, the bottles rinsed, and the wine then poured back into the original large bottles—and the wine was even better with the double aeration, both bottles being still in superb condition even when fifty years of age.

A Guide to Temperature	
Very sweet wines (including sweet sparkling wines)	8–12°C
Ordinary sparkling wines	10–12°C
Most dry whites. pinks	10–14°C
Certain light red wines	12–15°C
Red wines to be served at "temperature of dining-room" (before this heats up)	16–20°C

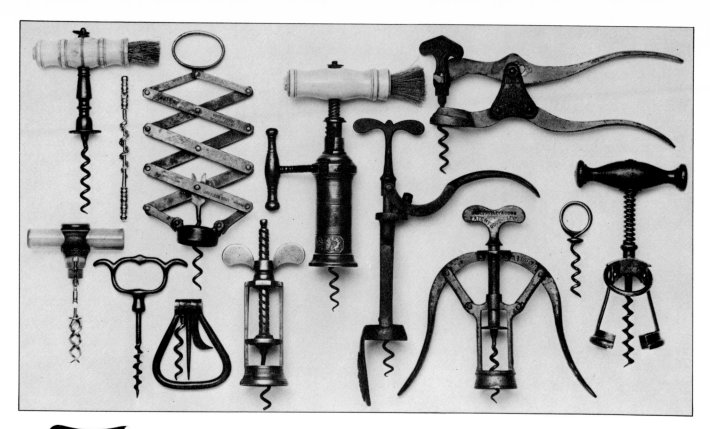

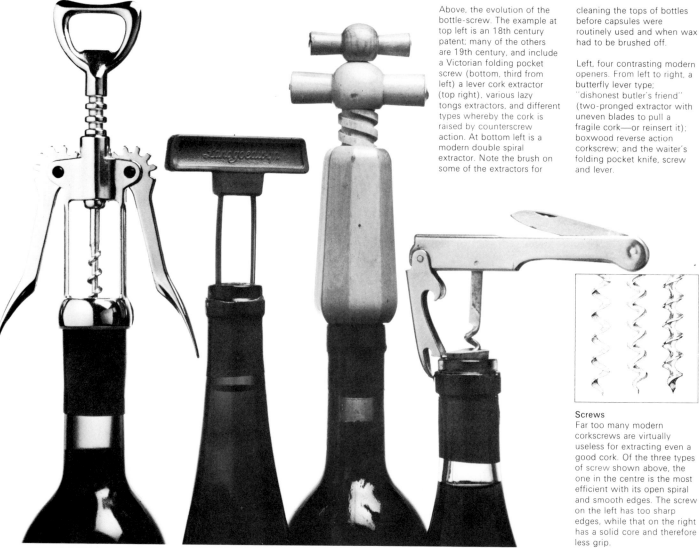

Above, the evolution of the bottle-screw. The example at top left is an 18th century patent; many of the others are 19th century, and include a Victorian folding pocket screw (bottom, third from left) a lever cork extractor (top right), various lazy tongs extractors, and different types whereby the cork is raised by counterscrew action. At bottom left is a modern double spiral extractor. Note the brush on some of the extractors for cleaning the tops of bottles before capsules were routinely used and when wax had to be brushed off.

Left, four contrasting modern openers. From left to right, a butterfly lever type; "dishonest butler's friend" (two-pronged extractor with uneven blades to pull a fragile cork—or reinsert it); boxwood reverse action corkscrew; and the waiter's folding pocket knife, screw and lever.

Screws

Far too many modern corkscrews are virtually useless for extracting even a good cork. Of the three types of screw shown above, the one in the centre is the most efficient with its open spiral and smooth edges. The screw on the left has too sharp edges, while that on the right has a solid core and therefore less grip.

Opening Wine

Never open a bottle in a hurry and never handle a bottle without having a napkin around it—these days bottles do not often split, but if one should do so you can be badly cut. In general, when picking up bottles, hold them at the top, so that you can see labels, possible brightness or deposit—"a bottle by the neck, a woman by the waist" is a wine trade maxim. The napkin should be clean and free of any extraneous smells—detergent, the inside of a cupboard (what the French call the *gout d'armoire*), and of course, scent—nor should your hands smell of soap.

Wipe the top of the bottle, and cut the capsule or remove it entirely; wine poured over a projecting capsule or a cork drawn through one are obvious impediments to enjoyment of a fine drink. Wipe the top of the cork after removing the top of the capsule; don't worry about polishing up the bottle—indeed, with a wine that has a sediment, do not attempt to clean it up or you will shake up the deposit—but the aperture through which the cork is drawn must be clean.

Insert the corkscrew slowly and without jerking, holding the bottle firmly with one hand, and turn the screw down into the cork, ideally aiming not to pierce it right through, as this may result in a few bits of cork falling into the wine. With a cork that looks as if it will be hard, insert the screw at an angle (see illustration). Pull steadily, without jerking, pushing down with the hand holding the bottle if you want extra leverage. When the cork comes out, wipe the neck of the bottle again. The wine is then ready to pour. The action of pouring the wine makes it assume the temperature of the atmosphere, so remember this if you want to give red wine a little more warmth—pour from a slight height, and slowly.

Cutting the capsule
An extra touch to impeccable presentation of a bottle: the centre of the capsule is cut out, a ring cut below the bottle lip and bent to one side, so that the cork can be inserted in this. Whether or not the wine is to be decanted, both bottle and cork are interesting. No wine must contact the capsule.

Removing a cork from the wine
When a cork has been pushed into the bottle it can be extracted either by a single string thickly knotted to lift it from below, or by a loop passed beneath the cork to pull it up. Use a stiff type of string. If you cannot manage this, hold the cork back in the wine with a wooden—not metal—skewer while you pour the first glassful, then the cork will float back in the bottle.

A sticking cork
A cork that sticks tight—as with young, recently bottled wines, where it will swell at once—is most easily drawn if you insert the corkscrew diagonally across the cork, giving greater leverage. Pull steadily and without jerking. For extra power, put the bottle on the floor and, while pulling upwards, press downwards with the hand holding the bottle. The diagonal pull can also be useful if a cork has broken off midway and you have to withdraw the remaining segment without risking pushing it into the wine. If the cork is likely to crumble in any way use the corkscrew almost as a fork, levering the portions of cork out of the bottle but not pushing them into it.

When opening sparkling wines, be scrupulous about never pointing them at anyone—or anything breakable. If they have been shaken up, they will be extra lively, so hold tight to the cork once you have removed the wire muzzle. Turn the bottle, never the cork, else you risk breaking it. You will feel the cork start to rise and eventually leave the bottle with only a discreet sound, and remain in your restraining hand, when you can immediately direct the wine into a glass, not letting it escape wastefully. An over-iced wine will have a very tough cork, so be prepared for trouble if you forget a bottle in the refrigerator. If for some reason you want to "pop" the cork, shake the bottle beforehand. Should you break off the top of the mushroom cork and cannot get it out by holding the bottle under the tap (see illustration), you must release part of the pressure inside the bottle by first piercing the cork gradually, letting out some of the gas, and then drawing it in the ordinary way.

When pouring do not touch the glass with the bottle—it can knock it over. Fill glasses only halfways or two-thirds up, so as to be able to swing the wine around. If you give the bottle or decanter a slight turn as you lift it from the glass there will be no drips.

Wine is conventionally served over the right shoulder of the drinker. Bottles and decanters usually circulate from right to left and port always does, but this, although associated with various rituals, is merely the easiest way for people to serve themselves. With port, the host is allowed a "backhander"—to help the guest of honour on his right—as otherwise they would have to wait until the wine has gone right round the table. It is thoughtless to let a decanter or bottle that is being circulated stand indefinitely before you—others may want to drink. Such an event may provoke the question "Do you know the Bishop of Norwich?", a reference to a former bearer of the title who was niggardly about passing the port. Naturally, if you do not want to drink you do not do so—but there are still a few very conventional tables where even a drop of port must be poured into the glass, traditional from the time when refusal to drink could be considered an insult.

Opening sparkling wine
When opening sparkling wine, always hold the bottle with a napkin. First, untwine the wire muzzle—usually in an anti-clockwise direction—then turn the bottle, not the cork (else you risk breaking off the top of the mushroom) for the quiet emergence of the cork while the mousse rises. If it is extra lively, as if the bottle has been shaken, the wine may tend to spurt, and surge out of the bottle. To counteract this, a brief touch with the palm of the hand on the neck will prevent it from overflowing down the sides.

Retaining the sparkle
If you wish to retain the sparkle in a sparkling wine before the bottle is finished, either use a stopper, such as the one on the right, or cut a wedge out of the original cork, force it back into the bottle and tie it down with string fastening under the flange of the bottle lip.

A sticking cork
If the cork of a sparkling wine sticks too tight for ordinary opening, do not bother with "nippers"—or wedging the cork in the door jamb or in the window. The simplest solution is to hold both bottle and cork, and let a stream of hot water run for a few seconds on the neck of the bottle. The increase of pressure due to the heat will cause the cork to rise easily. The pictures show the bottle uncovered by the napkin, for demonstration purposes, but ideally keep the napkin round the bottle. If the mushroom or top of the cork breaks off, and you are not near to a hot tap, try to pierce the cork gently, to release some of the pressure inside.

Decanting Wine

Hock bucket
Standard wine cooler
Claret jug

Decanting serves two purposes: it enables the wine to be poured off any sediment or deposit in the bottle, and it aerates the wine—sometimes helping a young or reserved, or even stiff, hard wine to show itself to advantage. If you have to serve a red wine while it is still really too young to be at its best, decanting will bring it on. In addition, a decanter looks well on a dining-table, and it is fair to say that an old wine deserves decanting, a young wine needs it. There are some who regard the use of the decanter as an affectation—the only way to make up your mind is to take two bottles of the same wine, decant one the length of time recommended in advance, and then compare this with the contents of the bottle from which you have just drawn the cork. Then decide. I know the Burgundians and many other wine makers seldom if ever decant their wines, but I am a traditionalist and prefer to decant nearly all my wines—including old white dessert wines, which sometimes throw a deposit. Vintage port must always be decanted, to pour it off its crust. (The techniques of opening and decanting port, and "cracking" vintage port, are illustrated on pages 120–121.)

How much time should you give a wine in the decanter? Obviously this depends entirely on the wine: very old, delicate wines should never be over-aired and, unless they are so delicate that you simply pour them from the bottle (pour out all the contents into a series of glasses at the same time so that you do not have to tilt the bottle up and down), it is probably wisest to decant such precious bottles only just before you drink them. You can wait for the wine to bloom in the glass, while if you leave it too long in a decanter you can only regret having lost it entirely. Again, some people like wines greatly aerated and, certainly with some ports and very fine, robust classic wines, it is possible to decant the dinner wines before mid-day, but you have to know the wines involved to risk this.

With most wines, I suggest decanting one to three hours ahead of the meal, the younger and tougher the wine, the longer the time. If possible, consult with the source of supply—there may be something quirkily individual about a particular wine, especially Bordeaux or Burgundy, that will affect the way you handle it. Even cheap reds are enormously improved by being put into a carafe or even a jug in advance of a meal. With fine wines, consider whether you should allow air to continue to reach the wine by leaving out the stopper of the decanter, or whether, from the time it goes into the decanter, it should be stoppered.

Prepare the decanter. It should have been put away clean and dry—any stale drains of

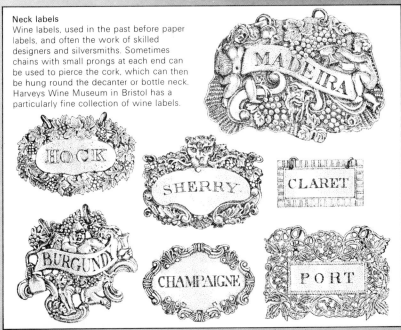

Neck labels
Wine labels, used in the past before paper labels, and often the work of skilled designers and silversmiths. Sometimes chains with small prongs at each end can be used to pierce the cork, which can then be hung round the decanter or bottle neck. Harveys Wine Museum in Bristol has a particularly fine collection of wine labels.

Short-necked decanter

Beaujolais carafe

Ship's decanter

Georgian port decanter

Modern magnum decanter

Modern ship's decanter

Typical
pot-bellied decanter

Victorian funnel

Modern decanter

Small pot-bellied decanter

Short-necked decanter

water will make it smell—with the stopper out. Stained decanters can be cleaned with various things, including anything that will clean false teeth, but they must then be very thoroughly rinsed and dried, or left to drain until absolutely dry inside. Put the decanter by the bottle so that both are at the same temperature. The bottle should have been standing up for at least 24 hours and preferably for longer, especially if the wine has a heavy deposit, so that this can slip down inside the punt.

Prepare all you need to decant—and resolve not to be interrupted once you start: corkscrew, napkin, a light (candle, bicycle lamp or unshielded table lamp), a glass and, if necessary, a decanting funnel, or piece of muslin to filter while decanting.

Cut the top off the capsule or remove it entirely, wipe the top of the cork clean, draw the cork, wipe the bottle neck again. Never pour wine over any part of the capsule. Hold the bottle so that the light shows you clearly either when any deposit moves into the neck of the bottle, or else—but only for the very self-assured—so that you can see any deposit in the flowing wine as you pour it against the light. Pour gently, slowly, ideally letting the wine slide down the side of the decanter without splashing (hence the curve in the funnel). Never tilt the bottle back, but, when you see any sediment appear, change to the glass to receive any final drains of bright wine. This can be added to the contents of the decanter —or, if you prefer, it can be used as a preliminary tasting sample.

In the illustrations on this page, traditional decanting procedure is seen with the use of bottle and light with decanter.

Next, wine is poured through clean muslin (*not* old handkerchiefs laid in lavender) and the resulting deposit displayed. The bottle of a fine wine should be shown to interested diners, and the bottle heel or dregs can be filtered and used in cooking.

The top set of pictures on the opposite page show how it is possible to decant from the edge of a table, without using the bin basket. If you find it easier to use a basket, remember that, once the bottle has been slid gently into it, you must hold it so that it does not slip up and down (and don't hold the edge of a wicker cradle or basket near a candle flame). Always keep the bottle at the angle at which it has been lying in the bin or rack even while you draw the cork. Here the wine is held in a piece of wood, the cork is drawn, and the wine poured into the funnel with the bottle very gradually inclined, one arm holding the bottle while the other lowers the decanter below the level of the table.

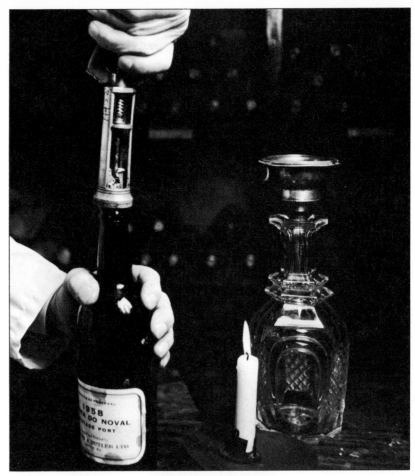

Opening and decanting port
Above, drawing the cork. Have a napkin ready to wipe the dirt away before pouring. Far left, a cellarmaster pours the first sample into a glass to check the wine is clear, before (near left) pouring the rest through the funnel into the decanter. The funnel is curved so that the wine will slide down the side of the decanter without splashing.

Filtering while decanting
Using a muslin filter in a plastic funnel, decanting port. Left, the wine is poured steadily through the filter. The candle, or other light source, is needed to see when the sediment appears in the shoulder or neck of the bottle. Right, the reason for decanting and filtering. In this illustration, the whole bottle has been poured into the decanter, to show what a port bottle may contain but normally the sediment or crust will remain in the bottle, and the dregs of the wine can be filtered later and kept for cooking purposes.

Opening and decanting without disturbing the sediment
Keeping the bottle in a horizontal position at all times gives less risk of disturbing the sediment or crust. Upper left, knocking the wax seal away from the neck and cork of a port bottle. Upper right, pulling the cork. Far left, before the cork is completely free, have the decanter and funnel ready below the bottle to catch the flow of wine that will follow the cork out. Near left, tilt the bottle gently, lifting it by the punt, as the bottle empties. Above, the results; and check that the wine is clear and bright.

The pictures on the right demonstrate taking the neck off a bottle of old vintage port, in which the cork may be fragile, crumbling easily. With a pair of heated bottle tongs, the neck is grasped and the top breaks off with the help of a hard tap with the back of a knife. Without tongs, you can use heated wire, or the back of a carving knife or similar instrument and, having scored under the neck ridge, strike upwards sharply, under the ridge, when the top will come off. If you wish, insert the corkscrew first, so that, as the bottle top breaks, you can lift off the entire top. But as all these procedures require some skill and practice, ask a merchant to decant for you (into a clean bottle) rather than risk ruining a bottle.

Decanting is far easier—and makes much more difference to wine—than it sometimes seems. The correct handling of wine is something in which the true wine lover takes great pride and drinkers appreciate in detail; but the greatest wine in the world can be ruined by maladroit decanting. Never decant in a hurry, break off in the middle, or let your movements become jerky. If you decant in front of guests, involve them in the small ritual. When they find that a wine they know seems better because of the way you have handled it, you will have your reward.

"Cracking" vintage port
For fragile corks, hot tongs are applied to the scored neck, which is then tapped, with a knife. The napkin is in case the bottle breaks. Then the top of the neck, and with it the cork, is gently eased away.

Wine Glasses

The plainness, the stem and the shape of the bowl of a wine glass make a great difference to the enjoyment of wine. In former times some people used tinted glasses to hide from their sensitive eyes the "flyers" in white wines; nowadays there are some who impair the view of a wine's beautiful colour by cutting or engraving, while others try to enjoy the bouquet of a fine wine from glasses triangular in shape, that simply direct the smell to the ear lobes of the drinker. Some people choose unnecessarily thick glasses. All these "refinements" can get in the way of the wine.

It is quite unnecessary to have different glasses for different wines, but, if you are comparing several, it can avoid confusion if you mark them, either with a chinagraph pencil or slip of paper stuck on the foot. Sometimes people find that a particular wine is always at its best in a certain sort of glass, but this does not necessarily mean that white wines need smaller glasses, red wines big ones, as is sometimes asserted.

The wine regions often have special glasses, such as the Treviris glass of the Mosel, of a shallow onion shape, with a particular pattern of cutting; there is the curved bowl of the Vouvray glass, the rounded Bourgueil glass, and the tranchette or Champagne pomponne (shown opposite) which has to be emptied before it can be put down, like a stirrup cup. But this is pleasant regional wine promotion, not essential to wine appreciation. Although it is probably wise to have one type of glass for everyday use and something finer for special occasions, suites of glasses are quite unnecessary. Many people wonder that a thin glass, preferably of crystal, is advocated for the finest wines—but if you compare drinking the same wine out of a cheap glass and a fine one, you will see how the delicacy and unobtrusive quality of the finer glass actually seems to make the wine taste better. Of course, everyday wine can be enjoyed out of a tumbler, a plastic goblet or a metal—even a precious metal —drinking vessel. But for a good to fine wine, the sight, smell and feel of the wine, as well as the flavour, are all ideally displayed in a classic wine glass, as thin as you can afford.

The Perfect Glass
Three versions of the ideal wine glass. Left, two examples of the tulip shape; right, the Paris goblet. Anything can be served from these to advantage, and they can cost pence from a chain store or pounds if made of finest crystal. The perfect glass is colourless, for you to enjoy the colour of the wine, on a stem so that you can swirl the wine round easily, and avoid warming a cool wine. It has a bowl of generous but not vast size, which is filled by two-thirds or a half. The bowl should curve inwards slightly, to hold the bouquet, but everyday wines may be served in glasses with straight sides. The thinner the glass, the less it obtrudes on the enjoyment of the wine —the finest crystal actually gives to the pressure of the hand. All the shapes shown are ideal for any wine—still, sparkling, fortified.

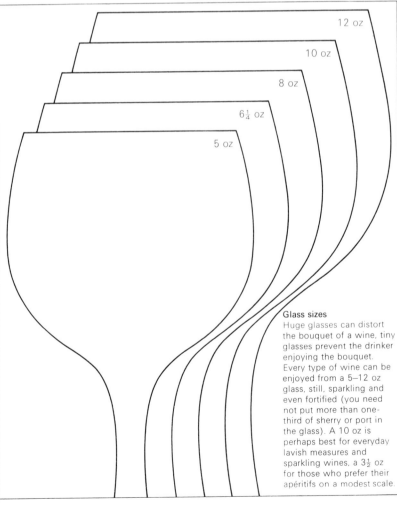

12 oz

10 oz

8 oz

6¼ oz

5 oz

Glass sizes
Huge glasses can distort the bouquet of a wine, tiny glasses prevent the drinker enjoying the bouquet. Every type of wine can be enjoyed from a 5–12 oz glass, still, sparkling and even fortified (you need not put more than one-third of sherry or port in the glass). A 10 oz is perhaps best for everyday lavish measures and sparkling wines, a 3½ oz for those who prefer their apéritifs on a modest scale.

Carousel
Traditional in the Palatinate, a carousel is a revolving frame, holding glasses in numbered sockets. At wine houses, and even at home, people can share a selection of wines served in a carousel, which may hold up to a dozen different wines for sip by sip appraisal.

Regional glasses
Some of the basic shapes that can provide a variation at table and enhance a progression of wines, together with all-purpose classic glasses.

Anjou
The squared-off rather shallow bowl is widely used for Anjou wines in the Loire.

Hock
Old style *römer*, nothing to do with rum, but the glass traditionally used formerly for Rheingau, Franconian, Nahe and some Mosel wines. The Baden *römer* has a shorter stem. These glasses can be very elaborate.

Baccarat crystal glass
The perfect glass for the finest red and white wines, made of crystal at the Baccarat factory in eastern France, and so fine that it will give slightly to the pressure of the hand and the bowl will sway on its stem.

Copita
The word means "a little mouthful" and this is the traditional glass as used in Jerez for sherry, ideal for appreciating the wine's bouquet.

Alsace
Like everyday German wine glasses, those of Alsace resemble a chopped-off onion. Often they have a green stem, as do Mosel glasses, whereas Rhine wine glasses may have brown stems, like the bottles.

Port or dock glass
This is the type of glass used in many tasting rooms; the international tasting glass has evolved from it, as the slight funnel shape of the bowl facilitates detailed appraisal of young wines.

Victorian cut-glass saucer
Just deep enough for wine but suitable for cups or deliberately pretty drinks. Some people like the effect of cutting and engraving on the wine's colour.

Tranchette
Resembling the stirrup cup, the tranchette was evolved in French inns so that travellers had to drink up and set the glass down empty. It was also a deterrent against stealing.

Cognac
Like the copita, dock and international tasting glasses, this is a perfect glass for any fine spirit and is traditional in Cognac, both for tasting and drinking.

Above, antique solitaire, used at table when several wines are to be drunk from the same glass, so that they can be rinsed, and dried on the napkin. Left, glasses ideal for sparkling wines, as contact with the air is kept to the minimum and the wine's vivacity prolonged. The inverted isosceles triangle, like the traditional flûte de Champagne, is also good.

Care of glasses

Ideally, never use soap or detergent on wine glasses, only hot water, but, if you must use detergent, rinse thoroughly—detergent on a glass can discolour a wine and give it an unpleasant smell. Dry only with clean cloths also wholly free of detergent and never used for anything except glasses. Store upright. If you turn glasses upside down, they may acquire the smell of anything on which they are resting; to keep dirt out of them, cover with paper or a clean cloth.

When you dry or polish a glass, do not put thumb or fingers inside, else you risk breakages—stuff the drying cloth into the bowl of the glass and work it round from the outside. A good polish is more easily obtained if you do not let the glasses drain and get cold.

Wine with Food

The selection of wines to go with food so that they together form a harmonious meal is at once one of the most fascinating and yet most difficult things to do satisfactorily. The wines and money available obviously influence the choice, but surprisingly often people pick wines almost at random to accompany certain foods or dishes without any thought as to the part they will play in the meal and progression of wines as a whole. For this reason, I think, many people never come to truly understand why wine is so fascinating, they have never had wines appropriately selected in relation to the food, the circumstances and the other drinks.

There are also those who are rigid in their choice of what to drink with what and are unwilling to experiment. This is equally limiting, and because a Frenchman would choose a French wine to go with a certain type of dish, or an Italian a wine of his own region, this is no reason for saying that their personal preferences should dictate the choice of everyone else. Once you make up your mind that there is only one way to choose wines for food, you may as well hand the whole matter over to a caterer, for there is no personal satisfaction in blindly following the opinions of anyone else, no matter how distinguished and authoritative.

But since hospitality and the sharing of food and drink should be planned with the aim of giving pleasure, it is helpful to know certain combinations and arrangements that through the times have proved enjoyable and therefore have established certain traditions. Once you know the rules and have gained a little experience, it is possible to bend, break and re-create them. The more you learn about wine, the more you will probably tend to choose food to set off wine rather than select wine after choosing food. It should also be an encouragement that, whereas it is possible to serve the finest wines in the world with very simple, but first quality food, second-rate pretentious food will never be made any better by the choice of second-rate pretentious wines. Indeed, wine is perhaps the supreme convenience food, because it can transform the most straightforward fare into a fine meal, yet the most elaborate and extravagant *cuisine* can do nothing to improve an indifferent bottle.

In general, the wine programme of a meal should be consistent: with a casserole something good in the everyday category; with a regional dish that comes from a wine region, the wine of that region; with what is often described as coarse fare, robust, straightforward, uncomplicated wines; and with superb simple food, fine and great wines, which on special occasions may be the stars rather than the food. Naturally, if you

Punch bowl, 1704, by Samuel Wastell. These bowls are sometimes called "monteiths", after a Scotsman who was said to have worn a scalloped cloak. Many had notched removable tops over which the glasses could be hung.

are giving a mixed party where only a few people will wish to talk seriously about wine, good rather than great wines are likely to be the most acceptable, with perhaps one special treat for those who can appreciate it, and for those who may suddenly realize how great a wine can be.

Apéritifs

When choosing wine for a meal, it is essential to consider all the drinks involved, and this means the apéritifs as well. Any very fine or delicate wine will be wasted on a palate already stunned by quantities of spirits or complicated mixtures of some piquancy. At the same time, something stronger than wine, even fortified wine, admittedly acts as a social ice breaker. If spirits must be served, I would suggest that the first course of the meal is a "blotting paper" dish and served without any wine at all. Some spirits do not seem to alter the palate as much as others: brandy, being a grape spirit, is traditionally permissible before wine, and vodka, which is very neutral, might come into the same category, as well as certain of the light or malt whiskies which leave the palate clean. In many instances, it is not the spirit itself that most affects the palate, but the additives, such as tonic, sparkling, fruit-flavoured drinks, and fruits themselves, such as lemons or limes. Much also depends on how much is drunk: after several double measures of any spirit nobody will be in a state of sensitivity to obtain much enjoyment from fine food and wines. A single dry martini, a gin and tonic, or even two, will not stun the palate. But it should be possible, on occasions when fine wines are to be served, to keep oneself ready to appreciate them to the full by settling for the appropriate apéritifs. There are plenty of suitable apéritifs, such as good dry, sparkling and still wines, dry vermouths and wine-based apéritifs, as well as the drier fortified wines.

Serving a single type of drink before a meal also simplifies entertaining, and many people prefer not to drink vast amounts before eating; those who inevitably crave for ultra-large amounts of strong drinks can indulge themselves before they arrive or put up with the two or three helpings of an apéritif which even the most generous hosts and hostesses consider ample.

The Sequence of Wines

Traditional rules decree that wines should be served in the following order: dry before sweet, young before old, and white before red, with the exception of sweet and dessert wines. Some people would also say Bordeaux before Burgundy, but I personally have reservations about the advisability of serving both at the same meal anyway.

Above, a pair of coasters, by William Burwash of London, 1813. Left, a Victorian tantalus. These could be locked to prevent the servants stealing the contents.

Dry wine before sweet makes sense because you cannot enjoy a fine dry wine if you have previously been drinking something sweet or even slightly sweet. The sherry served as an apéritif may have been vaguely categorized as "dry", but unless you have tasted it and are sure that it is drier than the Muscadet or white Burgundy to be served with the fish course immediately afterwards, choose a more robust white wine for the fish or change the sherry for one that is definitely dry. Similarly, white port, white vermouth and many wine-based apéritifs, although dryish, may be too sweet for a fine dry white wine to follow them satisfactorily, and the fact that they are higher in alcohol than the table wine may overwhelm it even more. Again, the finest sparkling wine will outweigh even a great white Burgundy if this is served immediately afterwards; ideally, a "blotting paper" course should be served between the two wines, or at least some substantial canapés with the apéritif. Canapés should be carefully chosen, however, as anything spicy, piquant or unctuous, such as stuffed eggs, can dull and eventually tire the palate. It is rather noticeable that when the wine trade entertain, there are seldom cocktail canapés apart from a few nuts or biscuits offered unless, of course, the occasion is more in the nature of a buffet.

Assuming that a very dry wine should usually not be served after even a slightly sweet one, it is equally logical that a bone dry wine should not be served at the end of a meal; if the wine served immediately before it has been fairly full-bodied and with a touch of sweetness about it, such as in fine mature Bordeaux or red Burgundy, a dry wine at the end will taste far less good than it should. For this reason, a bone dry Champagne or blanc de blancs, which is sometimes served as a toast with birthday or wedding cake at the end of a dinner, would probably be more enjoyable if it had been served earlier, and a slightly fruitier, sparkling wine substituted at the end. The finer qualities of German wines are sometimes served at the start of a meal, to be followed by a red wine that might otherwise taste perfectly good had it not been preceded by a slightly sweet wine, even just a Spätlese. Dry wine before sweet is generally a safe policy, providing that you can appreciate the varying degrees of dryness and sweetness.

Young before old is usually a wise course when the same type of wines are being considered because a wine that has undergone long-term maturation and is in its prime will make a young wine, not fully developed and perhaps not yet in harmony with itself, seem unsatisfactory afterwards. But I think that this principle should not be too rigidly observed; it is naturally sensible to progress from young to old if you are comparing red Bordeaux, Burgundy or German wines in the progression at a meal, but if a dessert wine is then served, its completely different character may well justify choosing something younger than the wine immediately before it; if the wine served as an apéritif or with the first course is older than the next wine but nevertheless vigorous and far from declining, old before young can be perfectly acceptable. For example, at the beginning of a meal, a white Burgundy, Alsatian or German wine might well be served that was three or four years older than the first red Bordeaux or Burgundy or whatever red wine was to follow. A large gap in years is unwise, however, as the first wine may then be so fine that anything coming after will be an anti-climax.

This leads to the important fact of constructing a meal so that the last wine served is the finest of all. There is something inevitably unsatisfactory about a dinner that starts with a superlative wine and then declines in quality. A good wine at the beginning of a meal must be followed by better wines as the dinner progresses. There is an added advantage to this, because, just as it is easier to taste in company with other people, so does a great wine invariably taste much better if it is introduced by one that is good but of lesser quality. Therefore, *at least* two wines of the same kind should always be served at what may be called "wine dinners"; interestingly, the first wine will also taste better if you go back to it after trying the finer one; they seem to show off each other's qualities.

As at a wine tasting, it is unwise to range too widely between wine regions in the course of a single meal. It is not necessary to stick rigidly to the wines of one country, but just as even the best peasant dish would not feature in a menu including a great classic dish, so some consistency as to the weight and assertiveness of wines is prudent. A white Burgundy may be a superb introduction to red Bordeaux, a certain type of white Rhône wine might precede a great red Rioja, a Balkan Riesling could precede an Italian Barolo, or a New World Chardonnay or hock-type white wine might go before a red Burgundy. But I would not vary the weights of wines so as to serve, for example, a delicate Mosel before a great red

Rhône, a fine Frascati before the best north African red, or an Alsatian Gewürztraminer before an ordinary Cabernet Franc, either from Europe or the New World. The palate becomes confused by constantly adjusting itself to such very assorted wines, however good each may be. The ideal is to progress from good to great, light to weighty, easy-going to important—and, usually, from inexpensive to more expensive.

Bordeaux and Burgundy

In theory, there is no reason why claret and Burgundy should not be served at the same meal, but I have never known it work. If the red Bordeaux is outstandingly charming, the Burgundy may seem obvious; if the Burgundy is weighty, the claret may seem too light—though no claret lover would ever admit that there is not a red Bordeaux wine for any and every occasion, even at need to overpower a great red Burgundy! The convention of former times, still occasionally followed at formal banquets, is to serve red Bordeaux or several red wines with that section of the meal that ends with the entrée or meat; thereafter will follow a sorbet, such as a neutral or very lightly flavoured water ice to refresh and change the palate, and often traditionally accompanied by a Russian cigarette. The game will then be served with the Burgundy or any other red wine. But if you want to compare two or three wines from great estates, famous shippers, or different vintages, you will be wise to stick to one type of wine chosen as the star of the evening. Side-by-side comparison of completely different wines for a study session dinner is naturally possible and can be most profitable to a serious taster, but is not something that I would recommend for a general party.

Number of Wines

Can one wine be served throughout a meal? To this question, the textbook answer is Champagne. But even in the Champagne region, a red wine will usually be brought out to accompany the cheese, which in France is always served after the last meat dish and before the sweet. Few people would enjoy a sparkling wine throughout a meal that consists of fairly substantial food, such as roasts or game, though such a wine is possible with fish or light poultry dishes. For an all-purpose wine for a light meal and possibly also for the apéritif, choose a wine made from the Riesling or Traminer grapes; for a heavier meal, a wine made from the Chardonnay; both are whites which will stand up to any type of meat.

The final number of wines depends on personal taste; it is not necessary to have a separate wine with every course, although it is enjoyable for a

Vase-shaped wine cooler, 1827, by John Bridge.

special occasion. However, wines of great quality served with the principal course, meat or fish, should ideally be finished before the sweet, and certainly before any salad. The French tradition of serving cheese with which to finish the wine is sound, but in Britain cheese is served after the sweet and at formal dinners not at all. Savouries, which, especially at men's dinners, often replace the sweet course, are usually of such a nature as to conflict violently with any fine wine.

Pairs of wines for comparison can be interesting with the main courses; few would want to do a serious comparative appraisal of several great sweet or dessert wines, although I have known both the Madeira and port trade to have two decanters of wines at the end of a meal—one to introduce the finer one—as I have suggested with table wines.

In conclusion, the number of wines with a meal is entirely personal; one wine may serve as apéritif and go on through the meal. There may be an apéritif wine and a single wine with the meal, perhaps a dessert wine afterwards, if not actually with the sweet. Or you may choose to have an apéritif, no wine with the starter and perhaps two red wines with a meat dish, or a white wine with the first course, followed by a single red. At grand occasions, with a fish course after the starter and before any meat or game, a second white wine may be served before a red one. For a wine lovers' meal, you may choose to serve two or more red or white wines with the main course for detailed comparison and appreciation. The wine that comes at the end of the meal should be equally important to what has gone before, but it may be more enjoyable to serve a dessert wine on its own. Served with the last course, a dessert wine should be as least as fine as the wines preceding it, and finer if possible.

In the picture of apéritifs opposite, the drinks include a pitcher of dry martinis (which could also hold Daiquiris), Champagne, fino sherry, Alsatian Riesling, Sercial Madeira, white port and a glass of dry vermouth. Other apéritifs might include a selection of vin blanc cassis, Lillet, Dubonnet, St Raphael, white vermouth, any dry sparkling wine, amontillado sherry or Pimm's No. I. It could also be Punt e Mes, any dry white wine, a brandy-based sparkling wine cocktail, a lightish straight malt whisky with spring water, or vodka and tonic. If any acidic liquids, such as tomato juice or unsweetened fruit juices are served, avoid any delicate wine immediately afterwards. Although any liquid can be poured over ice-cubes, a cocktail or mixed drink tastes vastly different when poured over finely crushed ice; rather than serve drinks "on the rocks", it is generally far better to chill the bottle.

Wine with Food

It is not essential to serve wine with a first course, even at an important occasion. There are certain foods that simply do not combine with wine, turning its taste into something unpleasant; these types of food include anything dressed in vinegar, especially malt vinegar, pickles in general, grapefruit and fruit cocktails. A touch of wine vinegar or lemon or a small quantity of mild pickle will not usually do any lasting harm to the palate, but it would be unwise to serve a delicate or fine wine. Any aggressively piquant foods, such as fresh peppers and heavy dressings of garlic or curry will tend to assault the palate; most egg dishes will dull it, and eggs even on their own can sometimes make a fairly robust wine taste strange and disagreeable. In considering wines for a first course, it is important to take account of the apéritifs served beforehand and the wines to follow with the main course. Immediately after apéritifs of spirit-based mixtures or of a fairly assertive wine, including Cham-

pagne, no ordinary wine can make even a moderately good impression. It is perfectly feasible to continue serving apéritifs with a starter or to accompany dishes, such as pickled herrings, with the spirits traditionally served with them in their homelands. Schnapps and vodka can be excellent with strongly flavoured fish.

Canapés served with apéritifs are often substantial enough to provide a type of starter, and many people welcome this form of "blotting paper" before the main dishes and wines.

The Chambéry vermouth shown in the picture on the left is utterly dry, fresh and stimulating with a delicate, herby back-taste, and could easily accompany such plain foods as creamed soups, asparagus, melon, artichokes and avocado pears. Dry Marsala, fino, amontillado or dry oloroso sherry, dry white port, Sercial Madeira or a dry, moderately full-bodied white wine of medium quality could also be served with these types of starters.

Starters

Thin Soups
No wine is necessary, but if a soup includes red wine, port, sherry or Madeira, serve the same wine.
Consommé: A spoonful of dry or medium sherry or ruby or tawny port can be stirred into each portion to enhance it. Do not, however, ruin the delicate flavour of a great soup with anything alcoholic unless the recipe specifies its inclusion.
Broths: These soups can take an addition of a little red or white wine, vermouth or fortified wine. If the broth is substantial, serve a full red wine with meat or game based soups, a fullish white wine or vermouth with fish-based soups. Fish soups including any spirit should be served without wine.

Thick Soups
Soups thickened with cream, eggs, flour, potatoes or pulses may be accompanied by an amontillado sherry, dry oloroso, dry Marsala or Madeira.
Creamed: Brandy, vermouth, dry sherry may all be added to these soups just before serving. It is not necessary to serve a specific wine.

Cold: These do not require any wine, but small quantities of any apéritif wine may be served.

Egg Dishes
These types of starters need a fairly assertive dry white wine to cut across them. A cold dish may need something robust, while a hot egg dish can take an ordinary red or white wine, according to the sauce to follow. Eggs in aspic with foie gras can take a slightly finer and fuller white wine; eggs in tomato sauce (*portugaise*) can be accompanied by a red or white wine of ordinary style. Eggs poached in red wine in the Burgundy style need a red wine, preferably an ordinary Burgundy. But as eggs change the palate radically, any delicate wine should be avoided.

Pasta and Rice
These are rather coarse foods and the seasonings may make them more so; coarsish wines should therefore be chosen. The basic components or meat or fish determine whether a red or white wine is served; if cooked with cheese and seasonings, either may be drunk.

Fish
Smoked: The assertiveness and oil of smoked fish make wine unnecessary; with smoked eel, serve Dutch gin, with herrings, schnapps, and with smoked trout certain types of straight malt. With smoked salmon, there are many possibilities from red wine, old Sauternes, fairly assertive white Burgundy or a Chardonnay, schnapps, London gin or any bone dry or dry white wine.
A *vinho verde* would be a good choice, but anything with moderate acidity will do.

Pickled: Serve with spirit-based drinks or neat spirits, such as schnapps or vodka.
Roes: Vodka, dry or still Champagne, fine dry *pétillant* or still white wines go with caviar; schnapps or ouzo suits taramasalata, lump-fish roe (mock caviar) and red caviar. With ordinary hard or soft roes, offer a fairly assertive but dry or bone dry white wine. With roes served as savouries, give whichever wine was served with the previous course, or the spirit to be served afterwards.
Fish Pâtés: These tend to be delicate in flavour, though fairly fat. Serve the type of wine you would offer with the fish that forms the basis of the pâté.

Cold Cured Meats
Curing usually makes meats unsuitable for any fine wine, but an assertive white or a moderately robust red may be served. Virtually any wine is wasted with ham with melon or pears, but schnapps or a spirit can be served in small quantities.

Frogs' legs: A crisp white wine goes well with fried frogs' legs, and something a little more full-bodied if the dish involves a sauce, especially if garlic flavoured.
Snails: As for frogs' legs. In Burgundy, a red or white wine of ordinary quality may be served with them, assertive enough to cut across any garlic butter.

Pâtés
A red Loire or a fullish very dry white wine are the most suitable with fatty pâtés, such as pork-based rillettes. With ordinary meat pâtés, a red wine of moderate quality would be a good choice, and with game pâtés a more assertive wine, especially if the recipe includes a spirit. Offer a delicate white or red

with liver pâtés, but with foie gras or truffled liver pâté, a type of wine that will cut the richness and balance the content, such as still Champagne, top quality Rieslings. With foie gras without truffles, serve a Gewürztraminer of especially stylish type, very dry big white wines in general, or by total contrast, the great Sauternes and Barsacs.

Vegetables
There is no need to serve any wine with cold vegetables (*crudités*), especially if these are dressed with a garlic-flavoured mayonnaise (*aioli*) or with spiced sauces. With asparagus served cold in a vinaigrette, do not offer any wine, but served hot with melted butter, this green asparagus can well be set off by a dry to medium dry white with moderate body, or with a carafe white. An assertive ordinary red or white wine is best with asparagus in hollandaise sauce.
A dry Marsala can be served with avocado dip or soup, but no wine is necessary for avocado vinaigrette or if they are stuffed with crab or prawns in mayonnaise.

Wine with Food

Shellfish are usually partnered with a fairly dry or even bone dry white wine with crisp fruitiness because most people find that this is most enjoyable with any slight saltiness retained in the fish. Champagne and quality dry sparkling wines are also possible, especially with shellfish served on their own as a luxury snack and not as part of a meal. Most *crémant* and *pétillant* wines are suitable with shellfish, though not, in my view, those made from the Moscato or similar fruity grape. Dryish pink wines, such as those of the Loire or Rhône, can be drunk with shellfish, and indeed any of the river wines, Loire, Rhône, Dordogne, Mosel, Ebro, provide some of the best accompaniments for all shellfish dishes.

With a platter of assorted seafood, including shellfish and crustacea, a moderately robust wine is good; it should be selected to partner the most important element in the assortment, crab, langouste, oysters or prawns. With local shellfish, try to drink a local wine; this is obviously possible in the Mediterranean, and the slight additional toughness and coarseness of some local wines is ideal. The more northern dry wines are better choices with cold-water shellfish, such as scallops; choose wines with a touch of distinct quality for shellfish of prime quality. I would choose a wine with a certain nervous intensity, such as estate Sancerre, some white Burgundies, even estate white Graves to go with the finest oysters, crab or lobster, served plainly.

The most important factor determining the choice of wine is the sauces, stuffings, garnishes and methods of cooking. Mayonnaise and egg sauces need a wine to cut through the unctuousness; with a vinaigrette, a big, obvious wine is suitable, and any dressing that incorporates strong herbs or piquant flavourings need a robust wine. Flambé shellfish made with a spirit which may also be in the sauce is best accompanied by an assertive, not necessarily subtle wine; a creamy sauce needs a wine with a certain delicacy, such as a young Mosel or a sturdy Franconian, or Rieslings in general if high in acidity. Wines made from the Chenin Blanc and Chardonnay are perhaps the most suitable of all.

In the picture on the left, a Muscadet accompanies the oysters; a Chablis, still Champagne, Loire or white Burgundy would have been equally suitable. Avoid dousing any type of shellfish with quantities of lemon juice, Worcestershire sauce, tabasco or malt vinegar; any fine wine will be wasted and will be better replaced with an agreeable, tough wine.

Shellfish

MOLLUSCS

Oysters
With plain raw oysters, serve a straightforward and not too light-bodied dry white wine, such as Chablis or Petit Chablis, a good Muscadet or wine made from the Chenin Blanc grape. Portuguese oysters are coarser in taste and need a straightforward, fairly robust wine. Champagne is excellent with oysters, especially if they are served as a single course or a luxury snack; ideally a firm-bodied or full-bodied type should be chosen. Other sparkling wines should be truly dry. Still Champagne may also be offered.
If oysters are served in a sauce, the predominant flavouring of this should determine the choice of wine.

Scallops
These are fairly delicate but fleshy shellfish and need a bone dry to medium dry wine, of good to fine quality. Wines made from the Riesling and Gewürztraminer are enjoyable with these shellfish, as well as those from the Chardonnay. Scallops in mayonnaise or a rich velouté sauce need an assertive white wine, such as a Loire or a Rhône.

Abalone
The method of cooking determines the wine, but a moderately fruity, dry to medium dry white wine is generally suitable. The fairly large-scale Rieslings, Chenin Blanc and Chardonnay in general can be served; a small-scale white Rhône is preferable if a strong garlic flavour is part of the recipe.

Clams
Served plainly, like oysters, any bone dry to medium dry white wine is suitable. Soups and chowders need no particular wine, but an extra glass of the apéritif wine can be offered. If sherry or vermouth is used in the recipe, the same wines make a good accompaniment. Clams that are stuffed or cooked in a strongly flavoured sauce can be accompanied by any of the white river wines, the style depending on the type of sauce.

Mussels
Served in a sauce, mussels can be accompanied by a bone dry wine with a certain amount of weight, or a dry to medium dry wine with definite fruit to cut through the sauce. If vermouth is used in the recipe, a glass of dry Chambéry or Marseilles vermouth is agreeable. Cooked with wine and herbs, stuffed or grilled, the wine in the recipe and the the type of herbs should determine the style of wine.

Cockles, Winkles, Whelks
With these small molluscs any everyday or local wine is suitable. When they form part of a seafood platter, select a fairly robust white that will go well with the most strongly flavoured shellfish in it.

CRUSTACEA

Lobster, Crayfish, Crawfish, Crab
If served cold, with vinaigrette or mayonnaise, suitable wines are not too expensive, dry to fruity whites, including Rieslings.
Lobster and crayfish that are cooked in a hot cream sauce are better accompanied by a moderately assertive white, such as a good Sancerre, estate Muscadet, medium-grade Burgundy and fair to good Chardonnays in general. Shellfish flamed with a spirit are best partnered by a slightly tougher wine. Dry Italian Frascatis and Riojas, and the finer Mediterranean whites are all good choices with large lobsters. More subtle wines, such as a good dry Graves, estate Sancerre, a white Jura or any wine with a little weight and finesse, are ideal with plainly cooked langouste and crabs.

Shrimps and Prawns
Simply cooked and served cold as a snack, these may be partnered by an everyday or regional wine; as a first course, a dry to medium dry white or even a quality pink wine, preferably with some elegance, can be served. With prawn cocktails which include a piquant sauce, serve the apéritif wine or a glass of dry and fairly robust white wine. For shrimp and prawn salads, choose a moderately tough white wine that will cut across the dressing.

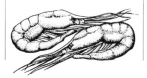

Wine with Food

The choice of wine with fish is wide and need not be limited to white wines; pink wines are much favoured with river and sea fish in many parts of France, and for certain recipes, such as *Saumon Chambord*, where the salmon is braised in red wine, it is logical to drink a red wine. Many people, however, find that a red or assertive pink wine takes on an unpleasant, often metallic flavour when accompanied by fish. The lighter reds with a certain amount of acidity, such as the red Loires, can be pleasant with plainly cooked fish, such as salmon, turbot or halibut, but most people will probably find a white wine most enjoyable.

Distinction must be made between river and sea fish, and between fish from cold and warm waters. As with wines from vines that have to struggle, fish from cold waters and rushing rivers tend to have more subtle flavours and greater delicacy of flesh; sea fish usually possess more fat, and the deeper and colder the waters, the fatter they tend to be. A river or lake fish will take on the characteristics of the waters; it is said that trout from different rivers are as subtly different as the wines from different plots of the same vineyard. Fish that have to fight against a current will be trimmed down to delicate succulence, those of

ponds and reserves are generally less complex in flavour. A sole from warmish waters will be quite different from a Dover sole, as different as the best Balkan Riesling from a fine Mosel.

The choice of wine is also determined by the relation of the fish course to other courses in a meal. Take into consideration the weight or lightness of the accompanying wine in relation to those, including the apéritif, that have been served, and those that are to follow. The method of cooking is equally important: anything fried in batter or served with a savoury butter or baked with additional flavourings should be partnered by wines that will cut through the fat. Sauces rich in cream and eggs need an assertive wine, from bone dry to medium dry and of fair weight, whereas a simply grilled or shallow fried fish can take a more delicate wine from any category except those of the sweeter wines. With piquant and fruit garnishes, choose a firmer wine; the bone dry and dry whites may be suitable, but the medium dry wines may be more acceptable with complicated fish dishes. Wines with a fair amount of obvious fruit are suitable for the plainer fish. In the picture above is an Alsatian Riesling, frequently an appropriate "when in doubt" choice.

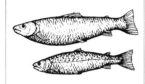

Salmon, Salmon Trout, Char
These sea fish are at the same time fairly fatty, yet delicate and moderately subtle in flavour. When they are served as main courses, a fairly important wine is necessary, such as some types of white Burgundy, big Rieslings from Alsace, German wines up to the Auslese category and including this as long as the accompanying sauce is not too rich. Baked or grilled and served with a white butter sauce (*beurre blanc*), a fine dry white Loire or a moderately weighty, southern white Burgundy would be suitable. For grilled steaks, a lightish red wine is possible, and the same type of wine can be served with plainly poached fish, although a dry white of some distinction is probably more acceptable. With sauces heavily flavoured with herbs, the wine must be able to cut across the strong flavours; choose from a large-scale white Burgundy, a white Rhône, a white Graves of some distinction or a bone dry wine of some weight, such as Chablis or great growth of Chablis, an estate Sancerre or still white Champagne. It is also possible to serve a sparkling, *crémant* or *pétillant* white wine with such dishes although a wine with a fair amount of body and fruit, such as some of the Palatinate wines, will be preferable to light and very dry wines. Estate Muscadets, Franconian wines, and the wines of the Jura and Savoie regions are alternatives for richly garnished dishes of these fish.

Trout
River trout should ideally be accompanied by a wine from the particular river region. Cooked plainly (*au bleu*) and served with melted butter, a Riesling from anywhere or a dry white Loire would be suitable. For trout bred on fish farms or in reserves, a Riesling, Sylvaner or Traminer would be good choices; they need not be of top quality. For trout with almonds or similar additions, or rich sauces and stuffings, such as banana with *Truite Caprice de Buffon*, a fairly fruity white wine is called for. Large-scale Traminer or Gewürztraminer, a dry white Bordeaux, one of the Italian wines made from the Trebbiano grape, or a Chenin Blanc wine from anywhere would be possible choices.

Sole, Plaice, Dab
Also known as game of the sea, sole should ideally be kept for 24 hours after being fished to concentrate its flavour. It deserves a fine white wine, such as a middle Loire or Burgundy unless cooked with elaborate sauces when a fruity wine, such as an estate Sancerre, is probably better. For deep-fried fish, choose a wine with more weight than for shallow fried or grilled sole. Garnishes, such as lemon, will affect the wine; *goujons* (fried strips of sole) with lemon can take a less fine and even a coarse wine, such as ordinary Riesling, Chenin Blanc or Muscadet. Plaice should not be considered an inferior version of sole, but a delicate fish in its own right; its light but distinct flavour can take the same type of wines as recommended for sole, but usually chosen from the slightly less expensive ranges: the Rieslings, Muscadets, white Italian and south-east European wines, and any from the Chardonnay and Chenin Blanc grapes are suitable. With sauces, such as hollandaise or sauce tartare, a tougher type of wine is probably better, such as one from north Portugal, the top of the Rhône or the inexpensive white Loires, or more ordinary Rieslings and Gewürztraminers. Dabs are usually simply cooked and can be partnered by delicate white wines as for grilled sole.

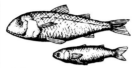

Mullet
Red mullet, which takes its name from the red scales, has white flesh with a delicate flavour. It is best grilled or fried and is often served with a garnish of lemon; so a moderately robust white wine, fairly dry, is ideal. Grey mullet is coarser and usually served with various cream sauces; any dry to medium dry white wine is suitable.

Whitebait, Sprats, Sardines
These small fish are fried whole and served sprinkled with lemon juice and sometimes with paprika. They are best with an easy going, dry white wine, such as ordinary Muscadet, any of the Rieslings or any agreeable light and possibly fruity white wine.

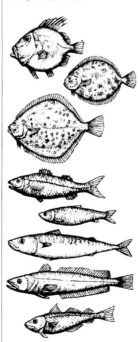

Whiting, Haddock, Brill, Bass, John Dory, Flounder, Hake, Herring, Mackerel
These sea fish usually have open textured flesh, and the choice of wine depends wholly on the way they are cooked. For simply grilled, poached or fried fish, choose a straightforward white wine, from bone dry to medium dry, in the inexpensive to expensive ranges, according to whether the fish is served as an intermediary or main course. With recipes involving strong seasonings, such as sea bass (*loup de mer*) grilled over fennel in the south of France, a moderately assertive, southern wine, such as white Bandol or certain whites from the centre of Italy, are agreeable. A glass of dry vermouth is excellent when these fish are served as a first course without any elaborate sauce or garnish. Fairly assertive, though not too tough whites are generally best with these types of fish, which seem to need the accompaniment of a wine that possesses both fruit and some acidity.

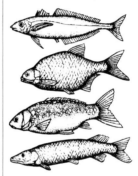

River Fish (Pike, Carp, Tench, Roach, Perch, Gudgeon, Bream, Barbel, Shad)
Pike is most often featured as fishballs (*quenelles de brochet*) and the wine must be chosen to accord with any of the traditional creamy sauces; in Burgundy, the choice would be a white Burgundy, but a still Champagne, any Chardonnay, a Franconian Sylvaner or Palatinate full-bodied wine are also excellent. The carp is a heavy fish requiring a weighty wine, possibly a white Rhône, but the fuller east-European Traminers are also possible. With other river fish, the way they are cooked and the sauces, which are usually necessary to enhance the somewhat dull taste of the fish, must be taken into account. Sauces heavily flavoured with herbs, onions and garlic need a markedly fruity wine; the white Bordeaux and many white Italian wines add great charm to river fish, especially when these are simply grilled, poached or baked.

Turbot, Halibut, Cod, Sea Bream
All these sea fish can take big wines, and even lightish types of fresh, crisp reds if they are poached or braised in red wine. The fat of the flesh enables them to be admirably partnered by the big white wines, from bone dry to medium dry in all ranges. Served with egg-based sauces, an assertive wine is required, such as a big white Burgundy, white Rhône or a white Rioja. With more everyday recipes, and especially for cod, take into account any onions, tomatoes or strong herbs before deciding on a suitable wine; good choices include southern white wines or fairly assertive, inexpensive northern whites.

Lamprey, Eel, Shark, Skate, Swordfish
The lamprey, an estuary eel-like fish, is usually cooked *en matelote* (stewed in red wine with shallots or garlic, and seasonings) in the Gironde, and is there accompanied by a medium personality red wine. Eel, skate, shark and swordfish can be accompanied by a dry, fairly robust, white wine. Served as a first course, pickled or with a piquant sauce, they may be partnered by a spirit like vodka or schnapps; wine is usually not suitable. Steaks from shark and similar big fish are often served with rich, complex sauces; these should dictate the choice of wine to accompany them, and assertive, even slightly coarse white wines are generally suitable, or lightish reds.

Wine with Food

Meat

There is a general supposition that white wines should be served with white meats and red wines with red meats. This, however, does not take account of the cooking methods, stuffings, use of herbs, sauces and garnishes, not to mention the accompanying vegetables. White meat is generally taken to include pork, veal, chicken and turkey, while the "reds" are beef, lamb, duck and goose. But roast white meat such as veal is partnered as well by a red Bordeaux as by a white Burgundy, and the richness of a navarin of lamb is balanced equally well by a full-bodied dry white Hermitage as by young Beaujolais or small-scale claret.

The wine, whatever it is, should complement the food. It should neither overpower nor minimize the dish but enhance its flavours and make a main course into a harmonious entity. Among the meats, beef and lamb have the most distinctive flavours and therefore can command the accompaniment of the finest red wines, but only when these meats are roasted and served quite plainly. Sauces incorporating fruits, such as oranges, gooseberries, cranberries, redcurrants and apples in small quantities may not affect fine wines adversely, but horseradish, mint, sage and onion, and caper sauces, pickles, heavy flavours of garlic, strong herbs and mustard will blunt the palate and make good red wines a waste of money. With such strong flavours, robust everyday wines are better.

With large, plain roasts of white meat—pork and veal—any white wines should be of equal importance to the meat, but consideration should also be given to the purpose of the wine. Is it meant to freshen and sharpen the flavour of the meat or is it merely an accompanying wine? In the first case, the wine should be fairly high in acidity, in the second predominantly fruity. Alternatively, choose a red wine of medium personality.

The suggestion of red wine with red meat and white with white meat and poultry does, certainly, break down as soon as cooking methods other than plain roasting, grilling and possibly frying, are used. Only the finest cuts of meat are suitable for roasts and grills, and it is therefore generally superfluous to add to their flavours with distracting garnishes, sauces and accompaniments, especially if great wines of delicacy and subtlety are to be served. But once piquant or rich sauces are added, together with creamed, highly flavoured or lavishly buttered vegetables, the delicate shades of great wines are lost, and wines of more robust character are preferable, as with very fatty joints. Much also depends on how long the meat has been hung and how it has been roasted. Well-hung meat will require a fairly forceful wine, and underdone beef and young lamb are best accompanied by fine though weighty wines.

Hot meats generally require wines slightly high in fruit, cold meats wines with definite acidity and some tannin, possibly including the better pinks. In extremely hot and sultry weather, chilled white or pink wines are often preferred, whatever the type of cold meat, though not by me. I would choose red wines that are lightly or distinctly fruity and may be served cool, such as Beaujolais or red Loire.

Informal types of dish, such as casseroles and stews, should be partnered by informal wines. If wine is incorporated in the recipe, the accompanying wine should be identical or of a similar type. Wines used for cooking should always be of good though not necessarily fine quality; as wine reduces in volume and concentrates in flavour in cooking, an inferior wine will display its negative character and taint the whole dish. Unless fairly good wine can be used in cooking, it is probably better to leave it out altogether. Casseroles, stews and ragouts based on beef and lamb and cooked without wine can be served with moderate to robust reds; fruity white wines may accompany stews of white meat, but I would always choose a lightish red wine, especially if strong flavourings are included. With very spicy dishes, such as goulash, a robust white, or red, such as Hungarian Bull's Blood may be served; with curry, beer or lager is more suitable than any wine.

Meat dishes in pastry can be partnered by straightforward, lightish red wines, although classic dishes of beef and lamb encased in puff pastry perhaps deserve finer Burgundy or Bordeaux for special occasions.

With "variety meats" or offal, which include kidneys, liver, sweetbreads, hearts and brains, the style of cooking determines the wine to be served. Variety meats are often braised or casseroled and served in a sauce; robust and fruity red wines are most suitable with sauces strongly flavoured with garlic, juniper berries and onions; for delicate cream and mushroom sauces you can also choose an assertive white, preferably from a region where the dish is traditional. Grilled liver is good with most classic reds.

The roast rib of beef illustrated on the right is served with a red Graves, Château Le Tuquet 1970. This is full enough to complement the great joint, yet at the same time subtle and sinewy. Other good wine choices for the beef include fine parish Beaujolais, fine or very fine Burgundy, not too weighty Côtes du Rhône or similar quality red wines, such as Cabernet Sauvignons, Shiraz and Grenache based wines from vineyards throughout the world.

Wine with Food

Chicken and turkey are often listed as white meats, although the latter, which has both white and brown meat, is usually roasted with a strongly-flavoured stuffing and served with rich gravy and trimmings. The wines chosen for poultry must ultimately be determined by the stuffings and accompaniments, but in general light red wines are suitable for roasts with fairly simple stuffings; with richer stuffings such as truffles, weightier wines should be selected.

Fatter poultry, such as duck and goose, may possibly be accompanied by white wines of assertive style and considerable weight, such as a great Riesling of a particular vintage, or a Gewürztraminer of special quality, so that the fruit as well as the acidity can cut across the fat of the birds and freshen the palate; these wines are particularly suitable when the accompanying vegetable is red cabbage. But regional traditions vary; in the south of France, for example, roast goose may well be partnered by a red wine of assertive style and weight, such as a great Hermitage or Châteauneuf-du-Pape. In eastern France, the traditional wine may be a fine red Burgundy or a Côte de Beaune of a good vintage.

The classic *Canard à l'Orange* is served in some regions with a good to fine red Burgundy or Bordeaux, while in others an assertive white Burgundy, a white Rhône, or a white Italian or Spanish wine is possible.

With more complicated poultry dishes, the style of cooking and the accompanying sauces and garnishes decide the choice of wines. Chicken in Champagne sauce obviously demands a very dry Champagne, while cream sauces and casseroles can suitably be served with a fairly tough, full-bodied white Burgundy, white Côte du Rhône or dry white Graves.

If wine is used in the recipe, a wine of similar style should be served although it is perfectly possibly to serve a little claret or similar red wine, or a young Beaujolais, Gamay, Zinfandel or Pinotage with a chicken casserole cooked with white wine. But where strong herbs and many spices are used, more robust, even coarse wines, red or white, or Mediterranean pinks are possibly better able to cut across the flavours.

Cold roast poultry served with various sauces are best accompanied by lightish, fairly assertive, everyday wines of any type.

In the classic *Coq au Vin*—chicken cooked in wine with onions, mushrooms and bacon—the wine is most often red; Burgundy, especially Chambertin, being the most recommended. Occasionally, *coq au vin* is cooked in Riesling, but whatever the cooking wine, the serving wine should be the same. In the picture above is a young full-bodied Burgundy; a Beaujolais, Côtes du Rhône or a quality Chianti would be equally appropriate for Mediterranean poultry casseroles.

Beef

The finer the cut, the finer the wine. In general, red wines always go best with beef, but with underdone, or even raw beef, such as *boeuf tartare*, the wine should definitely have some assertiveness. Wines of medium personality, inclined to weightiness, are usually best with roasts and grills. Bordeaux, Burgundy, Beaujolais, Côtes du Rhône, red Rioja and Chianti are good choices, as are any quality wines from good red wine regions. Very old clarets and Burgundies can be a little delicate for great roasts, but steaks, and especially entrecotes, can be admirable with them. With beef cooked in wine sauces, serve the wine used or a lightish red Rhône or any moderately robust wine.
For casseroles, the ingredients additional to the meat must be taken into consideration: peppers, onions and garlic need robust wines. With boiled beef, it would be possible to serve a big, dry white wine, such as a white Rioja, robust Chardonnay or Sauvignon, but a not too weighty red is probably preferable.

Veal

Plainly roasted veal can be partnered by a full-bodied dry or medium dry white wine, such as certain white Burgundies, white Riojas or wines from the Chardonnay grape and straight Sauvignons in general. But a light to medium-bodied red wine, which to me would be a Bordeaux, is preferable; the wine should not be too assertive in style to accompany this fairly delicately flavoured meat. The same applies to chops and escalopes, but here any sauce must be taken into account. With sauces based on cream, a full-bodied, dry white wine can be served, such as a suitable Burgundy or Alsace, especially if white wine has been used in the sauce. Brown sauces can be accompanied by most lightish to full red wines, but

if tomatoes are included in the sauce, something fuller, such as a Rhône, to counteract the acidity is probably a better choice.

Lamb

Plainly roasted or grilled lamb is one of the finest accompaniments to the finest and more important red wines. Sometimes recommendations are made for Bordeaux with lamb, and Burgundy with beef, but these are far too general in view of the varieties of wines. The finest and oldest Bordeaux are certainly well partnered by lamb, whether in the form of a roast or cutlets. Chops can be more fatty and a more substantial wine is better. Lamb roasted with rosemary should be only delicately flavoured to go with a sensitive red wine, but stronger flavourings can be used with the finer red Italian wines or Rhônes. The sweetness of the meat requires a certain subtlety in the wine. With young roast lamb serve a medium-bodied claret-type, but for older lamb and mutton, a more robust though equally fine wine is preferable.With cheap cuts, it is wise to choose red wines with fairly high acidity, such as red Loire, Bardolino, Grignolino, Hungarian Bull's Blood and most Gamays. Navarins, ragouts, moussaka, can be partnered by red wines of medium personality or full-bodied, not too fine dry whites. Boiled lamb with onion sauce is probably best partnered by any robust everyday wine.

Pork

Roasts of pork are rich, and a robust style of wine, high in fruit and acidity to combat the fat, are best. Dry white wines, such as Rioja, certain white Burgundies, Côtes du Rhône and Rieslings are possible choices, but medium to full-bodied reds (including Beaujolais) with moderate acidity and fruit, are equally suitable. I would not suggest any very delicate or subtle red wines, but the medium to fine bourgeois clarets and

Burgundies, and red wines of similar importance from wine regions throughout the world can all be served. Pork chops and cutlets also require a robust wine, red or white; grilled, they go well with the Italian Valpolicellas or Hungarian Rieslings, for example.
With casseroles, the wine depends on the other ingredients. Casseroles of pork, such as cassoulets, tend to include fairly robust ingredients like beans, so robust, straightforward red wines, such as the regional Corbières and Roussillons, are therefore appropriate.

Ham and Bacon

Here everything depends on how the joint is cooked; the saltiness of the meat can harm a delicate wine, but properly soaked before being boiled and baked, a joint can be accompanied by a full-bodied white Burgundy as well as medium personality red wines, such as Cabernets and Gamays.
A medium-quality Bordeaux or red Burgundy would be possible with braised ham wrapped in puff pastry, and with certain luxury recipes, such as ham cooked in Chablis or Champagne, the same wines are obviously appropriate to drink. With grills of ham and bacon, and with cold cuts, any ordinary reds or very robust white wines are suitable. Garnishes of peaches and pineapple, preclude delicate and subtle wines, but robust, everyday wines can be served.
Ham cooked and served in sauces based on white wine and creams goes well with dry, fairly full whites, such as Sancerre, Saumur and Mâcon blanc. But sauces flavoured with tomatoes, onions or peppers are best with robust southern wines, red or white.

Variety Meats

With plain grilled kidneys, a fine Burgundy or Bordeaux could be served, but with flamed kidneys, a Beaujolais or bourgeois growth might be a better choice. If cooked and served in a rich cream sauce with, for example, mushrooms, a parish Beaujolais of more robust character, such as Juliènas, might be suitable. With stuffed heart, braised oxtail,

and recipes using strong herbs, more obvious wines, such as straightforward Côtes du Rhône, are best. Grilled liver can be partnered by subtle yet firm wines that will complement the delicacy of the meat; good to fine red Bordeaux, Burgundy, the finest Beaujolais or estate New World reds are possibilities. Sweetbreads cooked in a creamy sauce may be accompanied by white Beaujolais, white Burgundy, dry Graves or any Chenin Blanc; cooked à la Normande, which involves calvados and apples, Loire or Alsatian Riesling is possible. Braised sweetbreads in a brown sauce are traditionally served with any red wine of medium personality, or a good Cabernet, Gamay or Pinot Noir. The same wine could be served with brains cooked in brown butter. If fried or with onion sauce, a weightier wine, such as any Pinot Noir, Grenache or wines made mainly with the Nebbiolo or Sangiovese, are possible.

Chicken and Turkey

With roast birds I would always choose reds, such as Bordeaux and Burgundies, or other classic reds, but white wines, such as Burgundies, most Loires, the lighter Rhônes, quality Chardonnays and Sauvignons, may also be served. Spring chicken and poussins without any stuffing may be accompanied by any moderately fine Riesling, those of Alsace being particularly suitable. With large roasted birds, bear in mind the ultimate flavours of any stuffing and select weightier wines than for plainly roasted birds. Fried and grilled poultry portions can be accompanied by the same type of wines, but if served with, for example, spiced rice, a weightier red, such as finer Pinot Noirs, estate Beaujolais, Riojas and Italian reds, might be more suitable. With boiled and poached poultry, white robust wines, of dry to medium dry quality, are usual, although it is also possible to serve a red wine of medium to weighty personality, preferably with some elegance.
Casseroles of poultry should ideally be accompanied by the same type of wine as used in the recipe.

Duck and Goose

These are fat-fleshed birds and often cooked with well-seasoned stuffings and sauces which must be considered when the wines are selected. For roast birds accompanied by not too strongly-flavoured sauces and vegetables, the best choices are red wines that will balance the fat of the meat, such as youngish bourgeois Bordeaux, light years of classed growths, certain types of Pomerol or St-Émilion, the Côte de Beaune reds or southern Burgundies and finer Beaujolais; the greater Italian reds, such as riserva Chiantis, fine Barolos and Bardolinos are particularly good with these fatty birds. Similar wines, but with higher acidity can be served with preserved joints of duck and goose (*confits*). Highly flavoured sauces, such as pineapple and orange, will deaden any very delicate, subtle wine, but assertive, large-scale dry whites would be suitable choices.

Sausages and Cold Meats

As partner to cold meats, any type of wine can be served, according to the meats. For example, with a selection of continental sausages, Franconian Steinwein would be admirable. Nothing very subtle should accompany salads, preferably a robust wine, white, pink or red. With pickles, chutneys and mustard, an ordinary red wine, such as a North African, will be the best choice as these flavourings will overpower anything moderately delicate. White wines are often served with cold poultry, and red or pink wines with cold red meats, but this is a matter of personal preference; a reasonably fruity, easily enjoyable wine is all that is required, and this can be red, white or pink, and in the cheap to medium-price ranges. Inexpensive, dry to fruity, sparkling wines are possible with most buffet foods and can, because of their acidity, cut through the fat of any fairly rich cold cuts, such as pâtés and terrines, or meats served with mayonnaise, similar egg-based sauces and dishes such as *Vitello tonnato*.

Wine with Food

Select wines in accordance with the style and quality of the meat: the finest wine with the finest game. Try to imagine the taste of the dish in advance, by taking into account such factors as marinading, stuffings, rich sauces and accompaniments of fruit, jellies and vegetables. There is never *one* single wine ideal for one single dish; it should simply be a fair complement to the food.

In the illustration on the right, the roast pheasant is served with a 1972 Volnay Champans, estate-bottled Marquis d'Angerville. This is a red Burgundy of fairly gentle style, with the breed of a particular site and the graciousness of a particular vintage. It would be equally appropriate to serve a fine Margaux of a great year. But if the pheasant had been cooked à la Normande—flamed with Calvados and served in a cream sauce with apples—a more definite, less complex wine would be called for. Here a red Burgundy, such as a Nuits-St-Georges Clos des Porrets 1971, a crisp Chinon, or a classed growth of St-Julien 1966 or St-Emilion 1964 might be suitable.

Wines with game need not inevitably be red. Although the assertive flavour of the meat requires a wine of fair weight, there is no reason why this should not be white. German wines, up to and including Spätlesen, the finer Alsatian Rieslings, certain white Burgundies, white Riojas and Chardonnays of vigorous character would be possible with roast game birds and waterbirds. Some people may even prefer a robust white wine with fairly high acidity to offset a rich game dish.

If the game comes from a particular wine region or is prepared and cooked according to a regional recipe, select the type of wine that would be served there.

Game

Small Birds
Wheatears (ortolans), plover, songbirds, figpeckers and snipe are usually roasted whole, in the oven or on the spit. A fairly firm, though not too weighty red wine is the most suitable, for example youngish bourgeois Bordeaux or one of the classed growths of light years. Alternatively, choose a Bordeaux such as Moulis or Listrac, a small-scale red Burgundy or a red Loire. More general wines include those made from Cabernet Franc, Merlot and Bardolino grapes, and the medium range of Italian reds. Eastern Mediterranean red wines are often served with small roast birds where these are local specialities.
With pâtés made from any small bird, a robust dry white as well as a medium-bodied red may be served, for example red or white "little" Rhônes. For casseroles, medium quality red wines of any kind are suitable.

Winged game
Young grouse and woodcock are usually roasted whole, and the great red Bordeaux and red Burgundies are traditionally served with them. Good wine choices for small game birds include

Côte de Nuits parish and site Burgundies, fine Médocs, notably those of Margaux and Pauillac, red Graves, St-Emilions and Pomerols. The subtle and more gracious red Rhônes are equally good. Outside the French wines, choose estate wines of moderate assertiveness, in the higher price ranges. Suitable wines of single grape varieties include the Cabernets, Gamays and possibly the Pinot Noirs as long as these are not too heavy.
For pheasant, choose a robust Côte de Beaune, a young St-Emilion or a medium-weight Pauillac. Well-hung game is best accompanied by a red, fruity wine, perhaps a fine Beaujolais, an estate wine from Morgon, Moulin à Vent or Brouilly and Côte de Brouilly, about three to six years old. In Spain, the red wines of finer quality are traditional with partridge. North Portuguese and local Italian and Sicilian reds, as well as the Cabernet and

Pinotages of Cape Province also go well with fine roast game birds.
Casseroles of game, at the end of the season, are better accompanied by less fine wines, such as Cabernets or Pinot Noirs.

Waterbirds
The flavour of waterbirds is less delicate than that of winged game, and when they are prepared with stuffings and rich sauces they generally need a red wine of assertive, medium-bodied style. Good choices are the southern Burgundies, such as Mercurey, Rully and Santenay, and parish wines from the Côte d'Or, such as Volnay, Nuits-St-Georges, Morey-St-Denis and Gevrey-Chambertin.
Classed growths of St-Estèphe, light Pauillacs and fine red Graves are other choices.
Teal, wild duck (mallard), wild goose and the American canvasback all have a certain amount of fat. The complementary wines should therefore be assertive enough

to cut across the richness. Large-scale white wines are possible, such as first or great growths Chablis, quality Alsatian Rieslings, estate Anjous, great Sancerres, Rhônes from the Viognier grape, Châteauneuf-du-Pape, Riojas and fine Franconian wines.
Good single red grape variety wines include the Cabernet, Shiraz and Pinot Noir, or any "Burgundy-like" wine. The young northern red Rhônes, young Barolos and red wines from central Italy are also excellent.

Ground game
The flavour of wild rabbit and hare depends to a great extent on their feeding grounds. For roasts, choose the same wines as recommended for waterbirds, the reds being more suitable than the white wines.
With casseroles, choose a straightforward, robust red wine, preferably of the same style as used in the recipe. Game pâtés are better with a lighter, more acid red wine, such as a Chinon.

Large game
This group includes venison (roebuck and deer), wild

boar, kid and other large-scale game. All, except kid, have a strong flavour to which substantial red wines are more suited. For roast game, excellent choices are big red Burgundies, such as the site wines of Vosne Romanée, Clos de Vougeot; and from Bordeaux, Pauillacs, certain estates of St-Emilion and Pomerol, red Graves and greater years of St-Estèphe. Red Rhônes, Riojas and Barolos are good alternatives. Fine, mature Cabernet, Grenache and Pinot Noir wines also go well with roast game, as do Nebbiolos and Sangioveses. Oven or spit-roasted kid can be accompanied by the same red wines as winged game and waterbirds. Where strong additional flavours have been incorporated, a more straightforward wine, a large-scale red Italian, or a Rhône is preferable.
Casseroled game can very well be served with any of the inexpensive red Balkan wines, ideally with a little bottle age, even six months.

Wine with Food

Wine is a happy accompaniment to cheese because the acidity in fine wine is complemented by the alkalinity of fine cheese. "We buy on apples, sell on cheese" say the wine trade, because cheese always seems to make wine taste better. The choice of wines with different types of cheese is entirely a matter of personal preference, but when the cheese board consists of regional specialities, the accompanying wines should be locally produced.

The prevailing custom in many English-speaking countries of serving cheese after the sweet course appears to have no sound gastronomic basis. It is impossible to taste a fine table wine (unless this is sweet) after anything sweet, and the sweet may well be a dish that includes a liqueur, or, even worse, chocolate, which is extremely detrimental to any wine. As a means of finishing the table wines that have been drunk during the course of the meal, cheese is the perfect conclusion, especially if two distinct and different types of wine, such as Bordeaux and red Burgundy have been served; it is quite acceptable to serve one with the main course or courses, and the other with the cheese. When several wines have been served, it can be a particular pleasure to discover how much better they can taste when flattered by the cheese at the end of the meal.

At this stage it may be pertinent to comment on the serving of salads with or after the meat course. Salads may be served in France, but in Britain virtually never at formal dinners, although they are permissible at luncheons. The vinegar or lemon in the dressing risks spoiling the taste of a delicate wine. Personally, I do serve salads, sometimes after a meat course, and sometimes with the cheese, but my entertaining is informal and always dictated by the wines to be served. Salad dressings composed of five to six parts oil to one of wine vinegar or lemon, as in my home, hardly affect the wine at all.

It should also be remembered that at formal dinners in English-speaking countries, cheese is usually omitted. Cheese tends to be a luncheon dish only, except at the time of year when, for instance, Stilton is in season. A cheese course accompanied by fine wines should come after the meat or fish main courses and before the sweets, when it can be a great pleasure.

It may seem surprising but it is nonetheless true that fine, often delicate wines are swamped by strongly flavoured cheese. A good cheese board selection should include a hard cheese, a fresh cream cheese, a blue cheese and a full fat or goat cheese. When selecting cheese for wine, the fat content is of great importance; the greater the fat content (*matière grasse*), which is often stated on the cheese label, the better the

cheese will go with subtle wines. Burgundy fat cheeses, such as the famous Epoisses, often have a fat content of 75 per cent, and most French Camemberts have 50 per cent. Blue cheeses can be very assertive, and the same applies to semi-matured cheeses, such as Brie; among the hard cheeses, the mild Dutch ones are popular with red wines, while the great hard cheeses, such as Double Gloucester and matured Cheddar, can overwhelm most wines. Lovers of great red wines would often choose goat cheeses to partner them; the Anglo-Saxon countries have a curious objection to goat although its milk makes delicate, elegant cheeses, ideal to accompany fine red and white wines. The great sweet wines can be well partnered by some of the great British matured cheeses; such a cheese course is virtually a meal in itself, but it is worth experimenting with, for example, a great Barsac served with a prime chunk of Wensleydale or Dunlop.

The processed and similarly convenienced packed cheese, while offering value to the consumer, cannot be considered in relation to fine wines; they are not outstanding cheeses, and any type of wine is suitable with them.

Cheese

Blue Cheeses

These are strongly flavoured cheeses and therefore need assertive, full-bodied red wines, of some weight. Stilton, blue Cheshire, German Edelpilz and Danish Blue in particular can have very strong flavours which tend to overwhelm any delicate wine. The softer, creamy blue cheeses, such as Bleu de Bresse, prime Roquefort, Gorgonzola and Dolcelatte, are less strong in flavour and suitable red wines can therefore be less weighty but they should still be robust and fruity.

Hard and matured cheeses

The great matured cheeses, such as farmhouse Cheddar,

Wensleydale, Lancashire and Gloucester, need a very weighty, robust red wine without much sublety; estate Riojas, old Barolos and fine Rhônes would all be suitable. Less strongly flavoured hard cheeses, including those made from goat's and ewe's milk, can take a good to fine red wine, fruity but not too robust. Gruyère, Emmenthal and mild German and Dutch cheeses as well as other cheeses of similar mildness, are well partnered by more delicate red wines. Used in cooking, such as soufflés and fondues, a more assertive wine is required to cut across

the obvious fat even in a mild cheese. With toasted cheese, and especially Welsh rarebit which includes beer in the recipe, any ordinary fullish red wine will be suitable as it will not be able to make any very strong impression above the cheese.

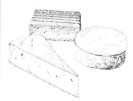

Soft, Full Fat Cheeses

The great creamy cheeses, such as Brie, Camembert, Carré de l'Est, Pont l'Evêque and Bel Paese, can, as long as they are in their prime and neither overripe nor too young, partner very fine red wines. With other soft cheese, such as Livarot, Swiss Fontina and Vacherin, Italian Ricotta and Austrian

Schlosskäse, less fine, more robust wines would be suitable. Full-bodied, bone dry and dry white wines are also agreeable with all creamy and soft cheeses, especially when fruits, such as peaches and table grapes, accompany the cheese board.

Fresh Cream Cheeses

These can be partnered by any type of wine, medium dry or even slightly sweet whites or lightish red wines. According to their main ingredients—cow, ewe, goat milk or a mixture of milks— the relative assertiveness should be considered. Cream cheeses with a predominant salty taste, such as the French Fromage de Monsieur and Greek Feta, and the herby cream cheeses like

Scottish Hramsa and French Boursin, need a more robust wine than the mild, almost bland Demi-sel types of cream cheese.

Novelty Cheeses

Smoked, semi-hard cheeses and those covered with nuts, dried black grape skins or peppercorns, are unsuited to any delicate or subtle wines. The same applies to cheese impregnated with strong flavours, such as garlic, the spicy Boulette d'Auvergne buttermilk cheeses and aniseed-flavoured Münster. Straightforward red wines, fairly robust, make pleasant accompaniments to all these types of cheese, as well as to the bland types of processed cheese.

Wine with Food

It is not essential to serve a wine with the sweet course of a meal, but it can be very agreeable to do so. If the occasion is one of celebration, such as a birthday or an anniversary, the toast will usually take place during the sweet course.

Many sweet dishes that are delectable in themselves, however, do not need any wine, and some may overwhelm or actually spoil the taste of a very fine or delicate dessert wine. Where a liqueur is used, either in the recipe, whipped into an accompanying cream, or used to flame a dish, as with pancakes, a fine wine is wholly superflous; but the same liqueur or a not too sparkling wine might be served. Sparkling wines are traditional for toasting, but most people would probably find a very dry one far too acid at this stage of a meal; a fuller, rounder type of sparkling wine is preferable, and this might be a sweetish Champagne, an Asti or a similar sparkling wine with a pronounced fruity flavour. A sparkling wine can be good to alleviate too much creamy richness, but it must be fruity enough to cut through the cream. Egg-based sweets, such as most custards, crème brulée, rich pastries or concoctions made with plenty of cream and eggs, require a definitely assertive wine. With the supreme examples of egg-based sweets, such as zabaglione or sabayon, I would suggest that the type of wine with which such recipes are made should or could be drunk with them. If a suitable Marsala, sweetish Madeira, or any *vin doux naturel* is not available, a not too fine, sweetish Italian or French wine is possible, notably anything made from the Muscat grape.

Certain fruits can be awkward with wine, notably the citrus and the pineapple and anything particularly acid, such as gooseberry and lemon. However, as fruits are often combined with cream, the acidity is diminished; apples, many berries and stone fruits can be good with the classic sweet wines, although I personally think that if the great German sweet wines are to be served, the sweet course should be as simple as possible so as not to blur the impression that these subtle, fine wines can make. The sweet Loires and Bordeaux, Monbazillac, and many Italian sweet wines, however, are sufficiently robust to withstand fruity sweets.

Wines do not go well with ices, liqueurs do. Sorbets and water ices are usually served between courses to cleanse the palate and possibly to prepare it for some fine wine with the sweet course. But the sugar content of the food must be taken into account before deciding on a dessert wine. If the food is very sweet, the wine, albeit sweet, may seem acid and unbalanced. Sugar in concentrated form makes it very difficult for the details of any fine wine to be appreciated side by side with extremely sweet food. The real enemy to wine with the sweet course of a meal, however, is chocolate, while curiously coffee does not seem nearly as much of a palate stunner. Chocolate virtually nullifies the flavour of any wine, both with the food and for some while afterwards. Spirits and liqueurs flavoured with chocolate, coffee or fruit, especially orange, may be served, but no fine wine should be wasted on a chocolate sweet. The open strawberry flan in the picture opposite is accompanied by a 1965 Château de Suduiraut, 1er Cru Classé Preignac, Sauternes, an interesting example of what was elsewhere a poor year for producing fine Sauternes.

Desserts

Ices
A liqueur is probably the best choice although a fruity type of sparkling or *pétillant* wine might be served. If the ice cream is part of a concoction of various other things, such as pastry, meringue or fruit, a medium-range sweet or sweetish wine is possible.

Egg-based Sweets
Liqueurs or spirits of some kind are often included in the recipes, and the same rules apply as for ices. If the wine flavouring is light, an

assertive, medium-range sweet wine may be served; alternatively offer the same type of sweet wine as used in the recipe.

Pastries and Cakes
The ingredients determine which wine if any should be chosen. Cakes that are mainly chocolate or liqueur-flavoured cannot take a delicate wine. A robust, sparkling or *pétillant* wine is possible, but a great Champagne would be a waste with such a dish; a

non-vintage Champagne might be suitable or a fine, sweet sparkling wine if the cake is fairly simple. With rich cakes, such as milles feuilles, profiteroles and éclairs, as well as any petit fours served at the end of the meal, a digestive in the form of some spirit would probably be welcome.

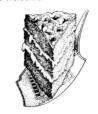

Fruit-based Sweets
The finest sweet wines can be served with recipes

involving fine fruit of a simple nature. Apples, dessert pears, berry and stone fruits are usually the best fruits with wine. With bananas and pineapple, spirits and especially rum (including Martinique rum), are possibly best. With fruit salads, steeped in a kirsch, maraschino or similar syrup, no wine should be offered, but if the syrup is based on a sweet white wine, such as a small-scale Sauternes, the same wine can be served.

Puddings
Heavy, everyday sweets, such as boiled, steamed or sponge puddings and dumplings do not go with wines of any type. With the traditional Christmas pudding, which has usually been flamed with a spirit, an inexpensive sparkling wine might be offered or a dessert wine after the pudding. The Malmseys, sweet Marsalas and Tarragona are usually too rich to drink at this stage of a fulsome Christmas dinner.

Wine with Food

Fruit

The pleasant tradition of terminating a meal with fruit can provide one of the best partnerships of wine with food. Grapes, apples, dessert pears and plums, cherries, greengages and, perhaps best of all, peaches and nectarines are excellent with all the dessert wines, sweet table wines and fortified wines, and to finish off good to fine red and white wines. Nuts in season during winter usually seem best with fortified wines. Berry fruits do not usually feature in dessert fruit selections, but strawberries, raspberries, loganberries, mulberries and even blackberries, soaked or dipped in red wine, are all good. Currants and dessert gooseberries in quantity can be rather too acid to go with most wines, and citrus fruits and pineapple are certainly too acid for all but the most ordinary dessert wines. A banana is neither good for wine nor wine for a banana. Perhaps the choice of stone fruits and pears in their prime is the happiest with fine sweet table wines. Port, dessert sherry and dessert Madeira are good with most fruit, and grapes usually go with any wine.

Ordering wines in restaurants

When choosing wine from a list where you are unfamiliar with the contents or lack the advice of an informed wine waiter, settle for the carafe or open wine, or the cheapest wine on the list. The wine two or three up from the cheapest will usually be the one the establishment is trying to push to customers.

For an important meal, the wine must be ordered well in advance, as no wine, white or red, can be prepared so as to be at its best in five or ten minutes. Order the meal before sitting down at table, and make sure the wine is ready, otherwise the hock may come with the meat and claret with the pudding. Be specific about the food so that the wine waiter can advise you. Instruct him about opening or decanting; corks should be drawn on white wines a few minutes before serving and youngish reds, whether or not they have a deposit, needs aeration. Most wine lovers are adamant that a wine cradle has no place on the table; it should be used only when a wine is drawn directly from the bin, for sudden decanting.

There are several basic rules about restaurant wine service: the bottle should be shown for you to check that it is what you ordered. The cork should be drawn in your presence, and you, as the host, should sample the first taste to check temperature, catch any bits of cork and to see that the wine is generally in good condition. Even with the cheapest wine, every bottle should be tasted in a fresh glass so that there is no risk of a corked wine being poured on top of a sound wine. With the finest wines, a fresh glass for everybody should ideally be provided with each new bottle. The waiter should not fill the glasses too full, subject white wines to near freezing in an ice bucket on a cold day, or serve a red wine that has been par-cooked by standing under a light, near a hotplate or been plunged into hot water. A bottle rejected as being out of condition—not necessarily corked but generally unsatisfactory—should be changed, at no extra charge.

Storing Wine

Cellars

Wine bottles must be kept lying on their sides, so that the corks are in contact with the wine and do not dry out, shrink, and possibly admit air. A very slight inclination of the bottle with its neck higher is permissible and keeps any deposit in the base of the bottle. Vintage port usually has a splash of whitewash, to indicate the side uppermost as originally binned, opposite where it formed its first crust, which should be allowed to re-form in the same way. Other wines should be binned labels uppermost—for ease in seeing what they are—and if the cellar is damp, tissue may protect the labels.

Wines require dark, stillness, a constant fairly low temperature, and ideally some humidity. A damp cellar is best for long maturation, 7–9°C temperature is ideal for red and white wines, but up to 10°C will not necessarily be harmful, providing there are no sudden and marked changes. At the higher temperatures, however, wine usually matures faster.

Check any "cellar" for vibration, direct rays of light, sun, draughts and anything (hot water pipes, an uninsulated roof) that may affect wines kept for more than a few weeks. If you have central heating, insulate against it; if you have a very dry, hot cellar, it is possible to install a humidified storage room, as for cigars.

The type of wine you store will be determined largely by your lifestyle and needs. You may normally wish to drink with food and/or between meals. The meals may be informal, when a less expensive wine will be appropriate, or lavish and requiring something altogether more important. Serious wine lovers will want serious wines, and the less experienced will want wine that is easily enjoyable. You may have a town apartment and a cottage in the country, each with different demands. You may simply prefer red to white or vice versa. My suggestions on the following pages are guidelines only.

Customers' reserves in the Wood Street cellars of Norton and Langridge, under Mitre Court in the City of London. Used for wine for well over a century, they were formerly a debtors' prison, established in 1555. The turnkeys' room, vaulted, was once the cellar of the Mitre Tavern, where Pepys bought his wine, and Wood Street is the route Shakespeare's Dark Lady took to visit her fortune teller.

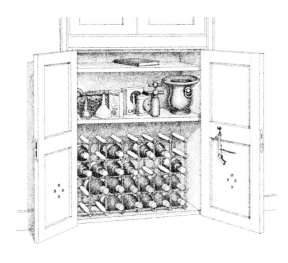

Basic cupboard cellar, with ventilated doors. The equipment includes decanting funnel, strainer, corkscrews, candle or bicycle lamp, basket, plastic funnel and filter paper, ice bucket, knife, stoppers for sparkling wine, cellarbook and plenty of clean napkins. If decanters are kept here, leave the stoppers out as stale air makes them smell—cover lightly with cloth or paper. Bin white wines at the bottom where it will be coolest.

Stocking the Cellar

The simple cellar

This may be arranged in a very small house, with no underground storage, or in an apartment, even a single room. If you have very limited space and certainly if you have central heating, a single dozen of assorted wines will probably be adequate, as you will be buying frequently and may

also be laying down wines in the custody of a merchant. A "cellar" can even consist of a single bottle. But it is always better to have two—and two bottles of any wine—because, although faulty bottles are rare, it is a disaster if you have nothing at all to replace the one that is undrinkable. Ordinary wine racks can be used in the cool corner of a kitchen, in a cupboard, corridor, or in the bottom of any storage unit that is not heated. Don't put wine in a drawer, as this will shake it, or on the top of a cupboard, as heat rises. Do try several sorts of inexpensive wines to gain experience, rather than cherish a single bottle of something so special the occasion for it may never arise—and you may be disappointed if it does.

The modest cellar

It is reassuring to know that several hundred bottles can be stored in a relatively small space. A cellar can be improvised in a loft (but insulate it against temperature changes), a garage (check for draughts, vibration and possible pilferage), under the stairs (if no hot pipes), at the bottom of a larder (if no draughts), or simply in a dimly-lit passage or boxroom. You need not buy in dozens, but remember that, if you want wines for meals, the standard bottle only yields six helpings— don't be mean; it is far better to be lavish with a modest wine than eke out something precious. Stock your cellar and broaden your knowledge with some unusual and small-scale wines: the rich and knowledgeable guest will be interested, and you will save by finding bargains and some novelties. Even for everyday purposes, don't always drink the same wine, however good or enjoyable it may be—you will widen your tasting experience and keep your palate alert with some changes.

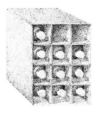

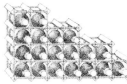

Wine can be stored quite simply, bottles being piled on each other, or in a carton tipped on its side; with a quantity, racks can be ordered to fit any convenient space.

The second cellar

If you have a second home—in the country, abroad, or even if you live mainly in the country and have a weekday working place in town—you probably need a different selection of wines. People who in one place delight in formal parties may enjoy informal and casual wines in another; those who can live partly in a wine region can keep stocks of all the local wines; those who drink mainly spirits and some medium quality wines in one home, can enjoy the change to finer wines and more subtle between-times drinks elsewhere. For casual living, have plenty of wines that can be served without preliminary preparation, with a few finer ones for special occasions. If you make a feature of a special type of cooking, select wines to go with the dishes you serve most often—whites for those who fish or live by the sea, robust reds for those who shoot or hunt game, wines to discuss at length if you enjoy long sessions of talk around the table.

The large scale cellar

Presumably you have actually got a cellar underground—dark, quiet, of lowish temperature and fairly damp—or else have been able to build a store for your wine that, by means of insulation and temperature control, will keep it in condition. Depending on the size, you may wish to use it for long-term laying down as well as for the

reserves on which you draw frequently. If you can divide the cellar, the smaller part will hold everyday fortified, sparkling and table wines, those of slightly more special importance, and the medium personality and weighty wines as they come up to their peak drinking seasons.

The greater part of this cellar will usually be made up of a selection of classic wines, unless you live in a wine region, when obviously there will be more of the local wines. But there are some wines of which it is not generally economical— either of space or money—to hold very large stocks, unless space and money are of no object. I would exclude any large quantity (five or more case lots) of non-vintage Champagne and sparkling wines, all but the finest white wines in general, all white wines that are most enjoyable when drunk young and fresh (unless you have an enormous establishment and give vast parties), the great sweet table wines (or not for more than 5–10 years, as you can usually buy these as and when you need them), ordinary fortified wines (unless you happen to be a devotee of old-bottled sherry) and all those red wines that are at their best when drunk fairly young. Your cellar will therefore logically be mainly composed of 60–75 per cent good to fine classic reds (including vintage port) with classic whites making up about 30 per cent, or half and half of each, according to your tastes. You will buy in case lots—an economy and something that facilitates re-sale; you can also watch the progress of a great wine as it ages.

The contents of your cellar
In compiling the suggestions for cellar stock I have seen no sense in nominating specific wines which may be unobtainable by readers, and are anyway in limited supply. Nor have I mentioned everyday wines that are sold under one name in one market and labelled as a merchant's brand in another. I have indicated types and styles—reference to the Classification will give a variety of examples. Generally, quality is indicated by the price range. I have not included half bottles, which are seldom truly economic; if you stopper any bottle of table wine and keep it in a cool place, it will be perfectly drinkable for 24 hours.

Ideally, any cellar should be selected with the personal advice of a wine merchant—and preferably several, for no one can know or stock everything. They will bin for you if required.

CELLARS OF DIFFERENT SIZE	Still Red wines	Still White wines	Others
Simple and cheaply composed cellars A cellar with not more than a dozen bottles should certainly include a moderately fruity dry white. This will provide for any-time drinks, serve as an apéritif and will go with most casual food, fish and light dishes. It could be the only wine kept.	1 or 2 bottles each of NON-VINTAGE, perhaps branded wine; MEDIUM PERSONALITY red, such as any made from the Gamay.	1 or 2 bottles each of DRY white with moderate fruit, such as Riesling, Chardonnay, Sauvignon or Chenin Blanc; DRY to MEDIUM DRY regional whites.	1 bottle each of DRY VERMOUTH; AMONTILLADO SHERRY or medium dry apéritif; CHAMPAGNE, non-vintage, for celebration or consolation.
Modest and medium priced cellars A more ambitious cellar of some thirty to sixty bottles should include apéritifs, sparkling wines and perhaps a dozen bottles each of everyday and medium quality wines, both white and red. There will be room for a few classics and special interest choices.	6 bottles each of STRAIGHTFORWARD everyday and medium quality reds. 2–6 bottles each of REGIONAL reds, possibly vintage, such as parish Beaujolais; CLASSIC reds, such as bourgeois Bordeaux, Rhônes, or southern Burgundies with medium personality and of interesting vintage.	6 bottles each of DRY to MEDIUM DRY everyday and medium quality whites. 2–6 bottles each of DRY whites of medium or fine quality, such as Rieslings or other lightish wines, and either Chardonnay, Loire or medium to fine white Burgundy. 1 or 2 bottles of SWEET white, good to fine quality.	2 bottles each of FINO or AMONTILLADO SHERRY; SERCIAL; DRY VERMOUTH; SPARKLING wine, dryish non-vintage; CHAMPAGNE, vintage; PÉTILLANT wine, white or pink. 1 bottle each of TAWNY PORT; CHAMBÉRY VERMOUTH; MANZANILLA; FINO SHERRY, straight solera.
Large scale cellars These cellars may be of any size so I will not attempt to be specific about quantities. You will already probably have the contents of the preceding cellars and should add to them as required. However it is now possible to also increase the range of your stock while keeping a sensible balance with the more commonly drunk wines.	ESTATE wines of the classic regions, and wines from other regions that are able to last long in bottle. Select these wines to afford interest as regards vintages, specific sites, growers and shippers. Also look for unusual small-scale reds and regional vintages.	As with red wines, choose ESTATE wines of the classic regions and elsewhere, making sure they will last well. Again, look for interest. INTENSELY SWEET Tokay and Sauternes can be included, as well as some Vouvrays, Quart de Chaume and the finer German sweet wines.	MONTILLA; WHITE VERMOUTH; SHERRIES, various; PORT, white, fine old tawny and especially vintage; DRY MARSALA; SPARKLING wines, a selection of white and pink; CHAMPAGNE, vintage and luxury, some magnums; Also rareties such as old Madeiras, *vins doux naturels* and old Commandarias.

Keeping a Record

It is important to keep a record of what wines you have, and especially important if they are not all kept in your home. In many merchants' cellars huge reserves exist unclaimed because their owners have died or the records have been destroyed. It is useful to know what you possess. The old type of cellarbook is still used by many, but often tends to be a stock book, for those who buy in dozens of dozens. If you can, combine your wine records with a set of tasting notes and possible with some kind of dinner book as well. It is up to you to set out the book in a format you can use easily.

A tasting book, which obviously may be carried about, cannot always be combined with a cellarbook, and sometimes people just file tasting notes from tastings they attend, or the diaries they keep when travelling in wine regions. It is useful to note the sort of reaction to wines used at meals, as this will enable you to avoid giving friends the same wines (and foods) on successive visits.

Remember, if you have stocks lying in a merchant's cellars, that these are not necessarily "under the shop" and he may need several days' notice to get them out. This is the sort of information you should note in your records, together with any reports sent to you on the progress of wines held for you elsewhere.

If you possess considerable reserves of wine, it is worth knowing their value: a merchant will give you an idea of what this is, and a professional valuation may be essential for insurance and tax purposes. Basic information in any cellar or record book should include: the wine's name, together with all relevant particulars; when it was bought and where; what was paid. Space for tasting notes should be allocated, and the date when tasted always recorded.

Laying down

Recently, people have tended to think of wine as an article for trading—and therefore as a long-term "investment". For anyone without considerable knowledge and experience, this is not only likely to be an abuse of a commodity that is perishable, but speculation in wine can force up prices and can often result in the original investor losing money.

What *is* always a good idea is to buy for laying down so that, in due course, some of the great classic wines are available for individual enjoyment, a saving having been achieved by buying them young and great interest being taken in their progress. Even the cheapest type of red wine, certain of the robust whites and non-vintage Champagne will benefit by a period of extra maturation after being bought; six to twelve months in a cellar will add enormously to their quality. Although the greatest white Burgundies and some German wines in the top ranges can be laid down usefully, their lives tend to be shorter than those of the great reds.

Vintage port, classed growth Bordeaux and certain of the finest red Burgundies are the obvious choices for long-term maturation, although lovers of the fine red wines of any region can certainly gain great pleasure from giving their favourites the benefit of slow development in ideal conditions. If you need to sell back your wine, then case lots (dozens) of estate bottlings are essential. You can acquire a good cellar by putting away even a modest sum per month or year for a merchant to use for you. If you want to drink your wines after a short rather than long time—drawing on your reserves frequently—then suitable wines can be bought for this. You may prefer to put away wines for ten or twenty years, but ideally the wine should then be in a merchant's own cellars, unless he has been able to approve your own. Any reputable merchant will deal with your orders even if you are on the other side of the world—and usually can give you a regular report on the progress of your own wines from the regular tastings they make.

The Cellarbook
Conventional types of tasting, bin, or cellarbooks have columns ruled for comments. Unless you have minute handwriting, it is my experience that the ready-made cellarbooks seldom allow enough space—a looseleaf book ruled up to your own liking is probably more satisfactory.

WINE	YEAR	QUANTITY	SHIPPER	DATE BOUGHT	PRICE PAID		DATE OF DRINKING	ACCOMPANYING FOOD	GUESTS	TASTING NOTES	BALANCE IN STOCK

Wine Regions
of the World

Wine Regions of the World

The vine can grow in places where few other crops will yield satisfactorily, but it flourishes in warm to temperate regions, and gives quality wines in areas on the borders of these regions, where it is at the mercy of variations of climate as well as extremes of heat and cold. Where the vine has to fight for life, fine wines may be made.

Regions where the climate is constant tend to make wines of constant quality, unlikely to excel in any particular way. A generally hot vineyard makes fullish red wines, and soft whites. Cold vineyards make whites that are high in acidity, and reds that tend to lack fruit. This is why the finest red and white wines tend to come from areas specially suited to them, and not always from a single region that can make the best of both red and white.

In terms of history as well as of present-day production, the main wine-growing countries are located around the Mediterranean and in western Europe, with Italy and France producing the largest quantities. More recently, vineyards in the Americas, Australasia and Africa have become of increasing importance.

The vine, in fact, is very widely grown, and produces wine in commercial quantities in countries as far apart as India and England, Canada and Egypt, as well as in those more commonly associated with wine production. Its cultivation is most varied, though, in parts of the world which are, or have been, most exposed to European influence.

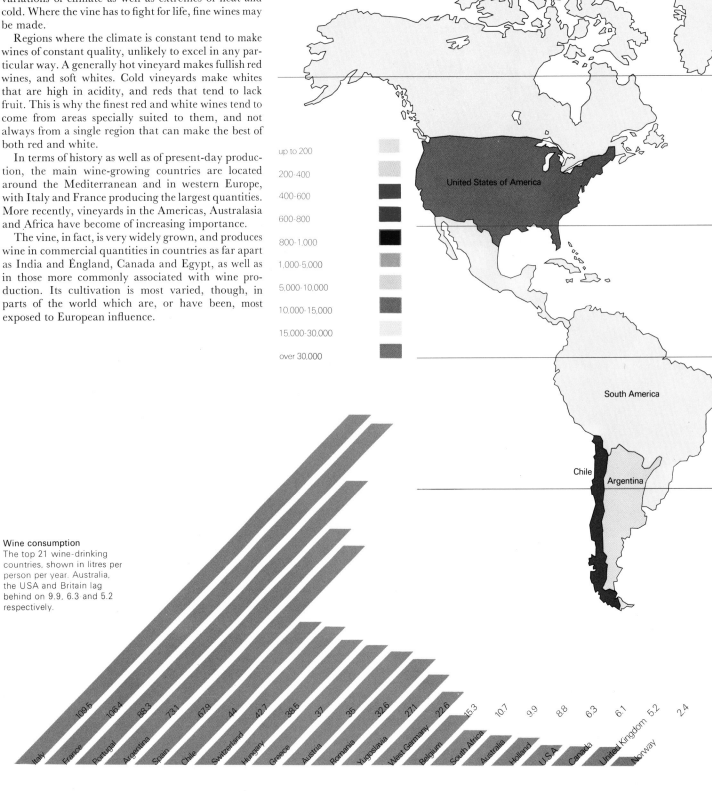

up to 200
200-400
400-600
600-800
800-1,000
1,000-5,000
5,000-10,000
10,000-15,000
15,000-30,000
over 30,000

Wine consumption
The top 21 wine-drinking countries, shown in litres per person per year. Australia, the USA and Britain lag behind on 9.9, 6.3 and 5.2 respectively.

Italy 109.6
France 106.4
Portugal 88.3
Argentina 73.1
Spain 67.9
Chile 44
Switzerland 42.7
Hungary 38.5
Greece 37
Austria 35
Romania 32.6
Yugoslavia 27.1
West Germany 22.6
Belgium 15.3
South Africa 10.7
Australia 9.9
Holland 8.8
USA 6.3
Canada 6.1
United Kingdom 5.2
Norway 2.4

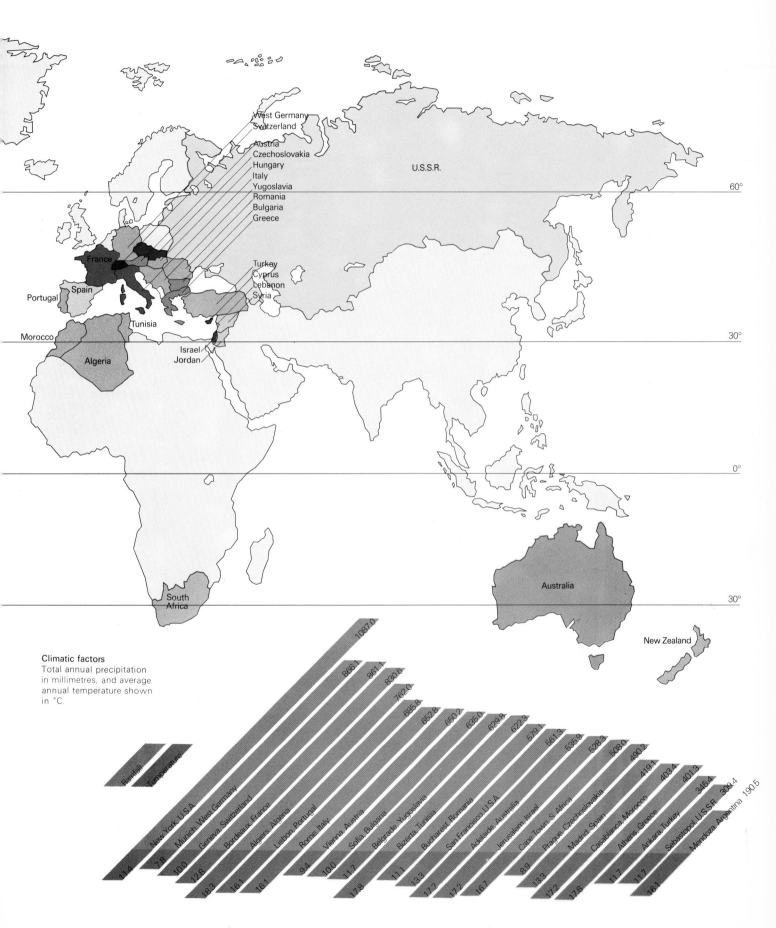

Climatic factors
Total annual precipitation
in millimetres, and average
annual temperature shown
in °C.

West Germany
Switzerland
Austria
Czechoslovakia
Hungary
Italy
Yugoslavia
Romania
Bulgaria
Greece

U.S.S.R.

Turkey
Cyprus
Lebanon
Syria

France
Spain
Portugal
Tunisia
Morocco
Algeria
Israel
Jordan
South Africa
Australia
New Zealand

60°
30°
0°
30°

Rainfall
Temperature

New York, U.S.A.   1087.0   11.4
Munich, West Germany   866.1   7.8
Geneva, Switzerland   861.1   10.0
Bordeaux, France   830.6   12.8   18.3
Algiers, Algeria   762.0   16.1
Lisbon, Portugal   685.8   16.1
Rome, Italy   652.8
Vienna, Austria   650.2   9.4
Sofia, Bulgaria   635.0   10.0   17.8
Belgrade, Yugoslavia   629.8   11.7   13.3
Bizerta, Tunisia   622.2   17.2
Bucharest, Romania   579.1   11.1   17.2
San Francisco, U.S.A.   561.3   16.7
Adelaide, Australia   536.9
Jerusalem, Israel   528.3   8.9   13.3
Cape Town, S. Africa   508.0
Prague, Czechoslovakia   490.2   17.2
Madrid, Spain   419.1   17.8
Casablanca, Morocco   403.4
Athens, Greece   401.3   11.7
Ankara, Turkey   346.4   11.7
Sebastopol, U.S.S.R.   309.4   16.1
Mendoza, Argentina   190.5

153

France

The Francophile will say that France can supply all the wines necessary for the enjoyment of life. It produces the supreme sparkling wine, the two greatest red table wines, and some of the greatest sweet wines, so it is natural to relate most tasting experiences to French wines, and impossible to write about wine without discussing France.

No one can know all the French wines, but every wine lover should try to get to know some. Luckily, many are available all over the world. There are good, even fine, wines made in many different countries, but in certain French vineyards some wines achieve a quality and interest, tried by time, which makes the study of wine far more than that of something merely to drink.

Appellation contrôlée

French wine production is strictly controlled. A government body, the Institut National des Appellations d'Origine des Vins et des Eaux-de-Vie (INAO) has charge of it. In general, INAO grants an AOC or AC (*appellation contrôlée*) in conjunction with the local syndicates of the various wine regions. The regulations define: the type of grapes planted; the method of pruning and training the vines; the number of vines planted per hectare; the maximum amount of wine that can be produced per hectare; the minimum amount of sugar in the must; the minimum degree of alcohol in the finished wine and, of course, the area.

The AC regulations can apply to an overall area (Beaujolais, Bordeaux), or a more limited area (Côtes du Rhône, St Emilion), with the type of wine (red, pink or white) often appended. Then there are the names of parishes within these regions. It is easy to see that the ACs fit inside each other. For example, Château Lascombes is an AC Margaux, as an estate in the parish of Margaux; it need not state anything more on its label, but Margaux itself is within the AC Médoc, and the Médoc in turn is within the ACs of Bordeaux Supérieur, and simple Bordeaux.

A label that bears the AC of a large general area will usually be lower in the category than one that particularises. At the extreme is the tiny Rhône estate, Château Grillet, which alone in France has its own individual AC. The only major French wine not obliged to indicate its AC status is Champagne, which uses the traditional "Vin de Champagne". The AC can be useful in sorting out wines with similar names: there is only one Château Latour AC Pauillac, but there are six other Bordeaux growths with "Latour" on their labels.

What is essential to understand is that the AC regulations only control where and how the wines are made; none is, and cannot be more than an indication of implied quality. A wine can be 100 per cent what its AC states, and not necessarily be what you enjoy or think good.

All the fine French wines are now AC, but much is still being done to sort out the anomalies. Dry wines made on the great Sauternes estates can only bear the AC Bordeaux Supérieur, because when the regulations were laid down all Sauternes were sweet. Or, in a suddenly successful vintage, much wine may have to be declassified to a lower AC just because too much is made—even though it may be identical with the higher priced wine with the higher AC.

Below the AC wines comes the Vins Delimités de Qualité Supérieur (VDQS), also subject to controls, though not quite as rigorous. They are becoming very important and, thanks to modern techniques, can be very good small-scale wines. Occasionally the category Appellation d'Origine Simple may be seen on old "little" wines. This, also below the AC category, is falling out of use. *Vin de pays* and *vin de table* are the next categories. *Vins de marque*, in spite of their high-sounding name, are branded wines, put out by companies offering consistent quality at moderate prices. They should not be confused with the *vins ordinaires* or *vins de consommation courant* (wines for everyday drinking), nor with the *vins de la région*.

Regional production of wine

Languedoc-Roussillon	40%
Bordeaux	9½%
Loire Valley	9%
Provence	6½%
Côtes du Rhône	6%
Bourgogne (Burgundy)	3½%
Dordogne	2%
Pyrenees	2%
Corsica	less than 2%
Alsace	less than 2%
Champagne	less than 1%
Jura	less than 1%
Alps	less than 1%
Rest of France	18%

Total annual production ('000 hl.)

1965	66,568
1966	60,935
1967	60,993
1968	65,120
1969	49,803
1970	74,373
1971	61,331
1972	58,498
1973	82,425
1974	75,482

World exports

West Germany	33%
Belgium/Luxembourg	14%
Great Britain	12%
Switzerland	8%
Netherlands	6%
U.S.A.	5%
Italy	4%
Rest of world	18%

E.E.C. exports

West Germany	46%
Belgium/Luxembourg	20%
Great Britain	17%
Netherlands	8%
Italy	6%
Denmark	2%
Ireland	1%

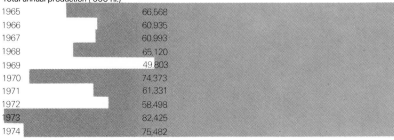

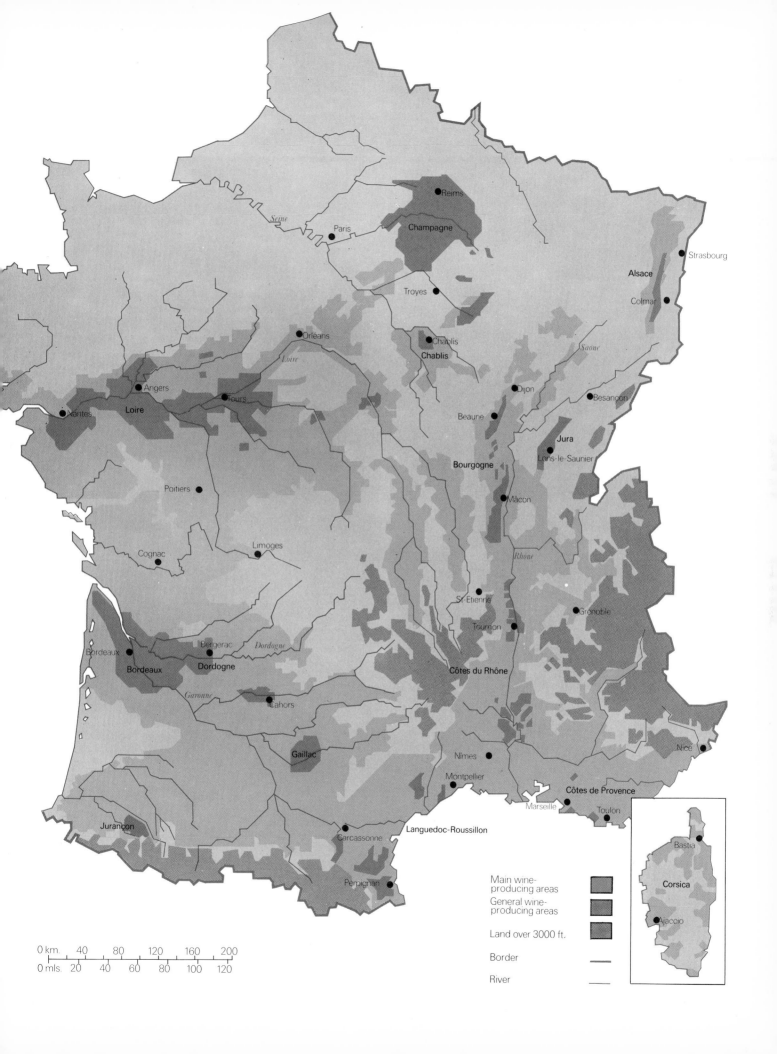

Reims
Paris
Seine
Champagne
Troyes
Strasbourg
Alsace
Colmar
Orléans
Chablis
Chablis
Loire
Saône
Angers
Tours
Loire
Dijon
Nantes
Besançon
Beaune
Jura
Bourgogne
Lons-le-Saunier
Poitiers
Mâcon
Cognac
Limoges
Rhône
St-Étienne
Grenoble
Tournon
Bordeaux
Bergerac
Dordogne
Bordeaux
Dordogne
Côtes du Rhône
Garonne
Cahors
Gaillac
Nîmes
Nice
Montpellier
Côtes de Provence
Marseille
Toulon
Juançon
Languedoc-Roussillon
Carcassonne
Perpignan

Main wine-producing areas
General wine-producing areas
Land over 3000 ft.
Border
River

0 km.   40   80   120   160   200
0 mls. 20   40   60   80   100 120

Bastia
Corsica
Ajaccio

France: Burgundy

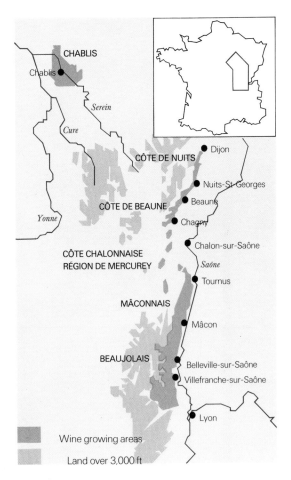

Nomenclature

In Burgundy there are the general vineyard areas, such as the Côte de Nuits; within them the parishes (*communes*), such as Nuits-St-Georges; within these are specific sites (*climats*) such as Les Saint-Georges, Les Vaucrains, and within the *climats* are specific plots or holdings, which may bear individual names too, or simply the name of the grower. The reputation of individual growers is as important as that of the individual plots. When it is remembered that a number of different people may possess holdings in the parishes, as well as in the sites and plots, that each will cultivate these and make the wine in an individual way (Clos de Vougeot has about 100 different owners) it will be appreciated that it is impossible to generalize about Burgundy. Usually, the great vineyard—for example, Le Chambertin—will have its name attached to that of the parish—Gevrey-Chambertin—but in the Côte de Beaune the white Corton-Charlemagne is greater than white Corton.

It should therefore be understood that, whether wines are bottled at their estates, at the shippers' establishments in the region, or elsewhere, their variations are enormous: in addition to differences due to the grower, the plot, the site, the vineyard, the region and the vintage, the wines from the many different establishments will all vary considerably in price and some in quality. It must be for the consumer to judge for himself as to what he likes best.

Vintages

Burgundy tends to mature faster than Bordeaux, but much depends on the way individual shippers handle their wines. It also depends in certain export markets on whether these are decanted off any deposit, which obviously shortens the wine's life. The southern Burgundies vary less sharply than those of the Côte d'Or from year to year, and a good year for reds is not necessarily the same for the whites.

White Burgundies

1970 good; 1971 fuller and more assertive, great in Chablis; 1972 goodish and promising; 1973 good drinking, likely to improve over the next two or three years (1976–78), some fine Chablis.

Grapes

White wines
Chardonnay for the quality wines (called Beaunois in Chablis)
Aligoté for other whites.
Red wines
Pinot Noir for Burgundies of quality.
Gamay for Beaujolais.
(Bourgogne Passe-tout-Grains is a mixture of about one-third Pinot Noir to two-thirds Gamay).
Pink or *rosé wines*
These are also made, those of Marsannay-la-Côte being the best known.

Red Burgundies

Red Burgundies
1967 lightish but with elegance, drink now (1975–76);
1969 keep for the future; 1970 stylish, though a little
lightweight, some to keep; 1971 small crop, some very
fine, definitely to keep; 1972 easy drinking, not perhaps
exciting; 1973 a great deal of wine, choice must be
careful to get quality.

Beaujolais
Usually most enjoyable within two to five years of
vintage, but ordinary Beaujolais and Beaujolais
Villages better drunk young. Beaujolais "Nouveau"
usually best drunk within six months of its vintage.
Parish wines and single estates can mature longer,
Brouilly, Côtes de Brouilly, Morgon and Moulin-à-
Vent usually being best with some bottle age.

Vineyards

Côte Chalonnaise/Région de Mercurey The central region
of Burgundy is a natural continuation of the Côte de
Beaune, and similar in soil and climate. The areas of
Mercurey itself, Rully, Givry, Buxy and Montagny
are the primary vineyards making reds and whites.

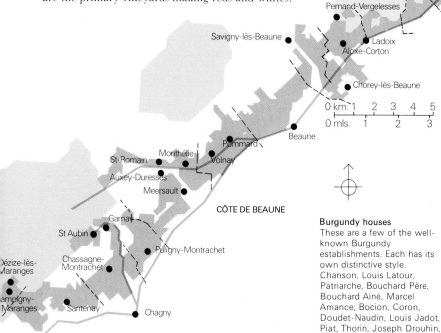

CÔTE DE NUITS

Chenove
Marsannay-la-Côte
Fixin
Gevrey-Chambertin
Morey-St-Denis
Chambolle-Musigny
Vougeot
Vosne-Romanée
Nuits-St-Georges
Premeaux

Principal wine
growing areas
Secondary wine
growing areas
Route Nationale
Parish boundaries

Pernand-Vergelesses
Savigny-lès-Beaune
Ladoix
Aloxe-Corton
Chorey-lès-Beaune

0 km. 1 2 3 4 5
0 mls. 1 2 3

St-Romain
Monthélie
Auxey-Duresses
Meersault
Pommard
Volnay
Beaune

CÔTE DE BEAUNE

Gamay
St Aubin
Puligny-Montrachet
Dézize-lès-Maranges
Chassagne-Montrachet
Sampigny-Maranges
Santenay
Chagny

Beaujolais-Villages (the wines from 30 communes
which may join their names to that of Beaujolais), and
the commune or parish wines: Saint-Amour, Juliénas,
Chénas, Moulin-à-Vent, Fleurie, Chiroubles, Morgon,
Brouilly, Côte de Brouilly, and nowadays there are
some specified estates labelling their own wines.

Chablis Includes the Grands Crus, Premiers Crus,
those simply labelled Chablis, and Petit Chablis. The
soil is light in colour, the climate can be wet and cold.

Côte d'Or Divided into the Côte de Nuits (making the
finest reds) and the Côte de Beaune (the finest whites).
The best wines come from half to two-thirds of the way
up the slope.

Burgundy houses
These are a few of the well-
known Burgundy
establishments. Each has its
own distinctive style.
Chanson, Louis Latour,
Patriarche, Bouchard Père,
Bouchard Aîné, Marcel
Amance, Bocion, Coron,
Doudet-Naudin, Louis Jadot,
Piat, Thorin, Joseph Drouhin,
Sichel, Prosper Maufoux,
Dépagneux, Georges
Duboeuf, Ropiteau, Viénot,
Albert Thierry, Remoissenet.

Mâconnais The region enjoys a milder climate than the
Côte d'Or and its light, often rocky vineyards make a
variety of excellent wines, both red and white. The
white Pouillys, Fuissé, Solutré, Vergisson, Loché and
Vinzelles, and white Mâcons, notably those of Clessé,
Chardonnay, Lugny and Viré are all worth attention,
and St Véran is a recently introduced AOC. The red
Mâcons, made from both the Pinot Noir and the
Gamay, often bear village names, and have an agree-
able crisp style.

Beaujolais Most of the wine is red, made from the
Gamay, although nowadays there is a little white,
made from the Aligoté. In ascending order of quality,
the wines are: Beaujolais, Beaujolais Supérieur,

Petit Chablis
Chablis
Chablis Grand Cru

Serein

CHABLIS

0 km. 1 2 3 4 5
0 mls. 1 2 3

Maligny
Lignorelles
Fontenay
Poinchy
Chablis
Fleys
Viviers
Chichée
Préhy

France: Bordeaux

No lover of Bordeaux—and there have been many since even before the Middle Ages—is capable of describing its wines in a few words. Each Bordeaux estate, including the bourgeois growths, possesses its own special individuality. However, if it is accepted that there are always exceptions, these comments on the Bordeaux regions may perhaps indicate the general styles of the different areas:

Bourg & Blaye Robust reds and medium quality whites. In good vintages the reds possess a full, slightly earthy flavour that appeals very much to many.

Fronsac These reds can have a lightness and elegance that makes them worth trying.

Graves de Vayres Can be light, almost elegant reds.

Entre-Deux-Mers Pleasant white wines.

Premières Côtes de Bordeaux Some distinguished small-scale whites and pleasant reds.

Cérons Lightly zippy, slightly sweet whites.

Ste-Croix-du-Mont Sweet whites on a small scale.

Loupiac Small-scale whites with a touch of spiciness.

Sauternes Full, luscious whites, beginning sweet, continuing sweet and ending sweet, with great profundity (and some dry but full whites that cannot bear the AC Sauternes which only applies to sweet wines).

Barsac Sweet, but with an odd, enticing dry finish (and some dry wines, as for Sauternes).

Graves The white Graves of the great estates have delicacy and depth, the reds great charm, spice and subtlety—not beginners' wines, but showing the pebbly character of the region and outstanding breed.

St-Emilion Full, often huge reds, sometimes called the Burgundies of Bordeaux, which to me always have a certain earthy back taste, of immediate appeal and often great length and fruit.

Pomerol The soil changes—and the wines show a pebbly finesse, often combining firmness with delicacy.

Haut-Médoc So many wines from such widely apart areas are included that it is impossible to make any statement—but some are very fine.

Moulis and Listrac Deserving of more attention—each individual, but both share a lightness and potential elegance.

Margaux Wines with fruit, charm, subtlety and graciousness—can be on a very large scale, but fine appealing classics for the beginner.

St Julien Close-textured bouquet, velvety wines, in my view ideal for the beginner in Bordeaux, because of their easy charm.

Pauillac Many different types of nobility—charm, reserve, magnificence, or, when young, a hardness and uncompromising style that is not always easy to understand. Do not treat a great Pauillac as casual drinking—you will not enjoy it.

St Estèphe For the slightly experienced, because they tend to be hard, slightly stalky until they mature, but they can possess great firmness and finesse in great years and sturdy appeal in the little wines.

Classed growths

Term chiefly used for certain Médoc growths which, with one red Graves (Haut Brion) were classified in 1855. The Sauternes and Barsacs were also classified in this year, the red Graves in 1953, the St-Emilions in 1955, and the white Graves in 1959 (Haut Brion Blanc not being included at the request of the owner). Mouton Rothschild, originally classified as a second growth, was reclassified as a first in 1973. It is not obligatory for an estate to indicate its classification on its label: Latour does, Lafite never has.

The thing to remember is that the classification was based on the prices the wines were expected to fetch, not as a direct indication of quality. But it is fair to say that, in spite of efforts to get a revised classification, the old one still serves, and most classed growths are, by implication, fine wines—or capable of being so. The vast improvement in quality of the bourgeois and artisan growths has led to proposals to include the outstanding estates of these in future classifications.

CLASSED GROWTHS
Médoc
Premiers Crus Ch. Lafite, Latour and Mouton-Rothschild from Pauillac; Ch. Margaux from Margaux; Ch. Haut Brion from Pessac (Graves).
Deuxièmes Crus from Margaux: Ch. Rausan-Ségla, Rauzan-Gassies, Durfort-Vivens, Lascombes; from St Julien: Ch. Léoville-Lascases, Léoville Poyferre, Léoville-Barton, Gruaud-Larose, Ducru-Beaucaillou; from Pauillac: Ch. Pichon-Longueville, Pichon-Longueville-Lalande; from Cantenac: Ch. Brane-Cantenac; from St Estèphe: Ch. Cos d'Estournel, Montrose.
Troisièmes Crus from Cantenac: Ch. Kirwan, Issan, Cantenac-Brown, Palmer; from St Julien: Ch. Lagrange, Langoa; from Labarde: Ch. Giscours; from Margaux: Ch. Malescot-St-Exupéry, Desmirail, Ferrière, Marquis d'Alesme-Becker, Boyd-Cantenac; from Ludon: Ch. Grand la Lagune; from St Estèphe: Ch. Calon-Ségur.
Quatrièmes Crus from St Julien: Ch. St-Pierre-Sevaistre, St-Pierre-Bontemps, Branaire-Ducru, Talbot, Beychevelle; from Pauillac: Ch. Duhart-Milon; from Cantenac: Ch. Poujet, le Prieuré; from St. Laurent: Ch. la Tour Carnet; from St Estèphe: Ch. Rochet; from Margaux: Ch. Marquis de Terme.
Cinquièmes Crus from Pauillac: Ch. Pontet Canet, Batailley, Haut-Batailley, Grand-Puy-Lacoste, Grand-Puy-Ducasse, Lynch-Bages, Lynch-Moussas, Mouton Baron Philippe, Haut-Bages-Liberal, Pédesclaux, Clerc-Milon, Croizet-Bages; from Labarde: Ch. Dauzac; from Arsac: Ch. le Tertre; from St Laurent: Ch. Belgrave, Camensac; from St Estèphe: Ch. Cos-Labory; from Macau: Ch. Cantemerle.

Red Graves
From Cadaujac: Ch. Bouscaut; from Léognan: Ch. Haut-Bailly, Domaine de Chevalier, Carbonnieux, Fieuzal, Malartic-Lagrevière, Oliver; from Martillac: Ch. la Tour Martillac, Smith-Haut-Lafitte; from Pessac: Ch. Haut Brion, Pape Clément; from Talence: Ch. la Mission Haut Brion, la Tour Haut Brion.

St-Emilion
Premier Grand Cru Classé
Ch. Ausone, Beauséjour, Cheval Blanc, Belair, Canon, Figeac, la Gaffelière-Naudes, Magdelaine, Pavie, Trottevieille, Clos Fourtet.
Grand Cru Classé
Ch. l'Arrosée, l'Angélus, Balestard-la-Tonnelle, Bellevue, Bergat, Cadet-Piola, Cadet-Bon, Canon-la-Gaffelière, Cap-de-Mourlin, Chapelle-Madeleine, Chauvin, Corbin, Coutet, Croque-Michotte, Curé-Bon, Fonplégade, Fonroque, Franc-Mayne, Grand Barrail, Grand-Corbin-Despagne, Grand-Corbin-Pécresse, Grand-Mayne, Grand-Pontet, Grandes-Murailles, Guadet-St-Julien, Jean-Faure, la Carte, la Clotte, la Clusière, la Couspaude, la Dominique, Larcis-Ducasse, Lamarzelle, Lamarzelle-Figeac, Larmande, Laroze, Lasserre, la Tour-du-Pin-Figeac, la Tour-Figeac, le Châtelet, le Couvent, le Prieuré, Mauvezin, Moulin du Cadet, Pavie-Décesse, Pavie-Macquin, Pavillon-Cadet, Petit-Faurie de Souchard, Faurie de Soutard, Ripeau, Sansonnet, St-Georges-Côte-Pavie, Soutard, Terte-Daugay, Trimoulet, Trois-Moulins, Troplong-Mondot, Villemaurine, Yon Figeac, Clos des Jacobins, Clos la Madeleine, Clos Saint-Martin.

White Sauternes and Barsac
Grand Premier Cru Ch. d'Yquem, from Sauternes.
Premiers Crus from Bommes: Ch. la Tour Blanche, Peyraguey (Clos Haut Peyraguey, Lafaurie Peyraguey), Rayne-Vigneau, Rabaud (Rabaud-Promis, Sigalas-Rabaud), Peixotto; from Preignac: Ch. de Suduiraut, de Malle; from Barsac: Ch. Coutet, Climens, de Myrat, Doisy (Doisy-Dubroca, Doisy-Daëne, Doisy-Védrines), Broustet, Nairac, Caillou, Suau; from Fargues: Ch. Guiraud, Raymond-Lafon; from Sauternes: Ch. d'Arche (d'Arche-Lafaurie), Filhot, Lamothe (Lamothe-Bergey, Lamothe-Espagnet).

White Graves
From Cadaujac: Ch. Bouscaut; from Martillac: Ch. la Tour Martillac; from Talence: Ch. Laville-Haut Brion; from Villenave-d'Ornon: Ch. Couhins; from Léognan: Ch. Carbonnieux, Olivier, Domaine de Chevalier, Malartic-Lagravière.

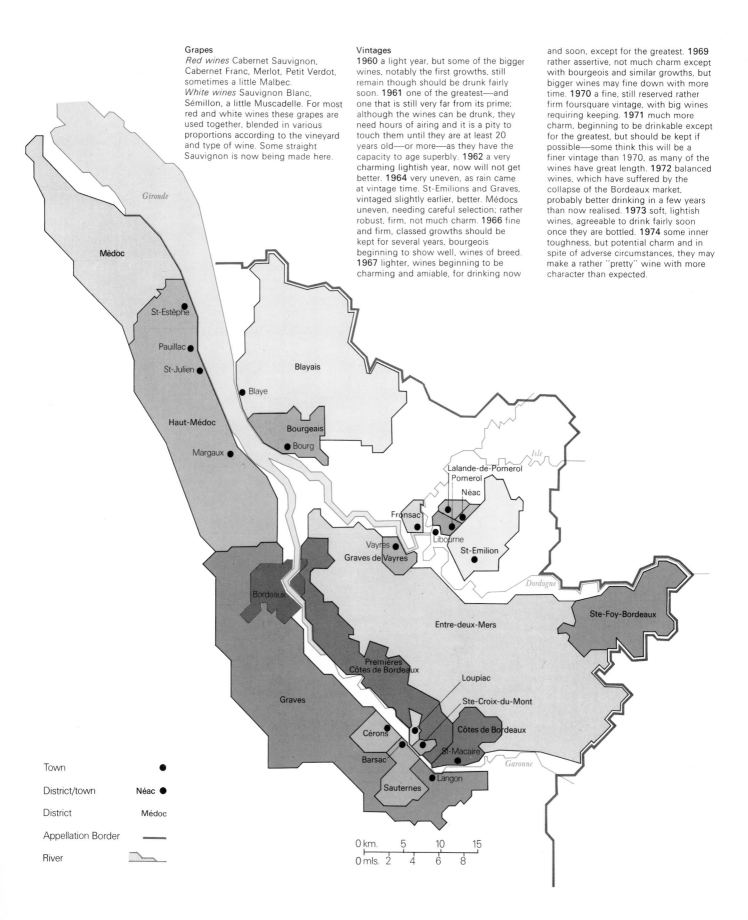

Grapes

Red wines Cabernet Sauvignon, Cabernet Franc, Merlot, Petit Verdot, sometimes a little Malbec.
White wines Sauvignon Blanc, Sémillon, a little Muscadelle. For most red and white wines these grapes are used together, blended in various proportions according to the vineyard and type of wine. Some straight Sauvignon is now being made here.

Vintages

1960 a light year, but some of the bigger wines, notably the first growths, still remain though should be drunk fairly soon. **1961** one of the greatest—and one that is still very far from its prime; although the wines can be drunk, they need hours of airing and it is a pity to touch them until they are at least 20 years old—or more—as they have the capacity to age superbly. **1962** a very charming lightish year, now will not get better. **1964** very uneven, as rain came at vintage time. St-Emilions and Graves, vintaged slightly earlier, better. Médocs uneven, needing careful selection; rather robust, firm, not much charm. **1966** fine and firm, classed growths should be kept for several years, bourgeois beginning to show well, wines of breed. **1967** lighter, wines beginning to be charming and amiable, for drinking now and soon, except for the greatest. **1969** rather assertive, not much charm except with bourgeois and similar growths, but bigger wines may fine down with more time. **1970** a fine, still reserved rather firm foursquare vintage, with big wines requiring keeping. **1971** much more charm, beginning to be drinkable except for the greatest, but should be kept if possible—some think this will be a finer vintage than 1970, as many of the wines have great length. **1972** balanced wines, which have suffered by the collapse of the Bordeaux market, probably better drinking in a few years than now realised. **1973** soft, lightish wines, agreeable to drink fairly soon once they are bottled. **1974** some inner toughness, but potential charm and in spite of adverse circumstances, they may make a rather ''pretty'' wine with more character than expected.

Map labels: Gironde, Médoc, St-Estèphe, Pauillac, St-Julien, Haut-Médoc, Blaye, Blayais, Margaux, Bourgeais, Bourg, Isle, Lalande-de-Pomerol, Pomerol, Néac, Fronsac, Vayres, Libourne, St-Emilion, Graves de Vayres, Dordogne, Bordeaux, Ste-Foy-Bordeaux, Entre-deux-Mers, Premières Côtes de Bordeaux, Loupiac, Ste-Croix-du-Mont, Graves, Cérons, Côtes de Bordeaux, St-Macaire, Barsac, Garonne, Langon, Sauternes

Legend:
Town ●
District/town Néac ●
District Médoc
Appellation Border ——
River

0 km. 5 10 15
0 mls. 2 4 6 8

France: Rhône and Loire

Rhône

Throughout the region, red and white wines are made, sparkling wines by the Champagne method at St Peray and Clairette de Die, and numerous pink wines, especially in the south of the area. The region has been under vines since possibly 600 BC, when the Phoenicians are thought to have brought the grape to Provence.

The Rhône wines taste as you would expect wines to taste from a fairly dramatic, north to south vineyard: the reds are generous and, as it were, warm-hearted, the whites full, buxom and varying from dry to full, with some sweet wines in the south. In the northern areas the vineyards are steeply sloped above the river; where the Rhône slightly alters course at Tain-Tournon they are dramatically terraced on both sides. Further south, the landscape opens out and can vary considerably. The vineyards of Châteauneuf-du-Pape, for example, consist partly of sand and of gravel, but most conspicuously of gigantic stones, like huge baked potatoes, golden-brown in colour and porous, so that they hold the heat of the sun. It is difficult to walk on them without risking turning one's ankle.

Red, white, pink and some sparkling wines are made, and certain fine dessert Muscats, such as those of Beaumes de Venise.

A wide range of grapes are also used, black and white grapes often being used for both red and white wines. The white Voignier is perhaps the most curious grape of the region, making the white wine to which it gives its name in the north of the region, and also that of Château Grillet, the only estate in France to have its own AOC, and which is under four acres in extent.

At the bottom of the valley, the wines in the eastern areas are slightly protected by the mountains and retain a certain inner freshness. Those on the west of the river are more sunbaked. The pink wines of Tavel are world-famous and perhaps the only pink wines capable of marked improvement with maturation over long periods; although most are made in co-operatives, some single estate wines are also made.

The wines of the middle region are very firm, but should never merit the description "strapping" which some apply to them. There are only a few growers, but their names are of great importance; most make both red and white wines. Indeed, white wines are made on several Châteauneuf-du-Pape estates, such as Château Rayas, and also in vineyards perhaps better known for their reds, such as Hermitage. Many Rhône whites have a slight straw tinge in their colouring. The reds tend to be very dark, even with some age, but it should be noted that nowadays, for economic reasons, few of them can be made so that they will last as long as the other great classic reds, which are also beginning to feel these pressures; however, if you can give any good Rhône red some bottle age it is certain to benefit.

AOC Regions
Côte Rôtie, Condrieu, Château Grillet, St Joseph, Crozes-Hermitage, Hermitage, Cornas, St Péray, Châteauneuf-du-Pape, Tavel, Lirac, Côtes-du-Rhône, and Côtes-du-Rhône-Villages. This last includes the parishes of Rochegude, St Maurice sur Eygues, St Pantaleon les Vignes, Vinsobres, Cairanne, Gigondas, Rasteau, Roaix, Segret, Vacqueyras, Valreas, Visan, Chusclan, Laudun.

VDQS Regions
Côtes du Ventoux, Côtes du Lubéron, Haut Comtat, Chatillon-en-Diois.

Grapes
A great variety of both black and white are used, 13 different ones being permitted in Châteauneuf-du-Pape, and often both black and white grapes being mixed. The principal black grapes are: Grenache, Syrah, Cinsault, Mourvèdre and Terret Noir. Whites: Marsanne, Roussanne, Viognier, Clairette, Ugni blanc, Bourboulenc, Picpoul and Muscat de Beaumes (used for Muscat de Beaumes de Venise).

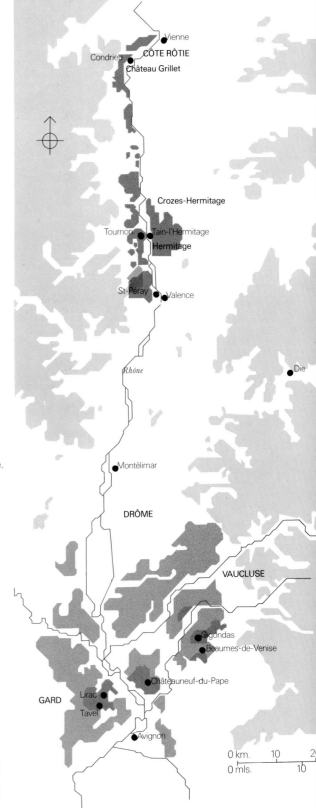

Main wine producing areas

General wine producing areas

Land above 1500 ft.

Loire

Red, white, pink and semi- and fully-sparkling wines are made, all types in the central region. The Champagne method is used for the sparkling wines, of which the best-known are Saumur and Vouvray; Vouvray makes *pétillant* and still wines too. The vineyards are mostly along the banks of the Loire and its various tributaries, and, at the upper reaches of the river, almost touch the Burgundy region.

The whole area has been under vines for centuries and, in the 12th century, it was the Count of Anjou, later Henry II of England, who, by marrying Eleanor, Duchess of Aquitaine, brought the whole of the south-west of France under the English crown. Rabelais, Ronsard and Balzac are only a few of the poets who loved the wines of the Loire, and Clemenceau, "le tigre", drank them. Others who must have done so include Mary Queen of Scots and the companions of Joan of Arc—it was at Chinon that she identified the disguised Dauphin.

The Loire, the longest river in France, flows east to west, between what is mostly a gently curvaceous countryside, with a few outstanding heights, such as those of Sancerre and Saumur, where notable white wines are made. It makes wines like its landscape—

with great charm and delicacy. The Loire is also a cool region and its wines reflect this coolness—many crisp whites and some sweet whites that possess an inner freshness, many very good and excellent sparkling wines, and fresh, fruity reds. It is important, when tasting Loire wines, to differentiate between the products of large concerns, some of which make admirable wines of all types, and the single estate wines, which naturally possess greater individuality.

The majority of Loire wines are not nowadays made so as to mature for long periods in bottle and, although both reds and whites can do so if made with this intention, the majority are intended to be drunk while young or fairly young. They seldom have vintage dates attached to them, simply because the makers prefer, with all except the finest single estate wines, to maintain a general quality standard which may involve blending. With the châteaux or named growth wines, the grower is of great importance, as the wines possess the special character of their estate or plot.

Muscadet sur lie is a wine bottled directly off the lees from the cask, which will retain some of the slight vivacity of youth, but it should be drunk within a year or two of its vintage. This may be given on the label simply to guard against it getting too old.

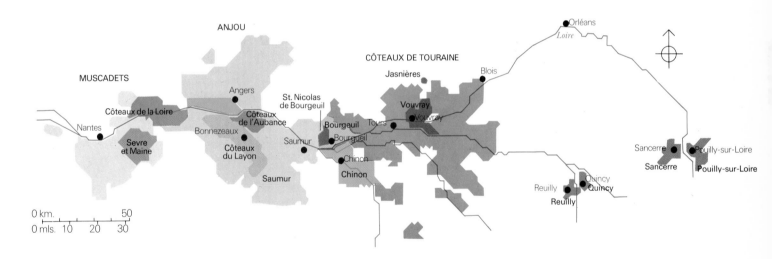

AC and VDQS Areas
Muscadet, sub-divided into Muscadet de Sèvre et Maine, Muscadet du Coteaux de la Loire and Muscadet; Gros Plant du Pays Nantais; Coteaux d'Ancenis; Anjou; Coteaux du Layon (including Quarts de Chaume, Bonnezeaux, Savennières); Coteaux de l'Aubance;

Anjou-Coteaux de la Loire; Saumur; Saumur-Champigny; Coteaux de Touraine; Bourgueil, St Nicolas de Bourgueil, Chinon; Vouvray and Montlouis; Coteaux du Loir and Jasnières; Reuilly and Quincy; Sancerre; Pouilly-sur-Loire; Menetou-Salon; Coteaux du Giennois; Orléannais.

Grapes
Red and pink wines: the Cabernet Franc for the quality wines, some Gamay in the Sancerre region, a little Pinot Noir, used mostly for pink wines, and some Groslot in Anjou for the cheaper pink wines. Pink wines from the Cabernet

Franc in Anjou are labelled Rosé du Cabernet.
White wines: the Gros Plant and Muscadet, and, for all the quality wines of the central regions, the Chenin Blanc, known locally as the Pineau de la Loire, which also makes the sparkling wines. But in Sancerre and

Pouilly-sur-Loire the quality wines are made from the Blanc Fumé (the local name for the Sauvignon), while others are made from the white Chasselas. This is why quality Pouillys are labelled Blanc Fumé de Pouilly, or Pouilly Fumé.

France: Champagne

Grandes Marques of Champagne
Ayala, Bollinger, Clicquot-Ponsardin, Heidsieck Monopole, Charles Heidsieck, Irroy, Krug, Lanson, Laurent-Perrier, Mercier, Moët et Chandon, G. H. Mumm, Perrier-Jouët, Piper-Heidsieck, Pol Roger, Pommery et Greno, Roederer, Ruinart, Taittinger.

Other Fine Champagnes
St Marceaux, Deutz & Gelderman, De Venoge, Boizel, Montebello.

Growths of the red wines
Ambonnay, Ay, Bouzy, Cumières, Dizy, Rilly, Verzenay and Villedommage. All of these are mainly or wholly planted with the Pinot Noir.

The Vineyards
Côte des Blancs Avize, Cramant, Le Mesnil-sur-Oger, Oger, Oiry, Bergères-les-Vertus, Chouilly, Vertus.
Montagne de Reims Ambonnay, Beaumont-sur-Vesle, Bouzy, Louvois, Mailly, Sillery, Verzenay, Tauxières, Verzy, Chigny-les-Roses, Ludes, Rilly-la-Montagne, Trépail, Vaudemanges, Villers-Allerand, Villers-Marmery.
Vins de la Rivière Ay, Dizy, Mareuil-sur-Ay, Avenay, Bisseuil, Champillon, Cumières, Hautvillers, Mutigny.

The Champagne region is "Champaign", or open countryside, with the vine growing on the broad gentle slopes around Rheims, Épernay and Ay. There are some forests, and down by the river Marne towns with attractive architecture. The main road through Rheims is a route from which it is difficult to see much evidence that this is wine country, unless you know where the vineyards are—such as those of Verzy. You can see more at Épernay, and a fine panorama of wine country from the road running between Rheims and Épernay, at the point where it overlooks the Marne valley.

The wine of Champagne has a long and colourful history, reaching back long before the time when it became famous for sparkling wine. Pope Leo the Magnificent, patron of Michelangelo, Raphael and Leonardo da Vinci, drank the wine of Ay, where "le vert galant", Henri IV of France, bought wine and Henry VIII of England kept a special commissioner to supply his cellars. The still or "nature" Champagne is still produced, both red and white. It is now known as Coteaux Champenois, and comes from several of the defined Champagne regions. The best-known of the still red wine is made at Bouzy and Cumières. For various reasons, it is not easily obtainable outside the region itself.

Champagne grapes are the white Chardonnay and the black Pinot Noir and Pinot Meunier. Some "Blanc de blancs" is made, purely from the Chardonnay, and "Blanc de noirs" solely from the black grapes, but for most Champagnes a combination of grapes is used—the white grapes giving finesse, the black giving body and fragrance.

Champagne-producing area

Major vineyards

Town ●

River ——

0 km. 10 20 30
0 mls. 5 10 15 20

Germany: Mosel, Saar and Ruwer

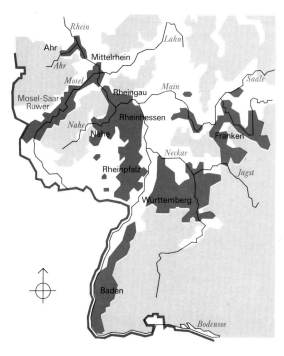

Mosel, Saar, Ruwer

Perhaps the most striking of the German wine regions are those on the river Mosel, and its tributaries the Saar and Ruwer. The Mosel is serpentine in its upper reaches, and very beautiful throughout, with steep valley sides and picturesque villages and towns, and ruined castles on the tops of mountains. Trier is one of the oldest wine towns, and full of historic interest.

The slate topsoil of the best vineyards and the Riesling grape give the wines of this area their distinctive quality and delicacy. The intricate windings of the river produce sheltered sun-traps, though the northerly location of the vineyards means that the wines may often be low in alcohol content, unless they are helped along by the wine scientists.

There are now literally hundreds of names that may appear on labels from the different vineyards and regions. The Mosel-Saar-Ruwer region and the area of Bernkastel contains no less than ten *Grosslagen*, or main wine districts, and in the *Grosslage* of Kurfürstlay, which includes Bernkastel-Kues, there are eleven *Weinbauorten*, or main sites, and 42 *Einzellagen*, or individual vineyards. This is probably a good thing, as the drinker will have to rely on the wine and its general area (and the name of grower and/or shipper).

The wines of Germany that are known to the world are its white wines, from three main regions: the region of the river Mosel, and its tributaries the Saar and Ruwer; that of the river Rhine, including the Rheingau, Rheinhessen and the Palatinate (also known as the Rheinpfalz); and the regions of Franconia (also called Franken) and Baden-Württemburg.

Some red wine is made—in the Baden-Württemburg region, a great deal—but it is the red of a cold country. The geographical location of Germany, so far north, makes it necessary for the wine makers to get as much assistance as possible from wine scientists, who can often bring out the essential characteristics of a wine, and help it develop, even in the most difficult circumstances.

As a result, the importance of the grower's name cannot be exaggerated. In the opinion of most authorities, the grower's name is more important than the vintage date, except in the very greatest years and with the very finest wines.

A great deal of sparkling wine is made, most of it by the sealed vat method, but a little by the Champagne method. In general, German sparkling wine is referred to as "sekt" (apparently from the 19th century actor, Ludwig Devrient, who played Shakespeare's Falstaff, and ever after called for "a cup of sack" when ordering his favourite sparkling wine). The finest sekt is always made solely from the Riesling grape.

Bottles

Mosel, Saar, Ruwer bottles are dark green.
Rheingau, Rheinhessen, Rheinpfalz, Nahe bottles are brown.
Franconian wines are put into the squat, flagon-shaped *boxbeutel*, of dark green glass.

Designated wine growing areas

Land over 1500 ft.

Rivers

International boundary

Grapes

A wide range is grown, but the grape for the finest Rhine wines, and Mosel, Saar and Ruwer wines, is the Riesling. The Müller-Thurgau is also widely used. In other regions, the Sylvaner, the Ruländer, Traminer, and Scheurebe are also grown. Red wine grapes include Spätburgunder (really the Pinot Noir), Blauer Portugieser and Trollinger, especially in the southern regions.

0 kms. 25
0 mls. 15

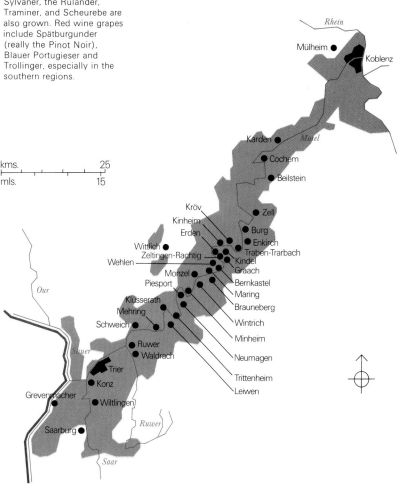

Germany: Rhine, Nahe and Palatinate

The Rhine and Palatinate

The Rhine is a much-used river, heavy with traffic, and the centre of some of Germany's most famous vineyards. The vineyards are comparatively small, and the northerly situation causes climatic problems.

The greatest vineyards are in the Rheingau region, between Lorch and Hochheim. They are on the north bank of the river, facing south, slightly above the river, but not steeply sloped. The Rheinhessen region, after the river turns south, is steeper, and characterized by a dark reddish type of soil, which sometimes imparts a fullness to the taste of its wines. The valley of the river Nahe is undulating and open, the vineyards yielding agreeable wines which, when they are well made, can be truly fine.

Further south, the Rheinpfalz (also known as the Palatinate), which is geographically the continuation of the Alsace vineyard region, is charming wine country, with villages on the mountain slopes, and vineyards below or alongside them. Other Rhine wine regions are the Ahr (red and white) and the Mittelrhein areas.

Franconia, Baden-Württemberg

Franken (Franconia) produces both red and white wines. It is best known outside Germany for the wines from the area of Würzburg, the centre of Franconian wine growing, a picturesque town with two hospices and a fine palace. The Würzburger Stein wines come from a steep slope above the town, with a limey soil. These *Steinweins* in the squat *boxbeutel* shape of bottle are often considered typical of the Franconian wines, though others are grown, notably along the river Main to the west of Würzburg.

The Baden-Württemberg wine country is also picturesque, with beautiful forests. This south German region makes large quantities of wine, white, pink and red. The finest part of the region is towards Baden-Baden, in the Ortenau region. There are some individual estates here, including the well-known Schloss Stauffenburg.

A speciality of the Baden area is the *Weissherbst* ("white gathered") wine, a very pale wine made from pressing bluish-skinned grapes as soon as they are picked.

Liebfraumilch, the best known name in German wines, is a wine created for export markets and unlikely to be available in Germany itself. Originally it probably was the wine of the vineyard surrounding the Church of Our Lady (Liebfrauenstift) at Worms, but legislation later prevented the use of the name for Liebfrauenstift wines. It is, in general terms, a Rhine wine attaining a certain quality: it differs in character according to the shipper, and it may be vintage or non-vintage, cheap or in the moderate price ranges, and can even be sparkling. Good Liebfraumilch can be a pleasant wine, but no one seriously interested in wine should confine their drinking simply to this type.

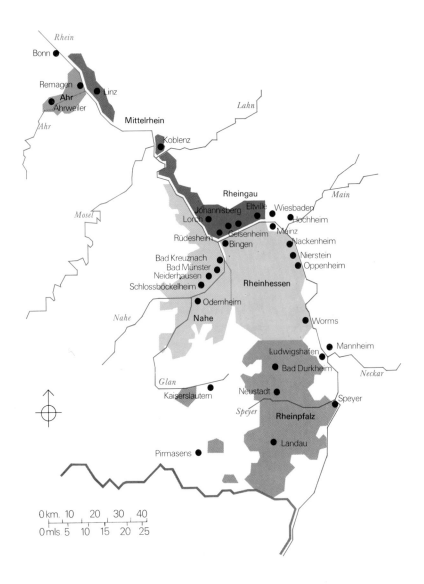

Areas	Hectares planted	Percentage of production		
Mosel-Saar-Ruwer	11,500	23%		
Ahr	500	1%		
Mittelrhein	1,000	2%		
Rheingau	3,000	3%		
Nahe	4,500	7%		
Rheinpfalz	20,000	22%		
Rheinhessen	20,000	24%		
Franken	3,000	3%		
Baden-Württemberg	19,000	15%		

Grapes
Mainly the Riesling, also the Müller-Thurgau; in the Palatinate, the Sylvaner and Scheurebe. The Spätburgunder for red Ahr wines.

Germany: Franconia and Baden-Württemberg

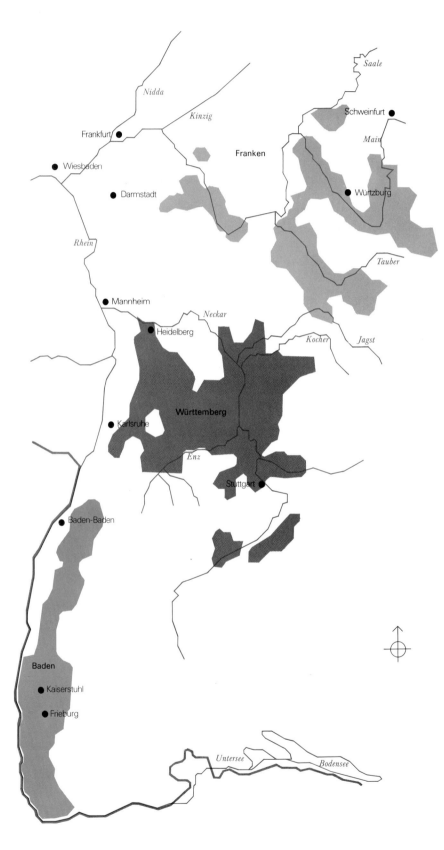

Wine Law

The German government has established a system of describing and labelling German wines for the consumer. There are three basic types of wine.

Tafelwein, which is ordinary table wine that must come from the river regions of the Rhine, Mosel, Main, Neckar and Oberrhein. Wines in this category do not bear site names.

Qualitätswein bestimmter Anbaugebiete (QbA), a term meaning quality wine of designated regions, comes from the following eleven regions: Ahr, Hessische Bergstrasse, Mittelrhein, Mosel-Saar-Ruwer, Nahe, Rheingau, Rheinhessen, Rheinpfalz, Franken, Württemberg, Baden. These regions are sub-divided into sub-regions, termed *Bereich*, and these again further divided, so that, for example, under the *Bereich* of Bernkastel there is the *Grosslage* (or composite area of similar vineyards) such as Badstube, with the *Einzellagen* (or small vineyards or sites) within it: Bratenhöfchen, Doctor, Graben, Lay and Matheisbildchen.

Qualitätswein mit Prädikat (QmP) means quality wine with title—such as *Kabinett*, *Spätlese* and so on. QmP wines must not be sugared, but the word *Naturrein*, formerly in use to indicate this, no longer appears on labels. The QbA and QmP wines bear a separate number, Amtliche Prüfungsnummer (AP), on their labels; it is important to note this detail, because only this number will now indicate where wines bearing exactly the same name, from the same grower and vineyard, may vary in quality—and sometimes very much in price. The term Original-Abfüllung is no longer used, the expression Erzeuger-Abfüllung indicating when the wine is cellar bottled.

In the QmP category are wines bearing the following descriptive terms: *Spätlese* (late picked); *Auslese* (selected bunches of grapes); *Beerenauslese* (individually selected grapes); *Trockenbeerenauslese* (individually selected grapes so overripe that they are more like raisins).

As far as the finest wines are concerned, their labels will give the fullest possible information and, when they are made literally cask by cask, there will be no blending of the casks, but the wines will be kept as separate as when they were made, and the cask number will appear on the label. The name of the grower and the shipper are of increasing importance today—indeed, in these northern vineyards, the vintage variations, except in outstanding years, can be of secondary importance to those who made and handled the wines.

Other terms that may appear on labels include *Kabinett* (special reserve), *Eiswein* and grape varieties. These last vary, naturally, according to the regions concerned but generally if the great Riesling grape is used for the wines in the medium and low grades, it will certainly be mentioned on the label. In some wines nowadays, several grape varieties may be mentioned.

Grapes

In Franconia, the Sylvaner; in south Baden the Ruländer and Traminer. For reds, the Spätburgunder, Blauer Portugieser and Trollinger.

Italy and Switzerland

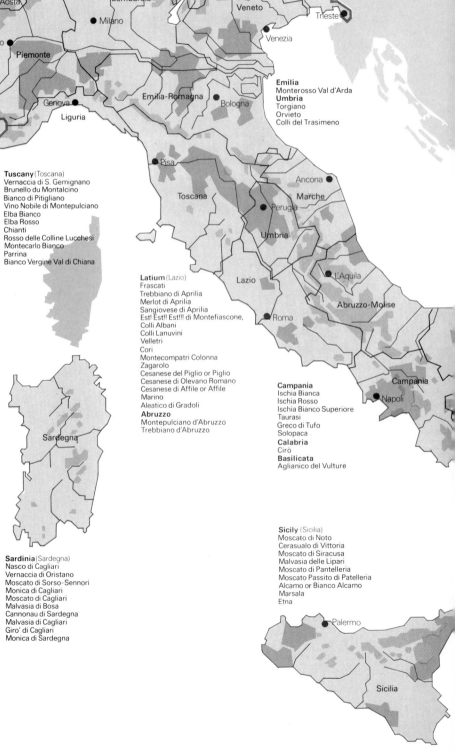

Valle d'Aosta
Donnaz
Enfer d'Arvier
Piemonte
Moscato Naturale d'Asti
Moscato d'Asti Spumante
Asti Spumante or Asti
Carema
Gattinara
Barolo
Barbaresco
Erbaluce di Caluso
Caluso Passito Liquoroso
Malvasia di Casorzo d'Asti
Sissano
Boca
Fara
Ghemme
Rubino di Cantanavenna
Barbera del Monferrato
Barbera d'Asti
Brachetto d'Acqui
Barbera d'Alba
Nebbiolo d'Alba
Dolcetto d'Ovada
Freisa d'Asti
Grignolino d'Asti
Malvasia di Castelnuovo Don Bosco
Freisa di Chieri
Grignolino del Monferrato Casalese
Dolcetto d'Acqui
Colli Tortonesi
Dolcetto de Diano d'Alba
Dolcetto d'Asti
Dolcetto delle Langhe Monregalesi
Dolcetto d'Alba
Dolcetto di Dogliani
Gavi or Cortese di Gavi

Trentino-Alto-Adige
Valle Isarco
Casteller
Santa Maddalena
Trentino
Meranese di Collina
Caldaro or Lago di Caldaro
Friuli
Collio Goriziano or Collio
Grave del Friuli
Colli Orientale del Friuli
Lombally
Franciacorta Rosso
Franciacorta Pinot
Lugana
Riviera del Garda
Botticino
Cellatica
Valtellina
Valtellina Superiore
Oltrepo Pavese
Tocai di S Martino della Battiglia

Emilia-Romagna
Sangiovese di Romagna
Gutturnio dei Colli Piacentini
Albano di Romagna
Lambrusco Gasparossa di Castelvetro
Labrusco Salamino di S Croce
Lambrusco di Sorbara
Lambrusco Reggiano
Trebbiano di Romagna
Liguria
Rossese di Dolceacqua or Dolceacqua
Cinque Terre
Cinque Terre Sciacchetra

The wines awarded a DOC are listed beside the map under their regions.

Tuscany (Toscana)
Vernaccia di S. Gemignano
Brunello du Montalcino
Bianco di Pitigliano
Vino Nobile di Montepulciano
Elba Bianco
Elba Rosso
Chianti
Rosso delle Colline Lucchesi
Montecarlo Bianco
Parrina
Bianco Vergine Val di Chiana

Emilia
Monterosso Val d'Arda
Umbria
Torgiano
Orvieto
Colli del Trasimeno

Latium (Lazio)
Frascati
Trebbiano di Aprilia
Merlot di Aprilia
Sangiovese di Aprilia
Est! Est!! Est!!! di Montefiascone,
Colli Albani
Colli Lanuvini
Velletri
Cori
Montecompatri Colonna
Zagarolo
Cesanese del Piglio or Piglio
Cesanese di Olevano Romano
Cesanese di Affile or Affile
Marino
Aleatico di Gradoli
Abruzzo
Montepulciano d'Abruzzo
Trebbiano d'Abruzzo

Campania
Ischia Bianca
Ischia Rosso
Ischia Bianco Superiore
Taurasi
Greco di Tufo
Solopaca
Calabria
Cirò
Basilicata
Aglianico del Vulture

Sardinia (Sardegna)
Nasco di Cagliari
Vernaccia di Oristano
Moscato di Sorso-Sennori
Monica di Cagliari
Moscato di Cagliari
Malvasia di Bosa
Cannonau di Sardegna
Malvasia di Cagliari
Giro' di Cagliari
Monica di Sardegna

Sicily (Sicilia)
Moscato di Noto
Cerasualo di Vittoria
Moscato di Siracusa
Malvasia delle Lipari
Moscato di Pantelleria
Moscato Passito di Patelleria
Alcamo or Bianco Alcamo
Marsala
Etna

Italy

Huge quantities of wine of many types are made throughout Italy and its islands. Virtually every region makes a wide range of wines, and it should be remembered that much of this may be made by the peasant proprietors for purely local consumption, as opposed to the large-scale concerns which supply international markets. The local wines can be full of interest to the traveller.

Of some of the better-known wine regions, Turin is the vermouth centre, Piedmont makes the best-known sparkling wines and some outstanding reds, and Tuscany makes the best-known Italian red wine—Chianti.

The landscape of the region gives a good indication of the sort of wine to be expected—white soil for white and light-charactered wines, undulating slopes for good reds, and terraced vineyards beside the lakes in the north for very light, mostly white, wines. The best white wines generally come from the central and northern regions, though with the techniques and skills of modern wine makers, good whites are now made even in Sicily.

DOC

In 1963 a law established the Denominazione di Origine Controllata or DOC, which is not exactly similar to the French AOC, but which endeavours to stimulate quality production. It comes under the Ministry of Agriculture in Rome, although the local

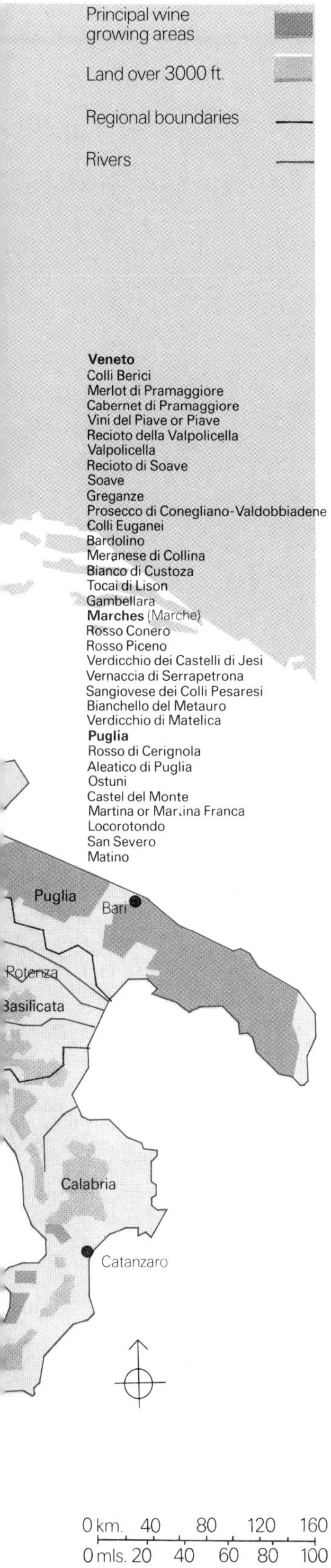

Principal wine growing areas
Land over 3000 ft.
Regional boundaries
Rivers
Veneto
Colli Berici
Merlot di Pramaggiore
Cabernet di Pramaggiore
Vini del Piave or Piave
Recioto della Valpolicella
Valpolicella
Recioto di Soave
Soave
Greganze
Prosecco di Conegliano-Valdobbiadene
Colli Euganei
Bardolino
Meranese di Collina
Bianco di Custoza
Tocai di Lison
Gambellara
Marches (Marche)
Rosso Conero
Rosso Piceno
Verdicchio dei Castelli di Jesi
Vernaccia di Serrapetrona
Sangiovese dei Colli Pesaresi
Bianchello del Metauro
Verdicchio di Matelica
Puglia
Rosso di Cerignola
Aleatico di Puglia
Ostuni
Castel del Monte
Martina or Martina Franca
Locorotondo
San Severo
Matino
Puglia
Bari
Potenza
Basilicata
Calabria
Catanzaro
0 km. 40 80 120 160
0 mls. 20 40 60 80 100

associations, or *conzorzii* naturally work with them. It applies only to wines bottled in Italy, and as it takes a considerable time for the DOC to be awarded, some of the most famous and respected names in Italian wine are not yet included. They should not be doubted because of this—a country so old in the traditions of wine has difficulty in defining both exact regions and methods.

The DOC specifies the area, soil and arrangement of the vineyards, the grapes used, and the proportions in which blends of grapes may be used, method of cultivation, production of the vineyard, yield of grapes and methods of wine making. It also specifies length of maturation—for example, Chianti must be a year in wood to have the right to call itself *vecchio*, two years to be *classico* (the "classico" region itself is defined, not being a grade of quality) and three years to be *riserva* (although Brolio Chiantis are always five years in wood). Bottles, including all regional bottles, and labels are controlled, words such as "type" cannot be used—which is why much wine previously called "Chianti" must now just be labelled Tuscan. Penalties for infringement of these laws are particularly severe, not merely fines or prison sentences, but closure of the offending concern.

A wine not yet awarded a DOC may be both good and exactly what its label specifies—and this of course applies to wines handled in bulk and bottled where they are to be sold. The DOC regulations cannot guarantee quality, which remains the responsibility of grower, shipper and merchant, but they certainly imply it and have been progressively improving the reputation of Italian wines in export markets.

Grapes

The classics, such as the Merlot, or Riesling are often named on labels. In Sicily, native white grapes include the Inzolia, Grecanico and Cateratto, and blacks the Pignatello, Nerello Mascalese and Frappato; in Sardinia, there are the black Cannonau and Nuragus. Sparkling Asti is made from the Moscato, though other sparkling wines use the white Pinot, and red sparkling Lambrusco is made from the vine of that name. In central Italy, the white Trebbiano and black Sangiovese are much used; Chianti may contain several types of grape, although the Sangiovese predominates. In Piedmont, the Nebbiolo is the great black grape, making Barolo and Barbaresco, and the Grignolino makes the wine bearing its name. For the sweet wines, a lot of Malvasia is grown.

Switzerland

Swiss wines are, as might be expected from the countryside and climate, mostly light and fresh. The main wine regions in Switzerland are around Geneva, the Valais, Chablais, Lavaux, Vaud and La Côte. The majority of the wines are white and many classic grapes are used to make them, although sometimes they have local names—for example, the Sylvaner is called the Johannisberger, the Marsanne the Ermitage. The Fendant, a type of white Chasselas, makes some of the best white wines; the reds, of which Dôle is the best known in the Valais, are made mostly from the Gamay and Pinot Noir.

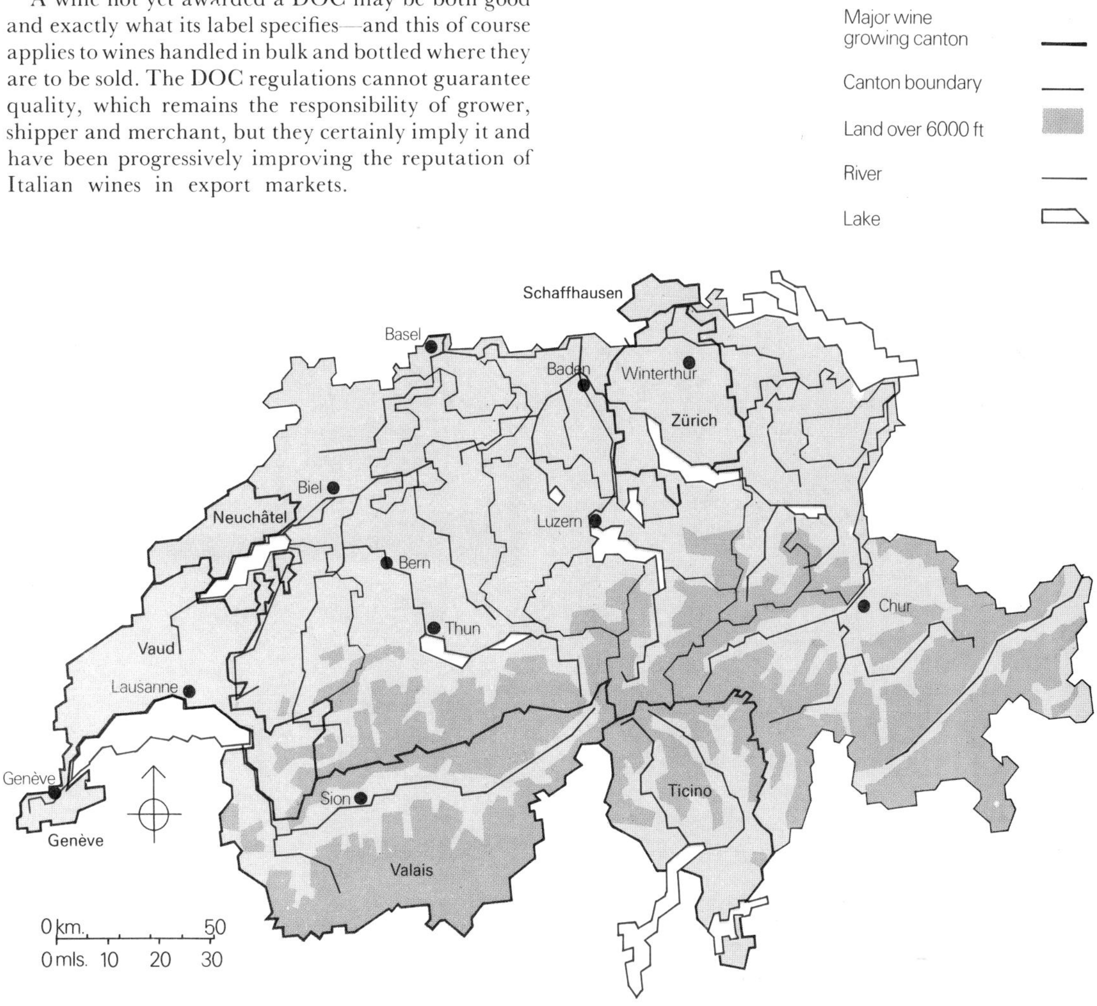

Major wine growing canton
Canton boundary
Land over 6000 ft
River
Lake
Schaffhausen
Basel
Baden
Winterthur
Zürich
Biel
Neuchâtel
Luzern
Bern
Thun
Chur
Vaud
Lausanne
Genève
Genève
Sion
Ticino
Valais
0 km. 50
0 mls. 10 20 30

Spain and Portugal

Spain

The landscape of Spain is variable, with extremes of climate. The Rioja Alta, for example, gets less sun than the Rioja Baja, and there is a marked difference in wines from different sides of the river Ebro.

The sherry vineyards are of three types, the most typical, and that producing the best finos, being of the almost shiny white *albariza*, very high in chalk. The other sherry vineyards are mostly clay or sand. The Valdepeñas ("Valley of Stones") area is appropriately named.

The Spanish Government and Ministry of Agriculture have established certain quality controls, detailed in a decree of 1970, and they have set up a chain of Consejos Reguladores de las Denominaciones de Origen, which establish and enforce standards for the following regions:

Allela and Panadés, Alicante, Almansa and Mancheula, Mancha, Méntrida, Carinena, Cheste, Utiel-Requena and Valencia, Huelva, Jarez-Xéres-Sherry and Manzanilla-Sanlúcar de Barrameda, Jumilla, Málaga, Montilla and Moriles, Navarra, Priorato, Ribera and Valdeorras, Rioja, Tarragona, Valdepeñas.

Portugal

The Portuguese vineyards near the coast, such as those near Lisbon and Colares, tend to be open and often sandy. It is the sand that has prevented the phylloxera from attacking the Colares vines. The Minho, the green wine country, is undulating with attractive forests; good ordinary red and white wines are also made here. Further inland, north from Lisbon, the wines show the character of the mountainous landscape. The Douro Valley, the port region, is wild and grand, the vineyards often on granite chips.

The establishment of controls began early in the 20th century, the main regions being defined as: Vinhos Verdes, Douro (producing port), Dão, Moscatel de Setubal, Colares, Bucelas and Carcavelos. Various other districts are now being considered for demarcation, including Torres Vedras, Ribatejo, the Upper Douro (at present only demarcated for port), Lafoes, Lamego, Pinhel, Agueda, Bairrada, and Lagoa in the Algarve. The government control is exercised through three bodies: the Instituto do Vinho do Porto, the Junta Nacional do Vinho and the Casa do Douro. The various regions have their special seals which must be affixed to the bottles.

Grapes: Spain

Sherry Palomino Blanco, Pedro Ximénez, Moscatel.
Montilla-Moriles Pedro Ximénez, and, to a lesser extent, Lairén, Baladí, Badalí-Verdejo, Muscatel.
Rioja White: Garnacho Blanco, Malvasia, Maturana Blanca, Moscatel, Viura (known in Cataluña as Macabeo). Black: Graciano, Garnacho Tinto, Maturána Tinta, Mazuelo, Miguel del Arco, Monastrel, Tempranillo, Turruntés.
Sparkling wine Sumoli, with smaller proportions of Garnacho Blanco, Xarel-lo, Dubirat-Parent, Pansé, Macabeo, Moscatel, Merseguera, Malvasia, Rosetí. Pink sparkling wines are made with some black grapes as well, such as Cariñena, Garnacho Tinto.
Málaga Moscatel, Pedro Ximénez.
Vega Sicilia Burdeos (Bordeaux) Tinto, Burdeos Blanco, Tinto Aragonés, Garnacho, and the white Albillo. These are mixed in the vineyards, which make only red wine.
Valdepeñas For red wines, Cencibel, Monastrel, Tintorera. For white wines mainly the Lairén, with some Palomino and Moscatel.

Grapes: Portugal

Port many different varieties, the most important being Alvarelhão, Mourisco, Tinta Cào, Tinta Francisca, Sousão, Touriga Nacional, Touriga Francesa.
Vinho Verde many different grapes, the most important black grapes being Vinhão, Borracal, Espadeiro and Azal Tinto. The most usual whites are Azal Blanco and Dourado.

Spain

Average % of total production	Wine produced	D.O.C. areas
0.15	Red, white & rosado	Alella
0.21	Red & white	Priorato
0.23	Red & white	Málaga
0.52	Red & white	Navarra
0.72	Red & white	Cheste
0.78	Red & rosado	Valdeorras
0.81	Red & white	Almansa
1.14	White & rosado	Ribeiro
1.15	Red & white	Méntrida
1.27	Red	Jumilla
1.29	Red	Alicante
1.75	Red, white & rosado	Cariñena
2.57	Red & white	Huelva
2.70	White	Montilla-Moriles
2.72	Red & white	Tarragona
2.89	Red & white (sparkling)	Panadés
3.19	Red & white	Utiel-Requena
3.69	Red & white	Valencia
3.74	Red, white & rosado	Rioja
4.20	Red	Manchuela
10.80	Red & white	Mancha
15.39	Red & white	Valdepeñas
38.09	Red, white & rosado	Other Areas
	Sherry only	Jerez

Portugal

Average % of total production	Wine produced	D.O.C. areas
0.002	White	Carcavelos
0.02	Red & white	Colares
0.08	White	Bucelas
0.20	White & red	Setúbal
5.18	Red & white	Dão
28.40	White & red	Vinhos Verdes
66.12	Red, white & rosé	Other Areas
	Port only	Douro

Sherry and port are classed as fortified wines, so do not appear in the percentage figures here. Note how much of the table wine is produced outside the DOC areas.

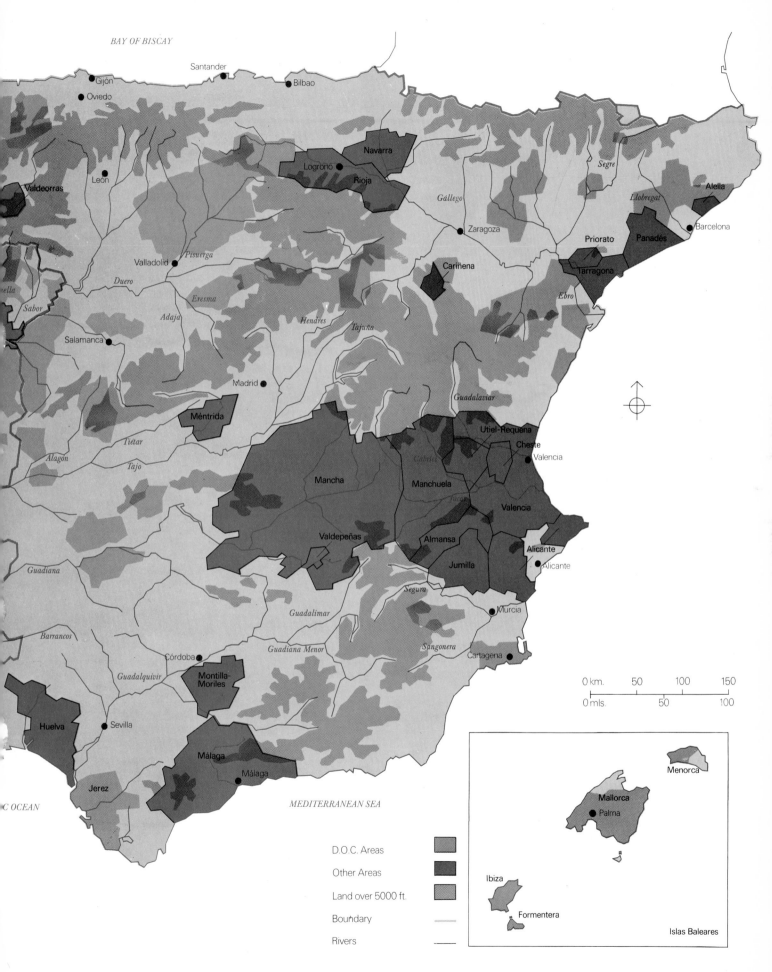

BAY OF BISCAY

Santander
Gijón
Oviedo
Bilbao

Navarra
Logroño
Rioja
León
Valdeorras

Segre
Gállego
Llobregat
Alella
Zaragoza
Barcelona
Priorato
Panadés
Valladolid
Pisuerga
Cariñena
Tarragona
Duero
Eresma
Ebro
Sabor
Adaja
Hendres
Tajuña
Salamanca

Madrid
Guadalaviar
Méntrida
Utiel-Requena
Tiétar
Cheste
Alagón
Valencia
Tajo
Cabriel
Mancha
Manchuela
Valencia
Jucar
Valdepeñas
Almansa
Guadiana
Alicante
Jumilla
Alicante
Barrancos
Segura
Guadiana Menor
Murcia
Guadalimar
Córdoba
Sangonera
Montilla-
Moriles
Cartagena
Guadalquivir
0 km.   50   100   150
0 mls.   50   100
Huelva
Sevilla
Málaga
Menorca
Málaga
Jerez
Mallorca
Palma
C OCEAN
MEDITERRANEAN SEA
Ibiza

Formentera

D.O.C. Areas

Other Areas

Land over 5000 ft.

Boundary

Rivers

Islas Baleares

169

Austria, Czechoslovakia, Hungary and Yugoslavia

In general this is all good wine country. Much depends on the local controls on the making of wine, and also on the demands of different markets. Some of the old traditions have been preserved, but in other regions large-scale wine production has superseded the production by peasant growers—often to the advantage of the consumer.

It is the inexpensive wines of many of these countries —notably Yugoslavia and Hungary—which have introduced so many people to the pleasures of drinking wine as an everyday routine. With the possible exception of Tokay, none of the wine nowadays is made to create a reputation like the great estate wines of western Europe, but both reds and whites can be good.

Czechoslovakia

Though the region has made wines for at least a thousand years, nowadays it has to import foreign wine to satisfy its needs, so exports are negligible. The majority of its quality wines are white, the most prolific region being that of Slovakia.

The grapes used include most of those cultivated in Germany, Austria and Hungary for white wines; and for reds the Blau Burgunder, Portugieser and St Laurent.

Austria

Increasing quantities of quality wines from Austria are making their effect on export markets, including some late gatherings (*Spätlese*) and even *Eiswein*. The labels indicate them as such.

Controls are strict nowadays, though the reputation of Austrian wines has been guarded for centuries. Indeed, the *heurigen* wines of the Vienna suburbs are to a certain extent still governed by the decrees of 1780. A more recent regulation is that permits must be obtained for taverns displaying green boughs—the sign that the new wine is on sale—if they are selling the produce of villages other than their own. In fact *heurigen* wines are found in many Austrian wine villages, but those of Vienna that are most celebrated are those of Grinzing, Heiligenstadt and Nussberg, and, in Weinviertel, Perchtoldsdorf.

The Austrian wine regions are: Lower Austria (Krems, Langenlois, Weinviertel, Donauland, Vöslau, Baden); Burgenland (Rust, Neusiedlersee, Eisenberg); Styria (Südersteiermark, Klöch-Osteiermark, West-steiermark); and Vienna.

A wide variety of classic grapes and those extensively cultivated in central and eastern Europe are used, but the native grapes are the white Grüner Veltliner, Neuburger, Bouviertraube and Zierfandler; the red Rotgipfler; and the black Blauer Portugieser, Blauer Wildbacher and Zweigelt. The *heurigen* wines are made from local vine varieties—Nussberg, Grinzinger and Sieveringer—and the more widely-known Neuburger.

Yugoslavia

The tradition of wine-making in Yugoslavia reaches back for thousands of years. Today, though there are various state and co-operative agencies, the bulk of the wine is from peasant growers, and it is remarkable how high the standards have become and how they continue to rise.

The Yugoslav wines come from Slovenia, Slavonia, the Istrian Peninsula and Dalmatia, Herzegovina, Vojvodina, Serbia, Kosmet and Macedonia. Regions are often named on the labels even of wine for export— such as Kapela, Ljutomer, Ormož and Maribor.

Many of the vines used are west European classics, such as the Riesling and Traminer, though the vineyards yield wines quite different in style, even from well-known grapes. There are also many of the grapes used in neighbouring countries, such as Austria and Italy. The Bouvier, for example, is the Ranina. Many of the names have, naturally, been translated into Yugoslav names, sometimes difficult to relate to the originals. Native vines include the white Plavac and Beli, the yellow Zuti, found in Slovenia and Istria-Dalmatia, and, for many red wines, the Mali Plavac and Prokupac Črni; in Slovenia the red Zametovka and Zametna; in Dalmatia the Maraština, Grk and Vagava for whites; in Herzegovina the white Žilavka and red Blatina; in parts of Vojvodina the Kevedinka for white wines, together with other better-known types; in Serbia the Smederevka, Plovdina and Začinka; in Macedonia a grape called the Stanušina for whites and a Montenegrin red called the Vramac, with other Yugoslav grapes; and in Montenegro itself a further local variety called the Kratošiva.

Hungary

This is where the finest wines of eastern Europe are made. The country has a very long wine tradition, and many natural circumstances such as topography and climate are highly favourable for good wine-making. State farms and co-operatives account for much of the wine produced, but the grapes themselves are mostly grown by peasant owners.

The main wine regions are: Tokaj-Hegyalja; Badacsony, Balatonfüred-Csopak and Balaton; Bársonyos-Császár and Mór; Eger; Mátravidék; Mecsek, Villány-Siklós and Szekszárd; Somló; Sopron; and the Great Plain, from between the Danube and the Tisza down to the frontier at Vojvodina.

The grapes used include many classic varieties. As in other Balkan countries, the Hungarian version of the name is often difficult to relate to the names used elsewhere (the Szürkebarat, for example, is the Pinot Gris). Hungarian vines include the Hárslevelü, Mézesfehér, Kéknyelü, Budai, Juhfark, Sarfehér and Szlankamenka for white wines. The black Kadarka is sometimes supposed to be a Hungarian grape, but although widely grown there it is common to many countries, and probably originated in Albania. The Ezerjó has been grown in Hungary for a very long time; at Mór it makes wine of great quality.

Bulgaria

Wine has been made since classical times, and today Bulgaria is beginning to export good wines, usually sold under a grape name or a merchant's brand.

Many of the grapes used are those found in other Balkan countries, and in Russia. Local varieties include the Tamianka and the red Gamza. They also make a blend of Wälsch and Rheinriesling, labelled Rosenthaler Riesling. Classic grape varieties are also cultivated widely.

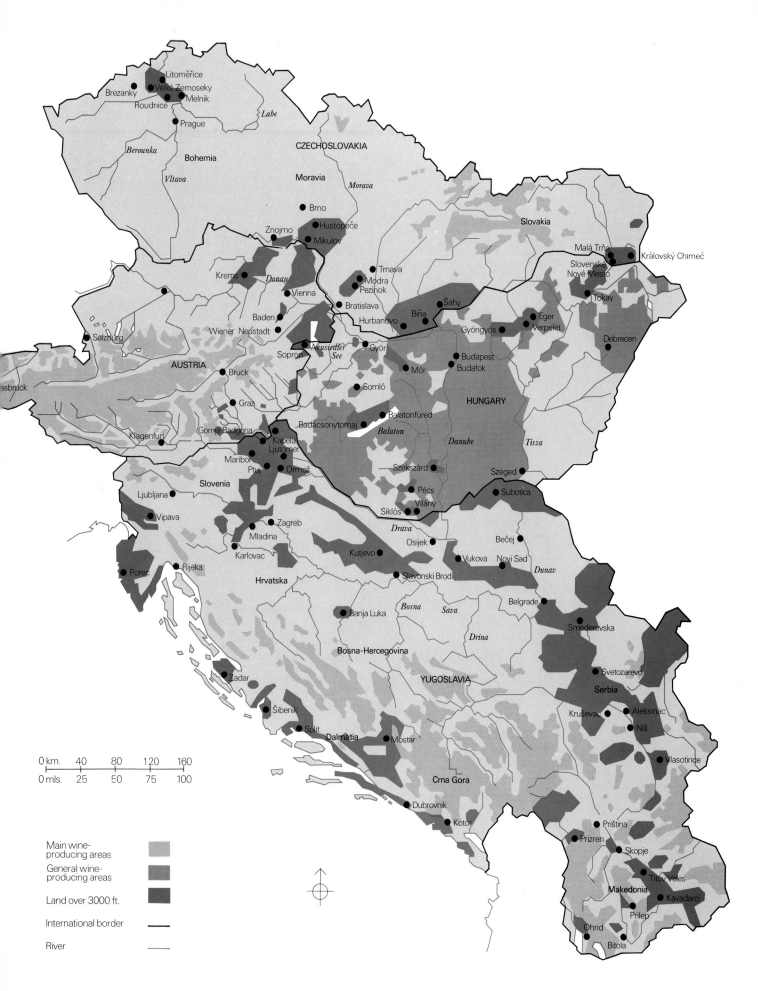

Litoměřice
Velké Žernoseky
Brezanky
Melnik
Roudnice
Prague

Labe

Berounka

Bohemia

Vltava

CZECHOSLOVAKIA

Moravia

Morava

Brno

Hustopeče
Znojmo
Mikulov

Slovakia

Malá Trňa
Královský Chimeč
Slovenské
Nové Mesto
Tokay

Krems

Donau

Trnava
Modra
Pezinok

Vienna

Bratislava

Baden

Hurbanovo

Biňa

Šahy

Eger
Verpelét

Gyöngyös

Debrecen

Wiener Neustadt

Salzburg

Neusiedler See

Győr

Budapest
Budafok

AUSTRIA

Sopron

Mór

Bruck

Somló

HUNGARY

nsbruck

Graz

Balatonfüred

Klagenfurt

Gornja Radgona

Badacsonytomaj

Balaton

Danube

Tisza

Kapela
Ljutomer

Maribor
Ptuj
Ormož

Szekszárd

Szeged

Slovenia

Pécs

Subotica

Ljubljana

Vilány
Siklós

Vipava

Zagreb

Drava

Bečej

Mladina

Osijek

Vukova

Novi Sad

Dunav

Karlovac

Kutjevo

Porec
Rijeka

Slavonski Brod

Belgrade

Hrvatska

Bosna

Sava

Smederevska

Banja Luka

Drina

Zadar

Bosna-Hercegovina

YUGOSLAVIA

Svetozarevo

Serbia

Šibenik

Split
Dalmatia

Mostar

Kruševac
Aleksinac
Niš

Crna Gora

Vlasotince

Dubrovnik

Kotor

Priština

0 km.   40   80   120   160
0 mls.   25   50   75   100

Prizren

Skopje

Titov Veles

Main wine-
producing areas

General wine-
producing areas

Makedonia
Kavadarci

Land over 3000 ft.

Prilep

International border

Ohrid

River

Bitola

Eastern Europe, Middle East and North Africa

North Africa

The vineyards of North Africa extend from Morocco to Egypt but most of the wine production is concentrated in Tunisia, Algeria and Morocco, in the more temperate areas along the coast or in the mountains. Since many of the installations everywhere have been taken over by the various state authorities, it has often been difficult to maintain sufficient quality of production to interest export markets.

All types of wine are made in North Africa, but the great heat makes the whites rather lacking in acidity and it is the reds that usually attain a pleasant, full-bodied and sometimes even charming style. The pink wines are very full-bodied and fruity, rather like small-scale reds. They should never be despised when they are featured on export lists, as they can offer agreeable everyday drinking at low prices, and are exactly what many northern markets require. Sometimes they are marketed under a firm's brand name abroad, but travellers will find them named according to the installations making them and occasionally even of localities or estates.

The Middle East

This is the region known as the cradle of wine making and enormous quantities have been produced here since the earliest times. Today few of the wines achieve more than medium personality and most are in the good to very pleasant everyday categories. The altitude of some of the vineyards, such as certain of those in Cyprus, does enable white wines of a certain crisp freshness to be made, thanks to the skill of modern wine makers, and there are some good dry whites made in Turkey, but it is the red and pink wines that are likely to appeal most immediately to drinkers already familiar with classic wines. The sweet wines, such as the Greek Mavrodaphne, Samos (where a dry wine is also made now), Cyprus Commandaria and many local whites generally described as "medium dry" for the benefit of tourists, all cater for the demands of active people for whom sugar and many sweet things come into the category of luxuries. Quantities of sparkling and fortified wines are also made.

USSR

Russia makes huge quantities of wine, including a lot of "champanski". Some of the best wines come from the Crimean region. Comparatively little is exported as yet.

The hybrids which were extensively planted after the phylloxera are now being replaced by various classic varieties.

Greece

It is lamented by wine lovers that as yet Greece makes only good and no fine wine, but this may change. Resinated wines (*retsina*) probably originated when the resin could form a film on the surface of the wine and prevent its oxidization. Most of the wines of Greece come from the Peloponnese, about 15 per cent from Attica, near Athens (Patras being the centre of the largest installation), and the rest from Macedonia. The islands of Rhodes, Samos, Santorin and Crete all make wine, much of it on volcanic soil.

There are many native grapes, including white Savatiano, red and white Muscats (Samos, famous for its Muscats, is protected as a name), and the Monemvasia vine (the ancestor of Malmsey) is said to have originated in the Peloponnese.

Cyprus

The wines of Cyprus have been famous since classical times. Nowadays the big wineries account for a large proportion of the exports. All types are made, each winery having evolved its house style, and, although export markets may know Cyprus mainly for its sweet sherry, they also produce dry Cyprus sherry, some of it made with a native *flor*, table wines of all types, including a *pétillant* and some sparkling wines, as well as fortified wines and the historic Commandaria.

Native grapes include the black Mavron, white Xynisteri and the palish pink Opthalmo. Experiments are now being made with many classic wine grapes which, because the phylloxera has not infected Cyprus, can be grown on ungrafted stock.

Romania

The wine business is in the hands of the state and much is being done to improve quality. The main areas are: Arad, south Oltenia, Drăgăsani and Arges, Transylvania, Dealul Mare estates, Cotnari in Moldavia, Odobesti, and Dobrudja.

Many classic vines are planted, and also a number of indigenous grapes, including the group related to the Grasă, a type of Furmint (sometimes called Coarna or Som), also the Feteasca, which makes both red and white from different types, and, for good whites, Leanyka, Tămîioasă Romaneasca and Friucusa.

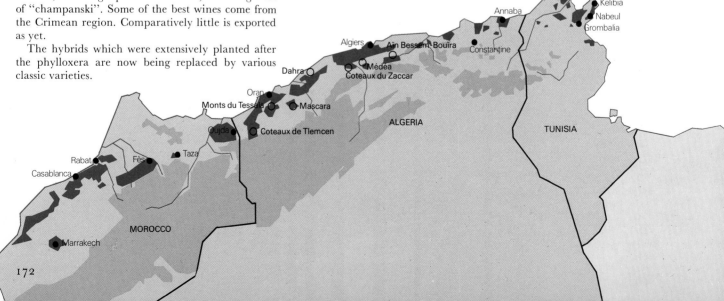

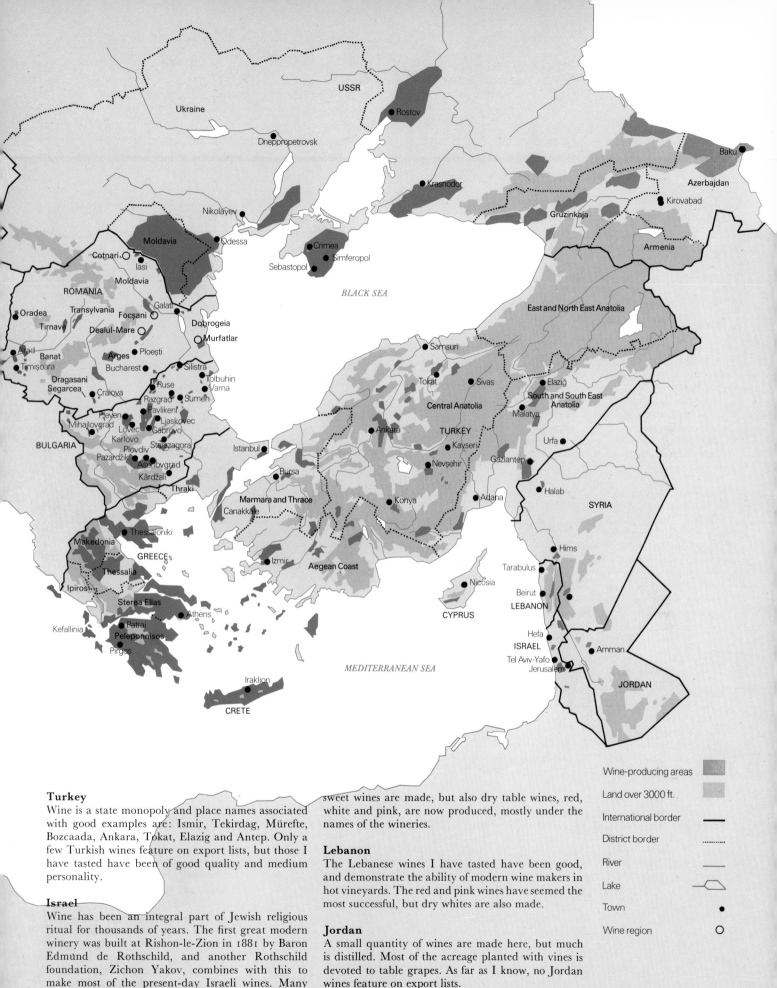

Wine-producing areas
Land over 3000 ft.
International border
District border
River
Lake
Town
Wine region

Turkey

Wine is a state monopoly and place names associated with good examples are: Ismir, Tekirdag, Mürefte, Bozcaada, Ankara, Tokat, Elazig and Antep. Only a few Turkish wines feature on export lists, but those I have tasted have been of good quality and medium personality.

Israel

Wine has been an integral part of Jewish religious ritual for thousands of years. The first great modern winery was built at Rishon-le-Zion in 1881 by Baron Edmund de Rothschild, and another Rothschild foundation, Zichon Yakov, combines with this to make most of the present-day Israeli wines. Many sweet wines are made, but also dry table wines, red, white and pink, are now produced, mostly under the names of the wineries.

Lebanon

The Lebanese wines I have tasted have been good, and demonstrate the ability of modern wine makers in hot vineyards. The red and pink wines have seemed the most successful, but dry whites are also made.

Jordan

A small quantity of wines are made here, but much is distilled. Most of the acreage planted with vines is devoted to table grapes. As far as I know, no Jordan wines feature on export lists.

South America

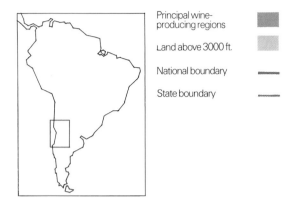

Principal wine-producing regions

Land above 3000 ft.

National boundary ——

State boundary ——

Argentina

Argentina is the fourth largest wine producing country in the world. Comparatively little is exported, but domestic consumption is high; quality can also be high, especially the wines of the Mendoza and San Juan provinces and the Rio Negro region. Both the Champagne and Charmat methods are used for sparkling wines and enormous quantities of vermouth are made.

Many classic grapes are grown, also the native Criolla, probably the Mission grape.

Chile

Most of the vineyards are on volcanic soil, at Huesca and Elqui in the north, the central region, including Aconcagua, Maipo, Cachapoal and Lontué, and in the south, Itata and Cauquenes; Llano del Maipo, near Santiago, is thought to make the finest wines but this is a matter of local opinion.

Classic grapes are used for all types of wine, still and sparkling, fortified and a lot of vermouth. But perhaps the most important thing about Chilean wines is that, never having been attacked by the phylloxera, they are grown from ungrafted vinestocks.

Brazil

Brazil's vineyards are mostly in Rio Grande do Sul on the Atlantic coast. Sparkling wines are made as well as table wines. A number of hybrids are cultivated, as well as a few classic vines.

Uruguay

Uruguay's vineyards are mostly in the region around Montevideo, making red, white and fortified wines.

Peru

Peruvian wines are produced around Ica, Locumba, Lima and the Sicamba River valley. Many classic vines are used.

Mexico

The vineyard regions are: northern Baja California, Laguna on the border of Coahuila and Durango, Parras and Saltillo in Coalhuila, Aguascalientes, San Juan del Rio in Querétero, Delicias in Chihuahua, and the Hermosillo area in Sonora.

The Criolla or Mission grape is still widely grown, but many classic varieties are now being used.

Fortified and sparkling wines, using the Charmat method, are also made.

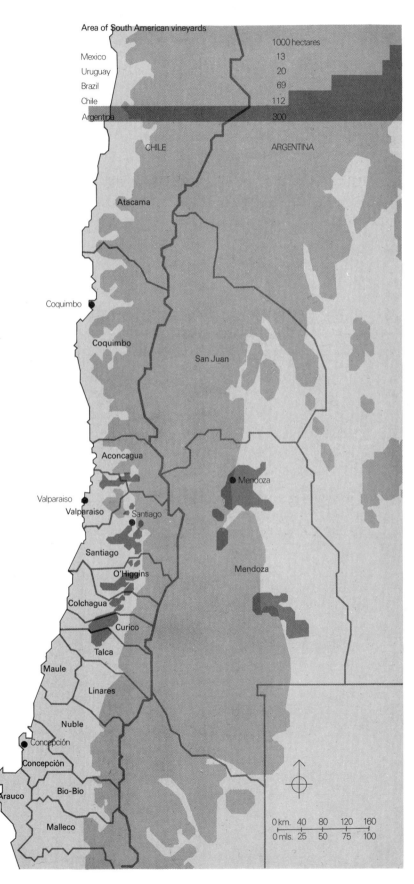

Area of South American vineyards

	1000 hectares
Mexico	13
Uruguay	20
Brazil	69
Chile	112
Argentina	300

USA: New York State

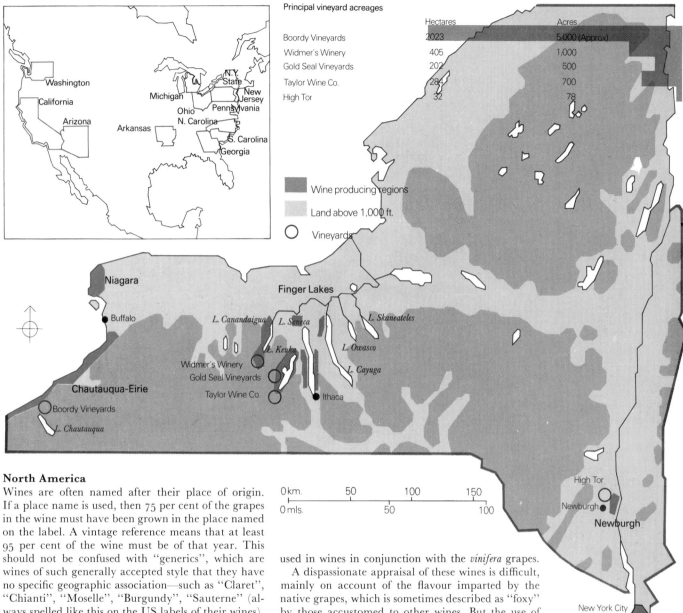

Principal vineyard acreages

	Hectares	Acres
Boordy Vineyards	2023	5,000 (Approx)
Widmer's Winery	405	1,000
Gold Seal Vineyards	202	500
Taylor Wine Co.	284	700
High Tor	32	78

Wine producing regions

Land above 1,000 ft.

○ Vineyards

North America

Wines are often named after their place of origin. If a place name is used, then 75 per cent of the grapes in the wine must have been grown in the place named on the label. A vintage reference means that at least 95 per cent of the wine must be of that year. This should not be confused with "generics", which are wines of such generally accepted style that they have no specific geographic association—such as "Claret", "Chianti", "Moselle", "Burgundy", "Sauterne" (always spelled like this on the US labels of their wines), "Champagne", and so on. "Varietals", or grape varieties, must, if named, account for at least 51 per cent of the wine. Wine labels must give the name of the bottler and packer, also where the wine was bottled and packed; if the term "produced" is used, then the wine maker named must have pressed, made, kept and bottled at least 75 per cent of the wine in the bottle. The word "made" is therefore often used instead—and can, of course, imply no loss of quality with a firm of reputable name.

Labelling is strictly controlled and terms used exactly defined.

Eastern seaboard

From the earliest settlements in the 16th century, wines have been made in the east of North America, huge plantations of wild vines being indigenous, including *vitis rotundifolia* and *vitis labrusca*, which are still used in wines in conjunction with the *vinifera* grapes.

A dispassionate appraisal of these wines is difficult, mainly on account of the flavour imparted by the native grapes, which is sometimes described as "foxy" by those accustomed to other wines. But the use of classic grapes and the skill of dedicated growers is obviously making a great deal of progress as regards quality. All types of wine are made, including a type of sherry in New York State, and sparkling wines, of which Great Western at Pleasant Valley is well known.

The wine regions include Canada (the Niagara Peninsula and a region in British Columbia), New York, especially the Finger Lakes, the Westfield-Fredonia region on Lake Erie and the Hudson River, and near Highland in Sullivan County. There are vineyards in Ohio from Sandusky to Cleveland along Lake Erie, in the Williamette Valley in Oregon, near Atlantic City in New Jersey, and in parts of the plain from Virginia to Florida in the south-east. There are also vineyards in Missouri (near Harman and in the Ozark foothills), around Benton Harbour in Michigan, and along Lake Erie in Pennsylvania, and some vineyards in Arkansas and Maryland.

0 km. 50 100 150
0 mls. 50 100

Grapes

The best known of the Eastern seaboard species are (according to Grossman's Guide) the white Scuppernong, black James and Misch, all Muscadines; the Delaware and Catawba, both red or pinkish, the former for white and sparkling wines, the latter for sweetish white and sparkling; the white Duchess and Niagara, and the black Concord. Many hybrids are also used and, nowadays, a range of classic varieties.

USA: California

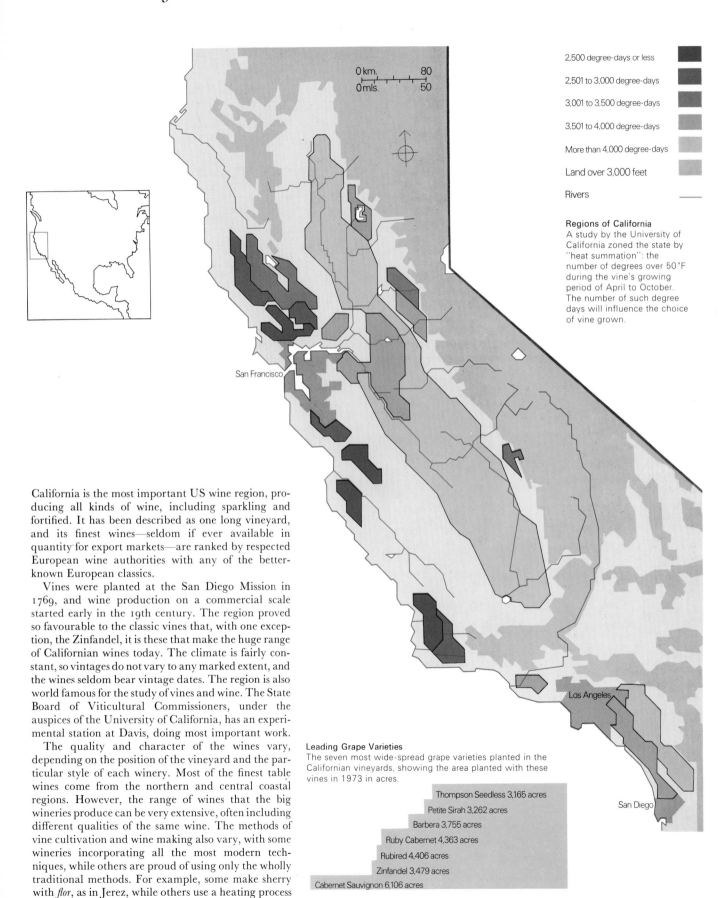

2,500 degree-days or less

2,501 to 3,000 degree-days

3,001 to 3,500 degree-days

3,501 to 4,000 degree-days

More than 4,000 degree-days

Land over 3,000 feet

Rivers

Regions of California
A study by the University of California zoned the state by "heat summation": the number of degrees over 50°F during the vine's growing period of April to October. The number of such degree days will influence the choice of vine grown.

San Francisco

Los Angeles

San Diego

California is the most important US wine region, producing all kinds of wine, including sparkling and fortified. It has been described as one long vineyard, and its finest wines—seldom if ever available in quantity for export markets—are ranked by respected European wine authorities with any of the better-known European classics.

Vines were planted at the San Diego Mission in 1769, and wine production on a commercial scale started early in the 19th century. The region proved so favourable to the classic vines that, with one exception, the Zinfandel, it is these that make the huge range of Californian wines today. The climate is fairly constant, so vintages do not vary to any marked extent, and the wines seldom bear vintage dates. The region is also world famous for the study of vines and wine. The State Board of Viticultural Commissioners, under the auspices of the University of California, has an experimental station at Davis, doing most important work.

The quality and character of the wines vary, depending on the position of the vineyard and the particular style of each winery. Most of the finest table wines come from the northern and central coastal regions. However, the range of wines that the big wineries produce can be very extensive, often including different qualities of the same wine. The methods of vine cultivation and wine making also vary, with some wineries incorporating all the most modern techniques, while others are proud of using only the wholly traditional methods. For example, some make sherry with *flor*, as in Jerez, while others use a heating process

Leading Grape Varieties
The seven most wide-spread grape varieties planted in the Californian vineyards, showing the area planted with these vines in 1973 in acres.

Thompson Seedless 3,165 acres

Petite Sirah 3,262 acres

Barbera 3,755 acres

Ruby Cabernet 4,363 acres

Rubired 4,406 acres

Zinfandel 3,479 acres

Cabernet Sauvignon 6,106 acres

Wine Regions and Vineyards
Below, seven Californian wine-growing counties, and their acreage under vines at five points over the last ten years showing how the vineyard area changes from year to year.

1965
1967
1969
1971
1973

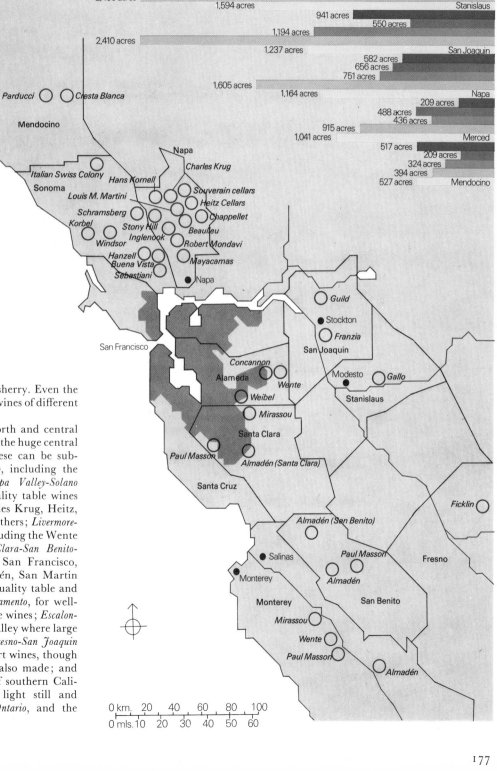

12,796 acres   3,027 acres

97 acres
204 acres
378 acres
Monterey

599 acres
490 acres
599 acres
1,284 acres
Sonoma

2,253 acres

565 acres
393 acres
518 acres
Stanislaus

2,406 acres   1,594 acres

941 acres
550 acres
San Joaquin

2,410 acres   1,194 acres
1,237 acres

582 acres
656 acres
751 acres
Napa

1,605 acres   1,164 acres

209 acres
488 acres
436 acres
Merced

915 acres
1,041 acres

517 acres
209 acres
324 acres
394 acres
527 acres
Mendocino

Grapes

The main classic grapes cultivated for wine are, for reds: Cabernet Sauvignon, Gamay, Pinot Noir; and for whites: the Chardonnay, Chenin Blanc, Folle Blanche (before the phylloxera the most important grape in the Cognac region) and the Pinot Blanc. But perhaps the most interesting grape is the native Zinfandel, a black grape, extensively grown and making quite distinctive red wines, varying according to where they are produced. Numerous other varieties of grapes are also grown; some of those known from other world vineyards include: Aleatico, Barbera, Carignan, Grenache, Grignolino, Merlot, Malvoisie, Valdepeñas, Aligoté, Gewürztraminer, Palomino, Melon, Müller-Thurgau, a number of different Muscats, Sémillon, Sylvaner, Trebbiano, Pedro Ximénez and the Sauvignon; several types of Riesling are also cultivated, including the Emerald, Franken, Grey, White and Johannisberg Rieslings, and a number of the port and Madeira grapes.

that gives a particular flavour to the sherry. Even the Zinfandel grape, therefore, will yield wines of different styles in different areas.

The three main regions are the north and central vineyards, around San Francisco Bay; the huge central valley; and southern California. These can be subdivided as follows: *Sonoma-Mendocino*, including the noted Buena Vista vineyards; *Napa Valley-Solano County*, very well-known for high quality table wines and famous wineries, including Charles Krug, Heitz, Beaulieu, Mondavi and Christian Brothers; *Livermore-Contra Costa*, east of San Francisco, including the Wente and Concannon vineyards; *Santa Clara-San Benito-Santa Cruz-Monterey* region south of San Francisco, which includes the Hallcrest, Almadén, San Martin and Martin Ray estates, producing quality table and sometimes sparkling wines; *Lodi-Sacramento*, for well-known fortified apéritif as well as table wines; *Escalon-Modesto*, in the middle of the central valley where large amounts of table wines are made; *Fresno-San Joaquin Valley*, the main region for good dessert wines, though some table and sparkling wines are also made; and finally the three principal districts of southern California, generally producing rather light still and sparkling table wines, *Cucamonga*, *Ontario*, and the *San Diego-Escondido* vineyards.

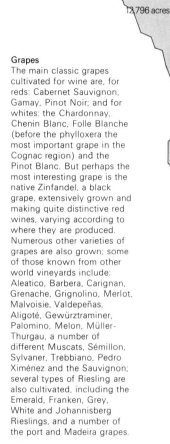

Parducci   Cresta Blanca

Mendocino

Italian Swiss Colony

Sonoma   Hans Kornell

Louis M. Martini

Schramsberg

Korbel   Stony Hill

Windsor   Inglenook

Hanzell

Buena Vista

Sebastiani

Napa

Charles Krug

Souverain cellars

Heitz Cellars

Chappellet

Beaulieu

Robert Mondavi

Mayacamas

Napa

San Francisco

Guild

Stockton

Franzia

San Joaquin

Concannon

Alameda   Wente

Weibel   Modesto   Gallo

Mirassou   **Stanislaus**

Santa Clara

Paul Masson

Almadén (Santa Clara)

Santa Cruz

Ficklin

Almadén (San Benito)

Paul Masson   **Fresno**

Salinas

Monterey   Almadén

Monterey   **San Benito**

Mirassou

Wente

Paul Masson

Almadén

0 km. 20 40 60 80 100

0 mls. 10 20 30 40 50 60

South Africa and Australia

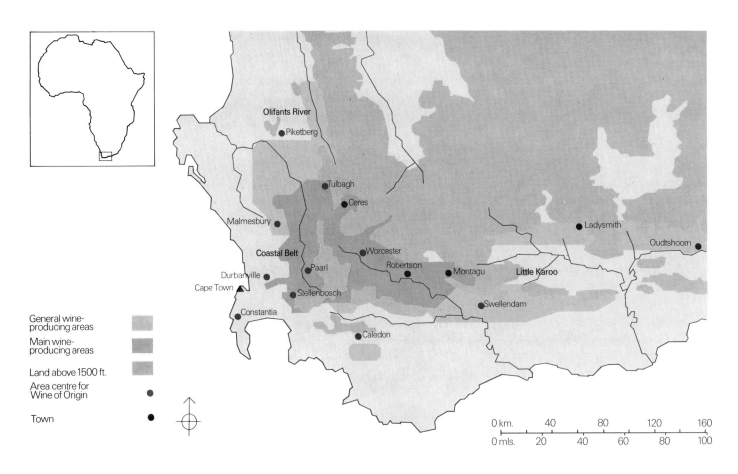

General wine-
producing areas

Main wine-
producing areas

Land above 1500 ft.

Area centre for
Wine of Origin

Town

0 km. 40 80 120 160
0 mls. 20 40 60 80 100

Grapes

For some time it was believed
that the Steen grape, making
some of South Africa's best
white wines, was either a
native grape or else a type of
Sauvignon, but it is now
decided that it is really a
descendant of the Chenin
Blanc. But wines are
marketed as the Chenin
Blanc name as well, and in
fact are different in style.
Other grapes in use include:
Palomino, Glourkatel,
Clairette Blanche, Riesling,
Hanepoot (Muscat
d'Alexandrie), Pedro Luis, as
well as the Chenin Blanc and
Steen for white wines; for
reds, Hermitage (the
Cinsaut), Cabernet
Sauvignon, Shiraz, Tinta das
Baroccas, various port
grapes, and the Pinotage, a
cross of the Pinot Noir and
Cape Hermitage or Cinsaut.

South Africa

Vines were first planted at the Cape of Good Hope in
the gardens of the Dutch East India Company in
1655, and made wine in 1659. Governor Simon van
der Stel established his farm at Groot Constantia, and
subsequent settlers, including many from France,
planted vineyards in Franschoek, Paarl, Drakenstein
and Stellenbosch. During the Napoleonic wars the
Cape wines became enormously popular in Britain,
but when Gladstone abolished the preferential rate of
duty in 1861, the trade collapsed and although, in
spite of phylloxera and many problems, the wine
business struggled on, it was faced with serious over-
production in 1917. In 1918 the Co-Operative Wine
Growers Association (known by its Afrikaans initials
KWV) was set up, and, by resolutely endeavouring to
improve quality, revived many of the markets. In
1972 it set up a system of delimited areas for wines of
origin and estate wines and, in 1973, issued seals
guaranteeing the origin, grape variety (cultivar),
vintage and quality of bottled wines.

The main regions of what must be among the most
spectacular vineyards of the world, are: the Coastal
Belt, Little Karoo and Breede River Valley, Olifants
River and Orange River areas. The dry white table
wines are mainly produced around Stellenbosch,
Paarl, Tulbagh, the reds in the Cape, Stellenbosch and
Paarl; the South African sherries of lighter style are
also produced in the Stellenbosch, Paarl and Tulbagh
regions, the more robust types from Montagu,

Robertson and Worcester, which also make good
Muscatels and a great deal of brandy and spirits.
Dessert wines are made around Paarl and Stellenbosch. Up to now it is the fortified wines, especially the
South African sherries, that have featured most on
export lists, but increasing quantities of table wines,
still, *pétillant* and sparkling, are beginning to be
known, although the red wines are so much in demand
locally that they tend to be in short supply; they benefit
greatly by being given bottle age. The makers try to
prevent the malolactic fermentation from taking place,
as they wish to conserve the malic acid in the wine, and
they do not usually let the red wines undergo a secondary fermentation for the same reason, but occasional
wines traditionally made, of some age, can be found.

The geographic areas for Wines of Origin are:
Caledon, Malmesbury, Paarl, Piketberg, Robertson,
Stellenbosch, Tulbagh, Worcester, Swellendam, Constantia, Durbanville, Olifants River, the Little Karoo,
and an area called Boberg (Paarl and Tulbagh
Divisional Council areas). The estates defined for
making Estate Wines of Origin are: Alto, Middelvlei,
Muratie, Neethlingshof, Overgraauw, Simonsig, Uiter-
wyk, Verdun, Koopmanskloof, Spier, Uitkyk, Ver-
gegezellen at Tulbath, Groot Constantia and Meer-
Backsberg, Oude Weltevrede and Johan Graue at
Paarl, Montpelier, Theuniskraal and Twee Jon-
gegezellen at Tulbath, Groot Constantia and Meer-
endal in the Cape Town area, and De Wetshof in
Robertson.

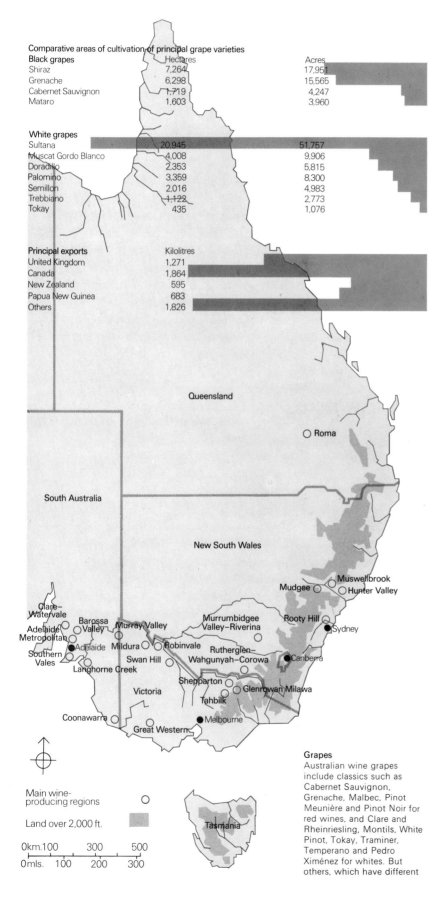

Comparative areas of cultivation of principal grape varieties

Black grapes	Hectares	Acres
Shiraz	7,264	17,951
Grenache	6,298	15,565
Cabernet Sauvignon	1,719	4,247
Mataro	1,603	3,960

White grapes		
Sultana	20,945	51,757
Muscat Gordo Blanco	4,008	9,906
Doradillo	2,353	5,815
Palomino	3,359	8,300
Semillon	2,016	4,983
Trebbiano	1,122	2,773
Tokay	435	1,076

Principal exports	Kilolitres
United Kingdom	1,271
Canada	1,864
New Zealand	595
Papua New Guinea	683
Others	1,826

Queensland

○ Roma

South Australia

New South Wales

Muswellbrook
Mudgee ○ ○ Hunter Valley

Clare–
Watervale
Barossa   Murrumbidgee   Rooty Hill
Adelaide Valley   Murray Valley   Valley–Riverina   ● Sydney
Metropolitan
Adelaide Mildura Robinvale   Rutherglen–   ● Canberra
Southern   Wahgunyah–Corowa
Vales   Swan Hill
Langhorne Creek
Shepparton
Coonawarra   Victoria   Glenrowan Milawa
Tahbilk
Great Western   ● Melbourne

Main wine-
producing regions   ○

Land over 2,000 ft.   ▓

Tasmania

0km.100   300   500
0mls. 100   200   300

Grapes
Australian wine grapes
include classics such as
Cabernet Sauvignon,
Grenache, Malbec, Pinot
Meunière and Pinot Noir for
red wines, and Clare and
Rheinriesling, Montils, White
Pinot, Tokay, Traminer,
Temperano and Pedro
Ximénez for whites. But
others, which have different

names in Australia, include:
Cinsaut, Mataro, Red
Hermitage (known
sometimes as the Black
Shiraz or Petite Syrah) for
red wines, and for whites:
Aucerot (the Chardonnay or
Pinot Gris), Blanquette
(Doradillo), Chasselas
(sometimes called
Sweetwater), Frontignac,
Gordo Blanco (the Muscat

d'Alexandria or Lexia),
Palomino (also sometimes
called Sweetwater, or Listan),
Sémillon (Hunter River
Riesling—very misleading,
this—or Shepherd's
Riesling), Verdelho, Waltham
Cross (white Málaga or
Rosaki), White Hermitage
(White Shiraz, Ugni Blanc,
Trebbiano, St Emilion).

Australia

Vine cuttings were brought by Captain Phillip to Port
Jackson in 1785, but the father of Australian wine
making is James Busby, who planted cuttings (as part
of his rôle as educationalist) in New South Wales in
1832, notably in the Hunter Valley, where the
phylloxera has never penetrated.

Today wine is made in many regions of Australia:
around the early settlements, such as Sydney, Melbourne, Adelaide and Perth; the Barossa Valley and
Hunter Valley, Rutherglen, Clare/Watervale, Coonawarra and Tahbilk; and settlements along the Murray
River and north of the Murrumbidgee, the Riverina.
The great wineries make complete ranges of wines,
each with their own individuality, and these are now
increasingly sold as such, instead of making use of
European names of types of wines. Sparkling wines—
that of Great Western being most highly reputed—and
pétillant or "perlwines" are made, together with
vermouths and fortified wines. Many of the better
wines are allowed long-term maturation in wood, like
certain European classics. The history of the various
wine dynasties and firms merits detailed study and the
Australian technicians are rightly proud of the fact that
they can hold their own anywhere in the world—in one
great Bordeaux estate in the very hot vintage of 1959,
an Australian visitor was able to advise the owner how
to make a particularly successful wine.

Some great Australian wineries: Sandalford, Valen-
cia and Houghton in Western Australia. In South
Australia, Seppelt, Gramp (Orlando), Penfold, Smith
(Yalumba), Saltram (Angaston), Buring (Château
Leonay), and the Kaiser Stuhl Co-operative; in the
Southern Vales, Reynella, Seaview, Hardy's Tintara;
near Adelaide, Magill, Maclaren Vale, Coonawarra,
Clare, Watervale, Modbury, Hope Valley, High-
combe; in the Murray Irrigation Area, Angove, Lyrup,
Waikerie, Renmark, Berri and Loxton are important.
In Victoria, the most important names are Tahbilk,
an estate making excellent wines, and Great Western,
famed for sparkling wines, the vineyards being owned
by Best and, predominantly, Seppelt. Other vineyards
are at Rutherglen, Glenrowan, Wahgunyah, Wan-
garatto and Mildura. In New South Wales, some of the
important estates are at Corowa, in the Murrumbidgee irrigation area and along the Hunter River,
with Penfolds, Lindeman, McWilliam the most important producers, and the estates including Cawarra,
Ben Ean, Dalwood, Glen Elgin, Mount Pleasant, Rose-
hill, Happy Valley, Bellevue, Tyrell's, HVD and
Lake's Folly.

Glossary

Wine Vocabulary

Hundreds and probably thousands of terms are used by the wine trade when wines are being analysed, appraised for specific purposes, or being taught at oenological colleges. These terms vary according to the language of the country, although it is quite common for a term to acquire international significance.

There is a difference between terminology that correctly defines something and between words and phrases that become jargon. Indeed, it is the careless use of wine expressions that has led to the assumption that anyone taking a serious interest in wine is a wine snob. As a layman, I have always found that the greatest authorities have been able to explain themselves in simple language; the wine lover will understand as much as he can and return after some experience to increase his understanding. Anyone who uses technical terms or descriptions current in the world of wine without understanding their significance, will soon cease to enjoy wine or wine talk.

There are three basic sets of wine terms. The first, which involves matters of fact—or sometimes opinions—refers to *what the wine is*: its general character, such as bone dry, sweet or weighty.

Secondly there are the general attributes of a wine; they include such things as body and fruit, and the less obvious qualities such as delicacy and finesse. As taste is subjective, it is not possible to be rigid about these terms, but with experience of tasting and a little knowledge of how other lovers of wine employ certain expressions, a common vocabulary eventually evolves.

Finally there are the descriptive terms that give some impression as to what the wine is like. In some instances, the most obvious words that may occur to the reader cannot be used because they have some specific wine trade significance, such as the terms "light" and "heavy". So these descriptive terms are derived from my personal experience in talking about wines with those that make and handle them; I have included those that I have found useful in teaching and writing about wines. Many people do in the course of time form their own personal vocabulary for describing wines, and this may subsequently enrich the terminology of others, providing it is used with discretion. (In my own tasting notes, I use the phrase "sucked peach stones" to describe certain fine white Burgundies from the Côte de Beaune, but this may sound like a joke to some and may be confusing to the beginner.) However, beware of using different terms for the sake of novelty; a set of terms must, like a language, be understood before one can break rules or compose new definitions.

Main Taste Categories

Bone dry Applied to a wine with no trace of sweetness, but with an assertive almost rasping dryness.

Dry Less obvious as a style than bone dry; there is no sweetness but there can be a mouth-filling, often supple character. Many dry wines are large-scale.

Medium dry Of wines that possess amiability; they are not sweet but often have a touch of softness, sometimes due to the grapes being markedly spicy or high in natural sugar, even if the wines are made to be truly dry.

Implicitly sweet Referring to an underlying or inner sweetness that is not assertive. Certain grapes and the way in which certain wines are made can result in slightly sweet wines that also have considerable freshness.

Sweet Possessing a distinct sweetness. This sweetness is not, in quality wines, produced by adding sugar, but by making the wine in such a way that it is naturally sweet. The method of gathering the grapes and making the wine has been aimed purposely at achieving sweetness.

Intensely sweet Having a pronounced, concentrated sweetness, which should never be cloying, sticky or in any way resemble alcoholized treacle.

Straightforward Applied to wines that immediately give what they possess for the drinker's enjoyment. The term in no way implies that they are superficial, dull or that the pleasure they can yield is of less importance than that of which other wines are capable. Straightforward wines make an impression at once; they are wines to be drunk with gusto rather than discussed at much length.

Medium personality Immediate enjoyment as well as something slightly more profound. Such wines can be explored and discussed a little; they often hint at the fine wine to which they may be related by being made in the same region or from the same grapes, and they are frequently small-scale versions of wines in the weighty category. Many of the wines are at the top of the quality range, and the choice is enormous.

Weighty Applied to wines that, when they are red, can include the greatest in the world. The term can refer to other wines that possess a certain complexity, even when they are straightforward, and which makes an additional impression to mere pleasure. Weighty wines are not taxing to drink, high in alcohol nor difficult to enjoy.

General Attributes

Assertive Possessing one particular, outstanding attribute, such as smell or taste resulting from the grape, climate, soil, etc. which makes an immediate appeal. The term should not be confused with aggressive, which is usually undesirable.

Body This term implies the general make-up or extract of the wine, which may be light, medium or full-bodied. It relates mainly to the flavour, although this may be indicated by the smell. A straightforward wine may be full-bodied, a weighty wine light in body, and *vice versa*.

Crisp Sometimes confused with fresh, but crispness is a permanent feature of the wine's nature and has a certain flick to it that at once stimulates all the senses involved with taste. Crispness is mainly found in white wines, although many red wines also possess it; crisp wines usually come from vineyards in which the acidity is of marked importance.

Delicate The opposite of robust. Wines that possess delicacy are endowed with extra shades of smell and flavour that are never assertive or obvious, but which greatly enhance the wine. The term should not be confused with fragility, for some of the most delicate wines are also profound, weighty, complex and long-lasting, and straightforward wines can also be associated with delicacy.

Elegant The term describes the fine proportions of both red and white wines as well as the way in which they display themselves to the drinker. Small and large-scale wines can possess elegance, which is more likely to be found in weighty wines or those of medium personality, and in the top ranges; it can also exist in straightforward wines.

Firmness Applied to wines that are, as it were, sitting down in the glass; they may sometimes verge on the weighty and profound. Many wines should be firm if they are well-made, but this characteristic does not preclude them from also being delicate and/or elegant.

Fresh Referring to wines that are at their peak when young, and to many wines in the straightforward category. They refresh the palate, whether they are red or white, and at whatever temperature they are drunk. A great wine in the weighty classification may have both freshness and crispness. However, if it is crisp by style, it will remain so throughout its life; if it is simply fresh, it may lose this freshness with some ageing, without necessarily losing anything else that makes it enjoyable.

Fruit A wine should have a good balance of acidity and fruit to give maximum enjoyment. Fruit or fruitiness is associated with the smell and taste of fruit rather than with anything else. Some wines seem more fruity than others, both because of the grapes and because of their individual characteristics. Generally, as wines age they tend to lose their fruitiness; with the greatest wines, this loss of fruit need not involve a loss of enjoyment, at least for some while, because the harmonious nature of the wine may result in the fruitiness developing into a remarkable profundity or subtlety. But a wine that is primarily attractive because of its fruit will be less pleasant as it ages. A fruity smell does not necessarily evoke the smell and taste of grapes; with some wines and some grape varieties, notably the Muscat grape, this may be the case, but generally wines rarely smell or taste grapey. Some people associate certain fruits with particular wines as aids to remembering them.

Heavy See **Light**

Light This term refers to the body of the wine, its individual character. A weighty wine can be light or medium-bodied as well as full-bodied; a wine in the straight-forward category can be full-bodied as well as light.

In the wine trade, the terms "heavy" and "light" refer to the alcoholic strength and acidity of a wine; in the wine classifications these terms are not used in such a context. A light table wine has an alcoholic strength up to 14°, a heavy table wine is above 14°.

Profound Fine and great wines, especially those classified as weighty, often possess profundity. The drinker seems to plunge down into many taste sensations when trying these wines and it can be noted in young wines as well as in those that are fully mature.

Robust Applied to a wine that makes a direct and plain appeal to the senses. Many weighty wines are robust, but the majority tend to be found among straightforward red wines or those of medium personality.

Descriptive Terms

Acid Several types of acids are found in wines; the worst type is *acetobacter*, the bacteria which turns wine into vinegar. If a wine smells of vinegar, it is acetic. However, some acids are essential to good wine, for they balance the fruit and result in crispness and freshness, preserve the wine and give it brilliance in tone. Without the right kind of acidity, a wine will be insipid and flabby. As alcohol is the skeleton of a wine and fruit the flesh, so acidity is the nervous system. Although types of acidity are primarily the concern of the laboratory, the more important ones are citric acid, malic acid, and, most important, tartaric acid.

After-taste An echo of the smell and taste that comes into the mouth, after you have swallowed the wine and are breathing out through your nose. This is like the shadow of the wine and should give pleasure, perhaps also reveal some extra attribute previously not noticeable, or indicate a distinct fault concealed earlier. The after-taste is not the same as the finish or the back-taste, and there can be a pronounced after-taste even in a wine that is short.

Aroma This has been admirably defined as "the smell of the taste". It is difficult to separate aroma from taste, one leading to the other.

Aromatic In wines relating to a concentrated, slightly spicy or actually herby smell.

Balance The relation of the components in a wine so that proportion is maintained. Some wines will be more enjoyable because of particular qualities such as fragrance, flavour, the way they build up to the after-taste, etc. A well-balanced wine will have the most notable attribute shown off to advantage, the other traits remaining in proportion with it.

Bouquet This has been described as the impersonal collection of smells given off by the wine, mainly the product of the maturing process. A very young wine may not possess any bouquet, but it will usually have aroma, it may have fragrance, and generally has a smell.

Breed Applied to a mature wine that displays all its qualities and subtleties of taste, in proportion and without any ostentation or over-assertiveness. It may well be possible to detect in a wine with breed, the refined details of the way it is made.

Bright The trade term that is used to mean a red or white wine perfectly clear of bits (if these are circulating in the wine they are known as "flyers"). A wine should generally be "star bright" in the glass, but many of the finest wines have particles in them which are not necessarily loose deposit. This is the result of the wines not having undergone excessive filtering, and it is not entirely a bad thing if a wine is not wholly star bright. The Victorians used tinted glasses for white wines, to spare themselves the sight of "flyers". Everyday wines can be so made that they are star bright, but with finer wines you should consider whether the presence of bits does affect the taste adversely, and remember that the greatest wines live on their deposit while maturing in the bottle. It has been said that each time a wine is sent through a filter, the bits may be taken out, but so may some of the character. The presence of bits in a glass may be due to careless service, and it may indicate that the wine is very fine and needs careful handling.

Broad The wine has a certain spread-out style throughout the bouquet, taste and after-taste.

Casky See **Woody**

Charm This implies a wine that appeals without ostentation or too obvious good qualities, like a person who smiles but retains a certain reserve. Any sort of wine

can possess charm, but even some of the greatest cannot be associated with it. I often associate it with wines that are at the top of their form in whatever category they come; they please without making demands, without overwhelming or puzzling the drinker. But some people do not rate charm in a wine highly and some even find it out of place in certain world-famous wines.

Chewy See **Crunchy**

Coarse Not necessarily used in a pejorative sense, but implying an obvious style, openness of texture, lack of depth, finesse or elegance. Some small-scale wines are naturally coarse, no fine wine should be —but some are.

Corked This is not always recognized immediately as it can take a little while to develop after a bottle is opened, and it can seldom be detected by smelling the cork when this is drawn. The presence of corkiness is generally to be suspected if a wine seems to lack any smell and if it tastes flat. In its extreme form, corkiness is an aggressive stink, which reminds some people of rotten cork or drains, and which to me evokes chlorine. It does not render the wine harmful to drink, and may occur because of a faulty or immature cork, damage by the cork weevil or by seepage through the cork. If a faulty wine is encountered, it is useful to try and register its smell and taste; there are distinct differences between corkiness, mustiness, and woodiness. The source of supply should always replace any bottle in which these faults are found.

Crunchy, chewy My personal term for wines that are so fresh and fruity that one feels able to squeeze them over the palate and press them in the mouth with extreme enjoyment. A chewy wine is one that feels big in the mouth and so substantial that it gives the impression of being slightly resistant to pressure. Many fine wines are chewy, especially when young.

Dead The state of a wine when it has wholly disintegrated and possesses neither smell nor taste. This can happen with very old wines and also with young ones that have been badly made or ill-treated, such as subjecting them to extremes of heat or cold for a long time.

Depth This is sometimes taken to mean profundity, but a wine can be deep without necessarily being profound. It may indeed possess the potentiality of being profound, which has not yet developed. Depth implies a wine into which the senses and the mind descend to seek more enjoyment.

Dirty It is difficult for the technically inexperienced to separate what is dirty in a wine, as it does not necessarily refer to the way it looks. Dirtiness is present when the taste impression is blurred, and one seems to detect an alien element. The wine has probably been badly handled at some stage before going into bottle, or a dirty bottle may cause the condition.

Distinction A slightly lower grade of praise than breed; a small-scale and even cheap wine may possess distinction when it is as good as it can possibly be.

Dumb Wines may go through phases when they do not "speak" to the taster and when they are virtually impossible to appraise. These phases may be due to certain stages in their maturation or due to treatment recently received. Bottles of wines may seem dumb and impossible to taste at the time the wine is flowering in the vineyard or at the time of the vintage. Wines may also appear dumb if they have just been moved or subjected to treatment, such as racking or fining. Wines may also go through phases of being dumb for no apparent reason, stay so for months, and then recover.

Faded Very old and sometimes even youngish wines can go off rapidly after being opened and exposed to the air; they usually lose their smell before their flavour.

Fat Many young large-scale wines have a pronounced surface taste, as well as an extra smell, that evokes good grease and which I describe as "fat". As the wines develop, they will shed this surface taste. It is in no way unpleasant, just a youthful exuberance of flavour and smell.

Fin It is not possible to translate the French word *fin* as "fine" as there is a difference in the significance, just as in the sound of the two words. A wine that is *fin*, no matter at what stage of its development, is aristocratic by nature and, as an individual wine, possesses in proportion all the qualities that will please the sensitive and perceptive drinker. Most, but not all the great wines are *fin*, although the ones that are *fin* are not invariably great. The attribute may also be possessed by quite modest wines.

Finesse This has been neatly defined as "the quality that makes you order the second bottle so as to discover what it really is". A wine possessing finesse will always retain some slight mystery, an indefinable fascination that draws the wine lover on to explore. Finesse is usually a quality only associated with great and very great wines, the product of many other attributes in successful harmony.

Finish The very last impression made by the smell and the taste. Whether a wine is on the short side or possesses great length, its finish should be both agreeable and distinct, not flabby or sloppy. Curiously, the finish can be different from the initial smell and taste, and in certain instances it may

indicate what the wine is likely to do in the future. Some wines have a delicious crisp finish, others seem to flourish their smell and taste vigorously once again at the drinker just before they end. One of the clearest examples of finish is in the sweet wines of Barsac as compared with those of Sauternes: the Sauternes have a sweet beginning, end and finish, the Barsacs begin and continue sweet, but at the end they finish dry.

Flabby A wine with insufficient acidity and often a coarseness resulting from too much fruit, such as occurs in many badly made white wines from hot vineyards. A flabby wine is unlikely to be able to be improved, much less improve itself.

Flat Term used to signify a sparkling wine from which all the carbon dioxide has been allowed to escape so that the wine is no longer sparkling. Also applied to an ordinary still wine of negative character.

Fleshy A good as well as a doubtful attribute; fruit insufficiently balanced by acidity can result in a wine being fleshy and out of proportion. On the other hand, a large-scale wine can, while still maturing, go through a phase when it may seem to possess a superabundance of fruit and roundness, even though it has plenty of acidity and an inner firmness. In time, this fleshiness will fade and the wine may develop well.

Flyers See **Bright**

Forthcoming The wine appeals, entices, shows itself to advantage but with discretion. This attribute can be appealing in a small-scale wine, it should not be overdone in a *grand vin*. The wine speaks— it comes to meet the taster.

Fragrance Applied to a smell that is slightly scented, with a crisp often elegant aroma. Many young wines and certainly many fine white wines are markedly fragrant.

Grand Like *fin* and "fine", *grand* and "great" are slightly different. A great wine can be great in potential, large-scale and undeniably good. But *un grand vin* possesses breed, charm, finesse, an aristocratic quality, which will, in my opinion, make a quite unforgettable impression on the drinker.

Green Often used in the scent business to describe certain fresh, almost sharp perfumes. In connection with wine, it can mean the agreeable freshness that some wines possess while very young. Many fine mature wines also have this delicious attribute, common to smell and taste, that refreshes the taster, and which evokes the atmosphere one breathes in a wood or garden after a shower, pungent and

profound. An excess of greenness in a wine, however, may indicate that it was made from young vines.

Grip Seeming to cling to the mouth, not in the least disagreeably.

Harsh Sometimes used in conjunction with the word "bitter", but I use it to signify something that appears to resist appealing to the taster—a wine that repels, in a fairly aggressive way.

Large-scale and **small-scale** An easy way of differentiating wines that have a great deal or only a little to give. In no way pejorative, because a good small-scale wine (such as a Balkan or New World Riesling) may be as good as its capabilities permit. A large-scale wine, such as a fine Mosel or Rheingau, should, potentially, give the drinker a much more important and detailed experience.

Legs The trails that slide down the inside of the glass after you have swivelled the wine round. They are related to the glycerine content, present in all wines and especially important in the sweeter ones. The presence of legs in a marked way is usually an indication of quality, either already evident or potential.

Length The time the various taste impressions of a wine remain with the drinker, both in the nose and on the palate. Certain authorities have timed the length of various wines, but this must be a personal matter, and it cannot always be agreed whether a wine is long or not. Some wines seem as if they were about to be long, and suddenly stop short in the impressions; others trail on and on, even for minutes. The impressions do not inevitably weaken with time, and may be compared to those left by the train of a woman's dress sliding out of a room after she has gone through the door.

Limpid This is my personal term for a wine with a positive brightness and clarity, and corresponds to the term "bright" in the wine trade. A limpid wine is alive in the same way as a glass of spring water is alive when compared with a glass of tap water.

Little A *petit vin* or "little" wine is not necessarily inferior, but can be very enjoyable. The scale on which it is made and the pleasure it can give will, however, be more modest than with wines that are *grand* or large-scale.

Lively Applied in the wine trade to a trace of sparkle in the wine, even though this may be hardly perceptible. Some very fine dry white wines may display this, especially while they are young. The liveliness may not be noted in the appearance of the wine, but be sensed by a slight feeling of rasp or prickle on the tongue.

Maderization The supposed resemblance of wines to Madeira. White wines, because of age or if badly kept, may darken and assume a brownish tone due to oxidation of the alcohol. This need not prevent them from still being pleasant drinks, but they will have changed. Full, rather soft wines can sometimes gain by maderization, crisper ones generally lose.

Mouth-filling Applied to certain good wines such as Beaujolais, when fruit is their chief attraction, enticing the drinker to fill the mouth.

Mushroom nose A term often used for very old wines that may have a smell of mushrooms or, to some people, truffles. It is a clean, almost fresh and very concentrated smell.

Musty Many smells, by no means unpleasant, are thought of as musty. But there is a vast difference between a healthy smell and the dank, vaguely rotting, stale smell that is truly musty; it is usually due to incorrect making or keeping of the wine.

Over the top A term used to imply that a wine is past its peak and will decline from now on; it may still continue to offer great enjoyment and much interest.

Oxidation The effect of the exposure of wine to the atmosphere. Up to a point it is sometimes good to air a wine, but eventually it will break up. Very old wines may oxidize as a result of the small amount of air in the bottle under the cork.

Pasteurization A process involving the heating of wine to a given temperature and keeping it at this temperature for a certain time. It is *not*, as is sometimes supposed, the sterilization of wine by boiling, as this would kill the wine completely. Pasteurization, named after Louis Pasteur, is used in stabilizing wines (preventing them from undergoing any changes that might adversely affect their ultimate enjoyment); at the same time the process will hasten the ageing of the wine. When correctly carried out, pasteurization can ensure wines reaching export markets in good condition and remaining so until they are drunk. Carried out to excess it can smooth out the individual characteristics of wines until they are merely insipid beverages. The insistence of some markets on wines being so safe as to be virtually neutral has caused sincere wine lovers to deplore the abuse of pasteurization. The finer wines of the world, however, are unlikely to be pasteurized.

Pinched Applied to wines that are mean in character; they never give generously, either of smell or taste, and they invariably disappoint. Their limited, measured-out style may be due either to the way they are made or to a particular vintage.

Pretty Many small-scale wines deserve this description; so do some of the finer wines made in off vintages and many wines that are most delicious when drunk young. There is as much difference between a pretty wine and a wine that is *grand* as between a pretty face and a beautiful face.

Proportion Used of a wine that possesses harmony. The proportions of a wine should be balanced so that acidity, fruit and alcohol combine harmoniously. Sometimes, through no fault of the wine maker, the proportions are not right, the smell being too much for the flavour, or the after-taste being out of proportion with the flavour. All the parts of a wine should remain in seemly proportions, so that the whole is pleasing.

Reserved Applied to a wine that is slow to reveal all its qualities, only gradually delighting the nose and palate. It is not synonymous with depth or profundity, nor complexity, although a reserved wine may possess all these traits.

Richness Need not invariably imply sweet, although sweet wines are often rich. But it can also be applied to a wine of great profundity, subtlety and possessing considerable fruit. In general wine talk, it will most usually be employed in reference to fortified and dessert wines and certainly in relation to the great sweet table wines.

Round Many people find it helpful to think of wines as having a shape. Some immature wines often seem to be angular, others seem straight up and down in slightly unripe vintages. A round wine has its skeleton (the alcohol) adequately and pleasantly covered with flesh (the fruit) and is enhanced by a good skin (the fragrance). Excess rotundity shows a lack of proportion, but many young wines possess a type of puppy fat which they shed later. How round a wine ought to be depends on the quality it should ideally attain; a great wine at its peak should be only gracefully curved, a good youngish wine in the medium ranges can be rather more curvaceous. Roundness is something felt as the wine passes over the palate and is held momentarily in the mouth.

Scented Sometimes the smell of a wine is markedly obvious and can be associated with the perfume of a flower, fruit or some other pleasure. Too much scent can, however, be out of proportion; a wine that positively reeks of roses would be halfway to being a perfume, not a wine.

Sensitive The French word *sensible* accurately implies the capability of a wine to unite with the drinker. A sensitive wine will be receptive to the nose, palate and mind of the drinker, and will bestow a multitude of impressions for those who can identify them.

Separating Sometimes, as the result of sickness in the wine or because of youth or great age, a wine's components seem to separate and be too clearly distinguishable for the wine to be a harmonious drink. Some fine wines can even at this stage be fascinating and enjoyable.

Shaded My personal version of the French word *nuancé*, implying that the wine possesses a variety of delicately subtle smells and flavours.

Shadowy Applied to a wine which, on account of age, is virtually a ghost of its former self; the attributes are still present, but only just.

Short The opposite of length. The taste of certain wines, including many in the straightforward category, remains for only a little while. Even among fine wines, particular vintage characteristics may make a wine short. The term does not necessarily imply a lack of quality, it is merely a description of the shape of the wine.

Sick If a wine seems in any way out of condition as regards appearance, smell, taste and after-taste, it may be sick and passing through some phase which the skilled technician should deal with. At certain times in their development and often after being moved, wines may become bottle sick, a condition that may range from their being disappointing to drink to truly unpleasant. There is no need to condemn the wine, but advice should be obtained from the source of supply. In many instances the sickness will pass and the wine will recover.

Sloppy Applied to wines that seem to be on the point of dribbling out of the mouth; they may also have been so ill-made as not to be unified. They often lack acidity, and sometimes they have been deliberately made sweet or appealing in a coarse way.

Soggy Reminiscent of licking a piece of wine-impregnated wood. This taste is occasionally present in an otherwise good or fine wine and indicates faulty vinification or keeping.

Stalky Related to the tannin content, although some people associate the term with greenness or youth in a wine. Think of biting the stalk of a grape and associate this with the adjective. A markedly stalky wine tends to be a little unbalanced, sometimes unripe, the inner toughness unlikely to develop into a harmonious wine. In very young wines, however, stalkiness can be attractive (their charm often lies in their freshness and bite), and there is a promise of softening in maturity.

Sulphur Sulphur dioxide (SO_2) is perhaps the most used antiseptic in the world of wine, for it will kill off harmful bacteria, wild yeasts and keep the wine in condition. Too much sulphur remaining in the wine is naturally undesirable, and interferes with enjoying the wine. The acrid fumes, like thick fog, sometimes noted in a winery and the catch in the throat when tasting young white wines can indicate the presence of sulphur. Used wisely, sulphur can protect wine, or help it through a difficult stage of maturation, but used without discretion sulphur will prevent a wine smelling of anything except sulphur dioxide and the taste will be neutral and dull.

Supple Amiable or mouth-filling. A truly supple wine has both these attributes as well as an easy-going drinkability. The very finest wines are seldom, according to my terminology, supple, for I do not associate this attribute with weight, but many of the most enjoyable wines in the straightforward and medium personality categories are deliciously supple.

Tannin A product of the skins, pips and stalks of the grapes, and the element that helps give long life to certain wines, notably the great red ones. In combination with other factors, tannin helps the wine to throw the deposit on which it will live in bottle. Tannin in young wines has a bitter, astringent taste and feel, slightly drawing the mouth, especially the sides of the tongue.

Thin Almost the opposite of round and an undesirable attribute. Wine diluted with water is thin. Similarly, a wet vintage may produce thin wines and, with great age, a wine may lose its fruit and gradually become thin, even skinny.

Tough Toughness can be a very good quality, especially in a young wine not yet fully mature, and may be a combination of tannin, stalkiness and sheer youth. It is also quite acceptable in the sort of inexpensive wines that are going to accompany assertively-flavoured informal foods.

Turned in Used about even fine wines that seem to be withdrawn and concentrating on making themselves. A wine that appears to be turned in can be presented as perfectly enjoyable and ready to drink by giving it a little aeration through decanting.

Two-dimensional My personal term that refers to a wine presenting two apparently unrelated impressions as regards smell and taste. The condition may be temporary, but it is also sometimes apparent in a wine that has been deliberately made like this for the purpose of making a strong commercial appeal.

Uncoordinated At some stage in their development the various attributes of young wines may seem to be unrelated to

each other. This does not necessarily involve lack of proportion or balance; a little tasting experience will provide the ability to detect how the unity may eventually develop.

Unripe Applied to wine made from unripe grapes, either because these have been deliberately picked before they have ripened fully, or because the vintage conditions have been such as to prevent them ripening well. Wine made from slightly unripe grapes can possess marked acidity and freshness as long as the grapes were not so unripe as to make it sour. In a wine for which the grapes should ideally have been fully ripe it may sometimes be possible to detect the unripeness in the form of too much acidity or a sharp flavour; sometimes the wine maker may attempt to remedy the lack of ripeness by sweetening the must or even the wine.

Vivacious My personal term used to describe a wine that has many attributes that are noticeably living, presenting themselves to the taster in a positive way. Vivacity may be associated with liveliness, to the extent of implying sparkle, but the term can, in my view, also be applicable to certain types of perfectly still wines.

Wet Detected in certain wines made when it rained hard during the vintage, the wine literally seems to have been slightly watered down as regards its flavour, although, of course, the alcoholic strength need not have been affected.

Woody Synonymous with a smell of wood. Sometimes the term casky is used for the smell relating to the cask, which may have been incorrectly prepared to hold the wine. It is not necessarily bad in a young wine, but it should not be present in a fully matured fine wine (see also **Soggy**).

Yeasty Applied to an undesirable smell. Although it is the action of yeasts that makes wine, the wine should never smell of yeast, though wines may at times legitimately do so, especially if they have only just been bottled. But if you get a flat, cardboard-like smell this may come from dead yeasts, and the wine has not been successfully treated. A yeasty smell is different from the flat, asbestos smell that generally means the wine has retained the smell imparted by the sheets of asbestos used in the filter.

Glossary of Wine Terms——
Terms that may be seen on wine labels or wine lists or used widely in descriptions

AOC, AC Appellation d'Origine Contrôlée —French system of wine controls.

Abboccato and **amabile** Italian terms, meaning slightly and medium sweet.

Auslese German wine term, meaning made from selected bunches of grapes.

BOB Buyer's own brand—wine either made and/or labelled for a specific outlet, such as a merchant or restaurant. Used particularly for Champagne.

Beerenauslese German wine term, meaning made from selected individual grapes.

Bereich German area; used on German wine labels under the new German Wine Law.

Blanc de blancs White wine from white grapes, not necessarily sparkling, and meaningless if applied to wine made from a single white grape.

Bourgeois growth French category of Bordeaux wines, just below the classed growths.

Boxbeutel Squat bottle used for Franconian and certain other wines.

Branded cork The finer wines usually have their corks branded with their estate names and vintages.

Brut Meaning "dry" and usually applied to Champagne with no dosage at all.

Claret Term used in England since the Middle Ages signifying red Bordeaux.

Classed growths Term relating to the various classifications of Bordeaux red and white wines, but most frequently referring to the classification of the red wines of the Médoc, plus Haut Brion, made in 1855.

Commune French word signifying parish or locality. A *climat* is a specific vineyard plot or site.

Crémant A wine with less sparkle than one that is fully **mousseux**, usually from 2.5 to nearly 4 atmospheres pressure behind the cork. Not to be confused with Cramant, a village and wine region in Champagne, where a Crémant de Cramant is made.

Cru Literally "growth", but the system whereby growths are allocated different categories relates to the classification of certain fine French wines, notably those of Bordeaux.

Cuve close Sealed vat or Charmat method of making sparkling wines.

Cuvée Literally, contents of a vat (*cuve*), but the expression *tête de cuvée* refers to the first pressings of a wine, which will by implication be superior.

DOC System for control of Italian bottled wines, and some Spanish and Portuguese wines (not exactly similar).

Edelzwicker Alsatian wine made from specified "noble" grapes in a blend.

Eiswein Wine from grapes late vintaged and frozen when pressed.

Erzeuger-Abfüllung Term now used to denote estate-bottling of German wines.

Etiquette French for bottle label.

Fiasco Flask in Italian. The use of the partly straw-covered flask for everyday Chianti may decline because of the cost of labour.

Frais Cool, but *not* frappé or iced, which wine should never be.

Frizzante, Spumante Italian for *pétillant* and sparkling; **Espumoso** is Spanish for sparkling, **Sekt** is German for sparkling.

Gay-Lussac The system evolved by the French chemist Joseph Gay-Lussac (1778–1850) for measuring the strength of alcoholic beverages in terms of percentage of alcohol by volume.

Governo The term *governo all'uso toscano* refers to the procedure whereby certain Chiantis and some other Italian wines are made slightly lively, almost *pétillant*, giving the impression of a type of secondary fermentation. Much liked in Italy, sometimes not cared for on export markets.

Hock English word used generally for Rhine wine, just as claret is English for red Bordeaux.

Liquoreux, moelleux Rich, sweet.

Millésime, vendemmia, cosecha French, Italian and Spanish for "vintage".

Monopole Used to imply an exclusivity, and often used specifically for the branded wines of certain producers—e.g. Calvet's Tauzia Monopole.

Passito Italian for wine made from slightly sun-dried grapes—i.e. sweetish.

Pétillant A wine with a very slight sparkle, sometimes only perceptible as a bead or two of bubbles in the glass and a sensation of a slight rasp on the tongue. The

vinhos verdes or "green wines" of Portugal are good examples of *pétillant* wines, which are sometimes also referred to elsewhere as "crackling" or "perlant". The slight sparkle may be a natural manifestation, but can also have been induced or accentuated by the wine maker.

Qualitätswein, QbA, QmP German categorizations of quality.

Quinta Portuguese for "estate".

Reserve, Riserva, Reserva French, Italian, Spanish terms indicating superior quality and, in some countries, subject to controls.

Sparkling, Mousseux A wine that has approximately 5.5 atmospheres pressure behind its cork. For the various methods whereby this is achieved, see pp. 100–101.

Spätlese Late-gathered grapes.

Spritzig The very slight natural prickle of liveliness in certain fine wines. The term will not be seen on labels, but the presence of this special type of pétillance in a wine must not be taken as an indication that it is "working" or fermenting.

Strength Calculated in various ways in different countries, it is simplest to understand in terms of percentage of alcohol by volume (Gay-Lussac). All types of table wines are about 7–14° (known as light wines; if they are over 14° they pay heavy wine duty); fortified wines are about 18–21° (categorized as heavy wines); vermouth and many wine-based apéritifs are 16–20°. No one can estimate the exact strength of a wine by tasting; this is a job for the laboratory.

Sur lie The wine has been bottled off the lees—that is, without racking or filtration but direct from the cask. Used especially of Muscadet.

Tastevin Shallow, irregularly indented tasting cup, still used in Burgundy, where there is little light in most cellars, to appraise colour. The Bordeaux *tasse de vin*, now obsolete, is slightly different in form. The Chevaliers de Tastevin is the Burgundy wine brotherhood, and the wines they select are usually labelled as such—i.e. *tasteviné*. This is a sign of the preference of the order, not an indication of quality.

Trockenbeerenauslese German wine term, meaning the grapes have partly dried on the vine and, usually, have been subject to the action of *botrytis cinerea*.

VDQS Category of French wines slightly lower than AOC.

Velenche, pipette, sonde Device used for drawing wine from the cask. It is a hollow

vessel, like a big syringe, which is inserted in the bunghole, then, with the finger over the top aperture, the wine can be lifted out in the vessel and, by altering the pressure of the finger on the aperture, directed into cup or glass.

Vin de marque A branded wine.

Vin de paille Literally, "straw wine", of the Jura.

Casks & Containers		Litres
Pipe	Port, Tarragona	522.8
	Madeira	418.
	Marsala	422.54
Sherry Butt		490.68
Aum	Rhine wine	136.50
Halbstück	Palatinate & Rhine	610.
Stück		1200
Halbfuder	Mosel	580.
Fuder		1000
Hogsheads	Bordeaux & Burgundy (barriques de transport)	221
	Barrique de Bordeaux (storing & maturation)	213–222
	Pièce de Bourgogne (storing & maturation)	218–231
	Barrique de Mâcon	214
	Australian hogshead	286.39
	American cask	223
Chablis Feuillette		136
Tokay Gönci		136

A container, a measure used for shipping inexpensive wines, may be either 2432 litres, or, in the form of stainless steel porter casks, 2659 litres—or, of course, it may be the entire hold of a specially built tanker ship.

Index

Figures in italics indicate illustrations.
All château names appear under Châteaux.

FOR FURTHER READING

There are many books about wine currently available. Some books, still often cited as authoritative, are however so dated as to the facts contained in them that they may well mislead the inexperienced, and I have omitted these from this list of suggestions. Where an author has something positive to give to the reader by way of lasting scholarship, historical research and a creative approach to wine, it will be rewarding to study what he says, although it should be borne in mind that the examples he cites may bear no relation to the wines most of us have a chance of drinking today. Authors such as Henry Vizetelly, Cyrus Redding H. Warner Allen, André Simon, Raymond Postgate, Morton Shand always merit consultation.

The following short list would make an interesting and reliable wine library, of books available in English. Many of these include lengthy and detailed bibliographies.

The Penguin Book of Wines—Allan Sichel, revised by Peter Sichel (Penguin 1971)
Written by a man who was a shipper, part owner of a great classed growth and an authority on French wines in particular, the first part of this book is an in introduction to wine that is highly personal, but already a classic in its field.

Encyclopaedia of Wines & Spirits—Alexis Lichine (Cassell 1967)
Encyclopaedia of Wine—Frank Schoonmaker (Nelson 1967)
A Directory of Wines & Spirits—Pamela Vandyke Price (Northwood 1974)
These are reference books, the first two large and detailed, the third for quick consultation, but with a very long book list.

A World Atlas of Wine—Hugh Johnson (Mitchell Beazley 1971)
Superbly produced detailed maps with a personal commentary on the wines.

Red, White and Rosé—Edmund Penning-Rowsell (Pan 1967)
The Chairman of the Wine Society writes factually for the beginner.

Wine—R. S. Don (E.U.P. 1968)
A very good practical approach.

Wines & Spirits—Pamela Vandyke Price (Corgi 1972)
For the novice, with special advice on how to buy wines.

The Concise Atlas of Wine—Wina Born (Ward Lock 1974)
A good basic introduction, with attractive pictures and maps.

Gods, Men & Wine—William Younger (Wine & Food Society 1966)
Dionysius, a Social History of the Wine Vine—Edward Hyams (Thames & Hudson 1965)
History of the Wine Trade in England—André L. Simon (1906, available in facsimile reprint)
A History of Wine—H. Warner Allen (Faber 1961)
The Enjoyment of Wine—H. W. Yoxall (Michael Joseph 1972)
The first two are very lavishly illustrated, the third a pioneer piece of research, the fourth a scholarly survey of wine from classical times to drinking as we know it. The last is a study of wines the author has drunk, including valuable opinions on combinations of wines and foods.

Champagne, the Wine, the Land & the People—Patrick Forbes (Gollancz 1967)
A superb and detailed study.

The Wines of Bordeaux—Edmund Penning-Rowsell (Wine & Food Society, revised 1971)
The most detailed commentary on the subject.

The Wines of Burgundy—H. W. Yoxall (Wine & Food Society 1968)
Less technical, but very useful for the traveller.

The Wines of Burgundy—Pierre Poupon & Pierre Forgeot (Presses Universitaires de France)
This English edition gives details of the ACs of each area.

Sherry—Julian Jeffs (Faber, revised 1970)
Sherry—Manuel M. Gonzalez Gordon (Cassell 1972)
These two deal in detail with this complex wine in different ways—both should be read.

The Wines of Spain & Portugal—Jan Read (Faber 1973)
Includes the basics of port, Madeira and sherry and is a very fine detailed survey of table wines, as well as spirits and liqueurs.

The Wines of Italy—Cyril Ray (McGraw Hill 1966)
Italian Wines—Philip Dallas (Faber 1974)
Both are practical and readable.

German Wines & Vines—Alfred Langenbach (Vista 1962)
Perhaps the easiest book on the subject.

German Wines—Heinrich Meinhard (Oriel 1971)
Agreeable and not technical.

Moselle—O. W. Loeb and Terence Prittie (Faber 1972)
Of great importance and interest.

Côtes du Rhône—Peter Hallgarten (S. F. & O. Hallgarten)
A modest booklet, but the best introduction to the wines and the region.

The Wines of Central & South Eastern Europe—R. E. H. Gunyon (Duckworth 1971)
Detailed and profound study of the wines, vines and wine history of these countries.

Spirit of the Vine (KWV 1968)
Deals in detail with South African wines.

Classic Wines of Australia—Max Lake (Jacaranda Press 1966)
Covers Australian wines most competently.

The Wines of America—Leon D. Adams (Houghton Mifflin 1973)
A most readable and detailed survey of wines and wineries in the USA, Canada and Mexico.

Massee's Guide to Wines of America (Dutton 1974)
Also includes Canada, Mexico and the South American countries, and is practical and authoritative.

Lafite—Cyril Ray (Peter Davies 1968)
Bollinger—Cyril Ray (Peter Davies 1971)
Cognac—Cyril Ray (Peter Davies 1973)
Mouton-Rothschild (Christie Wine Publications 1974)
All these give most valuable historical and background information as well as detailed accounts of the subjects.

The Great Wine Blight—George Ordish (Dent 1972)
An account of the phylloxera to fascinate even the non-scientific.

Wine-Tasting—J. M. Broadbent (Christie Wine Publications 1973)
Outlines the tasting technique of a member of the wine trade. Authoritative and detailed, I have learned much from it.

Acknowledgments

Hundreds of people, both in and outside the wine trade have contributed to my being able to write this book; a number of British firms have put the combined knowledge and resources of their staffs, literally from office to cellar, for me to draw on, trade associations and government departments, here and abroad, have been generous without stint, and many people, some of whom I have never even met, have unselfishly given up their time to obtain information and verify references.

My especial thanks are due to Baron Elie de Rothschild, of Château Lafite-Rothschild, who paid me the supreme compliment of consenting to write the foreword to this book.

Maison Sichel in Bordeaux and the firms of Sichel in London and Mainz have been my mentors for many years, and it was at Hedges & Butler and John Harvey that I was first able to learn some of the practicalities of wine. The following have allowed me to taste many special wines and have helped with much research: O. W. Loeb; Edouard Robinson; Hatch, Mansfield; Rutherford, Osborne & Perkin; Martini & Rossi; Charles Kinloch; Lay & Wheeler; Corney & Barrow; Berry Bros.; Norton & Langridge; Mentzendorff; French Regional Wines; Dolamore; Adnams of Southwold; Averys of Bristol; Cock, Russell; Laytons; G. F. Grant; Balls Bros.; Deinhard; Rawlings Voigt; F. & E. May; J. B. Reynier; Percy Fox; Gilbey Vintners; Grants of St James; Heyman Bros.; Findlater Matta; Rigby & Evens; Geo. Sandeman; Walter Siegel; André Simon; Stowells; Teltscher Bros.; Richard & William Teltscher; Williams & Humbert. The Italian Institute for Foreign Trade, SOPEXA, the Casa do Portugal, the Spanish Embassy, the Cyprus Trade & Tourist Office, the Australian Wine Centre have given help, hospitality and co-operation over a long period. To the South African Wine Farmers Association I owe the invaluable experience of being able to visit the Cape and learn about their old-established but essentially New World wines.

Of the many friends abroad, I particularly wish to thank M. Guy Schÿler, of Alfred Schÿler, Bordeaux, and Château Lafite; Martin Bamford MW, of Château Loudenne; John Davies MW, of Château Lascombes; Ronald Barton, of Léoville and Langoa-Barton; M. Edouard Cruse. In Burgundy the establishment of Louis Latour, in the Rhône M. Pierre Ligier of the Maison du Vin, Avignon, the vermouth houses of Noilly Prat at Marseilles and Sète, the Distillerie de la Côte Basque in Bayonne, the establishments of Rémy Pannier and Goblet at Saumur, the firms of Hugel, Dopff, Kuehn, Trimbach and Dopff & Irion in Alsace, and, in Champagne the CIVC, Moët et Chandon, Pol Roger, Mercier, Laurent Perrier. In Germany very many firms have been of special help, but most of all I would like to express my gratitude for the privilege of being able to consult Professor Becker, of Geisenheim. In Cyprus, my dear friends of KEO, SODAP, ETKO and The Vine Products Commission taught me a great deal about their historic and revivified wines, and so did the several authorities in Sicily whom I was able to visit and question. In Piedmont and Tuscany there are numerous firms and associations to whom I am indebted, in Portugal to the Gremio and the Association of Port Wine Shippers, and the Association of Vinho Verde producers, in Madeira to the Madeira Wine Association and especially to the late Horace Zeno and to Noel Cossart. In Paarl the KWV and many wine farmers likewise helped me very much.

Among the many friends in Britain who I remember with gratitude, the following have made special contributions to this book: Patrick Forbes, of Moët et Chandon, London; W. J. S. Fletcher, of Cockburn, Martinez, Mackenzie, John Lipitch of R. & C. Vintners; David Peppercorn MW; James Long of Gilbey Vintners; Sir Guy Fison, Bart. MW, of Charles Kinloch; J. W. Clevely MW, of H. Parrot; Jack Ward, of The English Vineyards Association; John Grinter MW, of The Four Vintners; R. Hawkey MW, of Grierson Blumenthal; Peter Hallgarten, of S. F. & O. Hallgarten; Pat Simon MW, of Pat Simon Wines; Clive Coates MW; Geoffrey Jameson MW, of Justerini & Brooks; David Rutherford, of Rutherford Osborne & Perkin; Gilbert Wheelock, of Martini & Rossi; Lionel Frumkin, of Southard; Jeremy Roberts, of Waverley Vintners; R. E. H. Gunyon whose great experience of east European wines has been most helpful; Julian Jeffs, whose work on sherry has been equally so; Jan Read, who enabled me to taste some of the exceptional Spanish wines about which he writes so well; Helen Thomson, of O. W. Loeb, who read the manuscript and compiled the index; and Mrs Margaret Bird, whose impeccable transcriptions of both tape and typescripts were of major assistance. I would also like to thank the staff of Dorling Kindersley, who enthusiastically and helpfully submitted themselves to the tasting techniques as these were worked out, and contributed much by their truthful and practical suggestions.

PAMELA VANDYKE PRICE

DORLING KINDERSLEY LIMITED would also like to express their gratitude to the individuals, companies and institutions named by the author, some of whom have given particular assistance in the creation of the original photography and illustration for this book. They would also like to thank the following: Amy Carroll; Counsel Ltd; H. Erben Ltd; Food from France; Guy Gravett; S. M. Groenbof; A. G. D. Heath; Albert Jackson; John Marshall; Saxon Menné; Paxton and Whitfield; Jean Peissel; The Portuguese Government Trade Office, London; David Russell; C. Shapland and Co.; Sotheby & Co.; The Turkish Embassy, London; Vitcovitch Bros.; D. A. Willis; The Wine and Spirit Association of Great Britain and The Wine Development Board; Wine Institute, San Francisco; Wines of Greece

The Taste of Wine
was conceived, edited and designed by
DORLING KINDERSLEY LIMITED

Managing editor
Christopher Davis
Art editor
Bridget Morley
Text editor
Lizzie Boyd
Designers
Derek Ungless
Malcolm Smythe
Picture researchers
Susan Elwes
Caroline Lucas

Cartographic work was undertaken by Harriet Bridgeman Ltd. (researchers: Edward Saunders, Rachel Hay), Jackson Day Designs and Arka Graphics

Consultants and Advisors
Clive Williams MW
Gilbey Vintners School of Wine
Helen Thomson
O. W. Loeb & Co. Ltd.
Terry Robards
The New York Times

Photographer
Philip Dowell
Artists
David Ashby
Roy Coombes
Michael Craig
Bill Easter
Andrew Farmer
Nicholas Hall
James Robins
Stephanie Todd
Owen Wood
Michael Woods

Picture sources
Barnabys Picture Library; Peter Baker Photography; Bodleian Library; Bristol University Dept. of Agriculture and Horticulture; Cockburn Smithes; Colorific; Daily Telegraph Colour Library; Robert Estall; Foto Fass; French Government Tourist Office; Grants of St James; Guy Gravett; Sonia Halliday; Michael Holford Picture Library; Mansell Collection; Mary Evans Picture Library; Moët et Chandon; G. H. Mumm & Co.; Andrew Morland; Picturepoint Ltd; Rapho; Ronald Sheridan; SOPEXA; Werner Forman; Wine and Spirit Education Trust

Typesetting
Tradespools Ltd.
Frome, England
TJB Photosetting,
London, England

Lithographic reproduction
L. Van Leer & Co. BV
Amsterdam, Holland